The Context
of Social Psychology

European Monographs in Social Psychology

Series Editor HENRI TAJFEL

EUROPEAN MONOGRAPHS IN SOCIAL PSYCHOLOGY 2
Series Editor HENRI TAJFEL

The Context
of Social Psychology
A Critical Assessment

Edited by

JOACHIM ISRAEL
University of Lund, Sweden

HENRI TAJFEL
University of Bristol, England

1972

Published in cooperation with the
EUROPEAN ASSOCIATION OF EXPERIMENTAL PSYCHOLOGY
by
ACADEMIC PRESS *London and New York*

ACADEMIC PRESS INC. (LONDON) LTD.
24–28 Oval Road
London NW1

US edition published by
ACADEMIC PRESS INC.
111 Fifth Avenue,
New York, New York 10003

Library of Congress Catalog Card Number: 70–185206
ISBN: 0–12–375150–O

PRINTED IN GREAT BRITAIN BY
C. TINLING AND CO. LTD,
LONDON AND PRESCOT

Contributors

Johan Asplund, *Department of Psychology, University of Copenhagen, Denmark*

Mario von Cranach, *Department of Psychology, University of Berne, Switzerland*

Claude Flament, *Laboratory of Social Psychology, Faculty of Human Sciences, University of Provence, Aix-en-Provence, France*

Rom Harré, *Linacre College, University of Oxford, England*

Joachim Israel, *Department of Sociology, University of Lund, Sweden*

Jaromír Janoušek, *Institute of Psychology, Czechoslovak Academy of Sciences, Prague, Czechoslovakia*

Serge Moscovici, *Laboratory of Social Psychology, École Pratique des Hautes Études, Paris, France*

Ragnar Rommetveit, *Institute of Psychology, University of Oslo, Norway*

Henri Tajfel, *Department of Psychology, University of Bristol, England*

Håkan Wiberg, *Department of Sociology, University of Lund, Sweden*

Contents

1

Introduction

Henri Tajfel

This book, the second in the series of European Monographs in Social Psychology, reflects preoccupations which, we think, are widely shared beyond the small group of the contributors. However one wishes to define or describe social psychology, there is no doubt that it is a discipline which, in principle, should be able to contribute a great deal to the interpretation of contemporary social phenomena; and, that its aim is either the "explanation" or the "understanding" (in the traditional sense of these terms) of the social life of individuals and of groups, large or small. The use of the phrase "interpretation of *contemporary* social phenomena" does not imply a belief on my part that applied research has some kind of priority over "basic" research or a theoretical approach. On the contrary, as stated in the third chapter of this book, the problem is not merely that of resolving the present tension between research which is oriented towards the solution of practical problems and research whose instigation is theoretical. We must concern ourselves with equally difficult problems relating to the *kind* of "fundamental" research that should be conducted with the help of the techniques we have evolved over the years. The questions posed throughout the book are mainly directed towards these problems. We ask whether, as social psychologists, we have succeeded in making a significant contribution to the debate about human social life. If we have failed we must find the reason for our failure. Social psychology is deemed to be concerned with the study of some of the roots of human social interaction, and is thus presently or potentially of great importance; consequently the questions we have raised should be of direct interest not only to those who are professionally engaged in one or another branch of the subject but also to their colleagues in other social (and biological?) sciences as well as to those who are not satisfied with some of the crude and simplistic notions about "human nature" that are widely bandied around as "explanations" of our most difficult problems.

It is not, however, the purpose of this book to discuss these problems directly. Its title, "The Context of Social Psychology", is meant to convey its indirect relevance to them. An assessment of the *context* of social psychology must be concerned with the purposes and instruments of the psychological analysis of human social behaviour and experience, with the role and origins of the values and presuppositions that may be embedded in this analysis, and with "models" of Man—old and new—that have been or are being used. These concerns are reflected in the titles of the three parts of the book. But before I go on to a survey of the contents, a little should be said about the origins of the book and the stages of its development.

In the spring of 1969, a plenary conference of the European Association of Experimental Social Psychology was held in Belgium at the University of Louvain. It became increasingly clear during the working sessions and in innumerable extramural discussions that, roughly speaking, two general points of view were represented—and sometimes even schizophrenically contained in views expressed at different times by the same people. Some of the papers delivered at the conference followed the long-established tradition of well-disciplined experimental research based on those ideas, methods and theories which have become familiar in the last twenty years or so. Others expressed dissatisfaction or searched for new avenues of theorizing and research. The discussions which followed the papers brought into the open something which can perhaps be described as a complex and conflicted collective state of mind. On the one hand, there was genuine respect for much that has been achieved through the well-tried methods of clear-cut empirical hypotheses and their experimental testing. On the other hand, many felt that an unquestioned acceptance of the assumptions—social, scientific and philosophical—underlying much of this research was a heavy price to pay for achieving a modicum of "scientific respectability" and even for making *some* gains in knowledge. It is possible that the "student revolution"—very much in evidence in the spring of 1969—had something to do with these conflicts. If so, this bringing to the surface of latent intellectual conflicts should be chalked up on the positive side of the ledger of the "unrest" (see Moscovici's chapter in this book).

But many of the questions discussed from various points of view in this book were with us long before the recent and present generations of students replaced the "silent generations" of the 'fifties. The most important refer to the following issues: the nature of theory in social psychology; the adequacy of the methods used for the analysis of "natural" social phenomena; the nature of the unstated assumptions, values and presuppositions about Man and society determining theories and methods of research; the relevance and significance of the results of science; the relations of theories, problems and methods of research in social psychology to those in the physical and in the natural sciences.

These problems came so clearly to the surface at Louvain that it was obvious that their discussion should be continued. The framework for such a continuation existed in the form of the "small working group meetings" periodically organized by the Association. The initiative for the one from which the present book developed came from Joachim Israel who took the responsibility for its organization after some preliminary discussions in Copenhagen with Serge Moscovici and Henri Tajfel. The meeting took place in April 1970 in Elsinore,[1] and if the Prince of Denmark had asked "how to be" instead of asking his other immortal question, he could easily have become one of the participants.

This Introduction is not the place to engage in a detailed discussion of issues which are taken up in the body of the book. But a brief introductory survey may be of some use.

Part I (the chapters by Moscovici and by Tajfel) presents, as it were, the "view from the inside" of social psychology. Moscovici is mainly concerned with the adequacy of sociopsychological theories *as* theories and with the fact that they neglect the social nature of Man. He asks the pertinent question (which may be considered impertinent by some): "What is *social* in social psychology?" He considers that social psychology has managed neither to study social conduct as an interaction between Man and society, nor to study Man *in* society. The most important differentiating feature of human social behaviour is the human use of symbols in social communication, and—proceeding from it—the creation and diffusion of ideologies which are produced by, and in turn

---

[1] We are grateful to the Danish Social Science Research Council and to the Tricentenary Foundation of the Swedish National Bank for their additional support which made this book possible. A grant from the Council helped considerably in the organization of the Elsinore conference; a grant from the Foundation enabled the editors to continue working together after the conference on the completion of the book.

contribute to producing, new conditions of social life and new modes of social conduct. But the proper study of communication in a social context and the study of ideologies have hardly made their appearance in contemporary social psychology. As most of the research in the subject is piecemeal, inductive and non-social, it has failed to promote a cumulative and systematic advance in knowledge. But it has also failed in another respect. The study of natural phenomena in the physical and natural sciences has transformed in many ways the nature of the phenomena studied: it has introduced *new* phenomena. Moscovici writes: "The aim of knowledge is not only to systematize that which exists but also to invent that which does not exist as yet." Social psychology has singularly failed in this task of discovery and invention of new alternatives. Moscovici therefore suggests that we should now concentrate on searching for new avenues of approach, particularly in the study of human social communication, without worrying too much about rigid conformity with the canons of experimental respectability. We need more ideas, not more experiments; *any* provocative theory would be preferable to the inductive collecting of bits and pieces that has become our respectable habit. The requirements for such a theory are outlined in his chapter which contains, therefore, as its main challenge, the affirmation of the need for a *social* theory of human social conduct.

Tajfel's chapter converges in many ways with that of Moscovici, although it is more sceptical about the feasibility of a "grand theory". He feels, as Moscovici does, that social psychology has studied the wrong kind of *homo* in its attempts to derive general laws of human social behaviour from the presumed "universal" and "pre-social" laws of individual motivation. Starting from a classification of experimental studies based on the opportunities of extrapolating from their findings to social phenomena at large that these laws presume though fail to offer, he widens his discussion to consider the three kinds of reductionism that have somehow succeeded in contriving the almost total disappearance of the "sociopsychological man" from social psychology. These are the biological, the psychological and the sociological versions of reductionism; and each has its own one-sided perspective. Ideally the central issue of social psychology should be the study of psychological processes accompanying, determining, and determined by social change. (This corresponds closely with Moscovici's plea for the study of social communication and ideologies.) One of the major sections in the chapter exemplifies the argument from the standpoint of a problem which presents a major challenge: the social psychological study of intergroup relations. It is pointed out that this challenge has either been taken up almost entirely at the level of "individual" theories or been practically ignored in the experimental studies of group behaviour.

Thus, Part 1 of the book maintains its chosen course on the "inside track" of social psychology. The two chapters remain in close touch with some of the recent theory and research. They present an argument for the transformation of what is being done at present into a genuinely *social* psychology which would have as its basis the idea that Man and society have a reciprocal effect upon the mode of existence and behaviour of each other; thus they call for the rejection of concepts implying a one-way causation, whatever direction the causation is presumed to take. Perspectives widen in Part 2 of the book to include considerations of the role of epistemological, ethical and social presuppositions in the construction and application of theories. Israel engages in a wide sweep of meta-theory exploring its implications for the social sciences. Rommetveit fights a battle on two fronts: against the behaviourist elimination of meaning from the study of human communication and against the encroachments of the new "hermeneutic-constructivist" approach (as represented by the influential writings of Apel and Habermas) in the day-to-day job of empirical research about the social context of human cognition (a complaint shared by Moscovici). Asplund goes back to Mead's symbolic interactionism in order to present a new approach to the *value relevance* of social scientific theories (as distinct from value determination or value freedom). Janoušek represents the Marxist point of view in his discussion of the role of Man's productive activities in the creation of an awareness of the self which is primarily of a social nature.

Israel starts from the concept that all social scientific theories are preceded by normative propositions about the nature of man, of society and of the relationship between the two. He attaches special significance to those propositions (or "stipulations") which are concerned with epistemological problems; that is, with the relations between the knowing subject and the object of his knowledge. After discussing various approaches to the study of Man and society, such as reductionism, holism and methodological individualism, he presents a model of the research process which includes various categories of propositions often neglected in social psychology and in the related disciplines. In particular, he contrasts the idea of "knowledge as a reflection of reality" with the idea of "knowledge as a construction", both on the level of an individual as a "social man" and on the level of scientific theories. Though they start from a different point, his conclusions converge in various ways with those reached by Moscovici and by Tajfel.

Rommetveit extends the discussion to problems of meaning and of psycholinguistics; and, more generally, to problems of social communication in Man. It is narrowed down again in the concluding section of his chapter in order to consider the adequacy of various psycholinguistic models (particularly that of Chomsky) for the analysis of human communication *in* social interaction. He is strongly critical of attempts, such as those contained in the writings of Apel and Habermas, to force a certain kind of philosophy of science on the social scientist. Whereas some of the other contributors stress the philosophical naivety of social psychologists who fail to recognize presuppositions of various kinds which underlie and determine their theories and research, Rommetveit attacks the scientific naivety of the "hermeneutic-dialectic" philosophers of social science who have, according to him, little understanding of the actual process of scientific research. As he claims, his contribution to this book "may be viewed as an empirically oriented psychologist's protest against the philosopher's persistent attempts to lure him into various traps inherent in monistic systems and views of the world". He wishes to reverse the relationship between the philosopher of science and the social scientist in which at present "the social scientist is requested to clarify his tacit philosophical assumptions in a terminology dictated by the philosopher". He supports this by pointing to important empirical issues the study of which would not gain very much from the application of "the novel commandment": "Thou shalt not seek knowledge about thine Brother that cannot be converted into self-insight in Him." As his alternative, Rommetveit develops a model of human communication from "deixis"; that is in the points of localization of the act of communication in time, space and direction. He describes three approaches to the act of communication and suggests the development of a "grammar of communication" which could build upon, and further develop, Wittgenstein's concept of "language as a game".

From Rommetveit's concern with the social scientist's independence from "monistic philosophies" we move with Asplund to the consideration of some *consequences* of social scientific theories which he considers inevitable. Just as one of Israel's main concerns was with presuppositions of various kinds that form the *background* of theories, so Asplund concentrates on their ethical and social *effects*, on the implications that they inescapably have for our manner of viewing social phenomena. He maintains that in this sense they are *value relevant* independently of the presence or absence of value presuppositions; and quotes several striking examples. He insists we should admit this relevance, despite the fact that we have been unwilling to recognize that often what appears to be a purely theoretical perspective cannot be divorced from its consequences in our social *Weltanschauung*. He points out that the classical social scientists were not afraid of acting simultaneously and explicitly as scientists and as moralists; and that we also act as moralists, but cling to the notion, mainly developed by the logical positivists, that we are able to make clear distinctions between statements which are descriptive and those which are normative. Asplund applies his notion of value relevance to several theoretical approaches amongst which Mead's symbolic interactionism acquires for him a central position.

The notion that theory and *Praxis* cannot be separated in the social sciences emerges in the chapters by Israel and by Asplund, and it also finds its place in some parts of Moscovici's discussion. It is taken up from a Marxist point of view by Janoušek as a central theme. The concept of *Praxis* in Marxism, as Janoušek writes, "refers to the activity of Man which aims at transforming the world as well as aiding his own self-development". Starting from this perspective, and from Marx's views about the role of production and exchange in social interaction, Janoušek discusses their relevance to the understanding of some of the major processes with which social psychology is concerned: competition, cooperation, the development of social roles, the development of social communication. In the course of his discussion, he undertakes an analysis of the implications for social psychology of the views developed by Marx as compared with the theories of Mead, of Homans and of neo-psychoanalysts such as Fromm and Sullivan. Some of the conclusions reached in his discussion are similar to those arrived at, in different ways, in some of the other chapters (Moscovici, Tajfel, Wiberg). One example is Janoušek's view about the weaknesses of the exchange theory in social psychology: ". . . free exchange is illusory even in a highly developed system of exchange. It appears free only as long as it is abstracted from the existing social conditions and relations which in reality determine the shape that exchange will assume."

The four chapters which constitute Part 3 of the book consider the methodological and substantive implications of several models for the study of human social behaviour. The models and methods discussed include game theory, ethological theories, mathematical representations of cognitive structures which operate in social interaction, role theories, and the "conceptual systems of role and rule". The chapters fall into two categories. Wiberg's chapter is primarily analytic and descriptive; the others contain proposals for methods and models for studying social behaviour which derive from three different approaches.

Wiberg's chapter is a broad *exposé* of rational and non-rational models of Man. He analyses the logic and validity of both kinds of model using game and decision theories as examples of the former, and instinct and motive theories as examples of the latter. The discussion of rational models, starting from a survey of concepts of "rationality", progresses from the simpler to the more complex, from decision under certainty to decisions and strategies under risk (including zero-sum games) to conclude with the mixed-motive games in which considerations of social interaction must, by definition, be included. As he proceeds, Wiberg points out the difficulties of empirical applications beyond, or even within, simplified laboratory situations. The instinct and motive theories are treated in a similar way, the "case of aggression and wars" being singled out as exemplifying the difficulties of their application. Though he adopts another perspective, some of Wiberg's conclusions converge with those found in several of the earlier chapters in the book (Moscovici, Tajfel, Israel). He feels that, on the positive side, the "roads of sophistication" have forced both kinds of models to take increasingly into account two sets of factors: the cognitive and the social. The cognitive factors are important since "our orientation towards the natural world is an orientation towards what we believe about it, towards the consequences that our behaviour will have". The social factors point to the need for a "decent theory of value"; although we do not have such a theory at present, both models "have had to take into account that we have some ideas about other people's values" and that these are acquired through social interaction. An "essential limitation" remains, however, and it is common to both rational and irrational models: "having a theory of Man often entails lacking a theory of men". From this follows "the indiscriminate use of both kinds of models for drawing conclusions about groups and societies".

Von Cranach continues the discussion of some of Wiberg's problems

but moves in a very different direction. His concern is with the applications to the study of Man, particularly social man, of one of Wiberg's
classes of "irrational models", the models used in ethology. But there is
one important difference between the subject matter of the two chapters:
although von Cranach discusses the application of ethology to the study
of human behaviour, he focuses his argument not on the issue of instinct
but on the more general problem of the relationship between animal
and human behaviour. His theoretical and methodological evolutionary
perspective does not cause him to deny the emergence of new structures
in Man, which are due to human cognitive and cultural development;
nor does it cause him to affirm that these structures are reducible to
those which came earlier in the evolutionary process. Nevertheless, he
warns us against attempting to analyse human behaviour without taking
into account the "structural integration . . . associated with the development of complex structures from the simple ones". Although many
patterns of social behaviour in Man must be regarded as "superordinate
systems with their own sets of laws" made possible by viable systems of
communication, "many innate (i.e. phylogenetically determined)
behaviour characteristics are largely integrated into the complex new
individual, social and cultural systems . . . They have acquired a
cognitive character and a cultural significance: in short, something new
has emerged." This brief summary with quotations from von Cranach's
chapter may leave one with the impression that there is no genuine disagreement between his views and those expressed by several contributors
who attack the validity of using reductionism of various kinds in the
analysis of human social behaviour. If such an impression has been
gained, I have succeeded in this Introduction in papering over the
cracks. For several other contributors to the book, the difficulties of
"integration", particularly in relation to what Wiberg calls "the use of
. . . models for drawing conclusions about groups and societies", remain
acute. Von Cranach does not deny these difficulties (see his Conclusions); but he argues, as does Moscovici in a different context, that
"no science can afford in the long run to let its problems be dictated by
its methods", and that it is imperative to find adequate comparative
methods in order to develop a proper study of human social behaviour.
The dilemma remains suspended on its two horns which are: the danger
of throwing away the baby with the bath water through concentrating
only on those aspects of human social behaviour which permit meaningful evolutionary comparisons; and the danger of forgetting the "animal

nature of Man" in theories of social behaviour. An adequate treatment of this dilemma would require us to edit an even larger book, or a different book altogether. It must be hoped that soon serious discussions of these issues between the biological and the social scientists will cease to display all the features, so habitual at present, of a dialogue between the deaf. For such discussions to be useful one essential requirement is that—to use von Cranach's terms—"biologistic" considerations ("misunderstood biological theories") which are so widespread at present should be replaced by a careful scrutiny of the theoretical and empirical implications of the studies of animal behaviour.

With Flament, we move from von Cranach's theme of homologies with animal behaviour to the other extreme of the largely unexplored areas of human social behaviour. Like Rommetveit in the concluding section of his chapter, Flament is concerned with certain specific aspects of the abstract and symbolic human social communication. It might be said that parts of Flament's contribution are an attempt to provide a (technical) answer to the question which persistently emerges in the chapters by Moscovici, Tajfel, Israel and Wiberg. In relation to Wiberg's chapter, it has to do with the construction of "a decent theory of value" which would enable us to take account, particularly in the rational models of Man, of people's knowledge about other people's systems of values; for the other three chapters, it relates to the discussions they undertake of the unwarranted generalizations (often presented in the guise of "laws") that are being made from theories and experimental studies of limited scope regarding the values and systems of knowledge that guide human social behaviour at large. Flament presents a model, derived from Boolean algebra, which should enable us to assess empirically the extent of overlap between any two systems of social representations.[1] He then goes on to show how this model can be applied to the "assymetrical" relationship between the cognitive structures of the persons being studied and of the scientist studying them. This meta-theory would, of course, lead logically to a meta-meta-theory of the relationship between the meta-theorist and the theorist who is the object of his analysis. But Flament reassures us that the process could

[1] Here, as in the translations of the two French chapters (Moscovici and Flament), we have decided to keep in the text the term "representation", widely used in French in conjunction with "cognitive", "collective" and "social", although it is not current in the social psychological literature in English. This decision was based on some of the meanings of "represent" listed in *The Concise Oxford Dictionary*: call up by description or portrayal or imagination; place likeness of before mind or senses; symbolize; stand for, etc.

not continue *ad infinitum* since only a finite number of levels is possible. In his conclusions he returns again to the issues raised in different ways in other chapters (Moscovici, Israel, Rommetveit, Asplund). In particular, he is in agreement with Rommetveit when he writes: "There is a belief that some kind of absolute truth has been obtained when the extra-scientific values, which make our knowledge relative, have been identified (as Einstein said: 'The only absolute is the relative'). It is my view that the identification of these extra-scientific values is itself a labour of cognitive analysis . . ."

Harré raises a controversy which we are no nearer to resolving than we are to finding a solution to the dispute raised by von Cranach. He is, like most of the other contributors, concerned with a *meaningful* analysis of social behaviour. He is also, like Rommetveit and Israel, concerned in his own way with the conflict between "explanation" and "understanding" (Rommetveit's *Erklärung* and *Verstehen*) in the approach to the study of social behaviour. But, unlike Rommetveit or Flament, he thinks it pointless to study *experimentally* the "interrelations of meanings as perceived by the interactors" which are for him "the mechanisms responsible for the observed patterns of social interaction". Nor would he agree with Tajfel that the non-experimental "approaches to the psychological aspects of social conduct [do not] present even as much solidity" as the experimental studies appear to have. According to Harré, social psychology has not yet reached the stage at which it can pass from "critical natural history" to science. This critical natural history should consist of an "analysis of episodes" for which Harré provides a conceptual framework as a form of "understanding" which is distinct from premature causal explanations in terms of factors extraneous to social interaction. His model is a "dramaturgical" one; it allows us to unravel "the ethogeny of an episode; that is, the rules and meaning which explain what is done and what is said". He outlines in detail the logic and substance of the model which, he explains, owes a good deal to the work of Goffman. Harré's system of analysis transcends the one adopted in role theory which he finds inadequate. He maintains that, in avoiding the determinism inherent in some of the parametric models of analysis, the new "ethogeny" of human social behaviour may be able to take into account more adequately than has previously been possible the choices, intentions and wishes ("decisions and wants") of the actors in social intercourse.

This brief résumé should make it clear to the reader that the book is characterized by a striking convergence of views as well as by obvious disagreements. It is difficult for us to be certain which of the two is more "striking" or more "obvious". But had we not thought that, in the long term, or even in the short term, the convergences were more important than the divergencies, the book would not have been published. It is easier to state this as a conviction than to support it in detail without plunging once again into a discussion of the contents. However, some of the major themes can perhaps be very briefly touched upon here but the rest will have to be left to the reader. All the contributors present views about social psychology which, although by no means uniform, manage to achieve two ends: to make explicit the reasons for a dissatisfaction with some of the dominant trends of contemporary work in a subject to which I referred earlier as being "potentially of great importance"; and to present constructive alternatives, some of which, as might be expected, are spelled out in more detail than others. We feel that the book as a whole reflects an important facet of the "wind of change" that is blowing through social psychology. Most, if not all, of the contributors would subscribe to the view that social psychology must become something of a "natural science of the *social* conduct in Man"; that it must take into account *explicitly* the interaction between the human individual and his social context; that it must not pretend to "objectivity" or freedom from normative and other presuppositions when it can be shown that these play a part in the construction of theories and the conduct of research; that, however, it is not enough to state this, or even to show it, as these systems of presuppositions must themselves be subjected to conceptual and/or empirical analysis; that meaning and the symbolic aspects of human communication can be eliminated from social psychology only at the cost of rendering the whole enterprise meaningless; that methods (experimental or any other) should not dictate the course of research and theorizing, for the opposite is a *sine qua non* requirement for a genuine advance in knowledge; and finally, that we must strive for a clearer awareness of the social significance of our work.

Some of these broad convergences of opinion are fairly obvious; but they would have been much less easily arrived at even a few years ago. From our point of view, the best that this book could achieve would be an extension in width and depth of future debates and of their connections with new theories and research. We decided not to place a dedication at the front of this book but had we done so it would have read: "To our students and colleagues who care, whether they agree or disagree."

To conclude, a word of warning: the chapters in this book were initially prepared in many diverse corners of Europe. The academic traditions of writing and exposition in Scandinavia, France, Germany, England or Czechoslovakia differ widely from each other. We decided that we should not try, in our editorial work, to force all this diversity into a common mould which would be more easily accepted or acceptable in one or another cultural or national context. The "cross-cultural" nature of this book is, to us, an important aspect that we wished to preserve. It is this diversity combined with mutual understanding that we see as being one of the foundations of the European contribution to an advance in social psychology which would acquire a significance independent of social contexts.

PART 1

Theories and Experiments

2

Society and Theory in Social Psychology[1]

Serge Moscovici

1 The day of the first judgement

We are, as European social psychologists, in a quandary; for most of us our science has just begun; but at the same time we belong to societies and cultures which have a long past behind them. This is why an intimate journal of European social psychology tends to be written as an autobiography inserted in an ancient civilization, while our American colleagues enjoy a conjunction of events which is an exact reversal of our own case.

What is at stake when questions are asked about what social psychology is or should be? First of all, there is no doubt that the answers which are sought are a reflection of the circumstances in which the questions are asked. This is why it seems advisable to begin by making these circumstances explicit rather than leaving them in the background. Two of them appear to be of major importance.

The first is the attempt to create in Europe a social psychology and the drawing together of a group of people who are trying—with varying

[1] Translated from the French by Henri Tajfel.

17

success—to achieve this aim. Many of us had to use autodidactic methods; we began by learning or reinventing procedures while consulting the only literature available to us, of which we knew neither the function nor the roots in its own society and in its own cultural tradition. Before us, ahead of us and around us there was—and still is—American social psychology. It is unnecessary to dwell on the role played in its development by people like Lewin, Festinger, Heider, Deutsch, Asch, Schachter, Sherif, Kelley, Thibaut, Lazarsfeld, Bavelas, Berkowitz and many others. But despite the respect we have for their work—and despite, in some cases, a network of personal friendships—it is no secret that acceptance is becoming increasingly difficult. As we read them and try to understand and assimilate the principles that guide them we must often conclude that they are strangers to us, that our experience does not tally with theirs, that our views of man, of reality and of history are different. Before my first visit to the United States there was little, save a few publications by Lewin, Festinger and Sherif, which did not leave me with the impression of strangeness.

Consider as an example the book on small groups by Thibaut and Kelley (1959) to which I shall return later. When I tried to read it for the first time several years ago, I could neither understand it nor find much of interest in it. As is well known, the book analyses all social relations in terms of transactions. These are based on an individual's rational calculation of how other people are likely to bring him most satisfaction, i.e. a maximum of rewards and a minimum of penalties. But as I read the book I thought of innumerable examples of social interaction which have nothing to do with an equation of supply and demand, such as the role of reciprocity and of values, or the reality of social conflict and of social identity. These gaps were disturbing, and I never managed to finish the book; yet I knew that it was considered to be an important book, though I could not understand why it should be. I encountered similar difficulties with some of the maxims implicit in a good deal of current research: "We like those who support us"; "The leader is a person who understands the needs of the members of his group"; "We help those who help us"; "Understanding the point of view of another person promotes cooperation".

This "social psychology of the nice person" was to me then—as it still is today—offensive in many ways; it had little relevance to what I knew or had experienced. Its implicit moral stance reminded me of another maxim (which is perhaps not as uncontroversial as it appears): "It is better to be healthy and rich than to be ill and poor". I knew from my social experience that we seek out those who differ from us and that we can identify with them; that we can love someone who is contemptuous of us; that leaders may impose themselves on others through violence or through following unremittingly their own ideals—and that often, in doing this, they are not only admired but also loved; and that, after all, is it not an opponent who often comes to know us best?

It was only after I had been to the United States and discussed these matters with American social psychologists that I began to understand their point of view and to see its background. I was then able to read the book by Thibaut and Kelley and gain some insight into its formulations and its maxims. But I also concluded that, in Europe, we must turn towards our own reality, towards our own maxims from which we must derive our own "scientific" consequences. The fact that social psychology is at present almost exclusively American constitutes a double handicap. From the point of view of American social psychologists, this cannot fail to set limits on the relevance of their results and to create uncertainty and doubt about the validity of the ideas and laws that they propose. For social psychologists elsewhere, this casts a doubt on the validity of their scientific attitude: they have the choice between building a social psychology appropriate to their society and culture or to rest content with the application to their teaching and research of a model from elsewhere which is highly restricted.

It must not be forgotten that the real advance made by American social psychology was not so much in its empirical methods or in its theory construction as in the fact that it took for its theme of research and for the contents of its theories the issues of *its own* society. Its merit was as much in its techniques as in translating the problems of American society into sociopsychological terms and in making them an object of scientific enquiry. Thus, if all that we do is to assimilate the literature which is transmitted to us—be it only for comparative purposes—we do no more than adopt the preoccupations and traditions of another society; we work in the abstract, to solve the problems of American society. And thus we must resign ourselves to be a small part of a science which is made elsewhere and to be isolated in a society—our own—in which we have shown no interest. We can achieve in this way scientific recognition as methodologists or experimenters—but never as social psychologists. It is true that we have many inducements for imitation.

But we must try to work in a spirit of contradiction, to become partners in a stimulating dialogue; the differences between the "big brother" and the "little brother" should become less marked with age; their persistence only shows that on both sides real maturity has not been attained.

This point of view is shared by others whose experience has been similar to mine; but despite our common background we have not succeeded in creating a language, a model and a definition of problems which would genuinely correspond to our social reality. It is not just this social reality that is shared; for many of us the ideas of, for example, Marx, Freud, Piaget or Durkheim are of direct relevance because they are familiar and because the questions that they were trying to answer are also our own questions. Thus, the social class structure, the phenomenon of language, the influence of ideas about society, all appear critically important and claim priority in the analysis of "collective" conduct though they hardly make an appearance in contemporary social psychology.

Confronted with this situation, some seek refuge in methodology and in the respectability that it offers, though they know full well that this is not a solution. The fact that there are so few of us is also important: it is difficult simply to continue writing for each other, to become isolated within our discipline and to be the only judges of what we do, while neglecting what happens elsewhere. Anthropology, linguistics, sociology, psychoanalysis and philosophy claim our attention; their practitioners demand that we communicate with them. It is impossible to ignore their questions and also those of the students who insist on getting answers. Social psychology as it is today is not of much help in confronting these pressures. It is an inward-looking pursuit and its development has been characterized by a neglect of the questions from which these pressures arise; or rather, it has developed in reaction to other pressures of which economics, behaviourism and industry are the most important.

The second major problem relates to what is now often called the "student revolution". There are many different opinions about the "revolutionary" character of the student movement and about how we should act towards it or react to it. My own view is that it has had a positive balance because it has helped us to confront problems which we have tended to forget. There is nothing healthier than to be brought face to face with one's own contradictions. We have been asserting for many years that science seeks truth, that its role is to promote civilized values, to extend the reign of reason, and to create human beings capable of objective judgement who would help to enact the ideals of democracy, equality and freedom. But the ideals dominated our discourse while reality judged us on our actions. Max Weber taught us that legitimate violence is the mainstay of the body politic, but we concerned ourselves with legitimacy while forgetting violence. The students took us at face value for they took seriously what we taught them. Thus, for them ideals are there to be implemented, and not just to be talked about. They are often blamed for their use of violence; but we must not forget the failure of another generation which aspired to be the counsellors of princes and became instead their servants. And, after all, who gave first the example of violence? Dictatorships, tortures, concentration camps were not born with the present generation of students. Phraseology alone becomes, sooner or later, empty of meaning, particularly when it distorts reality in attempting to convince the prisoner that he is free, the poor and the exploited that they live in an affluent society, the man who works fifty hours a week without any holiday that he is a member of a leisured society. No one ignores all this, but everyone helps in sweeping it under the carpet. Any visitor to a museum knows what is hidden under the fig-leaves and that their function has nothing to do with art. Why then attach a useless appendage to the human body? David's penis on the Piazza della Signoria in Florence is incomparably more beautiful. In their search for truth and sincerity the students turned against the sciences, particularly the social sciences, the institutions that shelter them and the men who practice them. Our disciplines do not appear to the younger generation as disinterested and objective as we claim them to be. They have taken it upon themselves to remind us of the ideological implications of what we do and its role in the preservation of the established order, as well as of the absence of social criticism in our work. They blame us for finding refuge in methodology under the pretext that using adequate methods is equivalent to scientific investigation. We assert that our interest is in the problems of society. They answer that we calmly ignore social inequalities, political violence, wars, underdevelopment or racial conflict. As far as they are concerned, we are safely ensconced in the "establishment".

Sometimes all this leads to the extreme view that social science is "useless". But a political movement which pursues long-term objectives cannot afford the luxury of withdrawing its support from science or of neglecting the contributions that science can make. No doubt many of us would have preferred to see the development of a science of "move-ment" rather than that of a science of "order"—to use an expression current in France. As Martin Deutsch (1969) wrote in his paper on the organizational and conceptual barriers to social change: "Indeed, many of the implicit assumptions of the social sciences buttress the barriers to change—or constitute major obstacles themselves" (p. 9). It is, however, unfortunate that neither Marxism nor the socialist countries have contributed to such a new social science of "movement". It is indeed a remarkable phenomenon, of which an explanation will have to be sought one day, that most of the social sciences such as linguistics, anthropology, economics or social psychology were founded or developed in the twentieth century without a significant influence or contribution from Marxism or the Marxists; this does not, of course, apply to Marx himself, whose ideas have had a profound impact. But the fact that such a science of movement does not exist today does not mean that its future development is not possible. And, as there is no *tabula rasa* in history, I would suppose that when it finally comes into being it will have to borrow a good deal from its predecessors. But this cannot be done if criticism remains unproductive. It is not enough to reinterpret—as is often done in France nowadays—a whole domain of research by showing that the social sciences, and social psychology in particular, depend upon implicit assumptions about society and upon an ideology which social psychologists have not been able to relinquish. This reinterpretation, which in the light of Marxist and Freudian ideas can be referred to as hermeneutic, led to the development in post-war Germany of a Freudian-Marxist ontology, while elsewhere in Europe (particularly in France) it resulted in a Freudian-Marxist epistemology.

The positivistic dream of a science without metaphysics—which today is often translated into a demand for a science without ideology—is not likely to become a reality. To my knowledge, no one has ever been able to show that as sciences were born they succeeded in pulling out their roots in social values and philosophies. If a change was created it was precisely in the transformation of these values and philosophies so as to forge links of a different nature. The notion of a complete independence of social science from pre-scientific conceptions is a fairy tale that the scientists like to tell each other.

The conference on which the present book is based was organized in response to specific pressures. We gave ourselves the task of considering a science which for some should not exist at all, and for others does not exist as yet. As I have already written, the social psychology that we ought to create must have an origin in our own reality, or at least in its relevant aspects. But this has not been, until now, the principal focus of attention. In addition—whether this is welcome or not—the role of ideology in science and the political relevance of science have become more salient than ever before. Some problems used to be considered by many as "extra-scientific", and science itself had the privilege of extra-territoriality. The time has now come to revise these notions. Science is a social institution and, as such, it is an object of analysis like any other, in the same sense as experimenters and their subjects are engaged in social interaction like everybody else. But even beyond this, the real question is simple enough though fundamental: we must ask what is the aim of the scientific community. Is it to support or to criticize the social order? Is it to consolidate it or to transform it? We are requested from all sides to state our position on this issue. There is little doubt that academic peace will not be restored for some time to come and that ivory towers will continue to crumble, one after another. It is therefore better to accept this as a fact of life than to regret a past which, after all, was not quite untarnished.

In the pages that follow, I wish to present a few ideas about the changes and transformations which appear to me necessary. I can foresee some of the objections that will be raised. It is my view, however, that some of the criticisms which originate from various political, philosophical or even scientific quarters can safely be ignored. They represent a solution which is both easy and facile as they derive from a lack of familiarity with the contents of the social sciences. My reference here is to some of the texts published by the Frankfurt School which are also discussed in this book by Ragnar Rommetveit. A similar movement exists in France: Kant, Hegel and Marx are taken up *ad nauseam*, compared and confronted; in turn, the authors confront their own "proper" image of the social sciences with that found in the "dominant" conceptions. Their victory on paper is assured and gives them the feeling of having helped in the advancement of social science. It would be an interesting experience to see them at work and to have them demonstrate how they would achieve what they propose. In science, as in other pursuits, it is not enough to point to a defect or to throw a stone at the sinner. It is foreseeable that if concomitant work of proof and validation is not done at some time or another all those texts written in fervour will soon be forgotten.

In much of the European writing there is a tendency to attribute to the Americans most of the responsibility for our failings and to confuse the criticism of social science with a criticism of the United States. This is easy for us: it is they who took all the risks. If we are "pure" it is because we have done very little and because we have not, as they have done, exploited the pre-war heritage of psychology, social psychology and sociology. I am convinced that if social psychology subsists as a discipline, the contribution to it of American social psychology will remain and last. In the sections that follow, I shall be critical of many American writers; the reason is that it is they who have done most of the work. In America, as in Europe, many social psychologists—particularly those of the younger generation—share a preoccupation with the same problems.

2   Who sets the problems and who provides the answers?

It is quite evident that the development of social psychology was directly influenced by concrete social events. For example, fascism and World War II led Kurt Lewin to his work on group decisions and on the democratic, authoritarian and *laissez-faire* types of groups. No great insight is required to understand that the needs of the market and of the manufacturing and service industries provide the background for much of the research that is done today. Nevertheless it remains important to analyse the manner in which research reflects these needs. It is here that we are made aware of one of the crucial requirements for a radical change. At present "society" (i.e. industrial and political groups, etc.) puts the questions and also suggests what kind of answers should be given. I shall illustrate this with examples from a few areas of research.

Let us begin with group dynamics. The central themes of research in this area are work efficiency and the functioning of a group in a given social environment. The real issue is the increase of productivity and the achievement of an optimal organization of industrial and military units. This is why all that was shown not to be directly linked to productivity, such as satisfaction in work, has been largely neglected. As Collins and Guetzkow (1964) wrote: "Since early studies failed to reveal a positive correlation between satisfaction and productivity, satisfaction appears to have lost its place as one of the central variables in social psychology." (p. 11.) The ideal which is aimed at is that of a good worker, a good foreman or a good officer; its content is determined by the management.

Thus, the networks of communication as well as the structuring of decisions and motivations are conceived within the framework of a system geared towards lowering costs and increasing profits.

The studies of change obey the same imperatives, as was clearly shown in the well-known experiment of Coch and French (1953) on the resistance to change. The aim was set in advance: it was the reconversion of an industrial firm. The management had difficulties with the workers and in order to achieve its aims it wished to reduce their resistance. In the Coch and French study, all that pertained to the attitudes of the workers was conceived as "resistance" while the intentions of the management were seen as fostering "change", and thus progress. In reality there was no question at all of a change in the overall functioning of the system; the aim was to achieve control of the transformation by the management which at the same time required that the workers should share its aims and its conception of the social processes which were involved.

What is the situation in the studies of conflicts and the game theory? The problems are set in advance in a perspective which is fully and specifically political: the antagonisms are based on a conflict of interests. It is the conflict between the United States and the Soviet Union which looms in the background. This is not a conflict in which representatives of two social classes or two social systems or different ideologies confront one another: it is a conflict of interest between two national states. The same kind of reasoning is applied to Vietnam. It is based on the idea that as soon as each of the opponents can achieve insight about the interests and the strategy of the other, the conflict becomes soluble. No doubt there are many disagreements amongst social psychologists about the mode of resolution to be adopted. In an excellent article Michel Plon (1970) analysed the debate on this subject between Morton Deutsch and Harold Kelley. The former has shown experimentally that reduction of threat and increase in communication during conflict can promote cooperation. The latter questioned this thesis in his own experiments and insisted that, in some measure, a show of force is needed to facilitate conflict resolution. But both "social psychological" hypotheses and the recipes that they imply are, in reality, a reflection of the two dominant political options: on the one hand, the liberal tendency, represented by Deutsch, with its stress on dialogue and the development of trust; on the other, Kelley's option of *realpolitik*, that is a strategy of negotiation supported by the realities of power. For the one and for the other the options existed before they initiated their research work in this area of social psychology.

My last example is provided by the marginalist school which is dominant at present in political economy. This school has worked out a refined model of market processes in which partners to an exchange have each their ordered scales of abilities or of preferences and, through a series of transactions, manage to establish a balance of prices, to distribute the goods and to satisfy their needs. I am not concerned here with the mathematical analysis used in this model or with its logical coherence. The real problem is that the model is based on a series of psychological presuppositions which are responsible for a vision of social reality that is profoundly individualistic. In fact, the book by Thibaut and Kelley (1959) which I have already mentioned elaborates the psychological counterpart of this theory; it accepts *en gros* its premisses and combines them with a behaviourist model of conduct. As is well known, Thibaut and Kelley assume that each individual has at his disposal a sort of internal "clock" or scale which determines the comparison level (C.L.) which indicates the profit that he might obtain if he engaged in a relationship alternative to the one in which he is engaged at present. If this profit is greater, he abandons the current relationship; if not, he stays with it. Thus, all social relations are capable of being translated in terms of supply and demand. The possibility that a demand which reflects the needs of an individual, or which he feels is his due, can be satisfied elsewhere on better terms defines the limits of the power that an offer may have. It is from this nucleus of ideas that Thibaut and Kelley proceed to the definitions of norms of work in groups, of power, etc. What appears to me significant is the attempt to construct a theory of collective processes on the basis of an individualistic theory; and this seems to be done through the assimilation of these processes into the functioning of a market economy. The market is a special social institution characteristic of a certain historical period; nevertheless, a general sociopsychological theory is founded on the principles of its functioning.

My concern is not at present with the logical basis of this trend of research or with the theoretical and experimental validity of its results. It is rather with what it excludes when it allows itself to be confined to the context just described. Thus, it is striking that in the field of group dynamics questions have never been asked about the manner in which the group is a product of its own activity. Groups do not just adapt to their environments; in some ways they create this environment and in others they treat it as a resource rather than as something that exists predeterminately. In other words, we are confronted with a study of group dynamics which, paradoxically, shows no interest in the genesis of groups (cf. G. de Montmollin, 1959, 1960). If we consider what happened around us historically we can see—and this is constantly being confirmed through ethological studies—that men always created the collective institutions and organizations which they needed. Productivity is, in reality, only a by-product: the first task of a group is not to function better but to function. Bavelas' networks—ingenious as they are—provide an example of this lack of interest in human creative activity, as it is expressed in society and in groups that create themselves. Some of the work done by Claude Faucheux and myself (1960) was concerned with the study of creating a system of social relations in an environment. Claude Flament (1965) has also tried to bridge the gap between the "genetic" and the "productivist" perspectives. More recently, in an experiment which has not yet been published, Jean-Claude Abric was able to show that the manner in which individuals conceive of a task leads them to create a form of social organization which is adapted to it.

Similar comments can be made about the study by Coch and French (1953). Social change cannot be envisaged solely in terms of techniques and of environmental constraints. There are always two factors in it, exemplified by those who initiate change and those who are at the receiving end of it. Together they constitute a system of intergroup relations with its special characteristics. This is a system of dynamic interactions in which each of the parts acts upon the other. In addition, resistance to change is a necessary ingredient of all change: it is not an abstract or a causal factor and it must be considered as a consequence of the social situation. As the process of change develops, resistance to it affects both its "receiver" and its "initiator". The fact that the management called in social psychologists in the case of the Coch and French study is proof in itself of some form of a modification of perspective in the initiator which was due to the pressure exerted by the other part of the social system.

It is indeed remarkable that the authors almost completely neglected the interactional aspects of the situation: they asked themselves no questions about the conduct of the management, its motivation or its intentions, nor did they investigate the history of the relations between the management and the workers. In this way, all the issues pertaining to the analysis of the total social system as such are by-passed and an *inter*group situation is transformed into one of *intra*group relations. All the issues are reduced to problems of motivation. The general perspective remains that of the management, since the stages of the process of change are defined as "resistance", i.e. as obstacles to the effective implementation of what *must* come. The issue of *who* wishes the changes to be introduced and *whose* interests they would serve is not even touched upon; nor is anything said about the possibility that resistance might be legitimate, that its roots may be in the objective situation and that perhaps it is a real necessity for those who resist. It must be stressed once again that the authors' reasoning implies that change could take place without anyone resisting it, or rather that it is the resisting group which is exclusively at the origin of the difficulties while it could take the option of simply accepting what is being proposed. Anyone who has had an opportunity of studying situations of this kind knows that the initiators of change, be they managers or administrators, are very often opposed to any change by which they themselves would be affected; if they request changes from others it is in order to maintain themselves even more securely in their own positions (Moscovici, 1961a).

To summarize: Coch and French adopted a partial definition of the situation which enabled them to consider social change as a means of ensuring social control; this in turn enabled them to consider resistance as a negative and accidental variable instead of recognizing that it is an aspect of the situation which is positive and necessary. Finally, they envisaged intergroup relations from an intragroup point of view. They were aware, however, of the intergroup nature of the problem as is shown in the following passage: "In this conflict between the power field of management and the power field of the group, the group attempted to reduce the strength of the hostile power field relative to the strength of their own power field. This change was accomplished in three ways: (a) The group increased its own power by developing a more cohesive and well-disciplined group. (b) They secured 'allies' by getting the backing of the union in filing a formal grievance about the new piece rate. (c) They attacked the hostile power field directly in the form of aggression against the supervisor, the time-study engineer, and the higher management. Thus the aggression was derived not only from individual frustration, but also from the conflict between two groups." But the authors have no interest in this conflict.

It cannot be said that the study of conflict in social psychology has been an example of an adequate scientific analysis of a problem. It has suffered from a narrow dependence upon game theory which itself contributed to the view that wars are a normal way of solving differences between nations and that they can be stopped through the use of an appropriate strategy—that is, a rational strategy. It is surprising that at a time when social and political ideologies play such an important role in human affairs so little interest is being shown in their effects on social conduct and in the definition of the nature of conflicts. Individuals or groups often have different conceptions of reality, and as soon as an appropriate analysis is made of the nature of these differences the conflicts of interests or of motives become secondary. It is then discovered that the opponents do not share a common framework, that they do not focus on the same aspects of the environment and that their weighing up of gains and losses is by no means identical. Because of all this, they do not have a common language or the will to communicate; if and when a dialogue does begin the conflict is already almost resolved. What then is the meaning of proposing a solution which consists of suggesting that attempts should be made to "understand" the other so that cooperation can replace competition? The implication is that the opponents were never strangers to one another and that the more they fight the more interest they have in becoming closely acquainted. It is only too well known that peace was never achieved in this way.

The same considerations apply to the relations between individuals and between small groups. I shall go even further: the alternative of competition–cooperation is unrealistic, or at least it is only one amongst several possible alternatives. Division of labour, definition of boundaries and the exercise of influence and of power all represent other modes of conflict solution which can be observed again and again in history as well as in everyday life. They deserve to be taken into account, analysed and assessed—at least in their theory if not in the design of experiments.

This brings me back to the economic conception which we have so easily and spontaneously accepted in developing the kind of social psychology imagined by the exchange theory and in our modes of thinking about decisions and conflict. Here also we are dealing with an individualistic conception in the sense that it considers all that happens in society in terms of individual choices and decisions. It confines the field of economic behaviour to processes of utilization of means that are considered as given in advance for the purpose of achieving aims which are also pre-established. This applies to the means that an individual has at his disposal and to his anticipations, as well as to the technical and social procedures which can be employed for reaching, in the long run, social aims and objectives. Thus, the aim of economic theory becomes the planning of distribution for the sake of an optimal satisfaction of pre-established aims and needs through the employment of pre-established means. One could say that, at the limit, the human individual becomes unnecessary. It was enough for Pareto to have a "photography of his tastes"; after that he could disappear. There is no room in this system for the agent of economic conduct nor for socioeconomic processes; there are only scarce resources and supernumerary needs which have to be coordinated. And even when the fact that a market economy has its uncertainties draws attention to the existence of people acting within it, no account is taken of the uncertainties that they may have about the resources available to them and about their reciprocal goals.

It is in this way that some economists have projected the attitudes and the norms of a capitalist society on the processes of exchange. Their "psychological" reconstructions belong in this context: human action is conceived as determined by the imperatives of a cash economy and of profit. But there is more to it than that: all that is social is simply excluded from this kind of economics. Collective investments, expenditure which is not channelled through the market or so-called external economics are not within its purview. In consequence, decisions which are truly collective, norms which determine the mode of utilization of resources and political interactions—which are very different phenomena from simple administrative deliberations leading to choices or to decisions that are of secondary interest—are also outside its competence; nor are the processes through which means of action become available and goals become defined within its province because in an individualistic perspective they are considered as "givens" in Man's nature. As a result of all this, this version of economics conceives of an immense area of human conduct as *irrational since within its practice all that goes beyond individualism and all that diverges a little from a capitalist model enters by definition the domain of irrationality*.

What is the background of this conception? First, it is a rationality which is purely Cartesian and mechanical: thus, conduct is rational in so far as it conforms to principles of conservation (the means are provided once and for all, and they are immutable) and of maximization (the search for optimal satisfaction). Second, the calculations are purely individual because they are limited to relationships between two individuals. But if psychologists adopt such hypotheses, which they have a perfect right to do, they must also realize that their intellectual universe comes to be confined within a very specific sector of the society and that they are only interested in a small and specific fraction of mankind. Reading a few anthropological studies or an acquaintance with other cultures would be instructive on this point. The gift, the reciprocity, the bonds of consanguinity and of religion are all there to indicate the limits of the law of supply and demand, and also of social psychological theories. In fact, the manner in which the processes of choice and of its evolution are envisaged in the theory of cognitive dissonance are not compatible with the premises of market economy. The remarkable experimental studies on needs carried out by Zimbardo (1969) prove that needs cannot be considered in advance as a "given". Mauk Mulder's research on power (1959) also contradicts in many respects a conception of this issue based on utilitarian principles.

But I should remind the reader that it is not my aim to criticize these theories and the research arising from them. I wish rather to demonstrate how much they are tied to the questions asked and the answers provided in a specific context. Our chances of progress and of renewal depend upon our ability to remain open to the problems of our collective reality. We have not been sufficiently receptive to them in Europe. Indeed, something important and precious can be learned from the openness and receptivity of our American colleagues. Society changes and invents, and its demands are an important source of stimulation. But it is for us to give the answers, or at least to attempt to find them. Because of our background, our functions and our traditions we are, or should be, in a position to analyse, examine and place the questions in a wider framework.

If the studies of conflict and of means to resolve it were placed in the perspective of all possible situations—that is of those enacted in history —and beyond the limited horizon of political interaction, they would lead to the formulation of answers which would differ from those that were until now envisaged. The same applies to change, to group dynamics or even to the very definition of what is social in human conduct. In fact, it is probable that, through a process of feedback, the questions themselves would be transformed. As of now—and this is what I wish to stress again—social psychologists have done no more than to operationalize questions and answers which were imagined elsewhere. And thus the work in which they are engaged—in which we are all engaged—is not the work of scientific analysis but of *engineering* with all the weight of methodology that this implies. The confusion between science and engineering is very marked in the social sciences, and particularly in social psychology. This is why it seems to me that if we must allow society to ask the questions—since this is implied in the nature of our activities—it is, in contrast, our duty to elaborate and redefine these questions ourselves. This is a necessary condition for establishing a real dialogue in which we can rediscover the freedom to analyse objectively all the aspects of a problem and to consider the various points of view emanating from the society in which we live.

3   The place of theory in a world of facts

3.1   THE TACIT COMPROMISE

It must be admitted that social psychology is not truly a science. We wish to give it an appearance of science by using mathematical reasoning and the refinements of experimental method; but the fact is that social psychology cannot be described as a discipline with a unitary field of interest, a systematic framework of criteria and requirements, a coherent body of knowledge or even a set of common perspectives shared by those who practice it. It would be nearer to the truth to say that it consists of a movement of research and methodology which periodically attracts a collection of diverse interests that sometimes succeed in enriching it in new and unexpected ways; but a solid foundation for the future has not been laid.

This movement is not one which proceeds steadily in a certain direction. From time to time the interests of the researchers are mobilized by themes or areas which appear new and important at the moment; but sooner or later these prove to be sterile or exhausted and they are abandoned. Thus, research spreads here and there in a haphazard fashion rather than accumulating and ascending to new levels. It oscillates between two poles. One consists of a collection of separate and unrelated topics; so that, for example, anyone interested in doing research on small groups or on networks of communication or on comparisons between individual and group performance will identify himself as a social psychologist. At the opposite pole there is an illusion of coherence since research is organized around general themes, such as the processes of social influence or of attitude change, but these themes remain eclectic and unstructured. The domain of the subject is split into "topics", "clans", "schools" and "establishments" which each have their own methods of asking questions, their own language and their own interests; what is more, each develops out of its peculiarities its own criteria of truth and excellence. Thus, social psychology is at the same time a field which is fenced in and a mosaic; our appearance of cohesion is due to external pressures, but our dependence upon diverse interests, techniques and sciences continues to separate us from one another.

It seems to me that the *creation of a system of theoretical activities* is essential for a coherent development of the subject. It is the absence of such a system that is the main obstacle in providing answers which would be relevant to the questions set to us by society. It is only a commonly shared framework of criteria and principles that can enable scientists to free themselves from external pressures, to take account of the relevant aspects of reality and to be critical both about their own activities and about the activities of those who are their patrons. Theories determine not only what is "interesting" but also what is "possible". But they do not originate *ex nihilo*; they are the result of a collective endeavour and of the collective inspirations of those who are the practitioners of a discipline. The point I wish to insist upon is that our entire "scientific ideology"—to take up a term used by Henri Tajfel—is an obstacle to this kind of development in social psychology. Three aspects of this ideology are, in my view, particularly important.

The first is the predominance of a positivistic epistemology. Its main tenets are that facts are "given" in the environmental reality, that they can be inductively isolated through a description of regularities, and that experimentation is the hallmark of science. In this perspective, theory is a language and a tool which is both subordinate to the empirical method and subsequent to it chronologically. We are not very clear about our identity; and therefore, in order to become "scientists", we try to follow as closely as possible the prevailing norms from which we derive our emphasis on experimental and statistical techniques and the ritualism that goes with them. Many of us work away peacefully in our own corners guided by the idea that it is essential for the moment to accumulate facts which will serve one day to build a conceptual structure.

In the second place, the neglect of theoretical activity results in a sort of *tacit compromise* whereby we avoid facing questions about the nature of laws with which our discipline is concerned and about their mode of validation. This is reflected in conflicts between observation and experimentation, and between the role of the "psychological" and the role of the "social". The dividing line between observation and experimentation is not due in our subject to a distribution of tasks or to a specialization of techniques of research; rather, it is due to a differentiation of research strategies determined by the nature of the problems which are being studied. It is a genuine split which divides the scientific community so deeply that one is entitled to ask if we are not dealing with two distinct kinds of scientists or two separate disciplines. To opt for one or the other of these methodologies is like becoming a member of a club which one can join on condition one adopts a *credo* that needs no justification or explanation. The game is all played out between these two clubs and mutual criticism eliminates all possibility of a *rapprochement* though attempts are still being made here and there to create it. The criticisms that each side makes of the other are well known. Experimental social psychologists are blamed for the artificiality of the situations which they use in studying social phenomena and thus for the fact that their scientific method is inadequate to take hold of social reality. Non-experimentalists are told that the complexity of social processes cannot be grasped in their "natural" context and that their simple collection of data is not a procedure capable of providing a rigorous verification of the hypotheses which may be suggested by observation. The argument against them hinges on the incompatibility of their vision of social reality with a properly scientific mode of procedure.

The real issue at stake in this debate is the definition of sociopsychological theory and its validation. To the experimentalists, the *post hoc* interpretations of observed facts—however coherent they may be—cannot result in truly scientific conceptualizations and cannot therefore provide the foundations of a science. The non-experimentalists find little interest in the hypotheses which form the background of experiments; efficient prediction is achieved, according to them, at the cost of neglecting most of the parameters and missing altogether the specificity of what is being studied. A common articulation of the two approaches becomes even more difficult in view of the fact that theories which lead to experimentation have a structure which differs from those which originate in systematic observation. And thus it is far more comfortable not to raise these problems too often, not to face choices or stimulate passions, and to leave the choice of future directions to the passage of time and to "natural selection".

But if a choice really had to be made, would our conceptual generalizations tend in a "psychological" or in a "social" direction? The acceptance of a psychological perspective essentially means that social psychology would become a specialized branch of general psychology whose function would be to deepen our knowledge of very general processes, such as perception, judgement or memory, which remain unchanged throughout their modes and conditions of operation and production. The data of social psychology would thus enable us to do no more than to specify in more detail certain variables in human or animal behaviour which, in the last analysis, are reducible to laws of "animal" or "individual" psychology, of psychophysics or psychophysiology. Thus, for example, social perception should be studied in the same way as auditory or visual perception; sociopsychological phenomena, such as processes of influence, of attitude change or of problem solution in groups, should be no more than special instances of conditioning or motivational principles to which the general laws of learning should be applied. The work of Zajonc (1966) is an excellent example of this tendency.

This kind of extension presupposes an implicit acceptance of three postulates. The first is that the difference between social and elementary non-social processes is only one of degree and that a hierarchy of phenomena can be established in which they are ordered from simpler to more complex, and from individual to collective. The second postulate is that social processes do not imply the existence of social phenomena governed by their own laws, but rather that they are accounted for by psychological laws which can at the same time be based on hypothetical laws of physiology. The final postulate is that there is no difference in kind between social and non-social behaviour: other people intervene only as a part of the general environment. The early doctrine of F. H. Allport (1924) remains the *credo* of many social psychologists: "The significance of social behaviour is the same as that of non-social, namely, the connection of individual's biological maladjutment to his environment. In and through others, many of our most urgent wants are fulfilled; and our behaviour towards them is based on the same fundamental needs as our reactions towards all objects, social or non-social." (pp. 3–4.)

Opposed to this tendency, though still timidly, is another trend of thought which tends to conceive sociopsychological processes from a sociological point of view. Examples of it are provided by research on the structures of small groups, on the hierarchy of roles and statuses through which are defined an individual's identity and his social position, on mass communications, on frames of reference and on intergroup relations. Social psychology becomes here a way of studying—if possible in the laboratory and with methods that have proved their usefulness—the social processes which exist on a wider scale in the society at large. The study of cultures is another example—though more marginal to social psychology—of a similar approach; it subordinates sociopsychological mechanisms to the cultural and social context of behaviour, to the social framework of the fundamental aspects of psychological functioning or to the cultural aspects of the processes of learning and socialization. By contrast—as Claude Faucheux (1970) has clearly shown—the cross-cultural studies in social psychology have completely neglected the properly cultural or social dimensions of comparison.

Amongst social psychologists it was undoubtedly Sherif who pursued most steadily the attempt to generalize from the laboratory to the society at large. The least that can be said is that, as a result, he has certainly not achieved much popularity. The proof needs to be sought no further than in the book by Deutsch and Krauss (1965) on theory in social psychology in which no reference is made either to his research or to his theoretical position. This lapse is obviously the result of a tacit consensus. If the problem of generalization had been taken more seriously, it would have been impossible to neglect this kind of orientation and to avoid an attempt to clarify the issues that it raises. In this book these issues are confronted directly by Israel, Rommetveit and Tajfel who each approach them from their own points of view; in doing so, they force us to face difficulties that many would prefer to forget and some might think of as being "old hat". Nevertheless, the problems are there and they remain permanently at the background of all our work. They need not perhaps be solved before we can run the next experiment; but we must find a solution to them if we wish to engage in building a theory.

Last, but not least, the avoidance of theory and of theoretical debate has also its emotional aspects. The social sciences, including social psychology, developed in confrontation with philosophy. As a result of this, there exists a kind of reactive fear of indulging in "philosophical" speculation. Manipulation of ideas is therefore acceptable on condition that it leads more or less directly to experimentation or, alternatively, if it is capable of a mathematical formalization which, however weak or dubious, offers at least an appearance of "respectability". Because of the prevailing insecurity, the milieu of the social sciences has become so repressive that it has made science completely uninteresting; the fundamental problems of Man and society are lost in a cloud of fragmentary "fields" and techniques which succeed in turning away genuine talent and in freezing all enthusiasm. Experiments play a negative role, as a barrier and a signal, only enabling us to prove to the world that we are doing science and not philosophy. If we lose this mark of identity, we will lose all our assurance and will not know whether our theoretical constructions can be recognized as "scientific". But all this is no more than a trap; neither methods nor formal languages have ever guaranteed the "scientific" character of anything. At any rate, why should we despair before we have even started. Not everything in science is "scientific": biological theories of the origins of life or cosmological theories about the structure of the universe have not yet reached this level.

3.2 SOME CONSEQUENCES FOR RESEARCH AND THEORY

The weight of positivism, the tensions between observational and experimental methods and the fear of speculation are the causes of the slow development of theory in social psychology. One of the consequences is the respect of good common sense, of the psychology of well-tried aphorisms. I shall not insist on this delicate theme; as is well known, it contributes greatly to the accusations of banality that are often thrown at us. I should like, however, to insert a few comments on the subject.

Common sense is reputed to be shared out more equitably than almost anything else in the world. It does not, however, necessarily reflect a stable and immutable set of data corresponding to the existence of a firmly validated version of reality. On the contrary, it is a product of culture which, in our society, is meshed in with scientific theories. In a study of the public image of psychoanalysis (Moscovici, 1961b), I described the extent to which psychoanalytic theory has penetrated common sense in everyday judgements, discussions and interpretations of people's actions. Claudine Herzlich (1969) analysed similar phenomena in our conceptions of health and illness. In the same way, Marxist vocabulary is part and parcel of our heritage and of, as it were, the spontaneous philosophy of millions of people. The same is true of behaviourism, of functional sociology, of economic models or of evaluation of actions in historical or in probabilistic terms. Thus, to respect common sense is to respect theories that we have implicitly accepted. But we must also learn to distrust the "wisdom of the people". The fact that it accords with our intuitions proves nothing but the existence of a consensus. The German socialist Babel used to say that he was always worried when he was in agreement with his opponents or when they agreed with him. I think that the social psychologist should have the same attitude when he observes or discovers that his results do no more than confirm something that is known to everybody.

This does not mean that we should strive to be original at all costs. And yet, in science it is only true discovery that is astonishing and original. This is why we must try to accept things for what they are in our discipline. In its beginnings, social psychology had the task of verifying certain hypotheses and interpretations even if they were not very different from what everyone would accept without difficulty. The time has now come to recognize that we must leave this first stage behind and go further. To multiply experiments in order to rediscover what is obvious can only lead to a paradoxical situation. In fact, the principal *raison d'être* of experimental method is to invent and validate *new* consequences of a theory or to produce *unexpected* effects. If we conduct experiments which do not have these characteristics and which do no more than confine to the laboratory what is already diffused in the culture, we proceed in a fully non-experimental fashion. Our experiments become then a kind of systematic survey aimed at inscribing in numbers and transcribing in books the beliefs which are transmitted by oral tradition. Thus, most of the experiments on social influence, on the effects of a majority, on leadership or on threat are no more than a long interview which we conduct with society about its social theory.

However, the reign of common sense is only one of the consequences of the absence of theoretical effort; the mortality and sterility of findings in some of the areas of research is another. Studies on group dynamics and on Bavelas' networks provide a clear example of this. I would not be far wrong in estimating that there must exist about 5000 articles on these topics; this figure is probably an underestimate. Most of these studies are no more than validations of industrial folklore and minia-turizations of real situations; they contain practically no valuable scientific information. The books that were written about these studies and the autopsies that were conducted on them revealed that, in most cases, they were completely devoid of any preoccupation with con-ceptual problems. As McGrath and Altman (1966) wrote: "The research production has kept mounting at an enormous rate. Theory was minimal throughout most of the 1950's and has continued to be so till the present." (p. 9.) For these reasons, the authors of the various reviews of the field were reduced to compiling bibliographies or, at best, presentations of classified lists of results; indeed, it cannot be said that what remains is a set of confirmed propositions or of properly defined variables. I have the suspicion that the same is true of the study of conflict.

The third consequence of the absence of interest in theory is the isolation of various areas of research, or rather the fact that no consistent efforts have been made to arrive at theoretical generalizations. With regard, for example, to the work on conflict, one may ask whether its main preoccupation was with processes of conflict—which are central to all psychological and social phenomena—or rather with particular actions said to be "conflictual". As is well known, the latter is true; no effort has been made to analyse the relations between this particular area of behaviour and the central processes of conflict or to see how they manifest themselves in various kinds of real situations. As I am not very familiar with this field of work, I shall not discuss it further; instead, I shall take the example of a subject which is nearer to my own interests and in which a great deal of work has been done in recent years: this is the phenomenon of "risky shift".

Let us first describe briefly the well-known paradigm used in these studies. The subjects are generally confronted with choices between various alternatives, involving a change in the situation, in the relations with peers, etc. of a person. Each of the choices represents various degrees of risk for the person who makes them. Working alone each subject makes ten or twelve such choices. Then the subjects are brought together in groups of various sizes and requested to select for each problem a level of risk unanimously acceptable to all the members of the group. Once the group discussion is completed, the subjects are again separated and asked again to indicate their personal preferences for the solution of each problem. Groups are generally found to favour riskier solutions than individuals.

This finding was arrived at by chance. In science and in technology chance findings of this kind have always been fully exploited. A good deal of attention has been drawn to risky shift because, from the time of the early experiments by F. H. Allport and by Sherif, it has been maintained that, in social situations, individual opinions and judgements tend to converge towards the mean and to shift away from extreme positions. Allport attributed this tendency to the rational nature of collective decisions which stand in contrast to the spontaneous behaviour of crowds characterized by extreme judgements and irrational actions. Thus, the results of the experiments on risk, which have been replicated many times, constitute an exception to a type of conduct which was thought to be universal. This brought in its wake two questions: the first concerned the conditions in which it was possible to produce a "conservative shift", and the second was the question of why groups took more risks than individuals.

Conservative shift was rarely obtained in experiments; when it did happen, it was through making more salient the ethical dimensions of risk. On the whole, it was disappointingly difficult to produce this phenomenon.

Diverse explanations of risky shift have been proposed. Wallach, Kogan and Bem (1964) offered the hypothesis of diffusion of responsibility in a group: as each individual in a group feels less responsible than he does when making decisions on his own he dares to take more risks. Brown (1965) started from the idea that in individual situations people are in a state of "pluralistic ignorance" which causes them to keep on the side of caution. When they find themselves in a social situation they abandon caution and take more extreme positions, particularly as risk has a positive value connotation in our society. Finally, Kelley and Thibaut (1969) took the position that there exists a "rhetoric of risk", i.e. that arguments in favour of taking a risk are made more convincing and are elaborated more than those preaching conservatism. In addition, some authors tried to show that risk-taking depends upon personality characteristics, and hence relates to the influence exerted on a group by its most extreme members.

My own view is that if all these theories have some truth in them, then one thing is certain: risky shift presents no interest as an object of study and does not deserve the efforts of experimental and theoretical analysis expended on it. Indeed, if it all comes down to a combination of questions of influence, of rhetoric, of personality and of conformity to norms, then risky shift is no more than a secondary phenomenon and it would be more useful to study influence or conformity directly. Judgements concerning risk could thus be seen as not differing in any way from judgements that are made about love, aggression or drugs. And if these show the kind of displacement found in the case of risk, the logic implied in the theories just mentioned could lead us to propose a theory of love-shift, aggression-shift or drug-shift. One could then multiply the examples indefinitely and finally arrive at a specific "theory" for each of these aspects of social conduct. To complete the picture, one could proceed to one of these "syntheses" or "comparisons", learning perhaps that the risky shift of the Germans is greater than that of the French, that there is no distinction between a "love-shift" and a "cuisine-shift", and finally that altogether more risks are taken in groups. Then, in a manner which is purely inductive and *post hoc*, we could reproduce *ad infinitum* a phenomenon which was first discovered by chance. All research would then be concentrated on risk without any new light being thrown on cognitive or on social phenomena.

But a very different situation arises if a strange phenomenon—strange in the sense that it contradicts generally accepted principles—leads to questions about the general implications that it might have. For example, when physicists learned about Roentgen's discovery they did not spend much time in questioning its validity or in searching for its various manifestations; they enquired immediately about its bearing on the theory of matter. When Kogan worked for a time in my laboratory we discussed his experiments; I adopted an attitude which seemed to me guided by the same concern for generalization and tried to go beyond the explanations specific to the phenomenon of risky shift and to keep at the level of its basic significance which is that it constitutes an exception to the apparently "universal" law about the influence of the group on an individual. This leads to the first question: Is this shift due to semantic content or to another property of this content? A brief analysis led to the formulation of a fairly straightforward hypothesis: the majority of studies which have shown the convergence of opinions in a group used stimuli which presented no significant meaning to the subjects and did not provoke any deep commitment.

It then became important to see if the same effect could be obtained by using judgement or attitude scales containing this feature of "significance" and of "commitment" which the previous scales had lacked. The next point was concerned with the difference between "risky" and "conservative" shifts: the only interest that it might have originates from a consideration of the semantic content; it is only through this that the direction of judgement becomes important and that we confront two distinct phenomena. In contrast, from the psychological or even from the social point of view, the main question is whether we are dealing here with one and the same phenomenon which is mistakenly being given two different explanations. This would amount to proceeding according to an Aristotelian type of epistemology which distinguishes between an upwards and a downwards movement, between circular movement and movement in a straight line, and which offers a separate theory to account for each. The Galilean treatment of the same problem abandons the descriptions of diversity and attempts to separate the unity and the common nature of the forces involved. Whether a body goes up, or down, it is always subject to gravity and it is gravity that must be studied.

In the same way, whether the judgement of a group is more conservative or more risky than that of its individual members, it reflects the same phenomenon; namely, a departure from the mean or a polarization of attitudes. Experiments on familiarization have, at a certain point of time, given the impression that individuals could show extremization in their judgements without any intervention of social interaction. This phenomenon was not confirmed in subsequent experiments. But in the experiment by Kogan and Wallach (1964), the validity of which has not been questioned by anyone, it was shown that individuals took greater risks after discussing the questionnaire of choice dilemmas and without having reached consensus. Therefore, all that can be said is that individuals reach more extreme opinions after social interaction; it cannot be claimed that groups take greater risks than individuals. Thus, the various theories mentioned above were so many attempts to answer a question that does not exist. But another question which has not been raised does exist and should have been answered since it motivated the initial interest in risky shift. Why, for example, does a group decision tend either towards a compromise (the mean) or polarization? In other words, why should either an effect of group averaging or one of group polarization be observed?

In relation to this question two points should be made which are of significance to the general modes of procedure in social psychology.

First, the question I have just formulated on a theoretical level has always been asked purely in technical terms. For example, the statistical analysis of risky shift is usually conducted as follows: first, the mean is calculated, i.e. the numerical value that would express consensus if individuals behaved according to the law of convergence; then, the difference between this "theoretical" consensus and the consensus that has really taken place is used as the measure of "shift". Consequently, the relation between group averaging and group polarization is considered in purely statistical terms.

The second point concerns obstacles to generalization. The restriction of interest to semantic content bars all progress towards more fundamental phenomena. Thus, if we focus entirely on risk we deal with an exception to a general law which can be distorted and turned about before we reach the point of analysing what is exceptional about it and why. The possibility of its serving to question a model or a theoretical concept cannot be exploited until we cease to concentrate on this particular aspect. In this way, the concrete imprisons the abstract. The experiments by Moscovici and Zavalloni (1969), by Doise (1969) and by Fraser et al. (1971) have shown that the polarization effect must be considered in a more general framework than the risky shift which is only a special case of another phenomenon. Other experiments have enabled us to study the conditions in which either group averaging or group polarization could be obtained with the items first used to demonstrate risky shift. But this was only possible because the issues raised at the beginning were modified to integrate the initial discovery into a wider context. It then became obvious that the modified phenomenon is of direct relevance to social decision. It is also relevant to processes of judgement and of attitude change, to the averaging and summation of social categories, and to intragroup—and even intergroup—relations in the formation of prejudice. The studies by Anderson (1968), Sherif et al. (1965), Tajfel and Wilkes (1964) and Fishbein and Raven (1962) confirm these views. Hence the present task is to find an explanation for the totality of these results, and the study of risky shift in isolation loses all its interest.

3.3 TOWARDS A PHLOGISTON THEORY

The respect of common sense, the proliferation of experimental studies lacking theoretical preoccupations, and the isolation of various areas of research in social psychology combine to explain the accumulation of facts and notions which do not amount to real progress since they are not conceptually integrated and since no theory is, in any real sense, disconfirmed or replaced by another. The concepts employed have their origin in other fields; theoretical models exist side by side in a relationship which neither constitutes real dialogue nor fertile contradiction. It is therefore not surprising that the empirically established facts are nothing but a heterogeneous collection, as are the theories on which they are supposed to depend. The experiments and empirical studies are not really capable of confrontation in a common framework; the contradictory results published about the same phenomenon rarely lead to a conceptual analysis which could provide a decision and transform our knowledge.

This situation is reflected in the textbooks. The most useful among them adopt a vague outline of structure enabling them, at best, to classify a few empirical results which are usually presented outside their theoretical context—assuming that such a context exists. Contradictory examples are rarely taken into consideration, and when they are it is in an abstract and remote manner. As a result, the student gains the impression of a well-ordered and fruitful discipline—for the very reason that difficult or contradictory points are ignored.

What happens when a theory does emerge? How is it presented, criticized or understood? The theory of cognitive dissonance is a case in point (Festinger, 1957, 1964). It is true thas this is not truly a sociopsychological theory; but there is no doubt of its importance as an intellectual discovery, its ability to stimulate research or its originality of perspective. In a properly constituted science, a theory of this kind would immediately become a point of departure for new concepts which would integrate it in a sociopsychological context and translate it into truly social terms. Its fate was radically different. With the exception of Bem (1965), interest was focused entirely on details of methodology. In a notorious article Chapanis and Chapanis (1962) devoted all their attention to the mode of selection of subjects and to points of statistics. Others reproached Festinger because he failed to provide a measure of dissonance and was therefore unable to make predictions. And it all stopped there. Many social psychologists continued to work on social reinforcement or on exchange theory as if the theory of cognitive dissonance did not exist and did not contradict the very principles of behaviour they took for granted. If they had really taken these principles seriously, a controversy created by dissonance theory should have been a centre of intellectual activity. Could one imagine the chemists calmly continuing research in their own little corners while some believed in phlogiston and others in oxygen? It is obvious to anyone familiar with the history of ideas that real progress emerges from theoretical confrontation and facts and methods play a role which is relatively less important. Even if Festinger and his pupils did not fully conform to the experimental ritual, the facts which they demonstrated retain their interest and importance. The facts established by Piaget on the basis of a solid and coherent theory also failed to conform to all the rules of the game—and yet they survived the passage of time and the attacks of the critics.

Festinger and his pupils were often reproached for their tendency to seek results which were not obvious, and which were at variance with common sense. This is an objection which is astonishing but significant: it shows how distant is our conception of experimentation from truly scientific thought. I wrote earlier that experimentation should always aim at invention and at creating new effects. The natural sciences are sciences of effects; as distinct from them, the social sciences—and particularly social psychology—remain sciences of phenomena and of appearances. The belief that everything or nearly everything about human conduct is already known from direct observation prevents our discipline from generating true discovery and from contributing data that would modify pre-scientific knowledge. And thus our knowledge takes the form of a refinement of pre-knowledge, and the banality of our results is concealed behind the refinement of techniques and methods.

It is not my intention to defend here the theory of cognitive dissonance for it needs no defence. But it is important to stress that when a theory of this quality appears in social psychology no serious attempts are made either to develop further its relevance to collective processes or to invalidate it. Even when attempts at disconfirmation are made they can hardly be described as scientific. Instead, theories of cognitive consistency are given uniform treatment as if they all had the same potential scientific impact; the recipe for this eclectic cuisine can be found, for example, in the recent book edited by Abelson *et al.* (1968).

It would not be very useful to discuss this situation in social psychology without attempting to outline how we might remedy the deficiencies. Practically all sciences have their theoreticians and their experimentalists, and also their theoretical and experimental journals. Why should we not accept the same kind of division and specialization? We could then let the theorists define their aim, their "culture" and the structure of their problems. At any rate, theory and experiment have never fully interlocked; the advance of knowledge is a result of contradictions between them and of the attempts to communicate made on both sides. In a study of the history of mechanics (Moscovici, 1968a), I was able to show that the essential feature of its evolution was not the predominance of theory or of experimentation but the tension that developed between the two. There is no reason why attempts should be made to avoid these tensions and the fruitful contradictions that go with them. Experiment and theory do not stand in a transparent relation to one another; it is the role of the theory to make experimentation unnecessary, and the role of experimentation to render the theory impossible. The dialectic relationship that exists between these two propositions needs to be properly used if knowledge is to advance.

But in order to achieve this, decisions must be taken about the kind of theories which should provide the frame of reference and about the intellectual tradition that should form their background. It is my opinion that more independence is needed from the predictive function of theory. As things stand today, whenever a concept or a model is proposed, it is evaluated exclusively in terms of its utility, of the phenomena which it is able to predict and of the experiments which it suggests. This results in the creation of restricted models which are more like reflections about certain aspects of a phenomenon than a genuine theory of it. Models of this kind are useful in stimulating a few interesting experiments but their application is limited since very soon a point is reached when nothing new is contributed by further experiments. In addition, it is often difficult to decide experimentally about the validity of the different models because they concentrate on different categories of variables pertaining to the same phenomenon; this is, for example, the case with models of group dynamics. This situation is reflected in a juxtaposition of experiments which are as numerous as they are inefficient; and it illustrates that an atheoretical science has no memory and is incapable of achieving integration of its restricted models. The usual progression of events can be described as follows: someone obtains data or proposes a hypothesis about, for example, "risky shift" or "social categorization". Once the findings are firmly established and the hypothesis confirmed, attempts are immediately made at further reproduction through varying such factors as age, personality, or cognitive style. The phenomenon is thus reduced to the context of individual or inter-individual psychology. In this way, the framework of social psychology is progressively abandoned. Instead of proceeding in depth, one proceeds by extension; instead of establishing links between sociopsychological phenomena, one makes them disappear through their absorption in processes which are not sociopsychological.

It seems therefore more useful to turn towards theories which are explanatory or which offer a systematization of a set of propositions. Should these theories start from fact and experiments? The answer could be "yes" and "no" at the same time. It would have to be negative if they were theories of a "Baconian" type consisting of a "critical review", a "synthesis" or a "clarification and definition of concepts". This is so for two reasons: first, there is not enough coherence in what we consider to be established knowledge in social psychology; second, it is Utopian to hope that a theory might emerge from a simple integration of parts which themselves do not bear the mark of a theory. The book by Collins and Guetzkow (1964), which summarized the experiments on small groups, showed the impossibility of such an attempt at integration.

But the answer could be positive if a theory offers a fresh perspective in which experiments or surveys are considered as no more than temporary expedients in sketching a new image of reality. Despite the criticisms which I made earlier of the book by Thibaut and Kelley (1959), it seems to me that it offers an example of a theoretical tradition that is worth preserving. The essential requirement is to have new ideas which can be outlined and developed. There is no need to search immediately and at all cost for empirical validation or to wait until one is guided by experimental data. As Novalis wrote: "If theory had to wait on experiment, it would never come into being."

To clarify my view, I should perhaps simply state my preference for *any* theory to absence of theory. As things are today in social psychology, we have—with a few exceptions—nothing but proto-scientific conceptualizations. It would be better to have at our disposal even something like the phlogiston theory than to continue with the lack of communication, dispersion and anomie which is evident at present. The phlogiston theory was useful in chemistry because it defined the central processes of the scientific undertaking, served as a guide for research, forced the scientists to confront each other and provided them with a common language. Social psychology could well use a similar intellectual discipline, and one might perhaps venture the suggestion that it is time to halt the collection of data. Henri Poincaré wrote: "An accumulation of facts is no more a science than a heap of stones is a house." We do have the stones, but we have not built the house. If we decided to abandon for a while the collection of new data, we could view them in perspective and reflect on what has been achieved; we might then be able to define better the nature of the questions we have been asking, the purpose of our search and the meaning of our findings. In exhorting our students to produce new data we reflect the pressures of academic and economic institutions whereas our efforts should instead be directed towards helping them to educate themselves. A basis for this education could be found in a return to Lewin and to the classical writers of anthropology and sociology; in taking into account recent developments in ethnology, linguistics and genetic epistemology; and in re-examining the approaches represented by the theories of exchange and of dissonance, with the object of transcending their individual and interindividual context in order to place them resolutely in a wider social framework.

The suggestion that we should aim towards, or at least not reject, theories which are proto-scientific, may be found offensive in some quarters. But the idea is not as scandalous as it may seem. Whether we like it or not, the ideas of Heider, the postulate of balance, and the notions of attribution are all pre-scientific. If we have to pay for our scientism by the absence of theory, then it is preferable not to be "scientific" when developing new theoretical ideas.

4   In search of a *social* psychology

"The determining cause of a social fact must be sought in social facts and not in the effects of individual consciousness." Durkheim.

4.1   ARE THERE ONE, TWO OR THREE SOCIAL PSYCHOLOGIES?

No theoretical study can be fruitless unless its objectives are clearly defined. Chemistry or linguistics, physics or economics became sciences only when their practitioners began to question reasons for the occurrence of the phenomena they observed. Certainly the aims of science are not immutable and theoretical advance depends upon an awareness of their progressive changing context; but there can be no further progress without a common definition of these aims.

There are many who think that general agreement about such a definition is no longer a problem in social psychology. In their view, social psychology is a science of behaviour—the science of social behaviour; hence they feel that the object of the discipline is identical with that of psychology in general, even if it is envisaged in a special context. It is this conception of the discipline which needs to be carefully and critically examined.

It is often forgotten that initially a strong impetus was given to the development of social psychology by the hope that it would contribute to our understanding of the conditions which underlie the functioning of a society and the constitution of a culture. The purpose of the theory was to explain social and cultural phenomena; the practical aim was to use the principles which it was hoped would be discovered in order to engage in a critique of the social organization. Thus, the domain of social psychology was seen to include the study of everyday life and relationships between individuals and between groups, as well as of ideologies and of intellectual creativity both in its individual and collective forms.

Seen in this perspective, social psychology offered the promise of becoming a truly social and political science. Such ideas were soon forgotten, however, when our science became a "science of behaviour". This new orientation shifted the basis of the argument from society to individual and inter-individual phenomena which were theoretically envisaged from a quasi-physical rather than a symbolic point of view. The field of research was drastically narrowed in its horizons as well as in its potential impact. It is perhaps worth recalling that, as James Miller once confessed, this change of emphasis to "behavioural science" was also meant to provide some reassurance in the quarters responsible for disbursing research funds because the idea of "social sciences" tended to create distrust and confusion. The label of a "behavioural science" appeared more acceptable.

But this change of terminology reflected a corresponding change in values and in interests. Indeed, workers in the new social sciences restricted their ambitions to searching for palliatives for the dysfunctions of society without questioning either its institutions or its psychological adequacy in the face of human needs. This narrowing of horizons is closely related to the restriction of the subject to the "study of behaviour". The close association with general psychology that this restriction represents conceals its social and political implications; it prevents us from viewing in their true perspectives the phenomena we are supposed to be studying and it even provides some justification for the opinion that we contribute to the alienation and to the bureaucratization of our social life.

Independently of all this, the notion of "social behaviour", however useful it may be in helping to define empirical indices, remains much too vague. Far from helping us to unify the subject, it has resulted in our having today not one but two or even three social psychologies.

The first of these is taxonomic; its aim is to determine the nature of the variables which might account for the behaviour of an individual confronted with a stimulus. This psychology ignores the nature of the subject and it defines "social" as a property of *objects* which are divided into *social* and *non-social*. Thus, the general scheme of the Ego–Object relation can be represented as follows:

Subject		*Object*
Undifferentiated	Undefined	Differentiated into
		Social Non-social

In this scheme, the aim of the study is the discovery of how social stimuli affect the processes of judgement, perception or the formation of attitudes; the fact that socially determined changes are themselves one of the basic aspects of these processes is not taken into account. For example, research in social perception has been mainly concerned with the classification of independent variables as perceived objects which are either "persons" ("human beings"—as in the experiments on person perception) or elements of a class of physical objects endowed with social value (as in the studies on the judgement of magnitudes of coins as a function of their value). Sherif's (1936) studies on the autokinetic effect also belong to this taxonomic perspective: modes of response are related in them to the structure of the stimuli. The same is true of the work of the Yale group (e.g. Hovland *et al.*, 1953), which aimed at accounting for persuasive communications in terms of the social characteristics of the source (such as its prestige, credibility etc.). This kind of social psychology is "taxonomic" in the sense that it limits itself to a psychological description of various types of stimuli and to a classification of the differences between them. It uses a definition of "social" and "non-social" in which phenomena that are inherently products of social activity are conceived as being, from their inception, a part of "nature". As its exclusive concern is with the enumeration of various kinds of reaction to the environment, it is bound to exclude from its range of interest the nature of the relationship between Man and his environment.

The second social psychology is "differential". Its principle is to reverse the terms of the relationship between Ego and Object and to seek in the characteristics of the individual the origin of the behaviour that is observed. On this basis, the nature of the stimulation is of little importance; the main preoccupation is to classify individuals by criteria of differentiation which often vary according to the school of thought to which the researcher belongs or the nature of the problem he is studying. Thus, subjects may be classified in terms of their cognitive styles (e.g. abstract–concrete, field dependent–field independent), their affective characteristics (e.g. anxious–not anxious, high or low self-esteem), their motivations (e.g. achievement motivation or approval needs) or their attitudes (e.g. ethnocentric or dogmatic) etc. The relationship between the subject and his environment can be represented as follows:

Subject	*Object*
Differentiated by his personality characteristics	Undifferentiated

Whatever kind of typology is adopted in this perspective, the aim is always the same: to find out how different categories of individuals behave when they are confronted with a problem or with another person. Ultimately, this tends towards the establishment of a differential psychology of responses and—at the limit—towards a description of the psychological composition of social groups from which their properties can be inferred. One example of this approach is a symptomatological analysis of subjects who are easily influenced, followed by a demonstration that the same individuals are highly suggestible when confronted with any kind of message. In the same way the social phenomena of leadership, risky shift or competition are perceived at the level of psychological traits of the individuals involved; what is completely ignored is that some of these traits may be no more than a reflection at the individual level of a phenomenon which is inherent in a network of

social relations or in a specific culture. Thus, it is evident that achievement motivation (McClelland *et al.*, 1953) is related to the imperatives
of protestantism and of economic rationalism, as was shown by Max
Weber. But to transform this ideal Weberian type into an individual
characteristic is to transplant it as a criterion for the differentiation of
a particular psychological structure which is then immediately assumed,
without any justification, to have some kind of universality. Very often
these personality descriptions are redundant and tautologous.

Like differential psychology which measures individual differences
in intelligence or in manual dexterity, this kind of social psychology
aims to measure personality dimensions or aspects of affectivity which
have only a tenuous relationship to social phenomena. It is because of
its attempts to explain what happens in a society in terms of the
characteristics of individuals that the interest of this social psychology
in the "social" is more apparent than real.

Finally, there exists a third kind of social psychology which can be
described as "systematic". Its interest is focused on the global phenomena which result from the interdependence of several subjects in their
relation to a common environment, physical or social. Here, the
relationship between Ego and Object is mediated through the intervention of another subject; this relationship becomes a complex tri-
angular one in which each of the terms is fully determined by the other
two. The situation can be represented in the following schema:

Subject

Object

Subject

It is, however, important to stress that this relationship between
object and subject in a common environment has been conceived in
two different ways, one static and one dynamic. In the former, the main
objects of study have been the modifications in the behaviour of individuals participating in interaction; in the latter, the interest was
focused more directly on the specific effects that these relationships
produce because they engage the total individual, the interactions
between individuals, and also their orientation in the environment. From
this distinction, two separate trends of theoretical and experimental
work can be identified. One is concerned with the processes of facilitation or of exchange and with an analysis, at the level of observable
performance, of the sequential progress of a relationship. It analyses

the modifications occurring in responses in terms of the mere presence of another individual, or of the relationships of dependence and in-dependence between two individuals; and it views these modifications as a function of the stimulation or the reward brought into the situation by the presence, the intervention or the response of another individual, or by the control that two individuals may exert upon one another. The work of Zajonc on social facilitation provides a good example of this tendency. The second approach considers a social relationship as providing the basis for the emergence of processes which create a sociopsychological field in which the observed psychological phenomena find their place and their origin. Examples here would be the work on small groups of the Lewinian school, the work of Festinger on pressure towards uniformity and on social comparison, and Sherif's work on the development of intergroup relations.

The three social psychologies—taxonomic, differential and systematic —today peacefully coexist in the textbooks. Perhaps this precarious equilibrium is understandable when one thinks of the requirements presented by teaching and of the absence of strong constraints which might upset the balance in one direction or another. The mixture remains nevertheless arbitrary and its ingredients are incompatible. Indeed, how can it be possible to outline and articulate the findings of differential social psychology together with those of systematic social psychology when, by definition, the former stands in contradiction to the latter? For example, if it is considered that individual differences in readiness to be influenced provide a sufficient basis for the under-standing of the effects of a message, nothing more needs to be done than to study the distribution of these differences in the population; there are no further requirements for a theoretical analysis of the mechanisms of social communication. In the same way, if one postulates that it is the presence of competitive subjects that makes a conflict situation competitive, then the study of conflict must be replaced by the study of the functioning of a certain personality type. If, on the other hand, one is genuinely interested in the nature of conflict or of communication, it is as useless to study personality factors as it would be to base the study of the laws of the pendulum on data about its humidity or the quality of its fibres. There is no doubt that these factors intervene as *parameters*; but to consider them as *variables* is to deny to sociopsychological phenomena the autonomy of functioning within their own specific system.

Some may think that I am flogging dead horses and that all these problems have long been familiar; this kind of argument is invoked each time someone questions the legitimacy of a consensus which, with the passage of time, has become second nature. My own view is that these problems are crucial and that, until they are resolved in one way or another, we shall not be able to guide our research in directions which would enable it to become the foundation of a sociopsychological science.

4.2   WHAT IS "SOCIAL" IN SOCIAL PSYCHOLOGY?

It would be difficult to outline here in detail the reasons for my view that it is only systematic social psychology which is really worth pursuing and that other approaches, which interpret social phenomena in terms of the properties of stimuli or of personality, do not have much to contribute. At any rate, this view has been brilliantly developed by now "classical" authors in social psychology and there is no need to repeat their arguments. I do wish, however, to push a little further the analysis of the manner in which our discipline nowadays attempts to define "the social" as an interaction between two subjects and an object; an examination of this issue will help us to clarify our views about what has implicitly always been, and still is today, the true object of our discipline.

The triangle Ego-Alter-Object is crucial to this discussion since it is the only scheme capable of explaining and systematizing the processes of interaction. However, the manner in which it has been used has not always contributed to the definition of social conduct or of the system within which this conduct is inserted. Two indices have often been implicitly accepted as reflecting the influence of social context on an individual's behaviour: the presence of another in his social field; and "numerosity". Thus, for many researchers, the behaviour of an organism becomes "social" only when it is affected by the behaviour of other organisms. Such a definition is equally valid for Man and for other species and it enables one to use a series of analogies in order to extrapolate across species.

Acceptance of these views led to the neglect of some fundamental aspects of social phenomena. Society has its own structure which is not definable in terms of the characteristics of individuals; this structure is determined by the processes of production and consumption, by rituals, symbols, institutions, norms and values. It is an organization which has a history and its own laws and dynamics that cannot be derived from the laws of other systems. When the "social" is studied in terms of the presence of other individuals or of "numerosity", it is not really the fundamental characteristics of the system that are explored but rather one of its sub-systems—the sub-system of inter-individual relationships. The kind of social psychology that emerges from this approach is a "private" social psychology which does not include within its scope the distinctiveness of most of the genuine collective phenomena. It can therefore be argued that, for reasons which are partly cultural and partly methodological, the systematic perspective in social psychology has not been truly concerned either with social behaviour as a product of society or with behaviour *in* society. This is not to say that there have been no attempts to analyse phenomena such as power, authority or conflict; however, the perspective of this analysis has always been inter-individual and consequently these pheneomena have been removed from the context to which they properly belong.

For these reasons, it is ambiguous to maintain that social behaviour is currently the real object of our science. From one point of view this assertion is justified since our preoccupation has been with one category of social acts and with one specific segment of social life; on the other hand, it has never been properly recognized that the "social" exists primarily in the intrinsic properties of human society.

This is why systematic social psychology must be renewed and redeveloped so as to become a real science of those social phenomena which are the basis of the functioning of a society and the essential processes operating in it. But—as it is obvious that not *all* such pheno-mena are within the purview of social psychology—it is important to select those that should be its main focus. The central and exclusive object of social psychology should be the study of all that pertains to *ideology* and to *communication* from the point of view of their structure, their genesis and their function. The proper domain of our discipline is the study of cultural processes which are responsible for the organization of knowledge in a society, for the establishment of inter-individual relationships in the context of social and physical environment, for the formation of social movements (groups, parties, institutions) through which men act and interact, for the codification of inter-individual and intergroup conduct which creates a common social reality with its norms and values, the origin of which is to be sought again in the social

context. In parallel, more attention should be paid to language which
has not until now been thought of as an area of study closely related to
social psychology. Present texts on psycholinguistics devote their
attention entirely to clear and scholarly expositions of linguistic phenomena as they relate to learning and memory or to phonetic and lexical
structures. They contain very little about the exchange functions of
language and about the social origin of its characteristics. It is taken for
granted that language is an essential feature of communication; but
this is not used as a basis for theoretical studies. In this way, the social
nature of language remains at the periphery of approaches to psycholinguistic problems; the implication is that sociopsychological questions
about language do not differ from those asked in psycholinguistics.
Rommetveit discusses in this book some of the general consequences for
psycholinguistics of this reductionist perspective.

The notion of ideology does have its place in contemporary social
psychology. Many phenomena which are at present being studied are
either inherent parts of ideology or theoretical substitutes for it. This
is true of habits, prejudices, stereotypes, belief systems, psycho-logic etc.
But this accumulation does not cover the full range of the major theoretical theme which still remains segmented. There are, however, some
signs that the study of the phenomenon of ideology may well be developed further; the promise of it is contained in the systematic analysis of
social thinking and in some of the work on cognitive dissonance, on the
unity of cognitive and non-cognitive processes and on social motivation.

Research in social psychology of communication has not advanced
very far, despite the fact that, as a discipline, social psychology is well
suited for this undertaking; it should be able to look at the basic aspects
of communication from the point of view of the genesis of social relationships and social products, and also it should be able to consider Man as
a product of his own activity—as, for example, in education and in
socialization. But in order to achieve this aim, we must go beyond
superficial explorations. To ask questions about the effects of mass
media, about the influence exerted by an authoritative or a non-
authoritative source, about the effectiveness of a message announced at
the beginning or at the end of a speech, is to confine our discipline to
purely pragmatic boundaries traced by the requirements of the owners
or the manipulators of mass media. The real problems are much wider.
They reside in questions about why we communicate and according to
what kind of rhetoric and about the manner in which our motivation

to communicate is reflected in our modes of communication. The mass media, whose object is to persuade, are a negligible part of the total network of communications. There is no reason why they should be given a privileged status as compared with the processes of exchange of information which takes place in social, scientific, political or religious communities, in the worlds of theatre, cinema, literature or leisure. Culture is created by and through communication; and the organizing principles of communication reflect the social relations which are implied in them. This is why we must envisage communication in a new and wider perspective. Until the present, it has mainly been considered as a *technique*, as a means towards realizing ends which are external to it. The study of communication can become a proper object of science if we change this perspective and conceive of communication as an autonomous process which exists at all levels of social life.

Social life is the common basis of communication and of ideology. The task of social psychology in the study of these phenomena is one for which the discipline is well equipped; it concerns the relationships between the individual and society. These relationships are a focus of tensions and contradictions, and they represent the meeting point of Man's needs for freedom and of his tendencies towards alienation; they are also the chosen battlefield of many political movements. Though it is true that social psychologists are aware of the problems involved, they do no more than eliminate their real interest and relevance when they reduce them to processes of socialization.

The views which stress the overriding importance of socialization can be summarized as follows: the child learns and internalizes a set of values, a language, and social attitudes; he models his behaviour on the behaviour of adults and of his peers. Finally, when he himself becomes an adult, he integrates into the group which prepared him so thoroughly for membership. When this stage is achieved, difficulties of adjustment only arise if the individual has not succeeded in the appropriate assimilation or the adequate application of the principles which he has been taught.

The development of this conception depends, in fact, on the acceptance of several postulates. The first is that the individual is a biological unit which must be transformed into a social unit; the second, that society is an immutable "given" encountered by the individual as a ready-made environment in the structure of concentric circles consisting of the family, the peer groups, and the wider groups and institutions in

c

which he moves and to which he must adapt. The third postulate is that the individual is inescapably absorbed by his social surroundings: he ceases to be an individual from the moment he becomes affiliated, submits to social pressures and becomes a role-player. Finally, it is assumed that society plays an equilibrating part in the individual's life, since it reduces his tensions and his uncertainties. In fact, these postulates imply a conception of the individual which is fully organic together with a conception of society which limits its role to that of a mediator for the needs of the individual organisms. In this conception society is not seen as a product of individuals nor are they seen as products of the society. The sociopsychological laws that emerge are not concerned with transformations that take place within the scope of the "social", but with transformations from the biological to the social. The primary interests of social psychology which mainly focuses on the processes of learning, of socialization and of conformity can be traced directly to these postulates and to their application.

And yet, the problem of the relations between Man and society intrinsically concerns both terms of the *rapport*; they jointly intervene in the economic, political and social processes. It must not be forgotten that the individual is not a "given" but a product of society because it is society that forces him to become an individual and to stress his individuality in his behaviour. For example, our market economy forces us all to become buyers and sellers of goods and services; our electoral democracy is based on the principle that each man represents a vote. But these are not universal principles, their boundaries are cultural. The antagonisms that capitalist societies created in bringing individualism to its highest peak are—in reality—a result of the close interdependence of all sectors of everyday life that is the mark of these societies. The system that has emerged combines the anonymity of urban life with physical, psychological and social interdependence; it also introduces a sharp cleavage between private and public life. The individual created by this society has very little in common with a purely biological organism. The jurists have been more successful than the psychologists in establishing a distinction between the moral person and the physical person. It is inherent in our society that individuals are primarily moral persons and as such they behave as parties to social encounters and as actors in their diverse milieux. For all these reasons, the notion of an "individual" is entirely relative: trade unions or political parties can be considered collectively as individuals who behave as such towards one another and in their relations with the society at large. Society produces individuals according to its own principles; thus it can be compared to a "machine" which socializes and individualizes at the same time. Its mode of action consists not only—as it is too often believed—of establishing uniformities, but also of maintaining and accentuating differences. Consequently, as the individual becomes social, so also does society acquire individuality; this is why there exists not one but many societies which differ from each other both in their origins and in the characteristics of social actors who compose and produce them.

This perspective enables us to understand the contrast between individualism and the tendency of the social actor to minimize his differences for the sake of pursuing his goals and interests and conforming to his notion of what is "good" and "true". The main question that social psychologists have been asking is: Who socializes the individual? They have neglected the second aspect of the problem contained in the question: Who socializes society? A new approach to the relationship between the individual and society will have to recognize two basic phenomena. The first is that the individual is not a biological datum but a social product; and the second is that society is not an environment geared to training the individual and reducing his uncertainties but a system of relationships between "collective individuals". This view of social dynamics has direct scientific implications as well as psychological and political significance; it forces us to envisage social control and social change in a common perspective rather than treating them separately as has been the case in the past. There is no reason at all why priority should be given to those aspects of socialization which tend towards the transmission of existing traditions and the stability of the *status quo*; the opposite tendencies which engender reforms and revolutions are just as important.

Our exclusive interest has been in the formation of "social objects"; and this is reflected in the conception we have of the individual organism as the passive party to a relationship that reaches its maturity in conforming to an immutable and pre-established model. The time has now come to insist on the formation of "social subjects" (Moscovici and Plon, 1968)—be they groups or individuals—who acquire their identity through their relationships with others. This change of perspective can already be seen in the work of Brehm (1966) on "psychological reactance", of Rotter (1966) on internal and external control and of Zimbardo (1969) on cognitive control. We must also recognize the essential role played in the formation of "social subjects" by "social solidarity" (i.e. social comparison and social recognition), decision processes (both social and individual), social organization and social influence. We already have a fund of theoretical notions and of experimental studies relevant to each of these phenomena. In order to reach a new level of understanding of the relations between Man and society, we must relate this knowledge to processes of communication and the influence exerted by ideologies. In this sense, control and change constitute two lines of development which must be analysed simultaneously in order to enable us to understand as well as to criticize the important aspects of social life. If we adopt this approach as a guide for research, we shall cease to consider our environment as an immutable "external" milieu and see it instead as the humanized background to the relationships in which men engage and a tool for these relationships (Moscovici, 1968b). This environment is not inherently ambiguous or structured, and neither is it purely physical or social; it is determined by our knowledge and methods of approach. Environment explains nothing; on the contrary, it stands itself in need of explanation, since it is both constructed and limited by our techniques, our science, our myths, our systems of classification and our categories. In most of the theories concerned with exchange or with influence, these processes are conceived as responses determined by resources present in the environment or by its organization. In consequence, questions concerning the genesis of social objects do not even arise. But progress in ethology, some recent studies on social influence (Moscovici and Faucheux, 1969; Moscovici et al., 1969; Alexander et al., 1970) and historical evidence about the transformation of the environment provide indications that the emphasis is changing: from a conception stressing the inertia of the material world we are turning towards the study of its significance.

In sum, the field of social psychology consists of social subjects, that is of groups and individuals who create their social reality (which is, in fact, their only reality), control each other and create their bonds of solidarity as well as their differences. Ideologies are their products, communication is their means of exchange and consumption, and language is their currency. This parallel with economic activities is, of course, no more than an analogy; but it enables us to define better those elements of social life that are most worthy of theoretical and empirical study; and it also underlines the need to introduce more direction and coherence in the definition of our potential field of investigation.

Where does "behaviour" stand in relation to all this? It also needs to be envisaged in a new perspective: instead of locating "social" in behaviour, we must locate behaviour in "social". In textbooks and other publications social behaviour is usually considered in the same way as any other kind of behaviour, the only difference being that social behaviour is supposed to include superimposed social characteristics. It is considered as being determined by the same psychological causes as other kinds of behaviour, and by the same systems of physical stimulation. From the point of view of the present discussion, social behaviour must be looked upon as a problem in its own right: its essential feature is that it is symbolic. The stimuli which elicit social behaviour and the responses engendered are links in a chain of symbols; the behaviour thus expresses a code and a system of values which are a form of language; or it could be said perhaps that it is social behaviour itself which constitutes a language. It is essentially social and it is created by social relations; indeed, there could be no symbolism confined to one individual or to one individual confronted by material objects alone.

Symbolic behaviour has often been confused with the general psychological processes referred to as "cognitive". Thus, theories which introduced the concept of consistency into the study of social influence or of motivation were classed as "cognitive" theories. The reason for this was that these theories were concerned with a symbolic mode of organization of actions, and "symbolic" has been subsumed under "cognitive". The difficulty of this view is not only due to the illegitimacy of assimilating the symbolic to the cognitive; it is also in the fact that, in doing this, one masks the distinction between the two terms. When the term "affective", "motor" or "motivational" are replaced by the term "cognitive", the underlying assumption is that one has done no more than move from one level to another. The focus of analysis still remains on the individual as a unit within the classical scheme of stimulus–response. But the fundamental aspects of symbolic behaviour consist of its verbal and non-verbal manifestations which are understood and become "visible" only in relation to the common meanings they acquire for those who receive the messages and those who emit them. Symbolic behaviour is supported and made possible by social norms and rules and by a common history reflecting the system of implicit connotations and reference points that inescapably develops in every social environment.

Social psychology is a science of behaviour only if this is understood to mean that its interest is in a very specific mode of that behaviour—the symbolic mode. It is this which distinguishes sharply its field of interest from that of general psychology. All that has been said in the present section concerns solely the development of this fundamental proposition.

5 A sociopsychological problem: the absence of dangerous truths

If the study of symbolic processes became our main object, we would be forced to explore the domain and boundaries of the social reality in which we live. Indeed, if we wish to grasp real social facts rather than individual facts in a social context, if we wish to abandon a vision of society in which individuals enclosed in the cells of their "primary" groups move as if at random, if we wish to destroy the illusion that we can one day achieve an empty universality of laws through getting to know general and abstract mechanisms without reference to their contents, then we must clearly admit that we have, until the present time, tended to ignore concrete social processes and their collective forms.

Despite its technical achievements, social psychology has become an isolated and secondary science (cf. Jaspars and Ackermann, 1966–1967). This judgement is certainly true for Europe, but I believe that it also applies elsewhere. This is probably the result of an intense desire to achieve professional recognition and academic respectability. Nevertheless, it is true that we have succeeded in conducting scientific experiments, in having our research programmes accepted by universities, in producing—though for a very limited market—students who know their literature, can employ statistical methods, manipulate apparatus and produce good dissertations. On the other hand, the gap that has been created between our discipline and other social sciences (such as anthropology, sociology, linguistics or economics) has led us into a situation of ignorant expertise. The questions we ask are most often very restricted; and if it happens that important problems are taken up, we manage to transform them again into minor questions.

But all this does not seem to disturb anyone, since it appears that we have achieved our principal aims of applying correctly the rules of the art of experimentation and of receiving for this success the approval of our own group. And yet, there is ample evidence that our control and *minutiae* have little significance for the really important aspects of the problems we are studying. For example, in their studies of primates the ethologists have never been able to use methods as refined as those we use in our studies of interaction. Despite this, they have courageously attacked crucial problems which are of direct interest both in the study of the social organization of animal species and of Man; they have produced a harvest of knowledge which appears richer and nearer to our present preoccupations than social psychology has ever been able to accumulate. By contrast, social psychology has become a psychology of private life, and at the same time it has managed to transform its practitioners into members of a private club. Even in the field of methodology, in which until recently we were well ahead, we have now been outpaced by other disciplines. It certainly cannot be said that there is a dearth of important problems: war, profound social change, race and international relations, individual alienation, struggle for political freedom, and violence. One might add the problems created by science, technology and the change of scale in the evolution of our world—and yet there is no trace of any of this in our journals and our textbooks; it is as if the very existence of all these problems was being denied.

It is not enough, however, to recognize that these issues are "relevant" in order to make them proper objects of investigation. They must also be approached in a manner which is "relevant"; that is, in a manner which would enable us to understand simultaneously how they concern Man and society, and how their study would contribute to a genuine advance of knowledge. A greater lucidity and a stronger intellectual commitment are indispensable for this task. For example, it will not be sufficient to discern in the social field only the work of forces that conserve, because forces that push towards gradual change or revolution are at least as important. History is not only made of societies that survive; it is also made of societies that die. We must learn to face these realities; an exclusive search for a science which would be but an art of compromise would, in the end, compromise science itself. It has become evident that social equilibrium and peaceful individual satisfaction are not the supreme achievements towards which men strive. Values are not only Utopias or useless appendages; the ideals of justice, truth, freedom and dignity have made live and die people who recognized in them their desire not to accept just any kind of life or death. It is difficult to see why we should forget, together with today's social psychologists, that the processes of revolution, of innovation, of the irreducibility of conflict are an inherent part of the evolution of human groups.

The second point I wish to stress is that social psychology must now come out of the academic ghetto or, perhaps one should say, out of the American ghetto that the European offshoots of this discipline have entered (Back, 1964). Meditation in a vicious circle has never expanded any horizons. One would have to be more than human to escape completely the influence of one's immediate surroundings and not to be affected by the perspectives in which questions in one's milieu are being asked. It is well known that the inhabitants of a ghetto share a common vision and do not resist strongly what is familiar to them. At present many of the arguments, judgements and research topics in social psychology reflect the values of the middle class from which most social psychologists have not yet become disengaged. Thus, they remain prisoners of a pragmatic culture which has for its main preoccupation the avoidance of what is called "metaphysics" or, in other words, of all the sombre and non-immediate realities of existence.

Most of the experiments conducted in England, in France or in the United States on social influence, on group polarization (risky shift) or on conflict employed students as subjects. No work has been done on the various regions of a country, on different social classes, on ideological, or on national, religious or racial groups. At the same time, few of us have been concerned with a careful study and an adequate formulation of the problems and preoccupations of these groups. Consequently, social psychologists find it difficult to see in proper perspective their own environment and values, and thus they cannot enrich and diversify their discipline. It is necessary and unavoidable that a science should sooner or later become an academic pursuit, but this does not mean that it should start by isolating itself either in the university or within the boundaries of a nation, a class, an age-group or a political movement.

Our discipline must now turn towards realities of which in the past it was unaware, and it must participate in social experiments and in the establishment of new social relationships. Social psychology cannot afford to remain a "science of appearance"; it must not only begin to discover the deeper aspects of social reality but also to participate in the general dynamics of knowledge through which certain concepts are

destroyed and new ones created. The aim should be not only to systematize existing knowledge but to postulate entirely new concepts. It is
now fully recognized that the exact sciences create new aspects of
nature; social sciences must create new aspects of society. It is only
the exploration of new realities that will enable social psychology to
progress and will take it out of the restricted framework of commercial
and industrial activities within which it is confined at present. Until
now its practitioners have preferred to concern themselves with the view
of the world current in some academic circles and to neglect what they
could be taught by artists and writers about human psychology and the
mechanics of a society. They have not taken as their guide the epistemological principles which lead to an analysis of what is rare and about
which little is known; it is this kind of analysis that helps to throw new
light on well-established and familiar phenomena. As Durkheim once
wrote: "If a science of societies is to exist, we must expect that it will
not consist of a simple paraphrase of traditional prejudices but rather
that it will lead us to see things in ways diverging from views currently
accepted."

The history of science shows that this principle is at the heart of all
discovery. The great intellectual innovations due to Descartes or to
Galileo were possible because of their serious interest in optical instruments which were familiar only to very few people at the time; the
majority of philosophers continued to practice a science based on everyday observations which had also been the basis of Aristotle's universe.
This is only one example amongst many; perhaps its importance is to
show that new and unexpected ideas in a science are not only due to the
inspiration and the genius of an individual but also to his readiness to
upset the conceptions which are current in his time. But this creation
of new departures also depends upon the susceptibility of a science to
new ideas and its capacity to remain open to conceptions which have
previously been considered to lie outside its field of interest. The classical
writers in social psychology were outstanding in their ability and willingness to receive a wide range of ideas. If we turn back to them, we shall
perhaps be able to achieve a better grasp of wider perspectives and to
dedicate ourselves to the pursuit of significant ideas rather than to the
pursuit of data. At present we respect the maxim that methodology
makes a science instead of remembering that science should choose its
methods.

It is only if we hold on to the belief that there *is* a royal road, and try to find it, that we shall be able to transcend the present limitations of social psychology and make it more than a secondary science. It is the destiny of all truth to be critical, and therefore we shall have to be critical. The present conjunction of events is favourable for such a mutation. In order that our discipline may become truly scientific its field of interest must remain free and its gates must be wide open to other sciences and to the demands of society. The aims of science are knowledge through action together with action through knowledge. It is unimportant whether these aims are reached through mathematics, experimentation, observation or philosophical and scientific reflection. But for the present, the terms "science" and "scientific" are still imbued with a fetishism the abandonment of which is the *sine qua non* of knowledge. Social psychology will be unable to formulate dangerous truths while it adheres to this fetishism. This is its principal handicap, and this is what forces it to focus on minor problems and to remain a minor pursuit. All really successful sciences managed to produce dangerous truths for which they fought and of which they envisaged the consequences. This is why social psychology cannot attain the true idea of a science unless it also becomes dangerous.

References

Abelson, R. P., Aronson, E., McGuire, W. J., Newcomb, T.M., Rosenburg, M. J. and Tannenbaum, P. H. (Eds) (1968). "Theories of Cognitive Consistency". Rand, McNally, Chicago.

Alexander, L. N., Zucker, L. G. and Brody, C. L. (1970). Experimental expectations and autokinetic experiences: consistency theories and judgmental convergence. *Sociometry*, **28**, 108–122.

Allport, F. H. (1924). "Social Psychology". Houghton Mifflin, Boston.

Anderson, H. N. (1968). A simple model for information integration. *In* Abelson *et al.*, op. cit.

Back, K. W. (1964). Le domaine de la psychologie sociale. *Bulletin du C.E.R.P.* **13**, 21–33.

Bem, D. J. (1965). An experimental analysis of self-persuasion. *Journal of Experimental Social Psychology*, **1**, 199–218.

Brehm, J. W. (1966). "A Theory of Psychological Reactance". Academic Press, New York and London.

Brown, R. (1965). "Social Psychology". The Free Press, New York.

Chapanis, N. P. and Chapanis, A. (1962). Cognitive dissonance: five years later. *Psychological Bulletin*, **61**, 1–22.

Coch, L. and French, J. R. P. (1953). Overcoming resistance to change. *In* "Group

Dynamics: Research and Theory" (Eds D. Cartwright and A. Zander). Tow, Peterson, Evanson, Illinois.

Collins, B. E. and Guetzkow, H. (1964). "A Social Psychology of Group Processes for Decision Making". John Wiley, New York.

Deutsch, Martin (1969). Organizational and conceptual barriers to social change. *Journal of Social Issues*, **25** (4), 5–18.

Deutsch, Morton and Krauss, R. M. (1965). "Theories in Social Psychology". Basic Books, New York.

Doise, W. (1969). Intergroup relations and polarization of individual and collective judgements. *Journal of Personality and Psychology*, **12**, 136–143.

Faucheux, C. (1970). Cross-cultural research in social psychology. Unpublished ms., Social Science Research Council.

Faucheux, C. and Moscovici, S. (1960). Etudes sur la créativité des groupes: tâche, structure des communications et réussite. *Bulletin du C.E.R.P.*, **9**, 11–22.

Festinger, L. (1957). "A Theory of Cognitive Dissonance". Row, Peterson, Evanston, Illinois.

Festinger, L. (1964). "Conflict, Decision and Dissonance". Stanford University Press, Stanford.

Fishbein, M. and Raven, B. (1962). The AB scales: an operational definition of belief and attitude. *Human Relations*, **15**, 35–44.

Flament, C. (1965). "Réseaux de Communications et Structures de Groupe". Dunod, Paris.

Fraser, C., Gouge, C. and Billig, M. (1971). Risky shifts, cautious shifts and group polarization. *European Journal of Social Psychology*, **1**, 7–30.

Herzlich, C. (1969). "Santé et Maladie: Analyse d'une Représentation Sociale". Mouton, Paris and The Hague.

Hovland, C. I., Janis, I. L. and Kelley, H. H. (1953). "Communication and Persuasion". Yale University Press, New Haven.

Jaspars, J. M. F. and Ackermann, E. (1966–1967). The interdisciplinary character of social psychology: an illustration. *Sociologica Neerlandica*, **4** (1), 62–79.

Kelley, H. H. and Thibaut, J. W. (1969). Group problem solving. *In* "The Handbook of Social Psychology" (Eds G. Lindzey and E. Aronson), Vol. IV. Addison-Wesley, Reading, Mass.

Kogan, N. and Wallach, M. A. (1964). "Risk Taking. A Study on Cognition and Personality". Holt, Rinehart & Winston, New York.

McClelland, D. C., Atkinson, J. W., Clark, R. A. and Lowell, E. L. (1953). "The Achievement Motive". Appleton-Century-Crofts, New York.

McGrath, J. and Altman, I. (1966). "Small Group Research: A Synthesis and Critique of the Field". Holt, Rinehart & Winston, New York.

Montmollin, G. de (1959). Reflexions sur l'étude et l'utilization des petits groupes: I Le petit groupe: moyen et objet de connaissance. *Bulletin du C.E.R.P.* **8** (4), 293–310.

Montmollin, G. de (1960). Reflexions sur l'étude et l'utilization des petits groupes: II Le petit groupe comme moyen d'action. *Bulletin de C.E.R.P.* **9** (2), 109–122.

Moscovici, S. (1961a). "Reconversion Industrielle et Changements Sociaux. Un Exemple: la Chapellerie dans l'Aude". Colin, Paris.

Moscovici, S. (1961b). "La Psychanalyse, son Image et son Public". Presses Universitaires de France, Paris.

Moscovici, S. (1968a). "L'Expérience du Mouvement". Herman, Paris.

Moscovici, S. (1968b). "Essai sur l'Histoire Humaine de la Nature". Flammarion, Paris.

Moscovici, S. and Faucheux, C. (1969). Social influence, conformity, bias and the study of active minorities. (Mimeograph). Center for the Advanced Study of the Behavioral Sciences, Stanford, Calif.

Moscovici, S., Lage, E. and Naffrechoux, M. (1969). Influence of a consistent minority on the responses of a majority in a color perception task. *Sociometry*, **32**, 365–380.

Moscovici, S. and Plon, M. (1968). Choix et autonomie du sujet—la théorie de la réactance psychologique. *L'Année psychologique*, **68** (2), 467–480.

Moscovici, S. and Zavalloni, M. (1969). The group as a polarizer of attitudes. *Journal of Personality and Social Psychology*, **12**, 125–135.

Mulder, M. (1959). Power and satisfaction in task-oriented groups. *Acta Psychologica*, **16**, 178–225.

Plon, M. (1970). A propos d'une controverse sur les effets d'une menace en situation de négociation. *Bulletin de Psychologie*, **23**, 268–282.

Rotter, J. B. (1966). Generalized expectancies for internal versus external control of reinforcement. *Psychological Monographs*, **80**, 1.

Sherif, C. W., Sherif, M. and Nebergall, R. E. (1965). "Attitude and Attitude Change: The Social Judgment-involvement Approach". W. B. Saunders, Philadelphia.

Sherif, M. (1936). "The Psychology of Social Norms". Harper & Row, New York.

Tajfel, H. and Wilkes, A. L. (1964). Salience of attributes and commitment to extreme judgements in the perception of people. *British Journal of Social and Clinical Psychology*, **2**, 40–49.

Thibaut, J. W. and Kelley, H. H. (1959). "The Social Psychology of Groups". John Wiley, New York.

Wallach, M. A., Kogan, N. and Bem, D. J. (1964). Definition of responsibility and level of risk taking in groups. *Journal of Abnormal and Social Psychology*, **68**, 263–274.

Zajonc, R. B. (1966). "Social Psychology: An Experimental Approach". Wadsworth, Belmont, California.

Zimbardo, P. G. (1969). "The Cognitive Control of Motivation". Scott & Foresman, Glenview, Illinois.

3

Experiments in a Vacuum

Henri Tajfel

1 Applied research, basic research and "relevance"

The aim of this chapter is a limited one. It attempts to express my pre-occupations as a social psychologist whose work has been almost entirely within the experimental tradition of the discipline and who continues to believe that, amongst the approaches to social behaviour open to us, theories which can be tested experimentally contain the least doubtful promise for the future. This belief may be no more than an act of faith or—worse—a demonstration that research can sometimes become a question of clutching at straws. But even if this is so, there are two important reasons for continuing on the straight and narrow path: the first is that a systematic study of social behaviour is an essential task, both intellectual and practical, for our times; and the second, that there is no evidence that other approaches to the psychological aspects of social conduct present even as much solidity as the experimental straw appears to have.

Experiments need not, of course, be understood as exclusively confined to laboratory manipulations. McGuire (1967), for example, pointed out that in several important recent publications "the magic word 'experimental' is not defined narrowly to exclude hypothesis testing in natural settings, or even testing in natural settings without manipulation by the experimenter of the independent variables. It is a happy portent of the peaceful emergence of the new development that I am predicting here that 'experimental' is taken in its etymologically correct meaning of 'to test, to try'—rather than in the misuse of it sometimes found in the less perspicacious (or less classically educated) followers of the establishment, who interpreted it as referring only to manipulational research, or still more erroneously, only to manipulative research in the laboratory." (pp. 127–128.)

The fact remains that, as of now, "manipulative research in the laboratory" dominates the scene. This is why it is appropriate to ask ourselves a few nagging questions about the present situation—even if we do not know the answers—before engaging in optimistic speculations about the future. As a matter of fact, it is this very domination of the field by laboratory experimentation—or a certain kind of laboratory experimentation—that provoked Ring (1967) to write a paper with the title "Some Sober Questions about Some Frivolous Values" and McGuire to publish his reply to it from which I have just quoted.

The two main problems that Ring raised and to which McGuire addressed his reply were the "tension between basic and applied research" in social psychology with the established dominance of what passes for "basic", and the *kind* of basic research which some people had done. The latter—according to Ring—is underpinned by "fun-and-games" values that reflect themselves in esoteric pursuits of interest to no one outside the charmed circle of the practitioners; and in the frantic search for "non-obvious" findings. McGuire agreed with many of Ring's criticisms, but he saw reason for hope in the present development of new and sophisticated techniques which might enable social psychologists to test their theories not merely in the impoverished environments of the laboratory but also in the concreteness and reality of natural settings. He was not much concerned with the allusion to "fun-and-games"; he argued that the quality of the research mattered more than the motives for doing it. Perhaps he took some of the more serious implications of Ring's discontent too lightly. As Ring wrote: "We are a field of many frontiersmen, but few settlers . . . A cumulative social psychology is not likely to be a product or even a by-product of fun-and-games values. Instead, we can expect our field to continue its erratic and yet curiously stagnant course, saturated with 'cute' experiments and petty quarrels between theorists . . ." (p. 120.)

Motivation for doing a piece of work need not be relevant to the scientific contribution that it makes; but—at least in the social sciences and perhaps in others too—the system of values from which a researcher starts is hardly likely to be irrelevant to his choice of problems or methods for dealing with them; this is particularly so when the purpose of the exercise is presumed to be a "dispassionate inquiry into the nature of social behaviour".

But this "frivolity" of values which some are accused of displaying is, as both Ring and McGuire seemed to agree, a symptom of a deeper malaise; perhaps, in the long run, it is not a very important problem. Sooner or later, as McGuire hoped, "class will show". I believe, however, that the first of Ring's problems, the conflict between pure and applied research, is also in the nature of a symptom. McGuire's solution, an increasing stress on sophisticated quantitative techniques applied to large populations or to great quantities of data from natural settings, is like burying the patient before he is quite dead in the hope that his descendants will present less of a problem. Experimental social psychology as we know it today is "irrelevant" only to the extent that it is a social science practised in a social vacuum and not because it is not applied. This vacuum is not due to the fact that we are attempting to do fundamental research; it is due to the social psychologists having often taken the wrong decision as to what kind of *homo* their discipline is concerned with: "biological", "psychological" or "sociopsychological".

Most undergraduate textbooks in social psychology contain in their first few pages some kind of a definition of the discipline. This usually includes at least three assertions: that social psychology is a scientific study of human behaviour; that the kind of behaviour it is concerned with is social behaviour (i.e. interaction between individuals, singly or in groups); and that this social behaviour is "a function of" or is "determined by" or is "related to" the social context in which it takes place. For example, in their "Theories in Social Psychology", Deutsch and Krauss (1965) are, not untypically, quite explicit about the issues involved: "Person-to-person relationships are distinguished not only by the fact that psychological events can take place on both sides of a relationship, but also by their *social* character [italics in the original text], that is to say, human relationships always occur in an organized social environment—in a family, in a group, in a community, in a nation—that has developed techniques, categories, rules and values that are relevant to human interaction. Hence the understanding of the psychological events that occur in human interactions *requires compre-hension of the interplay of these events with the social context in which they occur* [my italics]." (pp. 2–3.) They add: ". . . the social psychologist must be able to characterize the relevant features of the social environment in order to understand or predict human interaction." (p. 3.)

But reading those chapters in the book which are devoted to social psychological theories tested in experimental settings, one must search in vain for further references to the "interplay with social context" or for a characterization of "the relevant features of the social environ-ment". For example, the frustration-aggression hypothesis is presented in the introductory chapter as a typical (and influential) "middle-range" theory in social psychology; the presentation is concerned—as it must be in order to be faithful to the original product—with the logical relationships between derivations from the main hypothesis and with a brief analysis of some of the key theoretical constructs such as "aggres-sion", "interference", "goal response", etc. This is the beginning and the end of it; how then is this a *"social* psychological theory"?

Quite obviously, its various hypotheses must be tested through pre-dicted *regularities* in the observed social behaviour. One of the most important and pervasive social psychological problems with which we are confronted today is the explanation of the processes involved in intergroup behaviour; I shall return to it later in more detail. This is not a problem which can be characterized as "applied" or "theore-tical"; it is inextricably both at the same time since it involves some of the basic features of Man's behaviour towards Man as they are adapted to, modified by, and the determinants of the "social context" and the "relevant features of the social environment".

Claims are made that the frustration-aggression theory (or its various modifications) "explains" some of the aspects of intergroup behaviour, i.e. that it accounts for some of its observed regularities. Support for these claims is sought in data from experiments designed to test the various hypotheses. I am not concerned here with the issue of "truth" or "falsity" of the assumed relationships between the variables but with the validity of the claim that a transition can be made from the kind of experimental data that are obtained to intergroup behaviour at large. I shall return later to the issue of extrapolations from experiments. For the present it will be enough to recall that, in the case of frustration and aggression, the experiments range from inducing displaced aggression in frustrated rats to creating ingenious laboratory equivalents of a man berating his wife after having just been reprimanded by his boss. None of this can be relevant to a confirmation or invalidation of the hypotheses as they might apply to *any* social setting of intergroup relations. It is now well known that this cannot be done without taking into account the social reality which gives meaning and definition to "ingroup" and "outgroup", to what is and what is not "aggression", to the prevailing image of man that determines the range of application of acts the meaning of which can be described as "inflicting injury on another organism". LeVine and Campbell amongst others (cf. e.g. LeVine, 1965) have shown the close dependence of outgroup aggression upon the *kind* of network of social relations that prevails within the ingroup, and the impossibility of making efficient predictions about the former without a close analysis of the latter. And yet in texts on experimental social psychology the *setting* of discussions about experiments on frustration and aggression, as they relate to intergroup conflict, has remained very much the same as it was thirty years ago.

The objection that hypotheses stated in universal and asocial terms lack predictive power meets the argument that it is the business of science to provide laws of general application; and that no scientific theory can be concerned with particularities of individual cases or of sets of individual cases which contain unknown, unknowable and uncontrolled variables. What matters are the underlying processes which must be discovered and isolated—or, in Lewin's terms, the appropriate distinctions between genotypes and phenotypes. It was precisely this need to isolate the genotypic aspects of social behaviour which led Lewin to his insistence on the use of experimental methods and was thus responsible for the profound impact of his ideas on the subsequent development of social psychology. But the range of what is genotypic and what phenotypic for the purposes of formulating and testing laws of social behaviour is by no means immediately obvious.

The difficulty concerns the distinction between the "individual" and the "general" cases in social behaviour. If I conduct a social psychological experiment, I have groups of subjects who are placed in various experimental and control conditions. These groups can either be representative of mankind as a whole or of particular subsets of it from which they were drawn. If the former is true, then the observed regularities of behaviour are generalizable as a law of wide application. If the latter is true, they are generalizable to the subset. It should be made clear at this point that my concern here is not with the old and hack-neyed theme of "representativeness of samples" in social psychological experiments; there are good reasons why in many cases representative-ness may be quite irrelevant to the purposes of the investigation. What is, however, important is a clear realization that the "general" case is an impossible myth as long as human beings behave as they do because of the social expectations with which they enter an experiment—or any other social situation. If these expectations are shared—as they always are by definition to some degree in any social context—I shall obtain data from my experiment which are neither "general" nor "individual". The observed regularities of behaviour will result from the interaction between general processes and the social context in which they operate.

Without the knowledge of this context the data *may* be irrelevant to the confirmation or the falsification of a hypothesis. What is more, the extent to which the expectations are shared, and thereby the extent to which they determine the pattern of the results, is in itself an empirical question which must be answered before any conclusions can be drawn. If we are dealing merely with random individual differences, then the usual statistical tools will provide all the answers. If, however, the back-ground social context of the experiment and the social task that the experiment itself presents to the subjects provide enough common meaning to determine the observed regularities, then we must provide a kind of interpretation of the data that is specific to many problems in the social sciences, and for which distinctions between the "general" and the "individual" do not apply. This will have to be an interpretation concerned with specifying the interaction between what is assumed to be a general process in social behaviour and the conditions under which it may operate, or under which "phenotypic" differences may conceal "genotypic" similarities and vice versa. Thus, the observed regularities of behaviour in social psychological experiments fall somewhere in between the general case and the unknowable individual case. Their range of application is determined by the nature of human social behaviour in which lawful but diverse modifications of pattern occur as a function of interactions between groups of men and their social environment. A similar argument underlies many of the quasi-experi-mental and experimental techniques employed nowadays by etho-logists, particularly in their studies of the relationships between ecology and animal social behaviour. It applies even more strongly to the study of human social behaviour in which it can be ignored only at the peril of the continuing "irrelevance" with which Ring and McGuire were concerned.

Before proceeding, I should like to make it clear that the above argument is not a plea that experiments must be cross-cultural in order to provide valuable insights. The point is that *all* experiments are "cultural" and whether the "cross" adds to their value or not depends entirely upon the theoretical background from which they start. To go around looking for fortuitous "similarities" and "differences" may broaden the mind of the researcher as travel is presumed to do, but it will not add much to our fund of relevant knowledge (cf. Faucheux, 1970, and Frijda and Jahoda, 1966, for extended discussions of the cross-cultural issue). An experiment on, for example, conformity may be trivial because of the interpretation of its data in terms of such blunt theoretical instruments as "universal" needs for affiliation or for approval; and the observed differences between subgroups of subjects may become of little general sociopsychological interest if what we learn from them is that there are individual personality differences in the strength of these needs. On the other hand, one need not rush to other "cultures" in order to undertake an analysis of the contextual and background conditions which determine the subject's perception of what may be the socially appropriate behaviour in the quandary in which he finds himself when faced with a row of stooges who, to the best of his knowledge, are a random collection of moderately honest citizens.

Thus, the restricted range of applicability of the data from social psychological experiments has three main consequences. First, it places them in a special category which neither relates to the scientifically irrelevant "individual" case nor to the ideal and unobtainable "general" case. Second, this middle range of data means that, unless the characteristics of their context are specified, the data can neither confirm nor falsify a "general" law. Third, these characteristics are inescapably part and parcel of the experimental design. Therefore, a description of the "conditions" of an experiment must include the analysis or the description of those aspects of the social context that the researcher considers to be relevant to the conclusions he draws; also any conclusion about the confirmation or invalidation of his hypotheses must relate to these conditions.

The need to specify the characteristics of the range is not only due to the impossibility of obtaining amorphous and interchangeable populations of subjects in social psychological experiments. Control of an experiment in the physical or in the biological sciences means that the relevant properties of the substances or organisms on which the experiment is performed are assumed to be explicitly known. It is trivial to say that this is not the case in social psychological experiments. But it is perhaps worth restating that, without ever clearly acknowledging the fact, social psychologists have gone much further than Locke ever did in his dreams of a human *tabula rasa*; many of their experimental designs contain the assumption that the *categories* of subjects used are forever like a clean slate on which our experimental conditions can be written at will. Once again, this is not a plea for respecting individual differences or for what Moscovici calls in this book a "differential social psychology" for social psychology is not a catalogue of individual, or even group, idiosyncrasies of social behaviour. But, unlike the physicists or the physiologists, we cannot manipulate the properties of the materials which we study before we start the experiment. This need not trouble the "general" experimental psychologist concerned with, for example, perceptual constancies or short-term memory. There are reasons for believing that, provided certain conditions for obtaining responses are satisfied (and this can be ensured through appropriate preliminary tests), all human beings function very much in the same way. But we cannot assume that this is the case in social or socially determined behaviour.[1] Our experimental conditions are always "contaminated"; and the nature of this contamination is one of the principal objects of our study.

[1] But the "general" psychologist has his own problems, and they centre around a decision as to what is and what is not "socially determined behaviour". In this sense, the statement that "all human beings function very much in the same way" begs the question. Theoretical or empirical problems of this nature arise in the most fundamental areas of "individual" behaviour. In perception, there is the issue of experiential factors and of the consequent social and cultural differences (cf. for example, Segall, Campbell and Herskovits, 1966; and Tajfel, 1969c); in motivation, of the effects of free choice and of its constraints (cf. Zimbardo, 1969); in emotion, of the effects of cognitive and social factors upon the manner in which an individual labels his emotional states and behaves accordingly. As Schachter (1970) wrote in a conclusion to an excellent discussion about the identity between a physiological state and psychological or behavioural event: "If we are eventually to make sense of this area, I believe we will be forced to adopt a set of concepts with which most physiologically inclined scientists feel somewhat uncomfortable and ill-at-ease, for they are concepts which are difficult to reify, and about which it is, at present, difficult to physiologize. We will be forced to examine a subject's perception of his bodily state and his interpretation of it in terms of his immediate situation and his past experience. We will be forced to deal with concepts about perception, about cognition, about learning, and about the social situation." (p. 120.)

There are few social psychologists who have not at one time or another felt uneasy about the social vacuum in which most of their experiments are conducted. As already stated, the feelings of "irrelevance" to which Ring (1967) and many other people referred are not, in the last analysis, due to the "tension between basic and applied". They are directly related to the nature of what is presumed to be "basic". And this in turn is a relative matter and depends upon the fit between the kind of questions about human social behaviour that are being asked and the answers that are being provided. The fit between the questions and the answers is in turn reflected in the experiments being designed. I shall first discuss the experiments and then return to the more general question of what is "basic".

2   The social context of experiments

There is no reason why sociopsychological theories—or at least some of the hypotheses derived from them—cannot be tested in experimental settings, and there are good reasons why they should be. The main issue in deciding what can and cannot be done experimentally is not just the appropriateness of an experiment for the purpose of testing a hypothesis but also the relationship between the data obtained and the kind of extrapolations that are made from them, implicitly or explicitly, to social conduct in natural settings. I shall therefore attempt a rough classification of social psychological experiments from this particular point of view; that is, the principle of the classification is the role that the data play in the transition from the theory to the "natural" phenomena to which the theory is supposed to apply. From this point of view, the following three types of experiments can be distinguished.

a. "Modelling" experiments: the theory here is an integrated "model" of some aspects of social behaviour which generates a number of hypotheses. The selection and nature of the experimental situations are determined by the properties of the model. The theory contains explicit or implicit extrapolations to social behaviour at large. The question which arises is that of the locus of applicability of the experimental findings; we must discover whether these findings validate the hypotheses only within the range of events explicitly encompassed by the model or whether they also validate the extrapolations made to other events.

b. "Simulation" experiments: these are based more often on an "approach" or an "idea" than on an integrated set of hypotheses deriving systematically from a postulated set of relationships. The "idea" (in the form of a general hypothesis) may be concerned with the role played in social behaviour by a variable or set of variables which cannot be studied separately in "real" contexts. The experiments will then consist of creating situations in which the variables in question can be simulated so that their effects can be ascertained; in this sense, the experiment is a simulation of a truncated part of social reality. Therefore, the problem is that of the validity of the simulation.

c. "Naturalistic" experiments: these include arrangements which enable the subjects to exhibit behaviour which resembles as closely as possible what their reaction would be in the natural situation with regard to aspects of behaviour which are of interest to the experimenter. The obvious prerequisite for behaving "naturally" (unless very young children or animals are used) is that the subjects should not be aware of the true interests of the experimenter, i.e. that they should have no idea *which* aspects of their behaviour are being observed and recorded. The problem here is the somewhat limited range and scope of social conduct which can be encompassed by such experiments.

It is important to stress that this threefold classification is not meant to be exhaustive, neither is it mutually exclusive. Many of the "modelling experiments" simulate, and many of the "simulation experiments" are intended to conceal their "true" purpose from the subjects. Many experiments are both modelling and simulating. The classification is used here only as a convenient and provisional tool to examine the nature and scope of extrapolations made from experimental findings to "natural" social conduct. Thus, the "simulations" in the modelling experiments are theoretically determined by the properties of the model; and those in the simulation experiments by the assumed properties of the relevant aspects of the natural social conduct and/or environment. The concealment of the true purpose of the experiment in the simulation experiments usually does not aim at concealing from the subjects *which* of their responses are being recorded; what is usually concealed is the manner in which these responses are related to the experimental arrangements, so that the subject—presumably—is unable to guess the connection between the one and the other. In the "naturalistic" experiments, the subject—again presumably—does not know that some of his "spontaneous" responses, to which he is not paying any particular attention (an indispensable condition for these responses to remain

"spontaneous"), are precisely those which are the object of the experimenter's interest.

Recent work on non-verbal communication in dyads and on spacing
in dyads and small groups (e.g. Argyle, 1970) is the main example of
naturalistic experiments. This work has proved very useful in the
minute observation of regularities found in this kind of behaviour; but
it is very difficult to see how with the methods being used it will ever
be possible to go beyond the study of these subtle aspects of face-to-face
communication. The scope of social conduct encompassed by motor
adjustments to the requirements and objectives of social interaction is
strictly limited; even more limited is their capacity for being unknow-
ingly recorded in an experiment. Thus, we can either have an adequate
source of information about a preselected and narrow range of movements, in large part unintentional, in face-to-face encounters, or we can
have the full range of conduct recorded in "natural" situations which
present the usual difficulties of introducing adequate experimental
controls. Despite these difficulties, the latter alternative may well be one
of our solutions; but the experiments on "looking" and on spacing have
hardly until now provided us with much new guidance on the implementation of this solution. Though there is little doubt about their
potential diagnostic—and perhaps also therapeutic—value in some
clinical settings and in training (mainly for some of the smoother social
skills), it cannot be claimed that they contain the promise of the revolutionary advent of a "New Look" in social psychology.

Many of the experiments inspired by the application of game theory
to social psychology provide important examples of the "modelling"
category. Plon (1972) recently presented a useful discussion of some of
the theoretical difficulties inherent in this trend of work. One of his
principal arguments is that the "model" takes over without an attempt
being made to undertake an independent analysis of the phenomena
to which it is supposed to apply.[1] Thus, the assumptions that go into
constructing the model are bound to be validated in the experiments
inspired by it—without necessarily throwing new light on the phenomena to which extrapolations are being made. Following Bachelard's
discussion of the role of analogy in science, Plon argues that *if* social
conflict has the strategic properties of a game, then we should be able

[1] For a more detailed discussion of the background of the use of the game model and its
relation to a conception of social conflict in terms of a political and strategic conflict of
interests, see Moscovici's and Wiberg's chapters in this book.

to use a game model for game playing experiments, and thus be able readily to validate predictions derived from the theory. It is, of course, an entirely acceptable procedure to derive hypotheses from a model and to proceed to test them. But as long as they are experimentally tested in contexts which are selected on the basis of the properties of the model rather than those of the modelled phenomena, no extrapolations from the findings can be made to social conflict and no proof can be offered that social conflict is reducible to a strategic interaction. (Cf. Wiberg's chapter in this book for an extensive discussion of the "rational" model of Man.)

Some of the most eminent workers in the field of game theory go even further in their denial of its direct relevance to social conflict. Thus, it is clear to Rapoport (1970) that, as distinct from non-constant sum games, the "constant sum game paradigm" is inadequate even as a model of international conflict. On the other hand, the results of investigations in mixed-motive situations which led to a theory of rational conflict resolution rather than, as in zero-sum games, to a theory of rational conflict, "could be organized into a behavioural theory. The theory would explain or predict the choices of people *in that laboratory situation* (italics in the original text) and, of course, would not warrant any extrapolations from it to real life." (Rapoport, 1970, p. 40.) Its sociopsychological interest is, for Rapoport, in pointing to "what has been left out" after "the purely logical relations of conflict situations are uncovered and 'factored out' " (p. 39). More generally, as Rapoport wrote in the same paper:

> It is important to note that the principles of conflict resolution as they emerge in game-theoretic analysis have nothing to do with such matters as reduction of hostility, redefinition of goals or interests, or the like. Certain "equity" principles are, to be sure, involved in bargaining theory but only to the extent that they reflect symmetries in the strategic positions of the players—hence, purely structural features of the game itself, not the psychological characteristics of the players. In short, game theory is a "depsychologized" decision theory, dealing with situations controlled by more than one decision maker.
>
> p. 3

Thus, game theory provides the rational structure of non-zero sum situations which account for an overwhelming majority of real social conflicts. Experiments derived from it point, as Rapoport wrote, to departures from rationality in a highly restricted set of situations, the nature of which is determined by the theory. There is no doubt that an analysis of these departures could present a useful source of socio-psychological knowledge; but its limitations must be clearly kept in mind. They are of two kinds: the first, already noted, is the nature of the experimental situations used and the difficulty of extrapolating from them. The second is perhaps even more important: what kind of theory could enable us to engage in *any* form of extrapolation? Departures from rationality do not take place in a social vacuum; nor are experimental games conducted in a social vacuum, however "purified" the situation may appear to an optimistic experimenter. It seems fairly obvious that the most promising analysis of these departures would consist of relating to one another the two structures that are involved: expectations and evaluations "at large" as they apply to, and/or are modified by, parti-cipation in an experiment involving a "game". These issues will be discussed at greater length in later sections dealing with the distinction between "presocial" theories in social psychology and theories which explicitly take into account the context in which social conduct takes place. For the present, it will be enough to remind the reader that in published reports on the experimental studies of games there is very little evidence of this kind of psychological-contextual analysis.

By "simulation experiments" I do not mean the computer simulations which fall into the previous category since they are often a technically sophisticated version of the experiments on strategic interactions in the dyad. One example of simulation experiments is Sherif's work on the emergence of social norms and its subsequent replications and imita-tions. He worked on an idea rather than a detailed "model"; the idea was that the emergence and acceptance of social norms is a reflection of the human search for order and coherence in the environment. He then proceeded to create a physical and social vacuum—almost the primeval chaos—in which the experimental Adams and Eves (irres-pective of sex) met for the first time in complete darkness to generate shared wisdom about the extent of autokinetic movement. Convergence out of chaos represented the emergence of social norms.

The difficulties here are the same as those already referred to in the earlier discussion in this chapter about the "interchangeable" and "undifferentiated" experimental subjects. There is no such thing as a social vacuum in human affairs—be they experimental or not—and this was clearly shown in a recent study by Alexander *et al.* (1970). They assumed that Sherif's results could be alternatively explained by the structure of social expectations that the subjects brought to the experimental situation. Through a simple change in these expectations they brought about a reversal in one of the "classical" findings of social psychology: not a trace of convergence was found in the subjects' judgements. Once again, this does not mean that Sherif's views about the search for order and coherence through information gained from others need be abandoned as unconfirmed. But it does mean that these views must be tested in social situations that are analysed as such rather than assumed to be non-situations. As Alexander *et al.* wrote in the conclusion to their paper:

Ultimately, most of the human behaviours that social psychology will want to explain do occur in normatively anchored and socially defined situations. Thus, the inclusion of these variables in experimental measurement and manipulation can only facilitate the eventual and unavoidable task of generalizing experimental results to *specified* social conditions that differ in defined ways from the conditions obtaining in laboratory experimentation. Instead of wasting effort and imagination to create novel, unique and culturally irrelevant experimental situations, we might better attempt to control, measure and manipulate the socially validated interpretive frameworks—the situational meaning—that subjects use in defining experimental behaviours. Having learned these expectational structures through life-experiences, subjects apparently use them intuitively to structure their perceptions of and govern their responses to events—even in experimental situations.

p. 121

I do not agree with Alexander and his colleagues that the effort and imagination which goes into the creation of "novel" and "unique" experimental situations are necessarily wasted; nor—by definition— that an experimental situation can ever be "culturally irrelevant". Our task can be defined precisely as either to design experiments whose cultural relevance fits the requirements of our research problem, or to discover the cultural relevance of the experiments which have not been so designed; Alexander *et al.* succeeded in doing the latter in their own study.

Since I have objected to extrapolations from experiments to social conduct which do not take into account the interaction between social variables and "pure" psychological processes, it is only fair that I should add that similar shortcomings in prediction have been evident in my own work for very much the same reasons. Some years ago (Tajfel, 1959) I put forward a series of hypotheses concerned with the role of classification and of "value" in determining shifts of various kinds in social judgement. This work placed itself squarely in the tradition of derivation of principles of social judgement from the principles of psychophysical judgement—with the variables of classification and value thrown in for good measure to account for certain complexities in the judgements of other people not usually taken into account in the "classical" experiments in psychophysics. The aspects of social conduct to which extrapolations were being explicitly made were those of stereotyping and of other biases in social judgement. The experimental data from which these extrapolations proceeded consisted of certain regularities found in the judgements of physical magnitudes on which classifications were superimposed in a manner determined by the general theoretical scheme (e.g. Tajfel and Wilkes, 1963). In this sense, the experiments could be understood as belonging to the "simulation" category described earlier.

Some of these ideas have been recently taken up in a different context by Eiser (1971a, 1971b). Dissatisfied with certain straightforward applications of psychophysical principles to predictions of attitude change (e.g. Sherif and Hovland, 1961; Upshaw, 1965) and with the inconsistencies between the prediction of polarization of ratings of items and the data as they applied to judges who were at the "anti" and the "pro" extremes with regard to an issue, Eiser attempted to apply my earlier classification model to his own data. He was able to produce convincing evidence that the classificatory scheme yielded good predictions only if and when it was combined with an analysis of the semantic "value connotations" to the subjects both of the dimensions along which they were required to judge the items and of the items themselves. Eiser's own analysis of the value connotations remained *a priori* in his first experiments but this presents no theoretical difficulty for further research. A similar analysis explicitly conducted in one of my earlier experiments on person perception (Tajfel and Wilkes, 1964) also yielded fairly good predictions of ratings. The more general point is, however, succinctly made by Eiser (1971b) in his discussion of the relation between social judgement and the theories of cognitive consistency:

> [If the preliminary evidence is confirmed,] it calls into question the view that individuals with different attitudes differ simply along a dimension of favourability to unfavourability; rather they may differ in terms of the total frames of reference according to which they see the issue in question, in which case a description of an individual's frame of reference as such may tell one far more about his "attitude" than would any mere measure of favourability. It may, indeed, go some way towards providing an explanation of his attitude. For example, the "hawk" for whom the dimension "patriotic-unpatriotic" is most salient, might be said to support US policy in Vietnam *because* he sees the war as an issue of patriotism. If the dimensions

that are salient to an individual are those in terms of which he sees his own position as most securely positive, then they may also be those that touch most closely upon the system of values in terms of which he considers his own attitude to be justified. (pp. 450–451.)

Like everything else that happens in social conduct, experiments can be described as "episodes" in the sense of the term used by Harré in this book. Harré's solution is to classify the episodes on the basis of distinguishable modes of social conduct and to discover their meaning through observation, analytic interpretation and sometimes participation. But experiments can also differ in one important way from other episodes: they can be episodes which are caricatures of other episodes. I use here the term "caricature" in its sense of selecting and accentuating at will certain features of the object. The problem is to have caricatures in which their objects are still recognizable; and to have a clear purpose in the selection and accentuation of some of their features.

I shall not waste space by arguing that experiments remain one of the most efficient means of testing hypotheses; instead I should like to conclude this section with a restatement of a few points concerning experiments, all of which have been implicitly or explicitly made in the preceding pages.

a. Experiments cannot be conducted in a social vacuum. This implies: (i) that it cannot be assumed that anyone has ever succeeded in creating such a vacuum; (ii) that an analysis of the social context of the experiment and of the social situation which it represents must always be made; (iii) that specially designed experiments must be conducted for the explicit purpose of testing hypotheses about the features of the social context which determine, and interact with, the mode of operation of psychological processes. It would not be too fanciful to formulate a "law of compensation for the void of social psychological experiments"; the more novel, unfamiliar or strange an experimental situation is to the subject, the more he will tend to solve the problem that this creates for him by falling back on his own notions of what might be the conduct appropriate to it, i.e. the more will his conduct be determined by those of his norms and values that he perceives as being pertinent to the situation.

b. The "experimenter effect" cannot be considered without its counterpart, the "subject effect". This is a direct consequence of the "law" of compensation for void just stated. The notion of the experimenter effect (e.g. Rosenthal, 1966) can be defined for our purposes as the use of experimental procedures which may cause the subjects to entertain certain hypotheses about how the experimenter expects them to behave, and then to conform to these expectations. As is well known, this has already led to a substantial number of experiments about experiments. It is quite obvious that the experimenter effect, as defined here, cannot work "in favour" of the experimenter unless it is based on meanings and expectations which are shared by the experimenter and the subjects. That this phenomenon has important implications beyond the methodological growing pains of social psychology (and of the other branches of psychology) has been demonstrated in the recent studies by Rosenthal and Jacobson (1968) and in some of the work done by Katz (1968). On the basis of this work, the "subject effect" could be defined as the selection of experimental (or, for example, educational) procedures which may cause the experimenter (or the teacher) to persist in his previous expectations as to why the subjects behave as they do, and then to conform to these expectations in formulating his conclusions. Perhaps we need a research programme of experiments about experiments designed to relate the selection of experimental procedures to the nature of extrapolations made from them to social conduct in natural settings.

c. An experiment need not be the final link in the process of testing a sociopsychological hypothesis. This is in turn a consequence both of the law of void-compensation and of the interaction between the experimenter and the subject effects. It can be assumed that the sharing of meanings and expectations between the subjects (and also, in some cases, the subjects and the experimenter) leads to certain regularities in the observed behaviour. The analysis of these regularities is one of the tasks of a theory, and their prediction the object of the hypotheses formulated from the theory. There is no reason why a "cultural" analysis of norms and values which are thought to be relevant should not intervene between the theory and its experimental testing. This analysis (which could use a variety of methods) may have several purposes, such as achieving a definition of the meaning of the experimental situation, determining the kind of situation that will be used, or revising the hypothesis that will be experimentally tested. It is in this sense that an experiment designed to test predictions which follow from a combination of the theoretical and the "cultural" analysis can be conceived as a "caricature" of Harré's "natural" episodes. But there is no reason why the sequence could not be reversed. An experiment can follow directly from theoretical premises, and its data can be interpreted in the light of a subsequent "cultural" analysis.

It is, however, also possible to conceive of experiments which, through the pattern of their data, would *generate* hypotheses about the norms and values which could turn out to be relevant to a subsequent "cultural" analysis. This was the sequence which was forced upon us in recent studies of the effects of social categorization on intergroup behaviour (Tajfel, 1970b; Tajfel *et al.*, 1971). A scrutiny of the data disclosed the possibility that the most economical explanation of a complex set of results was the assumption that the subjects attempted to achieve a compromise between two norms and two values underlying these norms which, as far as they were concerned, were pertinent to the experimental situation. The norms were those of "groupness" and "fairness", and the values those of "solidarity" and "equity". A series of open-ended individual interviews clearly supported this construction, both with regard to norms and values and with regard to their relevance, in the subjects' eyes, to the experimental situation. These interviews helped in turn in the formulation of revised theoretical ideas about the interaction between the processes of social categorization and the functioning of social norms, as well as in the design of further experiments involving new caricatures of social reality.

Here I must stress that this account is not made in order to serve as a claim for a methodological "discovery". Similar combinations of laboratory procedures and interviews have been used in many social psychological experiments. But in many more no attempt is made at any form of cultural analysis. The main points relating to a systematic use of such analysis have already been made. What is perhaps more interesting is to ask why it is not being used in the great majority of cases. The answer to this question is not to be found in a discussion of points of research procedure. I shall now return to the prevailing conception of what is "basic" knowledge in social psychology.

3 Individual, inter-individual and social psychology

Questions about human social behaviour can be considered as being on a continuum which ranges from biological through psychological and sociopsychological to sociological. Whenever a statement of this kind is made, the current fashion is to add immediately that all these "levels" obviously interact; that not one of them can be studied without others being taken into consideration; that it has been hard enough to lower the barriers a little between the disciplines and therefore one should not make things difficult by erecting them all over again. The fact remains that "interaction" is merely a useless slogan unless it can be translated into a way of thinking about research problems and unless it determines the manner in which research is conducted.

It would be a pointless exercise to try to provide here formal definitions of these various levels. They are a matter of emphasis and focus of interest rather than clearly delimited boundaries. Thus, on the "biological" level, the questions concerning social behaviour tend to be about the genetic and physiological determinants of human adaptation to, and transformation of, the social environment, and answers are often sought in terms of evolution, ecology, their effects on the structure of the human organism, and the effects of this structure on its behaviour. An example here would be the work of the ethologists on the instinctive aspects of human aggression in their relation to, and continuity with, various forms of intraspecific aggression in other species.

The "psychological" questions are often addressed at the determination of social behaviour by those characteristics of the human species that are either unique to it or at least drastically different from those displayed by other species: language and other forms of symbolic communication, socially derived "secondary" motivation, the cognitive and motivational features of socialization. The answers are in terms of general laws of functioning, sometimes closely interacting with the "biological" level, and sometimes taking this level for granted as providing the range but not necessarily predicting the content of the processes involved. Amongst examples here would be, once again, the relationships between frustration and aggression, the various versions of the theory of cognitive consistency, the role of imitation in social development, laws of competition and cooperation deriving from various forms of the exchange theory, theories of achievement motivation and of affiliation, etc.

The "sociological" questions about behaviour are concerned with its determination by the social, economic and political structures. The answers often tend to formulate predictions from selected properties of these structures to observed behaviour, e.g. as in the relations between economic disparities and outgroup discrimination. Though psychologically derived concepts such as "relative deprivation" are sometimes used as a link between the independent and the dependent variables, their psychological context is not the focus of the theoretical analysis.

The sociopsychological man somehow manages to fall between these several stools. The lack of fit between the kind of questions asked about him and the kind of answers provided depends upon the professional identification of the researcher; so that sociopsychological questions tend to be given biological, psychological or sociological answers.

There could hardly be much disagreement with the suggestion that sociopsychological questions concern the determinants of human social behaviour and that the aim of sociopsychological theories is to explain and predict such behaviour. The determinants can be found, of course, at all of the "levels"; but this remains one of those empty "interaction" statements unless it can be shown to work when put to use in the business of explanation and prediction—and sometimes also of postdiction understood as "explanation" (cf. Popper, 1961). The lack of fit between questions and answers results from analysing human social behaviour *as if* it could be usefully reduced to the genetic and physiological characteristics of the species as it is in the case of the biological bias; or to non-social human behaviour as in the case of the psychological bias; or to a one-way determination by social structures as in the case of the sociological bias. I do not wish to overstate the issue: there is no doubt that certain aspects of human social behaviour can be usefully analysed in terms of any one of these reductions and I shall happily leave to the reader the task of finding relevant examples. My concern is with the large and crucial areas of social conduct which are uniquely characteristic of the sociopsychological *homo* in the sense that they present empirical discontinuities with his biological background, with his non-social psychological functioning and with the conception of him as being fully accounted for by the social system of which he is a part.

As is the case with other forms of reductionism, our three biases derive from a conception which is fundamentally useful. They provide the *range* of what is possible, i.e. research conclusions in social psychology cannot be incongruent with firmly established evidence deriving from those conceptions in biology, general psychology and sociology which have a direct impact upon the aspects of the functioning of the sociopsychological man that are being studied. But from then on he needs special treatment adapted to his own problems.

There are some distant parallels between this need for the acknowledgement of the emergence of new variables and systems of behaviour and the study of the emergence of new styles in the history of art. Styles in painting or in music consist, by definition, of certain regularities;

these must be isolated, described and analysed. Gombrich's (1960) descriptions of the use of "stereotypes" in the visual arts provide excellent examples of the use of a general psychological law for providing one important dimension of the range within which the analysis must be conducted. But he, or any other art historian, could hardly stop there. A study of the rules which enable us to refer to a group of painters as "impressionists" or "surrealists" or "fauvists" must be based on familiarity with their conception of what they intended to communicate, how they wished to communicate it, and why they chose their particular idioms. This in turn needs to be related to an analysis of what they were reacting to (or against), which may be conducted within the framework provided either by previous stylistic regularities or by the socio-historical background or by both.

The methods of acquisition of knowledge about regularities are, of course, different in the history of art and in social psychology; and so is the relative importance of contributions from a historical type of analysis. But the relationship between the boundaries traced by the range (of human communicative behaviour in the case of art) and the analysis of the nature of selected regularities is similar in both cases. It is undoubtedly useful and important to know that certain processes in perception and in reproduction (such as categorization and stereotyping) make it possible for styles in art to develop, and, at one remove, it is equally useful to know that without our visual apparatus, endowed with a capacity to perceive in perspective, and without our two hands and ten fingers, painting would not have been what it is. It is a far cry from the knowledge of these limiting properties of the range to the kind of knowledge that the art historian needs. If he is interested in style, he has the kind of "middle range" populations displaying regularities of behaviour to which I referred earlier when discussing populations of subjects in social psychological experiments. As a matter of fact, even in the case of the "limiting" feature of perspective, a socio-historical analysis of the development of communicative skills is a prerequisite for understanding how things happen. On the other hand, an excessive fascination with the fact that Man has two hands and ten fingers could provide us with propositions about the development of styles in art which would not be too far removed from certain unilluminating "basic" propositions in social psychology, such as that the more common goals the members of a group have, the more "cohesive" the group will be; or "the more often within a given period of time a man's activity

D

rewards the activity of another, the more often the other will emit the activity" (Homans, 1961, p. 54).

Equivalent to "stylistic regularities" in social behaviour are the conceptions that groups of men (selected according to criteria based on the researcher's theoretical interests) have about what they wish to do, their manner of doing it and the reasons for their choice of idioms. But the principal objection to this parallel of "stylistic regularities" is that it may imply a "clinical" and descriptive social psychology rather than a systematic science based on general theories of social behaviour. One possible answer to this is that perhaps we do not at present have such a science. In their book on theories in social psychology, Deutsch and Krauss (1965) wrote: ". . . being in its infancy [social psychology] is still largely dominated by theoretical approaches that are based on implicit conceptions of the nature of Man. None of these approaches is sufficiently explicit in its psychological assumptions, in its mode of logical inference, nor in its empirical reference to permit unambiguous testing of its implications. In short, none of the orientations is a 'theory' in the sense of theories in the physical sciences." (pp. 12–13.)

It is true, however, that some of the "approaches" or "orientations" that have been influential have led to the formulation of what Merton (1957) called "theories of the middle range"; these theories, without aspiring to the rigour of the physical sciences, were responsible for an abundance of good experimental research. The frustration-aggression theory is one example; others are provided by theories of cognitive consistency. In particular, Festinger's (1957) theory of cognitive dissonance has stimulated in the last fifteen years or so an enormous amount of research with an increasing range of application. There are many other examples, some of which bear witness to a sudden burgeoning of interest and research in "localized" and specific problems, such as has recently been the case with the work on "risky shift", on competition and cooperation in dyads, on the determinants of conformity in small groups or on non-verbal communication.

However, many of these theories present one of two characteristics: either they are not primarily theories of social behaviour, or if they appear to be, it is soon discovered that they are basically about individual, or at the limit, inter-individual behaviour.

Leon Festinger once said that he ceased to be a social psychologist long before he developed his recent interest in research on vision; as his work immediately preceding this interest was concerned with his theory of cognitive dissonance, this seemed at the time a highly puzzling utterance. But its original author must not be burdened with my *post hoc* interpretation which is based on a distinction between two types of theoretical questions about human social behaviour. One category consists of questions about what enabled Man, as a species, to become the kind of social animal that he is; the other concerns the behaviour he displays *because* he is the kind of social animal that he is.

Both types of question are relevant to the understanding of social behaviour. The first concerns the range of social behaviour rather than its content because it applies to processes that are preliminary to the social man, that are no more "social" in their origin than is colour vision or the generalization of conditioned responses. In other words, the relevance of these processes to social behaviour is theoretically of the same kind as the relevance to it of, for example, the psychophysiology of vision or of the role of secondary reinforcement in learning; social behaviour would not have been what it is if these processes were not what they are. But between them and social conduct, as it actually occurs, there are a variety of phenomena of social origin without the consideration of which predictions and explanations are bound to remain as "irrelevant" as they are often found to be. Itard's savage boy from Aveyron could have undoubtedly been shown, from the moment he was found, to conform to some lawful relationships between frustration and aggression; and to regulate his behaviour so as to avoid unrewarded effort. Truffaut's sober film about him (*L'Enfant Sauvage*) suggests the dramatic impact on his behaviour of the modification of these processes through social interaction. Some modifications of behaviour would also probably occur if one changed the social environments of the frustrated and aggressive rats in the experiments on the subject; or of the rats used by Lawrence and Festinger (1962) which "justified" the effort they expended by doing better work. As in the case of the boy from Aveyron, an analysis would then be required of the emergent variables without which an understanding of the behavioural transformations would not be possible. It should be clear that terms such as "transformation" or "modification" only make sense because in the case of the Itard story we start—uniquely—from something pre-social. In normal circumstances, the "social" is not a "transformation" of something that existed before its emergence: it interacts from the beginning with the processes defining the range.

The theories of the second kind are concerned with the behaviour that

Man displays *because* he is a social animal. The problems are directly those set by social interaction, such as communicating, competing, cooperating, or conforming. The theories from which the experimental hypotheses are derived and the design of the experiments can be considered from two points of view: the image of Man that is implicit in them; and the conception of the relation between Man's "individual" nature and his social behaviour.

The first of these issues is discussed at length from various points of view in other chapters in this volume (cf. the contributions of Moscovici, Harré, Asplund, Janoušek and Israel). It will therefore not detain me here. The second issue can perhaps be characterized by a quotation from an application by a psychologist for a grant to do cross-cultural research which I recently had the privilege to see. In one of its focal paragraphs it referred to "this set of environmental circumstances that we call 'culture' ".

This is very near to certain research conceptions of the relation between Man's "individual" nature and the social setting in which his behaviour takes place. The reasoning can be roughly described as follows: there is a bedrock of individual motives such as, for example, striving for reward and avoiding punishment (or striving for gain and avoiding losses); this determines Man's behaviour whether he is reacting to the weather, hunting for food, exploring a new phenomenon or dealing with other people. His capacity to profit from past experience (or learn from past rewards) and his "cognitive structures" intervene between what he wants and how he gets it. Other people present an additional complication: they too can profit from past experience and use their cognitive abilities. This is the principal reason for the complexities of social interaction. Otherwise, social behaviour is built according to the same matrix of gains and losses as "non-social" behaviour; in this matrix other people serve as means whereby these gains can be obtained or losses prevented. It is in this sense that they are "stimuli" which happen to be "social".

I know that this is a crude and oversimplified image; but it is not too far off the mark. Let me refer to one of the best and deservedly most widely used textbooks in experimental social psychology: that of Jones and Gerard (1967). After nearly 600 pages, we reach chapter 15 which gets down to "The Impact of Group Membership on Individual Behaviour". The title of the chapter is already of significance since it implies that human groups are in the category of "sets of environmental circumstances" somehow superimposed on individual behaviour. This is immediately confirmed in the first sentence: "We have travelled a long and winding road in order to record the major points at which the life of the individual is *touched* [italics mine] by the behaviour of other individuals." (p. 591.) The authors continue: "These other individuals have been characterized variously in preceding chapters as socialization agents, stimulus persons, comparison models, communicators, and actors *linked to the individual through contingencies of outcome* [italics mine]. Now we shall attempt to cope more directly with the phenomena of group life and no longer restrict ourselves to the dyad." (p. 591.)

It is indeed the dyad that has been, in previous chapters, the main basis for extrapolations to the wider systems of social conduct. The dyad serves as a model in two ways at least: *a* dyad stands for *any* dyad (in the sense of inter-changeability discussed earlier in this chapter); and relations within a dyad, such as, for example, those of competition and cooperation, serve as a model for the study of the psychological aspects of social conflict. Finally, there is only a short step from dyads to groups. Both are governed by the same instrumentalities. Thus: "Two or more persons become a group when the individual members feel that their purposes are served by continued affiliation. In some groups the members share the same purpose; in others the group holds together because it fulfills a variety of individual purposes." (Jones and Gerard, 1967, p. 591.) We join with others to accomplish our objectives. Hence: "To say that *A* is dependent on *B* or *C*, or the combination of *B* and *C*, implies that *A* requires the assistance of these others to achieve certain goals important to him." (Ibid., p. 591.)

Examples of this kind could be multiplied *ad infinitum*. It is true that in other chapters in the book there are discussions of communication in small groups and of the normative aspects of small group structure. But they are still reducible to the same model: Man's social behaviour is an adaptation of his general gain–loss strategy to the special requirements arising out of his being surrounded by other people. Thus, the second of the two kinds of theories referred to above—theories concerned with behaviour that Man displays because he is a social animal —can be reduced to the first: social behaviour is still considered in them in a "presocial" or an "asocial" perspective.

4   A perspective for a sociopsychological problem

The main theme so far discussed is that many of the theories which dominate the present research output in social psychology are not sociopsychological. It is therefore unavoidable that most of the experiments designed to test these theories should be equally impervious to the wider realities of social conduct and share their focus on the strategies of individual and inter-individual adjustments. It is in terms of these that we progress without a break from the individual to his relations with another individual in the dyad, then to the relations between a few individuals in a small group, finally to reach the problems posed by the relations between groups. But it seems that at this point the break in the continuity becomes too obvious to ignore. A simpler solution is then adopted: instead the problem itself is ignored. In a recent review of experimental work about group processes, Gerard and Miller (1967) devoted to it a dozen lines or so in a text of about 40 pages. The impact of these few lines is: (a) that indeed very little experimental work on intergroup processes is being done; and (b) that this is due to the methodological difficulties of creating intergroup situations in the laboratory. In the large volume by Jones and Gerard (1967) one must search in vain in the index for terms such as "intergroup", "ingroup", "outgroup", "identity" (social or any other). "Conflict" appears in the glossary at the end of the book as "a state that obtains for an individual when he is motivated to make two or more mutually incompatible responses" (p. 709). It is therefore not surprising that, for example, Sherif's "field" experiments on conflict between small groups are not even referred to.

Why should this be so? The puzzle becomes even greater if one recalls some obvious propositions, such as that the course of relations between human groups of various kinds is one of *the* fundamental social problems of our times; that in an infinite variety of situations throughout his life, an individual feels, thinks and behaves in terms of his social identity created by the various groups of which he is a member and in terms of his relation to the social identity of others, as individuals or *en masse*. It is equally obvious that this social conduct is determined to a large extent by the relations between the groups to which he belongs as well as other groups, and that the nature of these relations is in turn largely due to the socially shared regularities of intergroup conduct. This is therefore a social phenomenon which can be considered as an example *par excellence* of the interaction between the individual and his social setting. The social setting of intergroup relations contributes to making the individuals what they are and they in turn produce this social setting; they and it develop and change symbiotically. One would expect that the nature of this interaction could hardly fail to become a major focus of interest in social psychology and a point of departure for research and experimentation.

The reasons for the absence of such an analysis and for the poverty of the relevant research are not far to seek. If the "basic" processes with which social psychology is deemed to be concerned are confined to the motivational and cognitive functioning of an individual (and universal) human being, then intergroup processes can only be conceived in one of two ways: either they are fully explained through these individual processes or they present "special" problems the study of which would not add very much to our "fundamental" knowledge. The individual is seen as the genotype of social psychology; the social matrices which act upon him and upon which he acts are no more than a superimposition of phenotypes. As Berkowitz (1962) wrote:

> Granting all this, the present writer is still inclined to emphasize the importance of individualistic considerations in the field of group relations. Dealings between groups ultimately become problems of the psychology of the individual. Individuals decide to go to war; battles are fought by individuals; and peace is established by individuals. It is the individual who adopts the beliefs prevailing in his society, even though the extent to which these opinions are shared by many people is a factor governing his readiness to adopt them, and he then transmits these views to other individuals. Ultimately, it is the single person who attacks the feared and disliked ethnic minority group, even though many other people around him share his feelings and are very important in determining his willingness to aggress against this minority. Theoretical principles can be formulated referring to the group as a unit and these can be very helpful in understanding hostility between groups. But such abstractions refer to collections of people and are made possible by interindividual uniformities in behaviour.
>
> p. 167

The message is clear: "ultimately" it is the individual who is the unit of analysis; he reacts to others and others react to him—but otherwise nothing new has happened. Social conduct consists of interindividual uniformities made up of an algebra of individual cognitions and motivations. One possible analogy that this brings to mind is that of a ping-pong table on which many balls might be falling simultaneously from all directions and distances. The balls would, of course, bounce off in their individual ways; but in doing so they obey a few relatively simple laws. One of the essential requirements for these laws to have predictive power is that the balls should not modify each other or the table on mutual impact, nor should the table modify the balls. We thus have inter-individual uniformities of behaviour in a constant environment, with all the "elements" of the situation emerging un-changed and unscathed from their encounters. We might need two (or more) sets of balls for a "model" of intergroup conduct and perhaps, depending upon the problem, one, two or more tables.

Social psychologists still seem to be steeped in this kind of reduction-ism at a time when it is being abandoned, or at least seriously question-ed, in the very realm of individual behaviour to which they turn for their basic concepts. As Piaget and Inhelder (1969) wrote in a recent brief discussion of cognitive development:

> . . . an action consists in transforming reality rather than simply discovering its existence: for each new action the acts of discovering and transforming are in fact inseparable. This is not only true of the infant whose every new action enriches his universe (from the first feed to instrumental behaviour patterns, like the use of a stick as a means of pulling an object towards one), but it remains true at all levels. The construction of an electronic machine or a sputnik not only enriches our knowledge of reality, it also enriches reality itself, which until then did not include such objects. This creative nature of action is essential. Behaviourists study behaviour, therefore actions, but too often forget the "active" and transforming characteristic of an action.
>
> p. 128

There are several reasons for selecting the problems of intergroup relations to exemplify the arguments advanced earlier in this chapter. These problems are at the meeting point of the interests of the bio-logists, psychologists and sociologists. They involve social conduct in face-to-face interaction which is at the same time guided by highly abstract representations of social reality; they affect profoundly the social experience to which millions of individuals are exposed almost from the moment of their births.

And yet, as we have seen, there are good reasons for maintaining that an experimental social psychology of intergroup relations hardly exists. It is largely replaced by the *as if* approaches to sociopsychological problems to which reference has been made earlier. The focus of some of the biological (and most of the pseudo-biological) writing on the subject is on the evolutionary continuity of human intergroup behavi-our with intraspecific aggression and territoriality in other species. This is assumed to "explain" the less glorious aspects of the human past and present without ever, to my knowledge, an attempt having been made to put forward a set of hypotheses which would meet the criteria of falsifiability or pay serious attention to variables which are unique to human social organization. It would not be useful to return to a discussion of the asocial and presocial nature of these conceptions.

The psychologists have shown, on the whole, more scientific sophistication in considering these problems; or at least it can be said that as distinct from the previous case, their writings are based on some research on the subject. Roughly four trends can be distinguished in this research: derivations from theories of aggression (mainly but not exclusively centred around the frustration-aggression hypothesis); extrapolations from interindividual or small group competition and cooperation; a cognitive analysis of judgements, stereotypes, attitudes and beliefs about ingroups and outgroups; and studies of the genesis of prejudice in an individual based on its relevance to, and continuity with, his emotional experiences during early socialization. The first three of these trends of research are, in their own way, concerned as little with the emergence of social interaction and its role in accounting for the regularities of social conduct as is the biological approach. The fourth does take into account the diverse patterns of social relations as they affect early emotional development; but it explicitly focuses its analysis on the subsequent emergence of various types of personality prone to prejudice and thus it cannot, nor is it aiming to, encompass the wider aspects of the social psychology of intergroup conflict.

One way to characterize the approach to the same problems current in much of the sociological writing is to paraphrase the statement by Berkowitz which I quoted earlier (cf. p. 95). It could then read as follows: "Granting all this (i.e. the biological and the psychological considerations), the present writer is still inclined to emphasize the importance of considering the field of group relations in terms of social structure. Dealings between groups cannot be accounted for by the psychology of the individual. Governments decide to go to war; battles are fought by armies; and peace is established by governments. The social conditions in which groups of people live largely determine their beliefs and the extent to which they are shared. Ultimately, a single person's attack on an ethnic minority group that he dislikes or fears would remain a trivial occurrence had it not been for the fact that he acts in unison with others who share his feelings and are very important in determining his willingness to aggress against this minority. Theoretical principles can be formulated based on the individual as a unit and these can be very helpful in understanding hostility between groups. But such abstractions could only refer to unstructured collections of people and are only made possible by inter-individual uniformities in behaviour which are due to the fact that people live in a social context which has its own laws and structure."

This paraphrase is, of course, in many ways unfair to Berkowitz as it skates over some of the serious theoretical problems with which he is concerned.[1] But a critique of his views is not its main point. Rather, it is the fact that the paraphrased statement would readily command the agreement of many of our colleagues who emphasize the social determination of intergroup relations. To take two examples: it could easily be inserted in the recent and influential books by Banton (1967) or by Blalock (1967) without in any way creating inconsistencies with their general argument. But the difficulties it presents for a social psychologist are just as serious as those of Berkowitz's "psychological individualism". If this is the beginning and the end of the explanation of social conduct, then we have yet another *tabula rasa* on which nothing has been written about the convergence of the psychological and the social processes and the way in which they shape one another. In a sense, this is like a second sociological version of Skinnerian behaviourism which follows a different direction from the first version proposed by Homans (1961). It is the sociology of the "empty organism" which relates directly the inputs (e.g. economic situation) to the outputs (e.g. discrimination in employment) without concerning itself with the black box in the middle which contains the mysteries of human social functioning. Even this is not entirely true: unstated assumptions are often made about the black box; some relevant examples can be found in Moscovici's and Israel's discussions in this book of the relations between psychological and economic theories. (Also cf. Plon, 1972.) We are thus confronted simultaneously by the psychological individualism of the psychologists and a sociological or economic version of an implicit "naive psychologism".

[1] In particular, it ignores deliberately the inescapable fact that armies, governments etc. are composed of individuals who take decisions for themselves or for others. But this still does not mean that we are dealing here with the "individual" psychology of presocial men who form a society by coming together in a heap. Harré's discussion in this book of a man as a rule-follower is directly relevant to this issue. Also, cf. the discussion of methodological individualism in Israel's chapter.

It is not the purpose of this chapter to produce grand (or even minor) theories. But it is one of its aims to attempt a discussion of the kind of variables that a theory should include in order to fit the requirements of psycho-social reality. In the case of intergroup relations—and also in other cases, as, for example, in problems of social influence as they relate to the psychological aspects of social change—one could argue that we are confronted at present with a scientific system of separate tiers, with the means of access from one to another hardly ever used; or that we are witnessing something like an exchange of pre-packaged gifts, undoubtedly selected with the best possible intentions, but without any reference to the needs of the receiver or to the use that he might wish to make of them. The notion of flexibility in the relations between the human organism and his environment, grounded in biology and used in a great many ways in psychological theories and research on cognitive functioning, is the obvious perspective that should be common to ethological theories of intraspecific aggression and to the consideration of the emergent characteristics of human social behaviour. A similar role could be played by the notion of appropriateness of conduct in order to bring the "psychology of the individual" to a level adequate for many aspects of a sociopsychological analysis.

Very little needs to be said about flexibility. The most important evolutionary weapon of Man has undoubtedly been his capacity to modify his behaviour to accord with environmental requirements, and simultaneously to change the environment to fit his own requirements. And yet, as I have stated elsewhere (Tajfel, 1969a), the cognitive models employed to analyse human attempts to understand the environment, biological and physical, in order to act upon it have been ignored in most of the ethological and the psychoanalytic writing concerned with social environment.

It is as if we were suddenly dealing with a different and strange animal that uses some of his abilities to adapt to some aspects of his environment, and is quite incapable of using them in order to adapt to others. The prevailing model of Man as a creature trying to find his way in his social environment seems to have nothing in common with the ideas of exploration, of meaning, of understanding, of rational consistency. We have the rational model for natural phenomena; we seem to have nothing but a blood-and-guts model for social phenomena. In this new blood-and-guts romanticism so fashionable at present in some science and semi-science, Man's attitudes and beliefs concerning the social environment are seen mainly as a by-product of tendencies that are buried deeply in his evolutionary past or just as deeply in his unconscious.

Tajfel, 1969a, pp. 79–80

This applies particularly to problems of intergroup relations:

> It is hardly startling to say that the best way to predict whether a man will harbour
> hostile attitudes towards a particular group and what will be the content of these
> attitudes is to find out how he understands the intergroup situation. And it is hardly
> any more startling to say that this understanding will in turn affect his behaviour.
> This does not mean, of course, that emotional and motivational factors are unim-
> portant. But it is just as true that the greatest adaptive advantage of Man is his
> capacity to modify his behaviour as a function of the way in which he perceives and
> understands a situation. It is difficult to see why it should be assumed that he loses this
> capacity as soon as he confronts human groups other than his own, and that it is in
> these situations alone that most of his concepts, attitudes, beliefs and modes of thinking
> are no more than powerless and pale projections of instinctive and unconscious
> drives.
>
> Ibid., p. 81

The notion of appropriateness of conduct has more direct implications for current theories and research in social psychology. It derives
directly from the notion of Man as "a rule-following animal" which
underlies much of Harré's argument in this book and, among others,
Peters' (1960) discussion of the concept of motivation in psychological
theories. In a recent discussion of the primacy of abstract rules in the
determination of behaviour, Hayek (1969) wrote: ". . . all our actions
must be conceived of as being guided by rules of which we are not
conscious but which in their joint influence enable us to exercise
extremely complicated skills without having any idea of the particular
sequence of movements involved." (pp. 312–313.) This rule-integration
of motor skills is reflected at a different level in social conduct; or as
Peters put it: "Man is a rule-following animal. His actions are not
simply directed towards ends; they also conform to social standards and
conventions, and unlike a calculating machine he acts because of his
knowledge of rules and objectives." (p. 5.)

In the field of social conduct, "rules" can be described as notions
about appropriateness. This means quite simply that social conduct is
to a very large extent determined by what an individual deems to be
appropriate to the social situation in which he finds himself. His conceptions of what is appropriate are in turn determined by the prevailing
system of norms and values which must be analysed in the light of the
properties of the social system in which he lives. It is a crude over-
simplification to conceive of social "motives" as being capable of direct
derivation from a hedonic algebra of self-interest—real or fictitious—
based on a few "universal" human drives, whatever the choice of the

drives may be. To behave appropriately is a powerful social motive. It is in large part responsible both for the attempts to preserve or to modify one's conduct to fit a situation, and to change, reform or revolutionize a situation or systems of situations which interfere with the possibility (or the freedom) to act appropriately. This becomes clear if the motive to act according to certain internalized rules and the choice of the mode of action are placed in the context of social stability and social change, of social norms and values as they relate to individual calculations of self-interest, and of a social psychology as contrasted with one which is merely inter-individual. I shall briefly discuss each of these issues.

Notions of appropriateness reflect the system of social norms and values. One could define norms as being an individual's expectations (shared with others) of how others expect him to behave and of how others *will* behave in any given situation. But then—if the system of values were not brought into play—social conduct would consist mainly of unwavering and unchanging conformity. Values are the implicit and explicit ideologies of a society—political, social, moral or religious—and of the subgroups within it. I am not concerned here with the problem of how an individual acquires and internalizes his values, but with the fact that he *has* them. No change is possible in a society without serious tensions occurring between *some* of its norms and *some* of its values. Sometimes changes—e.g. technological ones—are accompanied by tensions, sometimes tensions create change; most often the two interact. If tensions exist, one way to resolve them is to redefine values to fit in with the norms, or to change the norms to conform more closely to values. But if enough individuals or groups—moved by common interests, or a common ideology, or a shared *Weltanschauung*—refuse to do the one or the other, the *status quo* is bound to be shaken sooner or later. In changing it, the individuals change themselves, since by removing one source of tensions they create another which stands in a new and different relation to what they are. Thus, to act "appropriately" is not necessarily to act in conformity with what is or has been. It is also to act as a rebel, an innovator, a saint, a revolutionary and—also—to be capable of genocide.

But to leave out of account motives and strategies of self interest would be to oversimplify as much as is done in the "inter-individual" psychology of gain and loss. The notion of "self interest" employed in much of the current research, unless closely analysed, is no more than the kind of self interest about which the researcher knows best because it forms a part of his own background that he assumes he shares with his subjects (as indeed he often does with the legions of undergraduates who gain "credits" by participating in his research); or if his subjects come from a background which is unfamiliar to him he must assume that he knows what their conceptions of self interest are. Of course, without independent evidence we shall never know if he was right or wrong in making this assumption. But how then can he pretend to verify "general" laws of, for example, competition and cooperation?

Even if he happens to be right in his unstated assumptions about his subjects, there are very good reasons why a simple view of "gain" and "loss" can only lead to "trivial" or "irrelevant" research. The system of values determines to a large extent the conception of gain and loss as soon as we leave the mythical pre-Aveyron "psychology of the individual" and treat him with respect due to a member of a species that created its own environment and its own complexities. In turn, the system of norms determines the strategies that are *acceptable* for achieving "gain". One of the important contributions to social psychology of Festinger's (1957) theory of cognitive dissonance lies precisely in the fact that it is capable of throwing additional light on the effects of the betrayal of a value on the genesis of subsequent norms. Otherwise, there is not very much excitement in knowing that subjects who expressed opinions contrary to their own for a reward of one dollar subsequently changed their original opinions more than those who did it for ten dollars (Brehm and Cohen, 1962). This finding, and others like it, are "non-obvious" only if we have finally and sadly reached a conception of the "obvious" which consists of ingredients taken from the simplistic versions of reinforcement theory and from the philosophy of life of a small-time businessman or politician.

The *shared* psychological processes of social change can be the subject of a proper sociopsychological theory only if betrayals of values, or discrepancies between values and emerging norms, or between norms and emerging values, repeated over a period of time, are seen as leading to the creation of new forms of acceptable conduct which themselves lead to a refitting of values or of their order of priority. This is how we can begin perhaps to understand why—at some points of time—many people may be ready to die because "it is for my country, right or wrong", and—at the other extreme—to take decisions to create concentration camps, to drop the first A-bomb, to burn Dresden or the

ghetto of Warsaw, or to kill "suspect" women and children in Viet-
namese villages. It is always possible to "explain" all these actions in
terms of motives of "self interest" or of an expression of the ubiquitous
"aggressive drive". This is just about as illuminating as to say that
mothers care for their children because they have a maternal instinct
and that we know that they have a maternal instinct because they care
for their children. The point is that even if this were true, it gets us not
a whit further—and the same applies to all explanations of social
conduct in terms of "basic" individual motivation.

A basis of "self interest", or of self-preservation, can be taken for
granted both in the actions of head-hunting tribesmen and of the
modern mass incendiaries. The aims of their actions cannot be understood without an analysis of their system of values; the means cannot be
understood without an analysis of the system of norms. The selection
of aims may or may not imply a conflict of values or a conflict between
values and norms; if it does, the processes of justification of actual or of
intended conduct come into play. The interaction between these processes and the system of norms may lead to modifications in the norms
if it takes place within a social system which is capable of an effective
diffusion of social influence and which also is characterized by the
existence of problems that are common to people who define themselves
as a "group" on the basis of social criteria, whatever these criteria
may be.

But this is not all that happens; as mentioned above, an action or
an intended action using means or aiming to achieve ends which imply
a conflict of values or a conflict between norms and values presents the
problem of refitting the system; and this is *one* of the determinants of
the creation of new ideologies which, if accepted at large, set the
process in motion all over again. For example, the diffusion of nationalist ideologies was (and still is) as responsible for the creation of new
nations as the "existence" of nations was responsible for the creation
and diffusion of nationalist ideologies (cf. Tajfel, 1969b and 1970a, for
a more extended discussion). In attempting to resolve its tortured
conflict of values, racism contributed more to the social significance of
"race" than did all of the genetic differences in the shade of skin or in
the shape of a nose. (The *presumed* genetic differences between races are
already part and parcel of the justifying function of the ideology.) Let
me make it quite clear that none of this is written with the intention of
denying or neglecting the intrinsic importance of economic, social and

political factors; but that the intention is to stake out a claim for the kind of contribution to the understanding of a tangled web of problems that can be made by a sociopsychological approach to some of its aspects.

The nature of this contribution becomes even clearer when one considers some of the psychological differences between categories of social conduct that could, for example, all be happily combined within the common denominator of one or another version of "universal" individual drives or "basic" motives and "secondary" derivations from them. Head-hunting or killing all prisoners of war can go on for centuries without causing the slightest tremor of change if it remains an unquestioned part of appropriate conduct in clearly defined categories of social situations. This cannot be so if similar actions take place against a background of potential and socially shared divergences in the interpretation of the appropriateness of modes of conduct: the *acceptance* of the establishment of concentration camps in the neighbourhood of large European cities or of dropping napalm bombs on jungle villages cannot go on for very long without considerable psychological repercussions on those who accept these actions as well as on those who do not. The seeds of sociopsychological change are both in the conflict between them and in the conflict within them. It is because of the socially derived, shared, accepted and conflicting notions of appropriateness of conduct, because of the social definition of the situations to which they apply, and of the social origin of their manner of changing and of relating to one another, that individual or inter-individual psychology cannot be usefully considered as providing the bricks from which an adequate social psychology can be built. The derivations need to be in the opposite direction.

It is true that, if we wish to formulate a theory, we must try to find some similarities of principle underlying the apparent diversity of attitudes and modes of conduct. It is also true that one such set of principles can be found, for example, in the relations that are shown to exist in individual behaviour between frustration, aggression, its inhibition and its displacement; and another in the processes of resolution of cognitive dissonance. My conviction that the latter is bound to be more useful than the former in a sociopsychological analysis is based on the fact that the concepts of commitment and of justification are inherent in it. These concepts are as social as they are psychological: they are capable of being analysed in terms of their social derivation, and they have their own derivations in the sharing, diffusing and communicating of conflicting modes of social conduct, i.e. in theories of attitude change.

This is not the case for theories which cannot transcend the limits of an analysis of individual and presocial motivation and of strategies of behaviour arising from it. To return for a moment to some problems in the psychology of intergroup relations and its analysis in terms of frustration, aggression and its displacements: as everybody's life is full of frustration and everybody's ingroup has its outgroups, we have reached the end of the road apart from a few technical embellishments and a few difficulties encountered here and there in defining our terms. Is it surprising therefore that we come up against complaints of irrelevance and triviality? A collection of individual frustrations is a very different matter from the socially shared *conception of the origin* of common difficulties perceived as common because of a notion of collective identity based on criteria of categorization which are again fully derived from their social context. Shared social conduct is not shared because we are all frustrated; it is shared by those who have all accepted basically the same theory of social causation. It is the analysis of the principles which determine the nature of these "theories", their diffusion and acceptance as well as their translation into social conduct that is one of the fundamental tasks of social psychology. If questions of this nature *are* the proper object of sociopsychological theories, it is difficult to resist the notion that explanations of intergroup conduct such as those provided by the frustration–aggression hypothesis and all other theories of "basic" individual motivation are a little like the grin without the cat that Alice saw.

5   Change and choice

The main argument of this chapter has been that:

a. The triviality of much of the current research in social psychology is in part due to the attempts to account causally for human social behaviour in terms of "general" laws of individual motivation.

b. These attempts are based on the assumption that the non-social laws of individual behaviour are the "genotypic" foundation of social psychology; through various kinds of reductionism they are also reflected in the extrapolations made from the study of a "presocial" individual to the explanation of the psychological dynamics of social phenomena.

c. This has led to the neglect of the interaction between the social context and the social conduct and to the formulation of "laws" in which this interaction plays no part in either the explanation or prediction of social conduct.

d. Many experimental studies in social psychology reflect all these tendencies. They are presumed to serve two functions: (i) to test hypotheses derived from theories or from "approaches"; and (ii) through the nature of their data to represent aspects of social conduct, however "purified", which are relevant to the hypotheses. The experiments are well adapted to the first of these tasks, but, owing to the "individual" nature of the theories and the absence of cultural and social analysis in the design of the experiments and in the interpretation of data, extrapolations to "natural" social conduct are often either not possible, or they are irrelevant or trivial.

Social psychology has certainly not succeeded in creating an intellectual revolution in the sense of deeply affecting our views of human nature as, for example, Freud and Piaget have done for individual psychology. Instead of a revolution, there has been a slight tremor. Amongst all the social sciences, ours is the only one which has managed to apply the techniques of laboratory experimentation to the development and testing of its propositions. This is not unimportant, but techniques, however advanced they may be, must be evaluated with the help of external criteria. Making faster cars for congested roads or devising and showing to millions of people an advertisement which will boost tenfold the sales of one washing powder rather than another are efficient techniques, though they seem to be a sad way of apportioning our resources. Like successful advertisements and faster travel, experimental social psychology has become in its own way an efficient technology—but its purpose often seems obscure. A friend reported to me recently with some pride that in the new jumbo jets used by his national airline there is one specially reserved seating section in which the passengers *do not have to watch a film*. This *reductio ad absurdum* of dubious "progress", this technological return "from shirt-sleeves to shirt-sleeves in three generations" brings to mind some of the experimental achievements of social psychology: we start with a proposition culled from day-to-day intuitions and horse-sense about, for example, the role played by the need for approval in determining conformity in small groups. We then devise complex experimental and statistical techniques to arrange and interpret an appropriate example, and we are able to show in the end that the proposition known to be true was indeed true.

This description obviously does not apply to all experimental research in social psychology; but there is enough to which it does apply to cause concern. It has always been my impression—although a gigantic review of the literature would be required to substantiate it—that the description applies mainly to experiments concerned with the "general" motivational aspects of social behaviour.

To study a phenomenon one must take a certain distance from it. It seems to me that in social psychology this cannot be done if we cannot see beyond motivational generalities about the interchangeable individual. The right perspective in the study of human motivation can only be achieved through an analysis of motivational and emotional phenomena in terms of concepts which are not a simple translation of individual experience. This is why the psychoanalytic and the psychophysiological approaches to the motivational and emotional roots of behaviour were capable of providing the quality of "surprise" not provided by the search for the basis of social conduct in motivational categories which have often consisted of a systematization of individual experience. Though we are able to make these categories more or less explicit to ourselves, we are much less—if at all—aware of their relation to, and determination by, the social context in which we live. They appear as "individual", and as self-generated rather than "social". It is perhaps for this reason that research such as that of Schachter (e.g. 1970) on the social and cognitive determination of emotional states contains more promise for the understanding of social conduct than any number of lists of "basic drives" or any motivational theories reducing social motivation to its presocial roots. Here we are faced with an interesting paradox: the "scientific" nature of social psychology precludes the use of introspection in the drawing of inferences from experimental data; but the theories from which the experiments derive often originate in conceptions based on what appears experientially "true", i.e. on the shared introspections of a generation of researchers. As Piaget (1967) wrote in another context:

... les approximations qui conduisent à l'objet ... comportent ... un processus essentiel de décentration, au sens de la libération d'adhérences subjectives ou de prénotions jugées au départ comme exactes du seul fait qu'elles sont plus simples pour le sujet. Dans le domaine des notions biologiques les adhérences subjectives seront, par exemple, les assimilations inconscientes ou voulues de données organiques à des schèmes tirés de l'introspection et les prénotions pourront être, entre autres, des schèmes atomistiques, si coercitifs dans les débuts de toute investigation avant qu'on en vienne aux idées de totalité organisée.

p. 80

The transcending of individual experience, the epistemological decentration of which Piaget wrote, is particularly difficult in social psychology—as long as social psychology is deemed to be concerned with the strategies used by an individual satisfying his "drives" in the face of social "pressures" and complexities. The "organized wholes" pertaining to biological concepts, to which Piaget refers in the above quotation, have their counterpart in social psychology; but it is even more difficult in social psychology than it is in biology to avoid the "coercion" of assimilating the more complex phenomena into the simpler ones.

The crucial problem of social psychology, which requires thinking in terms of "organized wholes", is that of the relations between Man and social change. This implies two notions discussed earlier in this chapter. The first is that change is *the* fundamental characteristic of the social environment, and, as such, is the most basic problem presented by this environment to the human organism. Social change is not only to be understood in terms of the large-scale transformations of techno-logical, social, political and economic structures which confront most men in most societies today and have done so, perhaps more slowly, in the past. It is also an inescapable ontogenetic phenomenon, in the sense that any change in an individual's life, including growing up and growing older, presents him with new requirements for reacting to the social environment and for acting upon it. The second notion is that the "acting" and "reacting" preclude a simple one-way perspective of response and adaptation to social pressures and circumstances which, as it is often said in social psychological texts, "impinge" upon the individual. By changing himself the individual changes the social environment; by changing it, he changes himself. He must create change, resist it, adapt to it or prepare for it; most often, he will do all these things at the same time in dealing with the diversity of tasks that he faces in his social environment.

There are two ways of approaching the study of this problem of interaction between social change and social conduct. One is to attempt to reduce the explanation of it to the laws of functioning of only one of the terms of the equation: and this is the case with the three kinds of reductionism, the biological, the psychological and the sociological, discussed earlier in this chapter. The other is to take certain things for granted and to start directly at the "higher" level. Thus, no one would deny that Man's social behaviour is determined by the genetic and physiological properties of the human organism, by its general learning, perceptual, and motivational characteristics, and by the input from the social conditions in which he lives. It is, however, equally undeniable that, in almost any circumstances, Man retains, because of his cognitive abilities, the capacity to *choose* between various modes of possible conduct—including choices which consist of changing his environment. Though these choices are, in the last analysis, "determined" by the constraining laws of the functioning either of the organism or of its environment, they are not predictable from them. The "need to affiliate" can result in continuous wars or in universal peace; the need to preserve one's self esteem can result in anything under the sun, including self-immolation and the creation of a gigantic business empire; the existence of sexual or aggressive cravings predicts very little about the characteristics of socially transmitted *changes* in the patterns of sexual or aggressive behaviour; economic deprivation predicts very little about reactions to it unless something is known of the range of choices that people perceive as being open to them; Piaget's early analysis of the moral development in the child (1927) owes nothing to laws of instrumental learning or of secondary reinforcement—but it does rely heavily on the interaction between the cognitive processes of progressive decentration, the nature of interpersonal exchange in the social environment, the peer group that enables these processes to function, and the changing nature of the same peer group set in motion in turn by cognitive decentration.

There is an interesting and perhaps unexpected parallel between the view of these interactions represented in some of the ideas of Piaget and of Festinger. In his *Biologie et Connaissance* (1967), Piaget summed up his conception of the assimilation of new stimuli to previously existing sensory-motor schemata of operations in a brief biblical paraphrase: *Au commencement était la réponse* (p. 17). The meaning of this theological excursion is that a stimulus becomes accessible to experience, acquires significance and co-determines a response only as it is assimilated into orderly systems (however primitive they may be) of previous actions which mediate between the organism and the environment, progressively determine the knowledge of the environment and also the capacity to transcend its here-and-now properties through the use of "reversible" cognitive operations. Festinger (with others) assumed the existence of a drive towards cognitive consistency. But the principal difference between his views and those of other consistency theorists is quite crucial; as for Piaget, for him also *la réponse était au commencement*. One of his main preoccupations is the analysis of the feedback of the response on the previously existing cognitive structures. The nature of this feedback is determined by the consonant or dissonant relations between the meaning of the response and the pre-existing structures; this relationship of meanings determines in turn the subsequent modification of structures—and thus it affects the nature of further responses. The central theme of both theoretical conceptions is the nature of the interaction between the requirements set by the environment, the pre-existing organized structures within the organism, and the effects of the resulting *changes* in both on further behaviour.

The social context of this formation and modification of structures gives them a unique quality, in the sense that they involve *sharing* on a cognitive level. To return for a moment to Piaget's (1967) ideas about decentration:

> ... du point de vue psychogénétique ces régulations interindividuelles ou sociales (et non héréditaires) constituent un fait nouveau par rapport à la pensée individuelle qui sans elles est exposée à toutes les déformations égocentriques et *une condition nécessaire de la formation d'un sujet épistémique décentré* [italics mine].
>
> p. 413

It is in this sense that sharing on a cognitive level, the capacity to perceive the world and act upon it in a manner which is dependent on one's social history and on the presence of others, defined in "decentred" social terms, is the *sine qua non* of human social life. It is here that the two major empirical discontinuities occur with other forms of conduct: human non-social behaviour and non-human social behaviour. Binocular vision or secondary reinforcement depend upon the physiological capacities of the organism and the feedback of its responses from the physical environment; the principles (though even here often not the content) of functioning are theoretically independent of social interaction. Non-human social behaviour is, of course, largely determined by the ecology of a species, including its social ecology—the presence of other members; but the new cognitive phenomena in Man related to the capacity of taking the place of the other and of defining oneself in terms of social interaction add up to a second major empirical discontinuity.

The term "sharing" has been adopted here as a shorthand description of these discontinuities of human social from human non-social and social non-human. It is this issue of discontinuities that is perhaps the crux of the disagreement between those who feel that the explanation of social conduct is reducible to non-social laws (primarily of learning and motivation) and those who feel that such reductions are not heuristic. In section 3 I described the reductionist "model" of human social behaviour in terms of gain–loss matrices in which other people are considered no more than a category of "stimuli" which happen to be "social", but which are otherwise "reacted to" according to the same laws as those which govern behaviour relating to other environmental events. I then referred to my description as being perhaps "not too far off the mark" but presenting nevertheless a "crude and oversimplified image" of such a reductionist model (p. 92). But perhaps one should drop these polite reservations and courageously join Arthur Koestler's "society for the flogging of dead horses". Here is an image emanating directly from one of the original sources:

> The propositions of behavioural psychology are believed to hold good of all men, and they are stated in terms of the behaviour of a single man: "If a man takes an action that is followed by a reward . . . etc." The propositions are particularly concerned with the effects of reward on behaviour. There is nothing whatever in the propositions to suggest that the effect of reward is different when it comes from another man than from, for instance, the physical environment. But when two or more men are interacting, when the actions of each reward (or punish) the actions of the other, phenomena of course appear that are different from those that appear when an isolated person is being rewarded by the physical environment. New phenomena appear, which may be called social, but no new general propositions are required to explain them—only the new given conditions that two or more men are interacting.
>
> Homans, 1970, pp. 323–324

The "sharing" to which I previously referred can be defined in terms of an individual's expectations about, and evaluations of, other people's behaviour. These are the individual counterparts of the systems of norms and values which is a notion used at a different level of analysis in sociology and in social anthropology. It is important—though obvious—to state that there could be no social groups and no social psychology without a modicum of *fulfilled* expectations about other people's behaviour and about other people's expectations concerning one's own behaviour; and without a modicum of *common* evaluations. I doubt that Homans—or anyone else—could disagree with this statement.

We thus have two undeniable statements about social behaviour, one concerning the effects of rewards and the other the existence of shared expectations and evaluations. Combining them we have the raw materials for a *Walden III* which might turn out to be even more ghastly to live in than *Walden II* must have been. Expectations and evaluations are, of course, learned. And we know from Homans' "Propositions of Behavioural Psychology" that actions leading to reward are those that are learned and that this process "explains" social behaviour. The question is: What kind of social expectations and evaluations would we learn? How would we expect other people to behave and how would we evaluate their behaviour?

The answers are fairly simple: we must *always* expect other people to behave so as to maximize their "rewards" and minimize their "punishments"; and we must always assume that other people will expect us to behave in this way. On the principle of reward, no other expectations can be learned and retained, at least not in the society at large, though there may be some "queer" and "maladjusted" exceptions. Evaluations present a slightly more complex problem, but it seems that they can be reduced to two kinds: evaluations of efficiency, and evaluations of usefulness. The first kind is in terms of the fit of another person's behaviour with *his* gains and losses: we can say that he has behaved stupidly or efficiently according to our judgement of whether his strategy was likely or not to lead to his obtaining the rewards which, as we know, are the prime movers of all his actions. The second kind is in terms of the usefulness of his behaviour to us: is it likely to bring us rewards or punishments?

Thus, in *Walden III* we have finally reached the transparent society: all expectations are, in principle, fulfilled and all evaluations have a common principle. If something goes wrong, if an expectation remains unfulfilled or an evaluation is not unquestioned, there still is a simple answer: a person has behaved in an unexpected way or he has not shared our simple and wholesome evaluation of his, ours or someone else's behaviour in terms of its relation to expected rewards (or to past rewards) because we made an incorrect assumption about his system of rewards.

As soon as this happens, the explanations of social conduct provided by the system of "behavioural propositions" as propounded by Homans turn out to be either tautological or false. Starting from them we can neither understand nor predict the behaviour of someone who has not fulfilled our expectations or shared our evaluations based on our common experience of the universal reward–punishment matrix; what is more, it is unlikely that it will be possible for us to understand or predict those aspects of our own behaviour which have suddenly, for reasons not directly accessible to our experience, taken a new turn leading to unexpected "rewards" or "punishments". We can, of course, explain all this *post hoc*: the rewards and punishments were there all the time and we could have understood if only we had known what they were. Why did William the Conqueror invade England? Homans provides a psycho-historical analysis: "William had a long record of success in his military enterprises in the past, and accordingly, by the success proposition of behavioural psychology, the probability that he would undertake military action again was apt to be high." (p. 322.) Why the French or the Russian revolutions or the Children's Crusade? Why are there powerful mass movements sometimes aiming to induce social change and sometimes to preserve the existing state of things? "When, as a matter of common knowledge, we can assume the values to be shared by many men, the rational proposition does very well in explanation. When they are somehow *queer* [italics mine] values, the rational theory is simply at a loss. But behavioural psychology, provided it has enough knowledge of a person's past experience, can sometimes account for the way values are acquired. New values, even queer ones, are acquired by being paired with older and more primordial values . . ." (Homans, 1970, p. 322.)

Homans' explanatory system of "behavioural propositions" is undoubtedly an extreme and therefore untypical example of psychological reductionism. His own aim in the paper from which the above quotations were taken is to present it as the substratum of sociological theory. One must assume that there is strong reason for its applying, in Homans' view, to theory in social psychology. It presents therefore a "pure case" and as such provides a justification for discussing it at some length here.

Homans' aim—and the aim of other similar systems—is to provide a scientific explanation of social conduct. But it soon becomes obvious that the activities of explanation and prediction—which should be inseparable according to Homans' own views—cannot but diverge when an attempt is made to apply empirical tests. Within the system, explanation is always possible *post hoc*; but the scope of prediction is strictly limited to two categories of events. There are only two bases for prediction from the "propositions". The first is that, given the occurrence of certain situations ("If in the past the occurrence of a particular stimulus situation has been the occasion on which a person's action was rewarded, the recurrence of stimuli in the present makes it more probable that the man will repeat the action", p. 322), social behaviour will be approximately the same as it has been in the past. The second basis for prediction is the assumption that other people share our system of values and will behave in the future as we know we would. Therefore, either we can predict social behaviour in conditions of stability and there is no way of predicting *any change*; or, if we do not have a sufficient knowledge of the past and present situations in which another person finds himself, we must extrapolate from our own experience in order to predict. The latter alternative is, of course, a cardinal methodological sin in the kind of "behavioural psychology" that Homans represents. The former enables us to make predictions of future behaviour in a mythical unchanging society. There is a third alternative; we can arrange simple experimental situations which leave no room for doubt about the nature of rewards and punishments: a hungry rat will depress the lever that previously produced a pellet of food, and it will avoid the electrified grid on which it was previously shocked. Thus, cardinal propositions have been "tested" in a manner which has no conceivable relevance to the predictions of social conduct or to any explanation of it which would be less than perfectly circular.

Behind the stark predictable stability of *Walden III* lurk other similar constructions. For a *Walden IV* we might take it as our cardinal proposition that, if we only knew enough details, social conduct could be explicable and predictable from, for example, the need to maintain body temperature; or to satisfy the unquenchable human passion for possessing a territory; or to give vent to periodic explosions of accumulated aggressive tensions; or to any combination of these and a few other "basic drives" thrown in for good measure. Any one of these combinations turns out on closer inspection to follow the pattern of Homans' "cardinal propositions": circularity of explanation, or extrapolation and projection (often implicit) of the theorist's cultural or personal experience as a vantage point from which his *Weltanschauung* parades as an abstract model of social man.

I have no grand theory to offer to replace these generalities, and I am nearly convinced that a grand "theory of social behaviour" is not possible. But there can be more modest insights into aspects of functioning of some important categories of social interaction, such as competition, cooperation, attitude formation and attitude change, social influence, social communication, social identity, perception of social causality, etc. The problems of intergroup relations provided an opportunity to discuss in section 4 some requirements for a possible theory of the socio-psychological aspects of one important social phenomenon. More generally, social interaction as we know it is mediated and made possible through expectations, fulfilled and unfulfilled, and evaluations, consensual and conflicting. By definition, every individual is capable of predicting the social conduct of others when his expectations are fulfilled and his evaluations unquestioned. Whatever social unit we may be concerned with, this system of shared and socially confirmed notions is the basis from which behaviour can be described and predicted. But this is an ideal baseline which is not reflected in any concrete social reality. As soon as anything changes in the environment, whether it is the individual himself, or his small private social world, or the social world at large, or the characteristics of the physical environment, some expectations are bound to go wrong and some common evaluations are bound to be shaken. The system of assumptions must be changed, or the environment must be changed to preserve the system. New causal inferences must be made, and in the face of conflicting expectations and evaluations, new choices confront the individual. The processes which underlie these choices, and thus constitute the psychological aspects of social change at all levels are the proper subject matter of social psychology. It is one of the principal contentions of this chapter that these new choices can best be explained and predicted from an analysis of conditions under which conflicts between and within the systems of expectations and evaluations are resolved in one direction or another and may at the same time give rise to the creation of new systems. Thus, for example, the progress of an experiment on competitive behaviour in a mixed motive situation may test a hypothesis and provide at the same time raw data for the generation of new hypotheses—provided that the interpretations are set in the context of social notions which determine the choices that the subjects will make. The same can be said of the other categories of social interaction mentioned previously. The usual theoretical alternatives—

general "presocial" laws or premature short-cuts to explanations in terms of various kinds of personality typologies—explain very little and predict less. Whatever else they do, they certainly do not amount to a psychological theory of social conduct.

Thus, social psychology could be redefined as the discipline concerned with interactions between social change and choice. What are the choices that are perceived by an individual as being available to him? What are the aspects of social change which contribute to an individual's perception that the universe which holds the alternatives open to him is a shrinking or an expanding one? What is the nature of the interaction of the social, the cognitive and the motivational processes which contribute to the formulation of his theories of social causation? What are the conditions under which these theories are or are not implemented in his social conduct—as a father, or husband, or student, or housewife, or employee, or a member of the electorate? And, finally, what are the determinants of the search for a wider or a narrower scope of choices, and the effects of this search on social conduct? Zimbardo (1969) has recently been working on this problem and this is how he saw one of its aspects:

> In place of true choice, which allows the possibility of a denigrating self-evaluation, one can give the appearance of choosing by putting himself in situations which force the choice or by arranging for others to act so he can merely react. It is only when the individual sees no exit, perceives that his freedom to choose is minimal, conceives of himself as helpless, victimized and passive, that he can be free in the negative sense of not being responsible. However, in this process of choosing not to choose, Man relinquishes a major part of his human integrity.
>
> p. 13

As I wrote in section 4, the issues of commitment and justification—which form the background of Zimbardo's experiments on the cognitive control of motivation—are amongst those that offer at present a promise of the introduction of social context into social psychological theories and experiments. This is not the case in Zimbardo's own studies and, in view of the general climate of opinion, it is hardly surprising that it should be so. As Newcomb (1968) wrote in his Introduction to the recent enormous compendium on cognitive consistency:

> Of the 54 contributors to this volume, not less than two-thirds have major interests in one or more aspects of social psychology . . . It is not inevitable that this should be so: after all, cognitive structures and the dynamics of cognitive organization are not in any *a priori* sense distinctively concerned with social phenomena.
>
> p. xvii

But perhaps social psychologists should be. I do not wish—and if I did, would not be able—to conclude this paper with a blinding flash of a "solution"; but it seems to me that if as much ingenuity went in the future into creating "simulation" and "modelling" experiments that would include genuine social "variables" of the kind discussed in this paper as has in the past gone into excluding them in order to create the mythical "controlled" vacuum, our problems would reach a new and more fertile level of difficulties.

This is where our real challenge lies. If it is not met, it is fully possible that—to paraphrase from another context—our discipline will have passed from infancy to old age (and death) without ever having reached maturity.

References

Alexander, L. N., Zucker, L. G. and Brody, C. L. (1970). Experimental expectations and autokinetic experiences: consistency theories and judgmental convergence. *Sociometry*, **28**, 108–122.

Argyle, M. (1970). "Social Interaction". Methuen, London.

Banton, M. (1967). "Race Relations". Tavistock Publications, London.

Berkowitz, L. (1962). "Aggression: A Social Psychological Analysis". McGraw-Hill, New York.

Blalock, H. M. (1967). "Toward a Theory of Minority-group Relations". John Wiley, New York.

Brehm, J. W. and Cohen, A. R. (1962). "Explorations in Cognitive Dissonance". John Wiley, New York.

Deutsch, M. and Krauss, R. M. (1965). "Theories in Social Psychology". Basic Books, New York.

Eiser, J. R. (1971a). Enhancement of contrast in the absolute judgment of attitude statements. *Journal of Personality and Social Psychology*, **17**, 1–10.

Eiser, J. R. (1971b). Categorization, cognitive consistency and the concept of dimensional salience. *European Journal of Social Psychology*, **1**, 435–454.

Faucheux, C. (1970). Cross-cultural research in social psychology. Unpublished. Social Science Research Council.

Festinger, L. (1957). "A Theory of Cognitive Dissonance". Row, Peterson, Evanson, Illinois.

Frijda, N. and Jahoda, G. (1966). On the scope and methods of cross-cultural research. *International Journal of Psychology*, **1**, 110–127.

Gerard, H. B. and Miller, N. (1967). Group dynamics. *Annual Review of Psychology*, Vol. 18.

Gombrich, E. H. (1960). "Art and Illusion". Phaidon, London.

Hayek, F. A. (1969). The primacy of the abstract. *In* "Beyond Reductionism: New Perspectives in the Life Sciences" (Eds. A. Koestler and J. R. Smythies). Hutchinson, London.

Homans, G. C. (1961). "Social Behaviour: Its Elementary Forms". Harcourt, Brace & World, New York.

Homans, G. C. (1970). The relevance of psychology to the explanation of social phenomena. *In* "Explanation in the Behavioral Sciences" (Eds. R. Borger and F. Cioffi). Cambridge University Press, London.

Jones, E. J. and Gerard, H. B. (1967). "Foundations of Social Psychology". John Wiley, New York.

Katz, I. (1968). Factors influencing Negro performance in the desegregated school. *In* "Social Class, Race and Psychological Development" (Eds M. Deutsch, I. Katz and A. R. Jensen). Holt, Rinehart & Winston, New York.

Lawrence, D. H. and Festinger, L. (1962). "Deterrents and Reinforcements: The Psychology of Insufficient Reward". Stanford University Press, Stanford.

LeVine, R. A. (1965). Socialization, social structure and intersocietal images. *In* "International Behaviour: A Social Psychological Analysis." (Ed. H. Kelman). Holt, Rinehart & Winston, New York.

McGuire, W. J. (1967). Some impending reorientations in social psychology. *Journal of Experimental Social Psychology*, **3**, 124–139.

Merton, R. K. (1957). "Social Theory and Social Structure". Free Press, Glencoe, Illinois.

Newcomb, T. M. (1968). Introduction. *In* "Theories of Cognitive Consistency" (Eds R. P. Abelson, E. Aronson, W. J. McGuire, T. M. Newcomb, M. J. Rosenberg and P. H. Tannenbaum). Rand McNally, Chicago.

Peters, R. S. (1960). "The Concept of Motivation" (2nd ed.). Routledge & Kegan Paul, London.

Piaget, J. (1927). "Le Jugement Moral de L'Enfant". Alcan, Paris.

Piaget, J. (1967). "Biologie et Connaissance". Gallimard, Paris.

Piaget, J. and Inhelder, B. (1969). The gaps in empiricism. *In* "Beyond Reductionism: New Perspectives in the Life Sciences" (Eds A. Koestler and J. R. Smythies). Hutchinson, London.

Plon, M. (1972). Sur quelques aspects de la rencontre entre la psychologie sociale et la théorie des jeux. *La Pensée*, **161**, 2–30.

Popper, K. (1961). "The Poverty of Historicism". Routledge & Kegan Paul, London.

Rapoport, A. (1970). Conflict resolution in the light of game theory and beyond. *In* "The Structure of Conflict" (Ed. P. Swingle). Academic Press, New York and London.

Ring, K. (1967). Experimental social psychology: some sober questions about some frivolous values. *Journal of Experimental Social Psychology*, **3**, 113–123.

Rosenthal, R. (1966). "Experimenter Effect in Behavioural Research". Appleton-Century-Crofts, New York.

Rosenthal, R. and Jacobsen, L. (1968). "Pygmalion in the Classroom". Holt, Rinehart & Winston, New York.

Schachter, S. (1970). The assumption of identity and peripheralist-centralist controversies in motion and emotion. *In* "Feelings and Emotions" (Ed. M. Arnold). Academic Press, New York and London.

Segall, M. H., Campbell, D. T. and Herskovits, M. J. (1966). "The Influence of Culture on Visual Perception". Bobbs-Merrill, Indianapolis.

Sherif, M. (1935). A study of some social factors in perception. *Archives of Psychology*, July, 187.

Sherif, M. and Hovland, C. I. (1961). "Social Judgment". Yale University Press, New Haven.

Tajfel, H. (1959). Quantitative judgment in social perception. *British Journal of Psychology*, **50**, 16–29.

Tajfel, H. (1969a). Cognitive aspects of prejudice. *Journal of Biosocial Sciences*, **1**, Suppl. Mon. No. 1; also *in Journal of Social Issues*, **25** (4), 79–97.

Tajfel, H. (1969b). The formation of national attitudes: a social psychological perspective. *In* "Interdisciplinary Relationships in the Social Sciences" (Eds M. Sherif and C. W. Sherif). Aldine, Chicago.

Tajfel, H. (1969c). Social and cultural factors in perception. *In* "The Handbook of Social Psychology" (Eds G. Lindzey and E. Aronson), Vol. 3. Addison-Wesley, Reading, Mass.

Tajfel, H. (1970a). Aspects of national and ethnic loyalty. *Social Science Information*, **IX** (3), 119–144.

Tajfel, H. (1970b). Experiments in intergroup discrimination. *Scientific American*, **223** (5), 96–102.

Tajfel, H., Flament, C., Billig, M. G. and Bundy, R. P. (1971). Social categorization and intergroup behaviour. *European Journal of Social Psychology*, **1**, 149–178.

Tajfel, H. and Wilkes, A. L. (1963). Classification and quantitative judgment. *British Journal of Psychology*, **54**, 101–114.

Tajfel, H. and Wilkes, A. L. (1964). Salience of attributes and commitment to extreme judgements in the perception of people. *British Journal of Social and Clinical Psychology*, **2**, 40–49.

Upshaw, H. S. (1965). The effect of variable perspectives of judgments of opinion statements for Thurstone scales: equal-appearing intervals. *Journal of Personality and Social Psychology*, **2**, 60–69.

Zimbardo, P. G. (1969). "The Cognitive Control of Motivation". Scott & Foresman, Glenview, Illinois.

PART 2

Presuppositions and Values

4

Stipulations and Construction in the Social Sciences

Joachim Israel

1 The nature of stipulative statements in social psychological and socio-logical theory

In all common-sense notions of a psychological or sociological kind certain assumptions about the nature of Man and the nature of society are implicit. Managers of factories have certain views about what motivates workers to work; school teachers have definite ideas about the capacities of their pupils; architects "know" the needs of people living in urban areas. Politicians tell us not only about Man's natural capacities and motivations ("without competition, no progress" or "if you increase taxes too much, you counteract the willingness to work") but also about the nature of society and of functional prerequisites for a society to survive. These common-sense notions not only reflect private biases; they also reflect stipulative assumptions on a pre-scientific level concerning Man and society which in fact may form the basis for social organization. Take one example: the use of punching-clocks at factory entrances reflects assumptions about the willingness of workers to go to the factory, i.e. about their basic motivation for working. These assumptions often function as self-fulfilling prophecies thus creating behaviour in accordance with what is assumed. This confers upon them not only the status of empirical statements but of *verified* empirical statements.

The situation which we find at a pre-scientific common-sense level does not differ too much from the situation we find when we move into the realm of social science. One example is the area in which "scientific theories" are applied for the management of people. Psychiatry and psychiatric treatment provide obvious examples. Thus the treatment of psychoses in closed mental hospitals may be based on certain diagnoses, which are derived from psychiatric theories. These diagnoses then may lead to a certain type of treatment, which in turn is to a large degree responsible for the behaviour predicted by the previous diagnosis. Scheff (1966) put forward an hypothesis that inmates in mental institutions are rewarded if they play the role assigned to them by psychiatrists and hospital staff and punished if they attempt to return to conventional roles. Thus, the patient's self-concept is brought into agreement with the diagnosis.

It seems that theories which have a direct application, such as those in psychiatry or criminology, operate with postulates which are similar to the common-sense notions of a psychological and sociological kind. The same, however, holds true for social science theories which can be located on a higher level of abstraction.

At least *three types of stipulative statements* can be distinguished in these theories. They are: assumptions concerning (1) *the nature of Man, including the nature of knowledge which Man has*, (2) *the nature of society*, and (3) *the nature of the relationship between Man and society*.

It is not some form of traditional essentialism that is being referred to here. This doctrine asserts that scientific theories should explain the "essence" or the "essential nature" of things and through this arrive at "ultimate explanations".

The statements concerning the nature of the phenomena to which I refer do not have the status of final explanations but of initial conditions. They are of a stipulative kind. They can be expressed in alternative ways. They are chosen (not necessarily consciously) and empirical theories are derived from them.

My main thesis is that these stipulative statements have regulative functions. They determine the type of empirical theories which are developed and these theories affect the research strategy used. Thus, the S–R model developed by behaviourism gives rise to theories which in turn are tested by experimental methods limited by these theories. Behaviouristic learning theories using rats and pigeons in experimental situations cannot be applied to the study of cognitive learning. However, the concept of "cognitive learning" may already have been excluded by the postulative assumptions made about phenomena with which theories deal and which precede the development of empirical theories.[1]

An attempt will be made to present a preliminary explication of the stipulative statements to be found in psychological and sociological theories. The content of these statements concerns the nature of Man, the nature of knowledge, the nature of society and finally the nature of the relationship between Man and society. These statements may often be interrelated in a theoretical system. In addition, such statements enter into empirical theories and are usually not clearly differentiated from descriptive statements. In fact, they are usually formulated as descriptive statements, thus veiling their true nature which is that of normative statements. These statements have a regulative function. They determine the content of empirical theories and, together with formal methodological rules, influence the procedures of scientific research, which themselves affect the theory. They can be relatively "freely" chosen among alternative sets of stipulative systems. Different sets of stipulative systems will give rise to different empirical theories. The choice of stipulative systems is in turn influenced by value-statements. The relationship between stipulative statements and/or systems and value-statements will be elaborated upon later.

To summarize: The statements discussed above are normative since the assumptions to be made concerning the nature of Man and society are stipulated. They are also normative in the sense that they can be replaced by alternative stipulations.

An example is provided by the stipulative assumptions concerning Man which are often used in economics. It is clear that "economic Man" is not a descriptive but a normative concept. Man is stipulated to be rational in the sense that his economic behaviour is guided by a striving

---

[1] When I mention "preceding" stipulative assumptions, I do not refer to temporary sequences. It may be that these postulative assumptions are formulated, if at all explicitly formulated, after empirical observations are carried out in order to give empirical theories a firm basis to stand upon. But once selected, they have regulative functions.

for maximization of his utility, i.e. he chooses among available modes of behaviour that which provides highest utility. Rational choice pre-supposes also that he has knowledge of all relevant alternative modes of behaviour, as well as their specific utility value. In addition, a rational choice presupposes that Man has absolute knowledge of the total market, i.e. complete knowledge of all goods and prices. Some-times it is also required that he should know the strategies available to other people with whom he interacts since the utility of his own behaviour may be dependent on others' behaviour. (For a detailed analysis of Man's "rational" behaviour see chapter 8 by Wiberg.)

2 Stipulations concerning Man's nature

2.1 PROBLEMS OF EPISTEMOLOGY

Traditionally two problems have been considered to be central in epis-temology. One concerns the conditions under which knowledge occurs. The second concerns the relationship between the perceiving and knowing subject and the object of knowledge. The two problems are not independent of each other; but in some cases the emphasis is placed on the first problem and in others on the second. "Empiricism" can be said to deal with *conditions* of knowledge, stressing the necessity of knowledge to be based upon experience. Those adhering to some form of "empiricism" do not necessarily take a stand on the second problem and on the question which may be derived from it: What is the nature of reality? Those epistemological orientations which assert the existence of an objective world external to the perceiving subject and prior to his experience are usually referred to as "materialism" or "realism". "Em-piricism" which does not take a stand on the question concerning the existence of an external world and on that concerning its nature becomes "positivism", which "refers to the phenomenalist tendency within the empiricist tradition" (Cohen, 1963, p. 105). "Phenomenalism" reduces experience to the phenomena of our senses, making sense data the central category of epistemology. "Reality" is only what can be experienced directly by our senses. "The truth cannot be sought externally to our experiences", wrote Philip Frank (quoted after Hofman, 1961). One central notion of epistemology in this case is pragmatic subjectivism. In opposition to what is judged as metaphysics, namely the idea that knowledge is the agreement between a judgement and that part of reality about which it states something, the truth of a judgement in pragmatic subjectivism is ascertained by its usefulness (Hofman, op. cit., p. 11).

The consequences of the subjectivistic attitude is not only phenomenalism in which "appearance and reality are identified" (Cohen, op. cit., p. 104). Another consequence is atomism. "The phenomena with which science deals were assumed to be isolated sensations, or single observations. The relations among the given phenomena were subjective matters of efficient but arbitrary ordering of data; hypothetical entities and relations were viewed as fictions or as shorthand; and the monadic character of atomic sensations was assumed *a priori* but made empirically plausible by a programme of reductive definition of scientific concepts in terms of individual observation reports." (Cohen, op. cit., pp. 110–111.) A system, being a totality, becomes a myth and therefore the explanation of the behaviour of elements forming the system can only be discussed from the point of view of the element. The opposite is true in a methodological attitude exemplified by general systems theory: the behaviour of the elements is explained in terms of the functioning of the total system.

The epistemological position I wish to stress becomes clearer when drawn against the background of positivism. Whereas positivism concentrates on sense data and therefore on perception, and in addition places emphasis on the problematic character of the subject, the epistemological position I wish to take stresses the reciprocal *relationship* between the knowing subject and the object of his knowledge. This implies that the subject is not only treated as a passive perceiving being but as an active, constructive, "sensuous conscious agent" (Cohen, op. cit., p. 107). Such a position is not only of importance for the scientific attitude and research methodology which derives from it. It has also a direct bearing upon the notion of the role of science. Whereas positivism claims to be neutral in relation to the existing social conditions—while its neutrality helps to maintain the existing conditions and thus has a clear conservative effect—the orientation taken here facilitates the attempt to assign to social science the role of carrying out a "rational critique of any given state of Man or society" (Cohen, op. cit., p. 106).

The "constructivist" approach in epistemology can be illustrated by referring to Marx's basic epistemological attitude. It is clearly expressed in the first of the eleven "Theses about Feuerbach" (Marx, 1964). There he maintains: "The chief defect of all previous materialism (including that of Feuerbach) is that things (*Gegenstand*), reality, the sensible world, are conceived only in the form of *objects* (*Objekt*) of observation, but not as *human sense activity*, not as *practical activity*, not subjectively." (p. 67.) Marx added that the idea of the cognitively active human subject was developed instead by philosophical idealism, which, however, identified reality with thought and products of cognitive processes.

What Marx asserts here is that the process of acquiring knowledge is an active, constructive one and that it is so in two ways. The sensing, perceiving and cognizing subject creates the objects of reality in two ways: (1) by confering meaning upon the object in the process of cognition, which on a higher level of abstract-symbolic actions means the development of theories; (2) by his own work as it is a part of the basic process of production. In this process he creates objects by transforming nature, and furthermore he creates the social conditions within which the basic process of production occurs. These processes Marx termed "*Praxis*". There exists a dialectic relationship between the cognitive constructive process and the practical process. The cognitive, constructive process is the basis for *Praxis* and *Praxis* in turn functions as a means of verification for the cognitive, theoretical process.

However, the picture is not yet complete. So far we have only pictured the role of the active, creative subject in the process of creating knowledge. The object, however, is not only created; it affects in turn the human senses; and it is perceived and cognitively worked upon. In addition, the objects of human work form the social environment of which Man becomes a product. Thus the relationship between the knowing subject and the object of his sense experience is one of reciprocal influence. (For a discussion of the Marxian theory of knowledge see Jordan, 1967, and Marković, 1967.)

The processes discussed can be pictured in the following simple diagram.

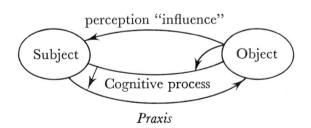

Praxis

Thus we find in Marx's model as interpreted here at least two dialectical processes functioning in the manner of feed-back mechanisms.[1] One is the basic process of acquiring knowledge, containing the reciprocal relationship of influence between subject and object. The other is the dialectical relation between the formulation of theories and practical action; this interdependent relationship is inseparable from the total process of knowledge.

I shall now turn to current psychology and compare two models of epistemology, one "dialectical" and the other in the tradition of empirical realism.

2.2 PIAGET AND SKINNER—TWO PSYCHOLOGISTS REPRESENTING OPPOSING VIEWS

To a majority of psychologists, problems of epistemology are located outside the domain of their scientific interest and enquiry. One of the most outstanding exceptions is Jean Piaget, who has dealt with these problems in his own research and who has advised psychologists that "they should certainly consider epistemological questions as legitimate problems of their interests" (Furth, 1969, p. vii).

The position taken by Jean Piaget comes near to the dialectical conception which characterized the process of knowledge in Marx's previously mentioned epistemological position.[2] Piaget's theory of knowledge can be summarized in the following way: (1) He considers epistemological problems from a genetic point of view, splitting the question "What is knowledge?" into two questions, namely, "How does knowledge develop?" and "What is the role of the subject in the process of the development of knowledge?" (2) Answering the second question, he considers knowledge as the relation between the subject and the object: "A thing in the world is not an object of knowledge until the knowing organism interacts with and constitutes it as an object." (Furth, op. cit., p. 19.)

Thus in these terms "knowledge" becomes an activity, a process; in this process the subject partly constructs the object. To understand fully the consequences of this position it will be useful to elaborate

---

[1] The model of language as developed by Rommetveit (see chapter 5) has similar dialectical features.

[2] Lucien Goldman (1959) is the first Marxist theoretician who, to my knowledge, pointed out the similarities in Piaget's and Marx's approaches.

briefly upon Piaget's concept of knowledge, and the theory of the development of knowledge.

Piaget assumes that knowledge develops in stages which follow a constant order of succession (Inhelder, 1962). Each stage is characterized by the attainment of a certain structure following a period of development. A structure is an organization of elements within the biological organism which responds to the external environment; and the development of a structure is a consequence of an inner organizing activity and of factors extrinsic to the organism: "A reaction of an organism is therefore not merely a response to an outside stimulation, but is always and at all levels also the response of the underlying structure within the organism." (Furth, op. cit., p. 13.) Hence, in order to respond to outside stimulation, the organism must have a certain, even if only primitive, structure, which in turn is influenced by extrinsic factors. This dialectical principle is underpinned by the concepts of "assimilation" and "accommodation". Knowledge, being an exchange between an organism and its environment, leads to the incorporation of external stimuli into an existing structure; this process of integrating external stimuli with an existing structure is called "assimilation". Accommodation is an outgoing process directed towards objects or some state of the surrounding world; in this outgoing process an existing structure is applied to a new situation. Through the process of assimilation the new elements are incorporated into the structure, differentiating it and developing it.

The diagrammatic representation used in depicting the Marxian epistemological paradigm could be applied to this theory giving psychological content to the arrow from the object to the subject and to one of the arrows from the subject to the object. The relation represented by the arrow going from the object to the subject indicates "assimilation", whereas "accommodation" can be represented by the upper arrow from the subject to the object. To summarize: knowledge is a *relation* of interchange between the structure of a biological organism and its surrounding environment. Through this relation the environment and "what it means to the subject" is shaped and reshaped and the environment affects, differentiates and develops the existing structure within the organism.

Now let us consider a completely different ontological view concerning knowledge, by comparing the viewpoint developed by Piaget with the one developed by Skinner. According to Skinner, "science insists that action is initiated by forces impinging upon the individual" (1955, p. 53). This statement *stipulates* an epistemological position implying the view that the subject is a passive recipient of (mainly external) stimuli. Thus, according to Skinner, stimuli impinging upon the subject are independent variables whereas the actions of the subject are viewed as dependent variables. The relationship between the independent and the dependent variables can be formulated in terms of causal laws; this excludes Piaget's theory in which the relationship between subject and object is one of reciprocal interchange. Piaget's viewpoint does not only reject the concept of the passive subject, but also substitutes one-sided causal relations by feed-back processes, cumulative interchange, etc. This makes the question of what is an independent and what is a dependent variable appear to be of the same quality as the one concerning the hen and the egg.

Let us for a moment return to Skinner's statement quoted above. As it is formulated in descriptive terms, it is presented as a theoretical statement. Also, a non-critical reader may take it as a true statement, i.e. one which has been proved. I suggest that it is a stipulation and in this I agree with Copeland (1964): "The view that the individual is always controlled exclusively by forces in his external environment, instead of being a scientific assertion, is simply the result of Skinner's *choice as to what ought* [my italics] to be emphasized." (p. 170.)

The next question then becomes: What is the basis of choice? In general we can say that choices are based upon preferences and preferences in turn represent values. I shall return to this problem in the concluding section of this chapter. Let me here just state one of the consequences of this interpretation: the epistemological position taken clearly stands out as a metaphysical stipulation prior to, and guiding, empirical research. Such stipulations will influence the research strategy, e.g. the way experiments are set up. And this restricts the selection of problems. Thus Koch (1965) concluded: "['Neobehaviourism' through its concern with] *general* laws of behaviour based on intensive analysis of animal learning in a few standard situations, [has] fled the subtler fluxions (not to mention certain obvious hard facts of human function) so vigorously that these matters were all but forgotten." (p. 30.) He adds that psychologists in their aspirations to be methodologically cautious have neglected relevant problems (the same could be said of sociologists) and have "allowed the rat to pre-empt the human" (Koch, ibid., p. 13).

Now let us return to Skinner's position: "[Behaviourism] is not the scientific study of behaviour but a philosophy of science concerned with the subject matter and methods of psychology." (1965, p. 79.) What then is the subject matter of psychology? The answer is behaviour as it is controlled by external variables. To the extent that these variables are thought of as *ultimate* causes (which Skinner probably does not consider them to be), the metaphysical nature of such statements becomes evident, as Copeland pointed out (op. cit., p. 170).

Skinner's philosophy of science emphasizes the desirability of explaining behaviour in terms of factors from outside influencing the organism and precludes physiological reductionism, though it does not preclude physical reductionism. Mentalistic expressions can, according to his view, be translated and reduced to statements of physical language, which will disclose their disguised meaning. A consequence of this attitude is the rejection of introspection as a source of knowledge, which brings us to what Malcolm calls the "Achilles heel" of behaviourism (1965, p. 147).

The problem is how one should treat sentences in the first-person present tense. Let us take as an example the sentence "I am excited". Is this a report of an observation the speaker makes about himself in the same manner as when he reports about a third person ("he is excited")? Malcolm asserts that first-person statements are not based upon observation. He goes on to say:

> The error of introspectionism is to suppose that they are based on observations of inner mental events. The error of behaviourism is to suppose that they are based on observations of outward events or of physical events inside the speaker's skin. These two philosophies of psychology share a false assumption, namely, that a first-person psychological statement is a report of something the speaker has, or thinks he has, observed.
>
> Ibid., p. 151

One can verify another person's excitement by observing his behaviour. However, as Malcolm states: "I do not verify in this way that *I* am excited. In the normal case I do not verify at all." (Ibid., p. 150.) Even if first-person sentences can be correlated with behaviour they usually go further. Malcolm asserts that sentences of self-testimony have an autonomous status. This has to do with Man's position of being a *subject* who can make utterances about himself without having observed himself before making them. Another point can be added to Malcolm's analysis: Man can certainly also be the *object* of his own perception, which enables him to make statements about what he is or what he experiences himself to be. *But that presupposes that Man is also a subject.* Thus Man can establish a dialectical relation with himself having as a subject a perception of himself as an object. These relations have been explored by George Herbert Mead amongst others. The experience of being an object of one's own perception may itself reflect upon oneself (the subject) and enable one to utter first-person statements. In any case, whether this is true or not, the basic behaviouristic fallacy is that first-person sentences are interpreted as if the person were an object of his own observation while behaviourism denies that Man can be a subject in this sense. This, it seems, is a central argument. Let us return once again to Malcolm who concludes: "Perhaps the best way to sum up behaviourism's shortcoming as a philosophy of psychology is to say that it regards Man *solely as an object.*" (Malcolm, op. cit., p. 154.)[1] The epistemological position of considering Man solely as an object not only excludes the subject–object dialectical relationship: it also excludes knowledge in the sense that *I* know something. It allows me at most to make statements concerning observations of the behaviour of others. But if one wants to stick strictly to behaviouristic methodological rules, these observational utterances cannot be interpreted as "something I know". Language thus becomes restricted to transmitting sounds, but not content.

2.3 STIPULATIONS ABOUT HUMAN NATURE—SOME GENERAL ASSUMPTIONS

There are at least two problems between which we ought to differentiate. The first one concerns ideas about the "historical nature" of Man; the second problem concerns ideas about Man taken out of their historical context to refer to Man "as he is now".

I shall first give a short account of the first problem and thereafter discuss some postulates about Man as found in current social psychology and sociology.

---

[1] The conception of Man as a passive object activated by external stimuli can be demonstrated in the concept of "operant response", being emitted by a subject, e.g. when pressing the bar in a Skinner box. The food pellet drops down as a consequence of an "operant response" and functions as a stimulus coming after the original "response". Now an "operant response" is in fact activity initiated by a subject. But in order to save the postulate that behaviour is controlled by stimuli in the environment, i.e. to save the postulate of the passive subject, operant behaviour is considered and treated as a "response". To quote Arthur Koestler: "The response responds to a stimulus which still is in the future—which, if taken literally, is nonsensical." (1970, p. 26.)

Two opposing views concerning Man's historical nature can be distinguished. One is the idea of Man having a basic biological nature which remains constant in spite of the change in the social and natural environment in which he lives. Thus, Man is considered to be a "naked ape" characterized by certain instinctive forces, e.g. "innate release mechanisms", as suggested by ethology (Hess, 1962).[1] There are various versions of this view, which can be differentiated according to their degree of sophistication. Common to all of them is the postulate of the more or less *unchangeable biological nucleus* of Man, inaccessible to environmental influences. Such postulative notions are often taken up again in conservative ideologies. "Ideology" is used here to mean "theories" or other types of explanations functioning to legitimize existing social conditions or to legitimize the necessity of social change.

Opposite to this "unchangeable biological nucleus" postulate is the one which Hegel termed "Man's self-creation". This postulate takes its point of departure in the assertion that what distinguishes Man from other animals is conscious, goal-directed production of means of subsistence:

> Men can be distinguished from animals by consciousness, by religion or by anything one likes. They themselves begin to distinguish themselves from animals as soon as they begin to *produce* their means of subsistence, a step which is determined by their physical constitution. In producing their means of subsistence men indirectly produce their actual material life.
>
> Marx *in* "The German Ideology", 1964, p. 53

The biological basis for production is to be found in the structure of Man's needs. This structure instigates productive work, the objects of which satisfy the needs. Production develops from a technique of using simple tools, like stones accidentally found, to a highly developed technology. The way the development of productive forces occurs can be pictured as an interaction between Man's needs on the one hand, which lead him to produce objects of need satisfaction, and the objects on the other hand, which do not only satisfy given needs but also create new ones. Thus the products created by Man's work basically affect and change those needs they were intended to satisfy, adding new needs to old ones or substituting old needs with new ones. Therefore one can postulate that the production of Man's life through work has a continuous influence on his "basic nature". As Man works and

[1] For an elaborated view of ethology, see the chapter by von Cranach, p. 370. See also Wiberg's discussion of non-rational models of Man, p. 340.

changes "nature" surrounding him, he changes his own nature (Marx, "Capital", Vol. 1, p. 127).

The process of human self-creation can be viewed as a phylogenetic as well as an ontogenetic process. In a phylogenetic perspective the following assertion has been made: "Uniqueness of modern Man is seen as the result of a technical-social life, which tripled the size of the brain, reduced the face and modified other structures of the body." (Washburn and Howell, 1960.) The same authors also state: "The tool-using, ground-living, hunting way of life created the human brain rather than a large-brained man discovering certain new ways of life." (Ibid.) If one looks at the phylogenetic development as a dialectical process, then not only did Man's way of life create the human brain, but the human brain in turn made possible more and more complicated ways of life. Ontogenetic self-creation can be illustrated by Piaget's model of acquisition and development of knowledge and intelligence.

The second position with regard to Man's historical nature has important consequences. Though it does not neglect biological structures within Man, it does not make any assumptions concerning the unchangeability of this biological nuclear structure. It can reject romanticist, Rousseauan ideas concerning "natural Man" and "Man's natural environment". (For a penetrating analysis see Moscovici, 1968.) To exemplify these romanticist ideas we may refer to Marcuse, who developed the notion of "repressive desublimation" built upon psychoanalytical metaphysics. Assuming that human instincts are basically asocial (a notion which seems strange when one ought to maintain that what is social or asocial depends on accidental norms and stipulations), he, like Freud, stresses the necessity of the repression and sublimation of instincts. Thus, the apparent liberalization of sexuality is regarded by Marcuse as "desublimation". This is shown by the fact that sexual behaviour often becomes exploitative and mechanized, and lacks erotic qualities.

Marcuse wrote:

Compare love-making on a meadow and in an automobile, in a lover's walk outside the town walls and on a Manhattan street. In the former cases, the environment partakes of, and invites, libidinal cathexis and tends to be eroticized ... In contrast, a mechanized environment seems to block such self-transcendence of libido.

1964, pp. 74–75

But for people for whom a car *is* the "natural environment", who never or seldom see or have access to flowering meadows and who never have seen town walls, the environment in which they make love may be as stimulating in its erotic qualities as environments of which they have no experience. An environment is "natural" if it is the one in which the individual grows up and lives, even if Man's actions systematically pollute this environment.

2.4   THE ROLE OF THE IMAGE OF MAN IN SOCIAL SCIENTIFIC THEORY

The stipulations concerning Man and his nature, though having varying content, seem to be related to three main issues. The first concerns Man's activity. Two main approaches can be distinguished. In the first Man is conceived as an object subjugated by social influences which he does not control. This view has a significant position within social psychology and sociology in which Man is often considered as executing his learned and internalized roles; but we will discuss this point later. In the second Man is thought of as being an active and acting subject, *and* at the same time an object influenced by his social environment. This reciprocal point of view is inherent in the epistemological position taken by Marx (see p. 128).

A third position could be taken, which, however, few social scientists would accept, namely the view which considers Man only as an active subject not influenced by his social environment. This view is sometimes held concerning certain people with certain positions within a social system. It easily leads to what has been termed "the conspiration theory of society" (Popper, 1969). This view states: "Whatever happens in society—including things which people as a rule dislike, such as war, unemployment, poverty, shortages—are the results of direct design by some powerful individuals or groups." (Ibid., p. 341.) Against such a view one can underline the fact that the actions of Man occur within a social system with certain properties and that these properties in turn have repercussions on him which may lead to unintended consequences. Thus also people with a high position in a power hierarchy are influenced in their actions by the functioning of the system in which they are elements.

The second issue is closely related to the first. It concerns autonomy versus social interdependence. Two views can be differentiated again: one underlines the fact that Man is an autonomous being and that his actions are a consequence of—perhaps innate—tendencies uninfluenced by social interaction; the other holds that Man is basically social, i.e. he is an individual who can develop his individuality only in interaction with other people. Marx expresses the idea of the basic social nature of Man by stating: "Man is in the most literal sense of the word a *zoon politicon*, not only a social animal, but an animal which can develop into an individual only in society." (Marx, 1964, p. 74.)

The third issue concerns the *rational* nature of Man and refers mainly to the question of how his action is initiated. Is it due to deliberate considerations to act towards certain goals or is Man and his action mainly instigated by motivational forces, which sometimes work on an unconscious level? The question is therefore whether Man is a rational being or irrational in his "basic nature" (see the chapter by Wiberg, p. 297, for a discussion of this problem).

2.5   STIPULATIONS ABOUT MAN IN SOCIAL PSYCHOLOGY

I shall restrict myself to two social psychological theories and the basic assumptions upon which they rest. The behaviouristic theories will not be included. They have not been excluded because they do not entail normative stipulations: they do. As already discussed, Skinner's views include postulative stipulations. Also other exponents of behaviourism, e.g. Hull (see Peters and Tajfel, 1957), use a mechanistic model and introduce metaphysical assumptions. The main reason for disregarding behaviourism is its relatively unimportant role for social psychological theory. Instead, I shall discuss two models of Man: one can be termed "a relational model", the other "the model of Man as a role-learning, role-internalizing and role-acting subject".

To illustrate the relational model let us start with Marx's definition of Man in the sixth of his theses on Feuerbach. There he asserts: "The essence of Man is not an abstraction inherent in each particular individual. The real nature of Man is the totality of social relations." (p. 68.) We should observe that Marx does not state that Man's nature is a consequence of his social relations, but that Man's nature *is* the totality of social relations; this difference is of great importance. Marx does not consider Man's nature to be a system or a collection of characteristics, traits or other qualities, which in turn are shaped by his social relations. Man's nature is equal to these social relations: he is not an object shaped and influenced by the social relations he establishes but he *is* in relation to other men, with whom he interacts. Therefore Man is both seen as an active subject when he interacts and a passive object when he is acted upon and these relations constitute him. The image of Man which Marx holds is in close agreement with his epistemological position as well as with his point of view regarding Man's interaction with his environment: "The materialistic doctrine concerning the changing of circumstances and education forgets that circumstances are changed by Man and that the educator must himself be educated." (Ibid., p. 67.)

There is a basic similarity between the images of Man held by Marx and by George Herbert Mead.[1] Mead was concerned much more than Marx with psychological processes, and thus went a step further than Marx. He makes a basic assumption of an ontological kind, which lays the foundation not only for a dialectical, but also for a consequent relational approach. The assumption is as follows: "A self can arise only where there is a social process within which this self had its initiation. It arises within that process." (Mead, 1956, pp. 41–42.) Hence, the emergence of the self presupposes social interaction; the self is initiated by this interaction. As Asplund has pointed out (1970; see also his chapter, p. 258), a traditional position in social psychology is to assume that interaction presupposes the existence of the self and of consciousness: certain mental phenomena are supposed to be the preconditions for social interaction. Mead reverses these assumptions. When the self emerges or is produced as a consequence of social interaction, it can be viewed not as a series of properties or traits but as a *relation* between the individual as an object of the actions of others, especially of the "significant others" within his environment, and his own actions towards the same social environment.

In fact, Mead makes it clear that the development of the self requires two stages: "At the first of these stages the individual's self is constituted simply by an organization of the particular attitudes of other individuals toward himself and toward one another." (Mead, op. cit., p. 235.) In this first stage the individual is a receiving object. This is, however, only one part of the dialectical process, necessary but not sufficient:

[The individual must also] in the same way that he takes the attitudes of other individuals toward himself and toward one another, *take their attitudes* [my italics] toward the various phases or aspects of the common social activity or set of social

[1] On the same subject see also the chapter by Janoušek, p. 279.

undertakings, in which as members of an organized society or social group, they all are engaged.

Op. cit., pp. 231–232

The attitudes of the others or of the "generalized other", to use Mead's term, are actively taken over by the individual, and together with the others' attitude toward him unite the self. Thus the individual is what his relations are.

The process of consciousness is intimately connected with language, referred to by Marx as "practical consciousness". Also in this respect there are some similarities with Mead for whom language is one of the preconditions for the development of the self. Mead considers consciousness as an activity and places it in opposition to "self-consciousness". The self is characterized by its unique quality of being able to become the object of its own perception. When the individual acts he does so only as a self constituted by the reaction of others towards himself and by his taking the role of the generalized other. Another component, however, can be added: if the self makes itself an object of its own perception, then "the self as an object becomes a part of the acting individual, i.e. the individual has attained what is called self-consciousness" (Mead, op. cit., p. 79). In this way, the dialectical relationship between the subject and his environment is supplemented by another one within the subject. There exists a subject–object relationship, the self being an object of its own perception. ◆

Perception of oneself like perception in general is considered by Mead as an act; perception in general relates a biological organism to its environment. Central to Mead's thinking is the concept of the "act", which is considered as an ongoing process: "An act is an ongoing event that consists of stimulation and response and the results of the response." (Op. cit., p. 76.) An act is goal-directed and therefore always has reference to the future. It also has a past, namely experiences of acts which in turn affect present acts. Social acts always involve other persons and thus interaction is seen again as a steadily continuing process which has dialectical properties.

It must be clear from this account of Mead's conception of human nature that one of the consequences of his position is non-reductionism. He does not try to explain social processes in terms of individual psychological laws, but, on the contrary, tries to explain individual behaviour or acts in terms of the social environment and the behaviour of the whole group of which he is a member "since his individual acts are involved in larger, social acts which go beyond himself and which implicate the other members of that group" (Mead, op. cit., pp. 133–134). We can now briefly summarize the stipulative notions concerning the nature of Man developed by relational theoreticians like Marx and Mead. Personality, or whatever the term may be to characterize the nucleus of Man, is not considered as a system of traits or properties, but Man's "personality" *is* his social relations; as he is steadily involved in interactions with others he is undergoing constant change. Therefore, the relational conception of Man's nature presupposes a process model and has to reject analysis in terms of static properties. Finally, the process of interaction is a process of reciprocal influence.

Now let us turn to *homo sociologicus*, i.e. Man as the bearer of roles. This idea has become so common in social psychology and sociology that it is taken for granted and its stipulative nature seldom questioned (Dahrendorf, 1967). The conception of Man as the bearer of roles is, however, a construction (see Dahrendorf, 1967, p. 17); the individual is viewed as being the sum of his social roles. According to Dahrendorf "roles" represent the "annoying fact" of society and its demands on the individual; thus one normative assumption is that society exists, as Durkheim has formulated it, *sui generis* and prior to the individual. The consequence of such a point of view is to regard Man as a product of social forces without necessarily stating anything about the character of these forces and their origin.

The central theme of role-theory is well known. Man has certain positions within the social system and related to these positions are normative expectations concerning the individual's behaviour and concerning relevant attributes. Positions are independent of a specific occupant. The same is true of the expectations directed towards a position; they are defined as the role of the incumbent of a position.

In this frame of reference roles are enforced upon the individual who is seen as a passive object exposed to social pressures. Sometimes an additional assumption is made to explain why Man accepts such pressures: he not only learns and internalizes role-expectations but a "normal" individual experiences satisfaction when he acts according to expectations and experiences disappointment and guilt when he does not (Parsons, 1964, p. 174). Two interpretations of such an assumption are possible: (1) Man does not only learn and internalize roles, but also learns and internalizes the meta-role to act according to internalized roles; (2) the alternative interpretation is that "Man has an archetypal basic need for determined patterns of behaviour and for adequate role-play" (Hartfiel, 1968, p. 251). Whatever interpretation one chooses they represent normative stipulations necessary to explain Man's behaviour as a passive role-bearer.

The idea of Man as the bearer of roles which are imposed on him faces one difficulty: observations show that two incumbents of the same role may exhibit varying behaviour. Several solutions of this problem are possible; and one is to differentiate between the "social" and "individual" role (see Rommetveit, 1954). This differentiation allows a "personal" contribution. Man's role behaviour is viewed not only as a consequence of social pressures, but also as influenced by his own "personality". If one does not wish to assume that "personality" refers to biological characteristics, it is necessary to introduce other assumptions about its nature. One solution is to consider "personality" to be the result of earlier learned and internalized roles (Israel, 1966). Here the distinction between "social" and "individual" roles refers to *social expectations* to which a subject is exposed at different periods of his life. Expectations which are learned and internalized earlier influence actions in later and different role-situations.

A second solution is to differentiate between *role expectations* and *role behaviour*. Role behaviour does not need to be identical in two subjects occupying the same position, since it can be asserted that role expectations do not state narrowly defined types of actions but only the *frame* of actions permitted, prescribed or proscribed (Rommetveit, op. cit.). One can explain existing individual differences in behaviour by reference to correct and false perception of expectations.

A third solution is also based on the differentation between *normative* expectations and *factual* behaviour. The term "role", however, is only used in connection with factual behaviour and does not refer to expectations. But in this case the original normative stipulation which makes "role" a "sociological elementary category, which is quasi-objective and in principle independent from the questioning of the individual" (Dahrendorf, op. cit., p. 49), is abandoned. The idea of the passive individual may likewise be abandoned. Instead "roles" become an individual's *behaviour patterns*, associated with certain positions; the term consequently refers to individual activities. Differences in role behaviour have in turn to be related to the individual's personality. Thus, when the term "role" applies to factual behaviour instead of to normative expectations additional normative stipulations concerning Man's nature are presupposed. The notion of role defined in terms of factual behaviour does not need to abandon the basic normative stipulation of Man as a passive individual, an object exposed to social influences; it merely gives him some personal freedom to act, which may be unimportant within the frame of strong societal pressures.

Dahrendorf discusses the consequences of such a "reified" image of Man. He points out that there are sociologists who are no longer aware of the hypothetical character of their artificial Man (op. cit., p. 73). He also asserts that sociology as a science of Man is inadequate. Man becomes indifferent to sociology if it is concerned with empirical observations of factual behaviour alone. Therefore positivistic sociology can correctly claim that it is a "behavioural science" in the literal sense and nothing else. If this is so it reduces sociology to behaviourism based on its own special kind of metaphysics (see Lundberg, 1939, who is an outspoken representative of this orientation).

The normative character of the notion of Man as a role-bearer is revealed most clearly by an analysis of the image of society into which such a view of Man fits. I shall return to this problem in the next section. For the present, it will be useful to illustrate these ideas briefly using the work of Parsons. One of his basic notions is that a social system has a given type of structure, which therefore is not questioned but accepted as non-problematic. The individual is born into this system, which has the monopoly on sanctions. Therefore it can force him to accept its norms: "It has been evident . . . that the dimension of conformity-deviance was inherent in, and central to, the whole conception of social action and hence of social systems." (Parsons, 1952, p. 249.)

The problem of social deviance is mainly seen from the point of view of those who represent the system and show conformity with its basic norms. Social groups trying to change the system are exposed to different social mechanisms, e.g. insulation. This mechanism restricts their impact on the rest of the social system (ibid., p. 309). It keeps conflict from coming into the open:

> The mechanisms which may be summed up as *isolating*, on the other hand have the function of forestalling even this structuring, and the development of appropriate cultural patterns . . . There are therefore two primary facets: the prevention of formation of group structures with their greater entrenchment of deviance, and the prevention of a successful claim to legitimacy.
>
> Ibid., p. 309

A social system is seen as being in, or striving for, a state of equilibrium. This is clearly a normative stipulation and not an empirical assumption. However:

> [When such a stipulation has been accepted it becomes clear that] fundamentally the problem is, will the personalities developed within a social system, at whatever stage in the life cycle, "spontaneously" act in such ways as to fulfil the functional prerequisites of the social system of which they are parts, or is it necessary to look for relatively specific mechanisms, that is modes of organization of the motivational systems of personalities which can be understood in direct relation to the socially structured level or role behaviour?
>
> Ibid., p. 10

Parsons thinks that the second alternative fits better into modern sociology. It is therefore clear that role theory is for him an integrated part of certain theories of society with their normative stipulations.[1]

3 Image of society: general remarks

This section will be devoted to a discussion of some of the problems which arise in connection with stipulations used about the nature of society. The first of these is the problem of different analogy models used in the social sciences. Secondly I wish to compare two of the more usual stipulative systems used in social science: the "functional-structural" model, also referred to as the "consensus" model, versus a dynamic model often referred to as a "conflict" model. The third problem concerns implicit assumptions concerning Man's role in society. Here I shall distinguish between an approach which assumes that the adjustment of the individual is a self-evident, or at least an unproblematic goal, and the approach which takes its point of departure in the concept of "Man's self-creation". This finally leads to the fourth problem: conflict between Man's need and the need of the social system.

3.1 ANALOGY MODELS USED IN SOCIOLOGY AND IN PSYCHOLOGY

The notion of the "social system" presupposes certain conceptions concerning its "nature" and its outstanding features. In reviewing the concept of "system", Buckley (1967) distinguished between three analogy models: the *mechanistic*, the *organic* and the *process* model. All of them start with certain postulative assumptions about the nature of

---

[1] Quite a different conception of "role" is found in the chapter by Janoušek, p. 291.

society, and in addition include certain formal rules for the determination of scientific activity.

Mechanistic models developed in social science as a consequence of the rapid development in physics and especially mechanics. An attempt was made first by "social physics" to interpret *"man, his mind, and society* [my italics] in terms of the same methods, concepts and assumptions as used in mechanics" (Buckley, op. cit., p. 8). Man was conceived of as a machine, or a mechanism—an idea which one can also find in the postulates of Man's nature used by psychoanalysis. Man is viewed as a physiological mechanism equipped with a certain amount of energy, which can be transformed etc. The strange notion of "sublimation" cannot be understood but in relation to such an image of Man.

Social systems were considered to be built of elements or atoms attracting or repulsing each other: "The physical concepts of space, time, attraction, inertia, force, power—which must be recognized as anthropomorphisms originally borrowed from everyday human experience—were borrowed back in their new connotative attire and applied to Man and society." (Buckley, op. cit., p. 8.)

Mechanical models using these concepts in modern social science have been developed by Pareto, among others, and some elements were taken over by Parsons and Homans. In psychology Lewin is an example: he used some of these concepts to construct analogies.

One special feature of mechanical models should be mentioned. This is expressed in the concept of "equilibrium" within a social system. Any changes which take place in such a system are assumed to be countered by other forces in order to restore balance, which is *postulated* as an important characteristic of a social system.

The idea of "checks and balances", the notion of "countervailing powers", or the notions of "inertia" and "equilibrium" as used in Parsonian theorizing belong here.[1] Another "balance hypothesis" is expressed in the assumptions concerning the relationship between "social differentiation" and "social integration". Thus:

> The problem for a society desiring to maximize its resilience is to balance social rank differentiation against social integration, so that the former is no more elaborated than needed for the task, but still sufficient to facilitate the upward flow of talent . . ., the latter to be neither so high that it challenges efficiency nor so low that it threatens cooperation.
>
> Svalastoga, 1964, p. 535

[1] These notions, however, are not solely based upon mechanical models, but also on analogies referring to organic models.

In addition to the normative use of "balance", hypotheses of this kind *implicitly* contain a conception of society as a closed system, an idea basic to mechanical systems. Even if it is stressed that social systems are looked upon as open systems, one has to conclude that they are treated as closed ones. This is due to the characteristics ascribed to such systems. Such problems as may arise, e.g. "the maximization of resilience", are usually treated as if they were not affected by factors external to the system. At best external factors are considered to be disturbing elements.

If one uses an analogy from mechanics and concepts such as "equilibrium" are used, then it is necessary to admit that theories based upon such models only relate to closed social systems. Consequently, a basic problem in the analysis of social systems is whether the analogy model used permits the treatment of the system as open or closed. In theories using mechanistic or organic models, social systems must be viewed as closed, self-sustaining systems. These theories therefore show a relative neglect of problems concerning the ways in which a system can deal with influences from external factors or with problems concerning the interaction of one system with another. Such questions are covered by theories which deal with open systems; these have to be founded on a "process-model". In the "closed system" approach, a system's main task becomes to overcome disturbances of equilibrium in order to reach a previous state of balance: "If the system should fail to do so, it would be interpreted as moving on to a new state of equilibrium . . . A careful scrutiny of the language used reveals that equilibrium and stability are usually assumed to mean the same thing." (Easton, 1965, p. 17.)

Theories building implicitly or explicitly on a "closed system" approach stipulate stability or equilibrium as a goal accepted by all members of the system. One can ask precisely why equilibrium and stability should be general goals in a social system. In fact large groups may strive to upset an existing equilibrium. Thus the emphasis on a system's generally accepted goals tends to be combined with a relative neglect of the problem of conflicting goals within it. In spite of the fact that they are presented in numerous theories as main societal goals, stability and equilibrium are stipulated goals and as such are problematic rather than self evident.

The functioning of an open system is determined by its capacity to take in, store, process and utilize information: "Final states may be reached from different initial conditions and in different ways. Such behaviour we call equifinality." (Bertalanffy, 1969, p. 40.) Final states within a system are achieved goals, which may be variable and even contradictory within the same system.

The choice of a theoretical frame of reference, involving either an "open" or a "closed" system, depends on the general model. The choice of a model is in turn strongly influenced by considerations of value, though again they may not be recognized as such. The assertion that one's own approach is value-free is partly due to the failure to make explicit underlying assumptions; and yet it is not difficult to demonstrate that the *concepts* used such as "integration", "balance", "stability" are strongly value-loaded. In addition the choice and the definition of goals postulated as being central in a social system presuppose certain values. In the example already quoted, the phrase "a society striving for maximum resilience" was used.[1] "Maximum resilience", however, cannot be defined in a meaningful way without reference to value criteria.

Finally, phrases like "a society desiring" may have a mystifying effect, since nothing is said about *who* or *which groups* may have such desires. That this is not stated may be a consequence of a stipulated assumption concerning general consensus in a society; and such a stipulation usually neglects or devalues the importance of conflicting interests, the existence of groups with different strategies and classes with contradictory goals. Consensus regarding values and beliefs is a prerequisite for equilibrium and therefore mechanical models not only include the concept of "equilibrium" but also of "consensus". At the same time "[such notions as those of] irreversible change of growth, of evolution, of novelty, and of purpose all [have] no place" (Deutsch, 1966, p. 26).

Certain formal rules of scientific method are connected with this type of model. Its concern is mainly with "two-variable problems, linear causal trains, one cause and one effect, or with few variables at the most (Bertalanffy, 1968, p. 12). It excludes multiple causality, interaction effects, feed-back mechanisms, etc.

Such models often deny directiveness or purpose; in fact teleological concepts are rejected as metaphysical in the sense of being "meaningless". They feature the assumption that systems usually function in an

---

[1] One could object that in this quotation nothing is said about the factual goals of a society: an hypothesis is only suggested. Nevertheless, it can be shown that what is expressed is a "technical norm" (for an explanation of this term see p. 178).

economic way, at minimum cost with regard to time and other expenditures. Bertalanffy stresses that assumptions of minimum cost depend on an utilitarian conception closely related to the economic outlook of the nineteenth and early twentieth centuries: "This is well known, for example, in the history of Darwinism: Struggle for existence and survival of the fittest are a biological version of the economic model of free competition." (Ibid., p. 18.) The conception of systems functioning in an *economic* way provides an excellent example of how certain stipulations are accepted as unproblematic and self-evident in the sense of being "empirically proved" even if this is not so and they are in fact anchored in metaphysical considerations. Bertalanffy's rejection of them is summarized in an alternative assumption: "There seem to be plenty of non-utilitarian structures and functions in the living world." (Ibid., p. 18.)

Let us now turn to the second type of analogy model, the *organic* model. Buckley distinguished between the "organismic" analogy and the more general "organic model" (Buckley, 1967, p. 11). When one applies an organismic analogy model, one strives to find a social analogy to the functioning of biological organisms.

Durkheim uses such an analogy to a certain extent when he contrasts "mechanical" with "organic" solidarity. The latter exists in highly differentiated societies where an elaborate structure of division of labour creates interdependence among subjects. This idea of differentiation of elements within a certain structure and especially their interdependence for "optimum performance" of the total system is essential to the model. The notion of interdependence of parts in organismic models implies that the total system is more than the sum of its parts.

In what has become "the functionalist tradition" in sociology, organic models referring to the individual organism often underly the theory. These theories stress "law and order", consensus, etc.

Organic models, like mechanical ones, imply closed systems, the main problems of which are *pattern-maintenance*, *integration* and *adaptation*, according to Parsons;[1] thus these problems refer to stabilization within the system and the restoration of previous states. In Parsons' classification

---

[1] Parsons (e.g. 1959) maintains that his model refers to an open system. "Open", however, means here only that the system's *internal* functioning is affected by factors outside the system. Open systems allow a flow of information in both directions. In open systems, therefore, interdependent functioning rather than internal functioning becomes the main area of interest.

there is a fourth category, goal-attainment, which could be seen to relate to dynamic qualities of the system. However, Parsons makes it clear that goal attainment also has a stabilizing function, which takes place when inertial tendencies within the system are disturbed by external influences. A goal is conceived of as "directional change" to reduce discrepancies between the system and the environment: "A goal therefore is defined in terms of equilibrium." (Parsons, 1961, p. 39.)

The problem of elaborating and changing the structure in an unstable system is almost neglected, since such events in the system as, e.g. conflicting goals and conflicting interests pursued by different groups and classes, are perceived as pathological phenomena in the organic sense, and not as inherent in the structure of the social system.

In addition to notions of pathology and normality, the model of a social system as an organism leads also to the introduction of "functional prerequisites" in theories building upon such a model. Functional prerequisites are conditions which make it possible for a social system to survive. What does the phrase "survival of the social system" mean? If we disregard self-evident interpretations such as the physical survival of its members or the survival of the total system as an autonomous political unit, the most meaningful interpretation is "survival with a given social structure". It has been pointed out that such an interpretation may easily become tautological since "social system" can be defined in such a way that changes of its social structure are equated with non-survival or death (see Carlson, 1962). Thus the suspicion is not completely unjustified that when one speaks about "functional prerequisites" for survival one refers to the survival of a *given* system with *definite* characteristics.

As an alternative one can assert that "on the sociocultural level . . . there is no specific structure, that is alone viable and normal for every society" (Buckley, op. cit., p. 16). If one accepts such an interpretation, the specification of functional prerequisites is not independent of a given set of values and goals which replace the general and vague notion of "survival". The formulation of functional prerequisites then corresponds to the establishment of certain technical norms or directives, i.e. norms which are concerned with *means* for achieving certain *ends* (von Wright, 1963a, p. 9).

Let us give one example: "Order—peaceful coexistence under conditions of scarcity—is one of the very first of the functional imperatives of *social systems*." (Parsons *et. al.*, 1951, p. 180.) If we consider this statement as containing a technical norm we can reformulate it in the following way: "If we want a social system with a given structure to survive under conditions of scarcity, then 'order', defined as peaceful coexistence, is necessary or desirable or useful as a means for reaching this goal." This technical norm states that peaceful coexistence tends to maintain a given social structure. Hence it is either a trivial description of a fact or a normative statement to which ruling groups and conservative people in general can subscribe.

Thus the reasoning of functional analysis with regard to functional "prerequisites" or "imperatives" becomes clear. First a given social structure of a social system is taken for granted or accepted as a universal phenomenon; then normative statements are made concerning how this structure can be maintained. Two obvious facts, however, are forgotten: (1) accepting a certain social structure within a given social system means that one is taking a *definite value position*, although this may be obscured by presenting the values and goals which are chosen as self-evident truths; (2) the presentation of functional prerequisites or imperatives, even if formulated as descriptive statements, corresponds to the construction of technical norms (see also p. 178). And so, by presenting values and goals as if they were universal and by formulating statements about functional prerequisites in a descriptive fashion, we are able to uphold the illusion of value-free science.

The third model is the *process* model. "The process model typically views society as a complex, multifaced, fluid interplay of widely varying degrees and intensities of association and dissociation." (Buckley, ibid., p. 18.)

Social systems are viewed as going through continuous *change* or *development,* and the term "process" may refer to either one of the two phenomena. The term "structure" refers in this context to relations existing between elements of a system at a *given point in time*. One question is whether the term "structure" can be used at all if a process analysis is carried out. "Structure" implies invariance and persistence. How can these characteristics be combined with "process", i.e. ongoing change? Nadel (1957) rejects this objection and asserts that "social structure is implicitly an event structure" (p. 128).

In order to sharpen the distinction between "invariance" and "persistence" as used by traditional structural analysis, and "variance" and "change" as used in process analysis, Nadel refers to a distinction by Lévi-Strauss between *micro-time* and *macro-time*. Nadel defines them in the following way:

Micro-time provides the time scale for events described a moment ago, that is for the shifts, movements and variations which still remain within the bounds of some overall constancy; conversely, macro-time contains the kinds of events which . . . change the pre-existing "structural alignment".[1]

p. 135

Dahrendorf (1959), in opposing Parsons' organic model, maintains that *social systems*, in contrast to living *organisms* in which structural change is accomplished from outside the system, are changed by the action of internal forces. He holds that besides the internal factors within social systems which tend to maintain the structure, there are factors which operate actively to change and supersede the existing structure even though they are constituents of this structure and function within it. Thus, like Nadel, he emphasizes the role of conflicts within a given structure in changing that very structure. This is equivalent to the dialectical principle which states that parts which make up a structure and which are thus interdependent can, at the same time, stand in a conflicting relationship to each other, e.g. when one part attempts to maintain the structure while the other tries to change it. This assertion is also the basis of the Marxist class-analysis. Thus, process models place emphasis on notions like "social conflict", "role-strain", "cognitive dissonance", etc. In addition they replace one-to-one variables with a multivariate approach, and they substitute interdependence, mutual interaction and feed-back mechanisms for one-sided cause-effect relations.

3.2 CONSENSUS VERSUS CONFLICT THEORIES

Buckley (1967) maintains that the controversy existing in current sociology between "consensus" and "conflict" theoreticians is associated with their use of different biological analogy models. The former use the biological organism as their analogy model whereas the latter, according to Buckley, use the species and the competitive interaction within it. It does not seem too strange to use interaction within a species as a basic model when analysing social systems, since social systems

---

[1] von Wright (1963a) when talking about "facts" differentiates between "events" and "processes". "Events", he says, are "a taking part": "processes" are "going on". (See also p. 190.)

are composed of elements belonging to ecological aggregates. One does not need, however, to accept additional postulates of organic models, e.g. the Darwinian "survival of the fittest", if one analyses society against the background of a model using ecological aggregates. In fact "survival of the fittest" becomes less and less a probable mechanism when Man develops complex productive forces and social institutions which provide security and protection.

There is, however, another and more important objection to Buckley's assertion. Whereas consensus theories usually apply a mechanistic and/or organic model, conflict theories use to a much greater extent the *process* models, as is the case in Marx's theories. Barrington Moore (1955) writes: "For a Marxist it is almost as difficult to conceive of a situation returning to a state of maximum harmony as it is for an equilibrium theorist to conceive of a self-generating cycle of ever fiercer struggle culminating in destruction." (Buckley, who quotes Moore, adds that the term "Marxist" could be exchanged for the term "process theorist".)

Accordingly, when we compare consensus and conflict theories we imply that their basic difference is to be found in the analogy model used: a mechanical–organic in the first case, a process model in the second. Both types of theories take their point of departure in a universal fact, namely conditions of scarcity existing in all societies.[1] These conditions certainly exist: they are not "postulated". I do not think that consensus and conflict theories differ with regard to the acknowledgement of this basic fact. The fundamental difference lies in the conclusions they reach when discussing scarcity; and these are in turn dependent on the model of society used and the assumptions made about Man and his nature.

---

[1] Moscovici (1968) has pointed out that sociological theories ought to be based on the stipulation that scarcity is built into our technology. To exemplify this one could postulate that the future "class-society" will be based upon such criteria as who is allowed to participate in space trips and/or who makes decisions concerning to whom permission for space trips should be given. Assume that one discovers that space trips will increase life expectations or that space trips carried out at a speed approaching that of light change the time scale so that a person returning from such a trip finds himself placed in another society and culture. A great demand for space trips may arise, which cannot be satisfied at the given level of development of Man's productive forces and resources in general. Therefore, inequality due to scarcity may arise which will then lead to the creation of new social classes.

The idea of scarcity, and therefore the existence of class differences built into our technology, fits the concept of "dialectical development" better than the messianic idea of a "classless" society in which dialectical processes come to an end.

The divergencies between consensus and conflict theories concern at least the following two points: (1) the way they look at scarcity and its consequences for conceptualizing conflicts in society; (2) the analysis of the role of inequality as a consequence of scarcity.

Let us briefly analyse the first point. I previously mentioned Parsons' statement (see p. 148): "Order—peaceful coexistence under conditions of scarcity—is one of the very first functional prerequisites of social systems." This statement was shown to be normative. It means that if scarcity is to be endured in a way which ensures peaceful coexistence between those who have access to resources and those who are deprived of them, then one ought to demand order and consider it as one of the necessary prerequisites for a social system. Problems of distribution of goods are secondary to the maintenance of order in such a social system. We should observe that Parsons' normative statement does not take into account that scarcity may, as is often the case, lead to conflict between groups or social classes, between those who have and those who have not.

The interesting point is that the normative character of this and similar statements is not recognized; it is taken to be a descriptive statement. From its acceptance, however, follows another normative assumption: If order is to be kept not by force but by consent, then one ought to establish consensus on values, especially on those leading to the acceptance of peaceful coexistence under conditions of scarcity. The next assumption may therefore be formulated in the following way: "A social system is always characterized by an institutionalized value system. The social system's first functional imperative is to maintain the integrity of that value system and its institutionalization." (Parsons and Smelser, 1956, p. 16.)

Consequently, Parsons provides us with another first functional imperative, i.e. another normative assumption. The third problem which arises is how to accomplish acceptance of the "common" value system. It is achieved by social control leading to consensus regarding opinions, attitudes, values and behaviour, which in turn will cause everyone to play the role to which he is assigned. Deviant behaviour must be eliminated and strong sanctions are needed to uphold consensus and uniformity. We come to a full circle when we are told that these conditions fulfil another of the prerequisites of the social system: to achieve and restore equilibrium.

Dahrendorf (1958) pointed out that such a postulative theoretical approach contains all the features which characterize Utopias from Plato's "Republic" to Orwell's "1984": (1) change of the total structure is absent; (2) universal consensus on prevailing values and institutional arrangements exists; (3) social harmony is to be found; (4) outsiders are not seen as products of the social structure, but as pathological cases of deviation; (5) processes which occur within the system as a consequence of its design follow recurring patterns; (6) isolation from other social systems, i.e. the notion of the closed system, is upheld.

In conflict theories scarcity and the consequent inequality of distribution of goods is assumed to lead to conflicts of interest, since certain persons cannot get more if others resist getting less. Conflicts concern the interaction between *groups* or between *classes* since people organize themselves when they have the same aspirations, goals and interests. In conflict theories a distinction is sometimes made between conflicts inherent in the social structure, which are termed "objective", and conflicts which are experienced by persons. The latter are termed "subjective". One problem in conflict theories then becomes the degree of agreement between objective and subjective conflicts or between "conflict in itself" and "conflict behaviour" (for an analysis see Bergström, 1970). Since in conflict theories groups and classes are opposed to each other, the idea of value consensus and uniformity of behaviour is substituted by the idea of multiple and contradictory value systems which affect behaviour. Conflicts, then, may be controlled by constraints and coercion, but they will continue to be enacted save under conditions of dictatorial enforcement of rules. In addition, conflicts are not solely considered to be negative phenomena in these theories, since it is postulated that they contribute to, and motivate, changes not only within the system but of the total system as such.

Several writers (see, for example, Allardt, 1970, and Lenski, 1966) have asserted that it would be possible to develop a theory which would integrate the two approaches. Conflicts arise in social systems, but there is also a certain amount of consensus, allowing for diverging values in varying groups and classes. I think that such an approach really misses the point. The question is not whether one can find through empirical studies conflict and consensus existing at the same time. The problem is what kind of stipulative prerequisites determine and delimit the development of certain theories. The basic difference between the two approaches can be summarized in the following way: in consensus theories conflicts are considered as disturbing elements, preventing equilibrium, which is considered as the "normal" state. In conflict theories conflict is considered as the "normal" state, whereas equilibrium is considered accidental. Reference to empirical results cannot be used to decide what is "normal" and what is not. This is a decision which has to be taken on normative grounds and when it is taken different consequences follow: in consensus theories the pattern is consensus→uniformity→equilibrium; in conflict theories the pattern is constraints→conflict→changes.

There is one thing which stands out from a study of the various consensus theories: they emphasize the necessity of uniform values and behaviour for the integration of a social system. They do not assert, however, that equality with regard to the distribution of material goods is a necessary condition for the integration of a social system. Generally there is a tendency to degrade the role of material needs and their satisfaction as functional imperatives and instead to emphasize certain *moral* factors. This in turn influences their treatment of the role of inequality in society.

Kingsley Davis's dictum about inequality may be quoted as a representative of the consensus theory approach: "Social inequality is thus an unconsciously evolved device by which societies ensure that the most important positions are conscientiously filled by the most qualified persons." (1949, p. 367.) We must still ask whether the criteria for the selection of the "most qualified" are social background, money, wealth, manners, intelligence or skill. Depending on which criteria are selected, Kingsley Davis's statement can easily be transformed into a tautology. The assumptions behind the statement quoted above are: first, that scarcity concerns foremost the number of qualified people available; second, that the positions these people fill have a special importance, that is a functional importance for society; and third, that they have to be motivated by material incentives and privileges to take over the "burden" of these functionally important jobs. None of the three assumptions are of an empirical kind. If education is made possible for all who wish to have it, a society may well have a redundant number of qualified people. Which positions are of more or less functional importance for the society can probably only be decided with reference to certain explicit values. If society is viewed as a system of interrelated positions with all contributing to its functioning, the question may even become nonsensical.[1] The stipulation that people in qualified positions have to be motivated by material rewards, status, etc. is itself founded on a certain image of Man which stipulates that Man is mainly motivated to work by the prospect of personal gains. Although this may be the case in our type of society, the question is whether the normative assumptions concerning Man's motivation do or do not create and maintain this type of motivation (for a detailed criticism see Tumin, 1953).

3.3 IMPLICIT ASSUMPTIONS ABOUT MAN'S ROLE IN SOCIETY

In his criticism of behaviourism Koestler (1970) summarizes what he calls the "four pillars of unwisdom" on which much of psychological thinking in our century has rested. The first is the idea that biological evolution is the result of random mutation; the second is that learning occurs by trial and error and by reinforcement of certain behaviour; while the third equates scientific method with quantitative measurement.

There is a fourth idea and this is the one which will concern us here If we accept the idea that "all organisms, including Man, are essentially passive automata controlled by the environment" (ibid., p. 17), the main task of Man within the social system becomes his adaptation to existing conditions. It is sometimes stressed that adaptive responses to external stimulation reduce tensions within the organism. Consequently we have two normative notions: (1) that Man's activity is mainly adaptive to external stimulation; and (2) that external stimulation (in addition to internal changes within the body) creates tensions which are reduced by adaptation to the environment. The second notion is sometimes supplemented by the hedonistic idea of Man's striving for pleasure and avoidance of unpleasurable experiences. This in turn makes it necessary to characterize tensions as unpleasurable, which is a doubtful assumption when presented in such a general way.

[1] A few years ago there was a strike of high-school teachers and university professors in Sweden at the same time as the garbage collectors went on strike in New York. After one week of strike the students had taken over the schools, encouraged by the central school administration. In New York, however, signs of disturbance of the social life of the city and risks of epidemics appeared. Should one conclude that garbage collectors are functionally more important for society than high-school teachers and university professors and that special incentives should therefore be given to them? In addition, it may be easier in highly industrialized societies in the near future to recruit high-school teachers than garbage collectors.

This standpoint has a number of consequences. If behaviour is considered as a response to external stimuli, then "emitted" behaviour can be controlled by manipulating stimuli or other aspects of the environment. Such control is facilitated when the individual himself becomes convinced and accepts that Man is a passive object exposed to external influences. Manipulation is easier with the consent of the manipulated; and this is usually obtained by characterizing as "socially adjusted" the behaviour which corresponds to imposed expectations. To express this in its extreme form, "social adjustment" is achieved when the individual acts in accordance with expectations and norms without questioning the validity, the relevance or the moral content of the demands made upon him. The normative content of the notion of "adjustment" becomes clear in the analysis of behaviour labelled as "maladjusted".

The stipulation concerning Man's passive adaptation to the demands of his environment has given rise to what has been termed the "managerial orientation" in social psychology and sociology (Bauman, 1969). The argument can be summarized in the following way: the development of productive forces has led to the creation of large organizations whose main problem is to manage their units and elements in such a way as to bring about "the highest probability of achieving the expected response" (ibid., p. 3). These responses are primarily judged from the viewpoint of the goals of the organization and not in terms of the goals and interests of the individuals who belong to them, and this in turn presupposes the assumption that organizational and individual goals do not coincide.

Managerial thinking is, as Max Weber calls it, formal-rational, i.e. concerned with the instrumental effectiveness of action for given goals. Managerial thinking therefore becomes technical thinking. It tries to "evoke more or less uniform, repetitive and therefore predictable responses" (ibid., p. 4) in the individual.

Since managerial demands are well organized and can rely upon strong support from the public, and since they can be bolstered by extensive material resources, they may influence quite easily the orientation of social science, not only by deciding what is useful research, but also by emphasizing certain stipulative claims concerning Man's behaviour. By stipulating that an organization is "concerned with what is restricted, 'realistic', relatively stable" (ibid., p. 4), one may direct research to be kept within given boundaries.

In contrast to this normative notion of "pragmatistic biotechnics", Bauman suggests an "anthropological" conception of Man based upon the stipulation of the active human being whose needs can be defined in reference to ethical norms. When these ethical norms are accepted, one main task becomes how to organize the environment so as to satisfy factual and prescribed or desired needs. The principal concern of theories with such a point of departure is how to adjust society to individual needs.

In fact, we can define two opposite views of the relation between Man and society: one could be termed "individual-oriented" and the other "society-oriented" (Israel, 1971). Both approaches make assumptions concerning conflicts between individual needs and societal goals. The difference between the two approaches is due to the attempt to "lay the blame" on either side; thus "individual-oriented" approaches use concepts like "self-realization" and assume that the organization of the social environment prevents the individual from realizing himself and his capacities and from satisfying his needs. The solution is therefore seen in the change of social conditions so that individual self-realization is made possible.

"Society-oriented" approaches, on the other hand, lay the "blame" on the individual and, in accordance with Hobbesian tradition, assume that "society exists primarily to protect men from each other and that culture was established to assist in preventing the break-through of primitive, selfish or destructive needs" (Zigler and Child, 1969, p. 471). The solution is the socialization of the individual to adjust him to the demands of society.

"Society-oriented" approaches can either view Man as a passive object responding to social stimuli, or as basically, i.e. biologically, asocial. In the first case the organization of society and its change are considered as the instruments by which Man is shaped to adjust to the needs of society. In the second, social organization is considered as a protective barrier against unchangeable inherent instincts, traits or other kinds of asocial characteristics within the individual. An outstanding example is the stipulated basis for Freud's theories. Freud considers Man to be basically asocial in two respects: (1) in accepting the Hobbesian position of the "evil nature" of Man; (2) in his acceptance of the hedonistic notion of Man's striving for pleasure and reduction of tension (in this respect he is joined by other influential figures in modern psychology, e.g. Clark Hull—see Peters and Tajfel, op. cit.).

Such a hedonistic tendency is considered to be asocial because it is seen as resisting social inhibitions considered necessary for all social life. In addition to these two metaphysical notions Freud's theory is based upon a model of Man as a machine equipped with certain energy which can be released, repressed and transformed. This is the basis of the idea of sublimation and the notion of "culture" as resulting from sublimation.

The idea that Man should be "basically" asocial seems strange, considering that what is "social" and "asocial" depends on the definition used, which changes as society changes.

There is another doubtful notion, basic both to the "individual-oriented" and to the "society-oriented" approach; that is the fundamental idea of an existing basic conflict between the needs of the individual and the prerequisites of society. Marx presents another view. He considers the process of material production as a consequence of Man's striving to reproduce himself. Here no conflict between Man and society exists. Instead, a struggle is assumed to take place between Man and "nature", i.e. his surrounding environment. He tries to transform this into objects of need-satisfaction; but the scarcity consequent upon insufficient means of production and/or means of distribution of available goods, leads to the transference of the basic conflict between "Man and nature" into a conflict between society and groups or classes.

4   Material rules

4.1   METHODOLOGICAL INDIVIDUALISM

"Empiricism sought criteria which would furnish cognitive agreement among equal and rational observers of the given world-order." (Cohen, 1963, p. 100.) This quotation succinctly states the basic attitude of a dominant empiricist position with regard to a meta-scientific programme. There are two points to be made. First, the empiricist doctrine in our century has been developed in intimate contact with natural science, especially physics; therefore the problem of a "world order" has not acquired any special prominence. Second, the doctrine developed acquires a value-bias when it is applied to the social sciences. It accepts the "world order" as given, and therefore has direct social and political implications. As distinct from the "world order" with which the natural sciences are concerned, the "world order" of the social sciences is constructed by Man and is consequently susceptible to change. Accepting the social "world order" as given and its empirical study as the task of the social sciences has several consequences: (1) it leads to a relative neglect of the study of problems of change; (2) it prevents or makes undesirable the *critical* analysis of the existing "world order"; (3) as a result, problems concerning the analysis and discussion of alternative goals of an alternative "world order" become non-legitimate.

Consequently, the empiricist orientation within social science either condemns itself to passivity and selects trivial but "non-controversial" issues as its main areas of research, or it offers the policy makers its services; if *they* can define their goals, the social sciences ought to be able to suggest the most effective means for reaching them. In this case the social sciences become "instrumental" in a dual sense. Scientific activity becomes instrumental activity and scientific theories can be reduced to instruments.[1] The position taken by Marx contrasts with the empiricist attitude of studying a *given* social "world order" with the aim of obtaining cognitive agreement among rational observers. His basic assumption is that "a rational and coherent social order within which all participant-observers would agree, is not yet given to experience; it must be created" (Cohen, op. cit., p. 100). "Rational" here does not refer to "formal" or "instrumental" rationality, but to "material rationality", to use Weber's concept. With regard to economic and social activity, material rationality can be defined only with regard to certain political, ethical, hedonistic, or utilitarian standards. In other words, values have to be introduced and taken into account. The social order which can be called "rational" in the Marxian sense is built in turn on his image of Man, which is closely related to the doctrine of "methodological individualism".

Its basic assumptions are: "No social tendency is somehow imposed on human beings from above (or from below)—social tendencies are the product (usually undesigned) of human characteristics and activities

---

[1] Popper attacks the idea that theories have only an instrumental value: "Instruments, even theories in *so far as they are instruments*, cannot be refuted as we have seen. The instrumentalist interpretation will therefore be unable to account for real tests, which are attempted refutations, and will not get beyond the assertion that different theories have different ranges of application." (1969, p. 113.) The more restricted view that the social sciences could deliver the correct means provided the politicians state the goal is also false. Among the reasons to be mentioned are: (1) means and goals are hierarchically ordered, and goals become means for goals higher up in the hierarchy; (2) the assumption has to be made that means have only instrumental value and nothing else, which in many cases is not true; (3) one forgets that specific goals may be realized by a variety of means. Each of these may lead to a number of consequences and implications, intended or not (see Israel, 1971).

and situations, of people's ignorance and laziness as well as of their knowledge and ambitions." (Watkins, 1968, p. 272.)

Thus, the central assumption of methodological individualism does not deny that Man can be influenced by tendencies intrinsic in certain social institutions or organizations. Even if an individual experiences these institutions and their influence is so strong that they seem unalterable, the fact is that they are created by human action and can be changed by it. Therefore the central assumption can be said to be that there does not exist any social tendency "which could not be altered *if* the individuals concerned both wanted to alter it and possessed the appropriate information" (Watkins, ibid., p. 271).

There are at least two problems in Watkins' view of methodological individualism: the first concerns the meaning of "social tendency"; the second relates to the constraints preventing Man from doing what he wants.

Let us start with a brief discussion of the first problem. Social tendencies are tendencies created by Man's action. To go to a beach on a sunny day is a social tendency; but to get tanned at the beach is not. To produce cars which easily get rusty is a social tendency (some say that it is especially pronounced in societies with a certain social system). However, the process through which cars become rusty is not a social tendency.

Let me turn to the second question: Why cannot Man "do as he wants"? Several reasons are usually given. One is the impossibility of envisaging all the consequences of human action; a certain intended goal may lead to unexpected consequences because of lack of knowledge, the complexity of the situation, or the inability of the brain to imagine or grasp the complexity and therefore to foresee. One type of human activity could be said to be intended to counteract these deficiencies: social-scientific activity. In fact one could, as Popper does, define the main task of theoretical social science as tracing "the unintended social repercussions of intentional human action" (Popper, 1969, p. 342).

The second reason why Man cannot do as he wants is that neither his actions nor his "will" are independent of interaction with others. Human action is always interaction. I would not have taken up this trivial matter had it not been for the fact that methodological individualism has sometimes been associated with liberal notions asserting the existence of autonomous individuals whose actions are guided by "enlightened self-interests", or similar motives.

The idea of the "autonomous individual" gives rise to the reified version of methodological individualism. By "reification" I understand the tendency to transform Man into an object, into a thing (Israel, 1971). This tendency can exist both on a societal and a theoretical level. On the societal level Man can be transformed into an object when he is regarded and treated as "working power" or as "consuming power"; he can then be manipulated through advertisement and propaganda and can become a tool of powerful bureaucratic bodies who may defend their actions in the name of economic growth or in the name of "the people".

On a theoretical level we may speak of "reified theories"[1] through which Man is *viewed* as a passive object. Thus the reified version of methodological individualism asserts that he is moved by his "self interests", which are regarded as his main motivating force. The reified character of this idea is concealed by calling action in accordance with "self interest" as "rational" behaviour. However, this reified version of methodological individualism is only a special case of the broader class of ideas asserting that Man is "steered more or less blindly, by his inner forces".

In opposition to the reified version of methodological individualism one can stress, as Marx did, that "the self interest in itself already is a socially determined interest, the goals of which can be achieved only within the conditions determined by society, which also provides the means" (Marx, 1953, p. 74). This can also be expressed by stating that Man's actions are determined by what Durkheim calls "social facts" (1966). They provide our third reason for explaining the constraints on intended human action. Social facts are defined as "ways of acting, thinking, and feeling that present the noteworthy property of existing outside the individual consciousness" (p. 2). In addition, Durkheim asserts, they have a power of coercion through which they control the individual's behaviour. Durkheim's concept of social fact has been used as a justification for placing his theoretical approach in contrast to methodological individualism. It has been described as metaphysical holism (Brodbeck, 1968). "Holism" assumes the existence of supra-

---

[1] A distinction has to be made between "theories about the process of reification" and "reified theories". The first type of theories are about social processes. The second type are classified as such according to certain meta-theoretical principles. In short, theories are reified when they do not allow for the notion of Man as an active, creative being but view him as controlled from "within" or from "without", from "above" or from "below".

human entities like "group-mind" or, to use another of Durkheim's allegedly holistic concepts, "collective consciousness".

As a short digression, I intend to show that Durkheim's notion of social fact can be interpreted in a way which does not contradict the basic ontological assumption of methodological individualism. Durkheim exemplifies his concept by saying that when Man fulfils his obligation as a husband, a citizen, etc. he is acting according to certain norms which, when violated, will be experienced as coercive. The explanation for this is that societies have a history, meaning that there exist traditional ways of behaving and that an individual born into such a society is thought to conform to those traditional ways of conduct, which are supported by sanctions "existing within society".

So far as I understand Durkheim, he does not assert that social facts are not created by human intentions, but that these facts are created by somebody else than the vast majority of those who feel coerced by them. Neither does Durkheim assert that those sanctions which cause social facts to be experienced coercively are created by supra-human powers. Nor is it necessary to explain "collective" consciousness as a supra-human entity. The concept can be interpreted as the collection of those social facts which, during the process of historical development, have been created and are still valid. Hence the interpretation in terms of methodological individualism makes it mandatory to emphasize the historical perspective. Such an emphasis on historical development does not imply the acceptance of some kind of historicism, e.g. the idea of "irrevocable historical forces", which belongs to the arsenal of metaphysical holism.

Marx, who is often accused of historicism, has clearly taken the position of methodological individualism in this respect:

> *History* does *nothing*; it "does *not* possess immense riches", it "does *not* fight battles". It is *men*, real, living men, who do all this, who possess things and fight battles. It is not "history" which uses men as a means of achieving—as if it were an individual person—*its* own ends. History is *nothing* but the activity of men in pursuit of their ends.
>
> 1964, p. 63

The fourth reason why Man cannot do what he will is due to the fact that Man not only interacts with others, but that he also creates complicated organizations and institutions, which in turn influence his behaviour. In the capitalist countries of the West the production and the distribution of goods and the allocation and reallocation of resources takes place in a most effective way—so we are told by outstanding economists—by the "forces of the market". I do not know of a better example to illustrate "metaphysical holism" than by reference to the notion of the "invisible hand of the market". Even if the forces of the market are created by human intention, they may, when in action, lead to unforeseen consequences which themselves affect human behaviour. Now these unforeseen consequences of human actions are often considered as "autonomous forces" affecting human behaviour. That they are unforeseen is not only due to lack of foresight but also to the fact that society is a system of interdependent elements which are organized in sub-systems, e.g. social and economic organizations, political parties, families and religious congregations. Only at the lowest level of sub-systems may the influence of each individual be visible. This does not imply that the total system and its sub-systems are not "run by men", but only that the functioning of the total system is so complicated that the effects of individual acts, carried out alone or in cooperation with others, in one's own name or as a representative of a large organization, often can no longer be understood as such and conceptualized accordingly.

Whereas expressions like "group mind" appear in the non-reified version of metaphysical holism, notions of the existence of invisible forces influencing Man represent the reified one. It can be summarized in this way: Man is pushed around by invisible and often powerful forces. The attempt to reformulate Marxism in terms of economic determinism is also an example of reified metaphysical holism.

This leads us to the fifth reason why Man cannot do as he wants. Individuals use holistic concepts and act, therefore, in accordance with the definition of the situation provided by these concepts. As Gellner points out: "When the holistic ideas of many individuals are coordinated and reinforced by public behaviour and physical objects—by ceremonials, rituals, symbols, public buildings, etc.—it is difficult for the social scientist, though he observes the scene from the outside not to use the holistic concept." (1968, p. 259.)

One of the most penetrating attempts to analyse holistic concepts and theories is Marx's analysis of the functioning of capitalist society with the help of notions like the "fetishism of commodities" ("Capital", 1965, p. 86). He asserts that commodities are presented as reified objects and not as the products of the social interaction of Man in the production process.

Marx makes a distinction between "phenomena" as they stand out and their "real" nature. The distinction can be interpreted in at least two ways: either as an expression of metaphysical essentialism or, which I prefer, as an attempt to translate phenomena described in the language of "holism" into the language of methodological individualism.

This idea of "fetishism of commodities" has been further developed in the previously mentioned theory of reification which holds that Man is transformed into an object by social tendencies prevailing in technocratic social systems. These social tendencies lead to the treatment of men as things. In addition, these tendencies are explained by theories which are themselves reified. They treat factual reification by referring to "forces inherent in technological systems" instead of presenting them as products of human activity. In this context, Gellner's observation that social scientists use holistic concepts is especially important.

There remains another important question. Does the principle of methodological individualism imply that the explanation of social phenomena has to be made by reference to psychological laws and that sociology therefore has to be reduced to psychology? Problems of reductionism are treated in the next section. Here I wish to point out briefly that "reductionism" can refer to two completely different problems. Firstly, it may refer to the issue of methodological individualism versus metaphysical holism. If holistic concepts, like "group-mind", are abolished and group properties defined in individual terms, we have the first type of "reductionism", namely from metaphysical holism to individualism. Secondly, "reduction" may refer to the issue of whether the *laws* of sociology can be deduced from the laws of psychology. It should then be possible to differentiate between reductionist and non-reductionist approaches.

The first type of reductionism, i.e. from "metaphysical holism" to "individualism" concerns the *description* of social events. It tells us what social events are and what their identifying characteristics may be. The second type of reductionism concerns the *explanation* of social events. It enables us to discover why the described events occur and attempts to formulate generalizations and laws.

We can now combine the different approaches on the descriptive and on the explanatory level into a three-dimensional matrix (see p. 165).

The matrix gives us eight cells. It has often been pointed out that holists also are non-reductionists. Logically one can, however, be a holist and a reductionist at the same time, when one assumes that "unanalysable

	Descriptive level			
	Methodological individualism		Metaphysical holism	
	Reified	Non-reified	Reified	Non-reified
Reductionism *Explanatory level*	1	2	3	4
Non-reductionism	5	6	7	8

properties of groups are connected by empirical laws to the behaviour of individuals in groups" (Brodbeck, op. cit., p. 244). More usual, however, is the position where methodological individualism is connected with non-reductionism.

Gellner expresses this position by saying: "History is *about* chaps. It does not follow, that its explanations are always in terms of chaps." (Op. cit., p. 268.)

We can now give reasons why the acceptance of the basic epistemological position presented earlier (p. 128) also requires the acceptance of the non-reified version of methodological individualism *in combination* with a non-reductionist approach on the explanatory level. The position of methodological individualism accounts for the notion of the active, creative human being. It stresses the role of the subject. The non-reductionist approach tries to explain human action in terms of the total social situation, e.g. considering society as an open system. Accepting the position of methodological individualism alone may sooner or later lead to the acceptance of one of its reified versions. Accepting the non-reductionist approach alone may lead to the neglect of human action as an independent variable and may lead to metaphysical holism. Thus combining the two approaches allows for theories in which human actions as well as social events may be treated as independent variables, and in which their interaction is emphasized.

4.2 ON REDUCTIONISM

The discussion in the preceding section makes it clear that I am rejecting the position of metaphysical holism. I do so for two reasons: (1) the position of metaphysical holism makes necessary the acceptance of such concepts as "group-mind", which contradict most of the knowledge collected within the social sciences; (2) the position of methodological individualism plus non-reductionism is assumed for reasons of logical consistency with the basic epistemological model presented earlier (p. 128). In this model the relationship between the subject and the object was characterized as being one of mutual influence and interdependence. Thus, the issue concerning metaphysical holism versus methodological individualism can be removed from the agenda. The issue of reductionism versus non-reductionism, however, has to be analysed, since it comprises many problematic points.

We must first of all ask what the problem of reduction refers to? "Reduction is something that takes place, if at all, between two *theories.*" (Addis, 1968, p. 232b). The same author also mentions that reduction as a problem has arisen in four cases: the reduction of particle physics to quantum mechanics, of chemistry to physics, of psychology to physiology and of sociology to psychology. Obviously we are concerned most with the last one.

"Reduction" refers to the question of whether phenomena of one science can be explained in terms of theories of another science. Can phenomena of sociology be explained by psychological theories? "Explanation, in one firm meaning of that term, is achieved by deducing what is to be explained from true premises." (Brodbeck, 1968, p. 286.) Statements serve as premises and as conclusions in a process of deduction. Since reduction is a certain type of explanation, it implies deduction: "The deduction by which reduction is achieved also serves to explain. Explanation is in fact a major reason for reduction. It is consequently a matter of laws and theories and not of terms or concepts." (Brodbeck, ibid., p. 287.)

To make the issue clearer we will start with an example and some theoretical considerations. It has been asserted that women's emancipation in Sweden was caused by women's aggression which had its sources in sexual frustration (Sjöwall, 1968). Such a statement attempts to explain a social phenomenon, "women's emancipation in Sweden" in terms of psychological hypotheses. Intuitively the hypothesis seems unreasonable. This would become clearer if the term "Swedish women" was substituted by the term "Swedish workers", but let us instead argue about the matter in question.

It may be that some women who are sexually frustrated may publicly demand women's emancipation. On the other hand there may be some women demanding emancipation who are not sexually frustrated. Finally, there may be some sexually frustrated women who do not at all demand women's emancipation.

We may now formulate two common statements in the language of psychology, which may account for a part of the hypothesis mentioned above: (1) sexual frustration leads to aggression; (2) individual aggressions are directed against persons, groups, social institutions or specific social conditions (e.g. the discrimination against women in Swedish society). These psychological statements offer an explanation of why some frustrated women may demand equality; they still do not explain why non-frustrated women may do so. Also we have to formulate a statement explaining why frustrated women direct their aggression against existing social conditions and not against their husbands. One hypothesis might claim that psychological states must be explained by reference to sociological statements, e.g. about existing social conditions. Such an explanation may be formulated as a statement like the following: Existing social norms allow men to act in a way which makes their wives frustrated. A statement of this kind endeavours to explain individual psychological states in terms of social conditions; this is surely a case of what may be termed "counter-reductionism". Sometimes an additional statement may be formulated, asserting that social phenomena as contrasted to psychological ones are "ultimate conditions" or "more basic", or "decisive in the last instance" etc. Such statements imply assumptions concerning the causal significance of sociological variables. The risk with such explanations is one-sided determinism, e.g. economic determinism as in some vulgar interpretations of Marxist theory. The objection which I have raised against the explanation of sociological phenomena by reference to psychological statements could also be raised against the type of explanation which has been called "counter-reductionism". This becomes clear by objecting to the explanation presented above on the grounds that it does not account for the fact that certain husbands, though they are influenced by the same social norms, do not sexually frustrate their wives.

We could now drop the whole matter and claim that the hypothesis concerning the relationship between women's sexual frustration and social tendencies for women's emancipation is false (which it most probably is). Such a step would be of little value for helping to solve the problems with which we are concerned and which can be formulated in the following way: (1) Can the behaviour of individuals be explained solely by reference to psychological laws (which I think is one of the central questions of social psychology)? (2) Can social facts be explained by reference to psychological laws? The answer to the second question is "no" if we accept a non-reductionist position. It will become clear why when we have answered the first question.

Psychological laws establish connections between properties or characteristics (often between certain values these characteristics may assume) in individuals. They also establish connections between relational properties or "descriptive relations, since, like properties of single individuals, they refer to observable characters of things" (Brodbeck, op. cit., p. 281).

Sociological laws can refer to two separate classes of phenomena. They can contain: (1) assumptions concerning the connections of properties or relations of *aggregates* of human individuals; (2) assumptions concerning complex wholes like social institutions, and properties or relations characterizing these complex wholes.

Theories about the first class of phenomena may lead to the establishment of laws which are only true if statements about individuals composing the aggregate are true. "The cohesiveness" of a group can be explained only in terms of the attraction of the members to each other and to their common activities and goals.

Complex social wholes, however, "can indeed exist only if their parts exist—that is indeed the predicament of all wholes—but their fates *qua* fates of complexes can nevertheless be the initial conditions or indeed final conditions of a causal sequence" (Gellner, 1968, p. 263). In such complex wholes we could arrange the sub-units according to level of complexity, where complexity refers to the number of elements making up a unit. Laws formulated at the least complex level may be called "microscopic" in relation to laws formulated on a level of greater complexity which may be called "macroscopic", e.g. the laws of physiology in relation to the laws of psychology.

The reduction of macroscopic laws to microscopic laws presupposes certain conditions which make possible the formulation of *process laws*.[1] Imagine a universe composed of a given number of elements and a given number of quantitative properties of elements, which thus enable it to assume certain values. If we have a complete set of properties (or variables), i.e. all properties which make a difference are included, and the values for all elements at a given state are enumerated, then we have a state description. If, in addition, the set of variables interact only among themselves and with nothing else, we have a closed system. Under conditions of completeness and closure "the values of *any one*

[1] I am here following the reasoning of Addis (1968) and Brodbeck (1968).

variable at any time can be computed by means of the laws from the value of *all* the others at any other time" (Brodbeck, op. cit., p. 289). Such laws are called process laws. Process laws have another specific feature: they are reversible with regard to time, which means that "any two states of the system can be inferred from each other, quite regardless of which comes first in time" (Brodbeck, op. cit., p. 290).

Assume that one variable within the closed, complete system varies and that this change is paralleled by the variation of a variable in another system. Then the laws of one system can be translated into laws concerning the other system. Laws which express the connection between parallel variables are called cross-sectional laws, i.e. connecting one variable in one system with a variable in another. Reduction is therefore possible if cross-sectional laws exist. Since, as mentioned above, reduction implies deduction, the reduced and the reducing theory must have common terms or variables.

The laws of a system to which those of another are reduced must be process laws in the sense defined. In other words that system to which another system is "reduced" must be closed and complete. But the systems studied by psychology are neither closed or complete; nor is there reversibility. Therefore, the laws of sociology cannot be reduced to those of psychology. Neither is the reverse operation termed "counter-reductionism" of psychology into sociology possible, since the systems studied by sociology are not closed nor complete. Consequently the problems of psychology and sociology are problems of *open* systems (I will take up the notion of "open systems" later). This means that the behaviour of individuals cannot be explained in terms of individual properties without the influence of the social context also being taken into account (see on this problem the chapter by Tajfel).

Before we present an alternative argument one brief comment should be made in order to meet a possible objection. Assume that we have three people in a group and we have been able to formulate laws concerning their interaction. If these laws also explain the interaction of ten persons in a group, they may be called composition laws. Such laws make it possible to predict from a simple to a more complex situation. Suppose, however, that the number of persons in the group exceeds ten and the law no longer holds. It will then be necessary to formulate another composition law which may break down at still another level of complexity. In that case we should have an instance of *explanatory emergence* referring to laws of group behaviour which are "not derivable from the laws, including whatever composition laws there are, about individual behaviour" (Brodbeck, op. cit., p. 301).

Explanatory emergence is not unusual in the social sciences because composition laws often break down at a certain level of complexity. But an explanatory emergence may be transferred into a composition law, implying the possibility of substitution of composition laws. However, this could lead to the suggestion that composition laws may, in this case, be meaningless. The idea implicit in them is that it should be possible to compute the values of variables in a complex situation from the values of the variables in a less complex one (Addis, op. cit., p. 326). But this is prevented by explanatory emergence. Since in a given system there is a maximum level of complexity, one may favour another strategy. It implies starting an analysis and, consequently, an explanation, at a fairly complex level of a system viewed as open. Then laws or law-like statements can be established to explain the functioning of sub-systems in terms of interaction within the total system. Nevertheless, this does not preclude the additional possibility of studying sub-systems on their own and formulating laws which explain events *within* a sub-system.

From a knowledge of the state existing in the total system the states of the sub-systems can be found. On the other hand, knowing the state of one sub-system does not necessarily help us to discover that of the total system. But this does not preclude us from studying the sub-system and its functioning.

In order to clarify the problem further, I wish to refer to a distinction provided by Mandelbaum (1957–58). He differentiates between "abstractive" and "global" laws. In the former an attempt is made to establish relationships between certain elements, components or aspects of a system and "to state this relation in such a way that it will be applicable in all cases in which these particular aspects or components are present" (ibid., p. 645). The specific nature of a certain state in which the elements are found does not enter the law, but represents limiting conditions of the type "given that and that".

Global laws consider entities as wholes. It may then be possible to formulate "law-like statements concerning changes in their global properties, or concerning relationships between the nature of the system as a whole and the manner in which its component parts behave" (ibid., p. 645). Reference to the properties of the system are in this case included in the law.

The strategy suggested, i.e. to formulate laws "from above", implies that one takes into account the functioning of the social system or its institutions when trying to explain group or individual behaviour. Such a strategy has certain consequences for social psychology. It may get a *mediating* function between individual psychology and sociology. The variables that individual psychology treats as dependent, namely behaviour, ought to be treated in social psychology as independent; and the variables which sociology treats as independent, e.g. institutional functioning, ought to be treated by social psychology as dependent. From the point of view of the epistemological model (see p. 128), individual psychology and sociology may treat the person as an object: then social psychology should treat him as an active subject, an agent. Addis writes: "[The idea we have tried to develop has been called] the thesis of total social interactionism. That means that within the social realm literally everything which occurs at a given time 'makes a difference' to what occurs at any other time." (Op. cit., p. 332.)

I want to end this section by presenting a heuristic reason for this approach, a reason suggested by Rapoport (1969). He stresses the speed with which social changes occur today. The radical change of society has reached such a point that changes have become visible within the normal span of a lifetime. Rapoport asserts therefore that we ought to turn to holistic system description and analysis and renounce, at least for the moment, analytical methods concentrating on details. He claims that this is a methodological justification of holistic description and analysis which implies the primacy of sociology over psychology.

Another consequence of this methodological standpoint may be mentioned. It will not be sufficient to analyse total systems or parts of them as if they were unchanging. "Structural" laws, both of the abstractive and global kind, have to be supplemented by genetic laws taking into account change and development. However, not only should the objects of research be studied in a genetic way, one also ought to analyse on a meta-theoretical level which "genetic state of development" has been reached by theories and methods.

4.3   SOME REMARKS ON THE GENETIC-HISTORICAL APPROACH

In the previous section the necessity of the application of "genetic laws" was stressed as a consequence of the subject matter of social science: the rapidly changing social world. Genetic-historical explanations can account for "processes" going on in a system leading to "change" which may take the form of "development". The term "process" refers to ongoing actions of, and interactions between, the components of a system (Buckley, 1968). These actions and interactions occur according to certain patterns, which may be labelled "structure of the system". A structure persists for a certain period of time, dissolves and changes. "Change", roughly speaking, is a transformation of a state of affairs into another state (von Wright, 1968; see also the discussion on p. 205). In order to analyse changes we must determine initial states and end-states. "Development" is a special type of change in which the end-state is usually considered to be more complex than the initial state. "Complex" may refer to such characteristics as "degree of differenti-ation" or "degree of integration" of component parts, or to both.

With regard to individuals, according to our basic epistemological model, the central problem is the study of the individual's interaction with his social and physical environment viewed as a continuous process. In this process biologically determined structures within the individual influence interaction with the surrounding environment and are in turn influenced by this environment. Interaction is viewed not only as a continuous process; it is also thought of as affecting structures within the individual which change from one level to another. Development can be interpreted in this way. Piaget asserts that there is a progressive transformation of simpler structures and their substitution by more complex ones in the individual. In his theoretical scheme "develop-ment" means change from sensory-motoric structures determining interaction with the environment to structures of concrete and later of abstract and symbolic, logical formations.

Theories of process and change in social structures are more difficult to analyse. Historical explanation attempts the reconstitution of struc-tures to make them understandable in a system as it is "now". Thus, we can "use the term 'synchronic social now' to refer to that period of time within which the given sociocultural system remains more or less stable" (Goldstein, 1960, p. 617). The study of the general condition of change can then be labelled as a "diachronic social study", the task of which is to discover how synchronic social "nows" develop from previous synchronic social "nows" (ibid., p. 619; see also the discussion on "macro-time" and "micro-time", p. 150).

The diachronic social studies are then concerned especially with: (1) the organized social condition in the system into which the individual is born; (2) the organized social phenomena which exist independently of him but nevertheless influence his behaviour. Examples of the first type of organization are the social sub-systems in which the basic process of production occurs; also the kinship system in societies in which kinship matters belongs to the same category. The structure of language systems, and that of the system of social control including norms, customs and other rules which the individual obeys, belong to the second category. The latter, together with social institutions of education and mass-media, also form the structure for the system producing "the consciousness of the individual". It is typical of all these systems that the individual may not be aware of their structure and still behave according to their rules.

From this it seems that diachronic studies should concentrate on the genetic-historical aspect of structures. Laws which might be developed within such a framework may be termed structural-genetic laws. One example is Marx's attempt in "Capital" to lay the basis for "the economic law of motion of modern, capitalist society".

The aim of such structural-genetic studies could then be formulated to "trace the unintended social repercussions of intentional human actions" (Popper, 1969, p. 342).

4.4 OPEN SYSTEMS AND THEIR PROPERTIES

A system can be defined as a complex whole, consisting of elements related to each other in certain ways. The first problem after identifying the boundaries of a complex whole is specifying the type of relations existing between elements in complex wholes. But, as Nagel (1968) stresses, the term "whole" is ambiguous and often used in a metaphorical way. Still more ambiguity is introduced if assumptions are made concerning the relations between the elements of "complex wholes", such as: "The whole is more than the sum of its parts." Nagel distinguishes between eight different ways of using the term "wholes". The definition which comes closest to my own ideas about "complex wholes" is: "Any system whose spatial parts stand to each other in various relations of dynamic interdependence." (Op. cit., p. 383.) "Dynamic interdependence" implies that elements or parts in such a whole "do not act, and do not possess characteristics, *independently* of one another" (ibid., p. 391). Any change in one part, its removal, or the addition of a new part affects not only the other parts, but the whole as such.

So far we have tried to clarify the use of the term "system", defined as a "complex whole". Two additional problems characterizing the use of the term have to be explicated: first, we must attempt a definition of an "open system"; and second, we must understand the meaning of the phrase "elements in a complex system may stand in conflict with each other or assume contradictory positions". The second problem refers to one of the central assumptions of dialectics.[1]

The concept of an "open system" has been introduced and mathematically defined by Bertalanffy (1969) as follows: "A system is closed if no material enters or leaves it; it is open if there is import and export, and therefore change of the components." (p. 70.)

Open systems are thus characterized by import of energy or other kinds of resources, e.g. information, which may "furnish signals to the structure about the environment and about its own functioning in relation to the environment" (Katz and Kahn, 1966). Closed systems do not have this input of energy, information, etc.; therefore they reach equilibrium at the cost of losing structure and do not attain a maximal degree of entropy.[2] In an open system the import from outside causes negative entropy. This import may increase differentiation of the existing structure or facilitate changes in the structure of the total system. The increase of negative entropy, however, is dependent on the existence of "information processing centres"; these may partly establish negative feed-back loops which keep certain characteristics of the system within the limits of given values. They may also partly initiate positive feed-back or deviation-amplifying tendencies, leading to the above mentioned changes in the structure of the total system.

When talking about "structure", one should distinguish between "structure" as exhibited by the temporary interrelationship of the components, and the system as such:

Making this distinction allows us to state a fundamental principle of open, adaptive

---

[1] "Dialectics" is no less an ambiguous term than "complex wholes". It can refer to "characteristics of the elements of a system" and it can also refer to a method according to which a system and its elements can be analysed (for a discussion, see S. Hook, 1953).

[2] This is in fact what the Second Law of Thermodynamics states, namely that in a closed system, entropy, which is a measure of "disorder", will always increase until equilibrium is reached. Thus, in thermodynamics equilibrium means maximum entropy. The mechanical models used in the social sciences (e.g. Parsons' approach) view equilibrium as a state of order achieved by consensus and control of deviant behaviour. These models, however, as pointed out before, use terms like equilibrium, order, stability to a large extent as normative and not as descriptive terms.

systems: *Persistence or continuity of an adaptive system may require, as a necessary condition, change in its structure*; the degree of change being a complex function of the internal state of the system, the state of its relevant environment, and the nature of the interchange between the two.

Buckley, 1968, p. 493

Another characteristic of open systems is *equifinality*, as defined by Bertalanffy. In inanimate systems final states of the system are determined by its initial conditions. Living systems display different characteristics. "Here, to a wide extent, the final state may be reached from different initial conditions and in different ways. Such behaviour we call equifinal." (Bertalanffy, 1969, p. 76.)

Closed systems do not display equifinality. They may have certain *functions* but do not show *purposive activity*. Churchman and Ackoff (1968, p. 245) distinguish between three teleological categories: (1) Systems which accomplish certain objectives by functioning in an invariant way in a wide range of environments have *extensive function*. The clock is a prototype of this functioning; (2) Another type of closed system exhibits *intensive function* and thus may change its behaviour when external conditions alter but exhibits in general only one type of behaviour in a given environment. An example is the thermostat or a servo-mechanism; (3) In addition to these two different modes of functioning, a system may have *purpose*. Purpose can be said to exist in open systems, which accomplish their objectives by different types of behaviour, even if the environment remains constant. A system which has "purpose" must always make *choices*. But choices presuppose alternatives, and in complex systems like societies, alternatives may exclude each other; therefore conflict may arise. Thus "conflict is endemic in organic systems. It is at its most complex and acute in men and societies" (Vickers, 1968). Therefore complex, open systems like societies have "dialectical qualities".

I am trying to define "dialectical" in a way which I hope will make the term useful. We have assumed that there exists a dynamic interdependence of parts or elements within a complex system. Let us assume at least two elements which, within the functioning of a system, are interdependent, but which in a choice situation choose different and mutually exclusive alternatives. These elements can be individuals, groups, classes or other categories. Their relation of interdependence means that both are necessary for the functioning of the system. Furthermore their relationship may also be symmetrical, but can and will often be asymmetrical, where the terms are used as applied in formal logic. Asymmetry of relations is assumed to be a consequence of an uneven distribution of resources and/or power, which in turn is a consequence of the previously mentioned basic characteristic of social systems, namely scarcity. In addition to interdependence and asymmetry (or symmetry), their relationship may be characterized by a third *descriptive* relation, i.e. one referring to observable characteristics. The elements have conflicting goals. These can be of two kinds: (1) they can be mutually exclusive; (2) they can be mutually exclusive and exhaustive, which means that a third alternative does not exist.[1] Conflicts of the second type are considered to be more severe than conflicts of the first type. (I imagine that Mao Tse-tung's distinction between antagonistic and non-antagonistic conflicts can be interpreted in the way it has been suggested here.)

In summary, a system has a dialectical property if at least two of its elements, *interdependent* for the functioning of the total system or subsystem to which they belong, have an *asymmetric* relation to each other (in weaker cases a symmetric one) and at the same time goals which are *mutually exclusive and/or exhaustive.*[2]

5   A model

5.1   WHAT IS THE NATURE OF STIPULATIONS?

I have tried to show in the previous analysis that certain types of stipulative assumptions enter or precede the formulation of empirical theories concerning human behaviour and the functioning of social systems. I shall now develop a model in which I wish to include those categories of statements distinguishable when analysing social psychological or sociological theories.

---

[1] The two types of contradicting *social relations* correspond to two types of *contradictory sentences*, distinguished in formal logic: (1) mutually exclusive; and (2) mutually exclusive and exhaustive sentences. In the German and in the English languages *logical* contradictions are denoted by the same term as *social* contradictions, namely "contradiction" (in German *Wiederspruch*). I believe that this semantic confusion is the cause of other confusions, e.g. when it is claimed, as some Marxists assert, that traditional logic cannot be applied when analysing dialectical social relations. Instead one asserts that a special "dialectical logic" has to be used. So far I have not been able to find out what such a "dialectical logic" means (see also Popper, 1969, chapter 15, on this problem).

[2] Professor Mihailo Marković has pointed out in a personal communication that this explication is sufficient for static but not for dynamic states.

I have referred to "stipulative sentences" in a manner which has intentionally been unprecise; reference has also been made to "normative assumptions" and to the well-known distinction between "formal" and "material" rules. Thus, all the terms used have seemed to refer to *normative* ideas. I shall now try to be more precise and in this attempt I shall draw heavily on an analysis carried out by the Finnish philosopher von Wright.

Von Wright distinguished between three major groups or types of norms which he calls *rules, prescriptions,* and *directives* (1963a, p. 15).

He divides "rules" into three sub-groups, one of which has a special importance in our context: this sub-group is called "rules of a game". Let us assume that scientific activity, e.g. social psychological research, is "a game", played by more or less competent players. (The idea that research should be considered as a game may entail two notions: one is that it follows certain rules; the other, which I think is no less attractive, equates "games" with "playful activity". The idea of research as an activity which is only laborious, pedantical and strict could never win my acceptance.)

Von Wright points out that rules of the game *determine* the way a game is played, i.e. its moves "and thereby also the game 'itself' and the activity of playing it" (ibid., p. 6). The category of *formal rules* seems to fit this explication. How about the category of material rules? They have been termed "regulative principles" because they state certain rules concerning the content of premisses included in an empirical theory. One example of such a rule discussed earlier is the doctrine of methodological individualism. We can assert that even material rules are rules of the game since they determine the specific game which is played by a certain science, in this case the social sciences.

Our stipulations about the nature of Man and society are also of a normative kind and do not differ too much from material rules. I would therefore say that they also can be considered, at least in part, as rules of the game. To some extent they may have another character, namely what von Wright calls "praxeological statements" (1968, p. 12) to which I shall return later.

Material rules and stipulations can be considered as rules of the game because once they have been chosen they *determine* the content of theories which are used in empirical research. They do not, however, *determine* theories in the same sense as formal rules which define the *correct moves* in scientific activity. The stipulations belonging to the category of material rules have a delimiting function: they *permit* certain types of theories and exclude others.

There is one problem connected with identifying stipulations and material rules with norms. The type of norms which are called rules gives rise to a certain linguistic behaviour. Norms are usually expressed in terms like "ought to", "must", or "may". However, material rules and stipulations about human nature and the nature of society are usually not expressed in normative terms, but in descriptive ones. I think that this has a psychological explanation. The idea of a value-free science has so deeply permeated the minds of scientists trained in the positivistic tradition that it also influences their language behaviour. Consider the following sentence: "If a system is to constitute a persistent order or to undergo an orderly process of developmental change certain functional prerequisites must be met." (Parsons, 1952, pp. 26–27.) Is Parsons stating here an empirical hypothesis? As the previous discussion has indicated, I do not consider that he is. One interpretation of the sentence is the following: "One *ought* to think of systems as being constituted as a *persistent order* or *as undergoing an orderly process of developmental change*. Therefore certain functional prerequisites must be met." By formulating the sentence in this way one expresses a rule for how we ought to think about social systems. The first reason why stipulations are usually not formulated in a normative language is that they are not recognized as rules of the game.

Another way of interpreting the above quotation is to consider it as a *directive* or *technical norm*. Then the sentence could be formulated in the following way: "If we wish to consider a system as constituting a persistent order . . . then we ought to formulate certain functional prerequisites which ought to be met so that a system can be considered in such a way."

Von Wright considers conditional sentences as the standard formulation of technical norms. In the antecedent of the conditional sentence something is mentioned which is *wanted*: the consequent concerns "something that must (has to, ought to) or must not be done" (1963a, p. 10).

A second reason for believing that statements of the type mentioned are not stipulative, i.e. normative, but descriptive may depend on the fact that they can be formulated as technical norms and therefore may be confused with conditional statements stating a natural or logical necessity. These statements, which von Wright calls *anankastic statements*, may have a logical connection with directives or technical norms. However, it would "be a mistake . . . to identify technical norms with anankastic propositions" (ibid., p. 10).[1]

Our stipulative statements therefore seem to be "rules of a game" or "technical norms". That they are not recognized as such may be due to the predominant tendency to assert the "value-freedom" of social science. It may also be due to a lack of analytical interest in the statements which form the basis of social psychological and sociological theories.

There may be a third reason. We mentioned earlier that stipulative statements in the social sciences are able to function as self-fulfilling prophecies (see p. 124). This function is due to their normative character and as such they can contribute towards change in agreement with the content of the statement.

There is also a fourth reason why stipulative statements are not considered to be normative. We may ask: How are stipulations selected? Is it done randomly or is there a basis for selection? My answer would be that the choice expresses the preferences of the researcher, consciously or unconsciously. But preferences reflect values. Given a certain valuation we prefer certain types of stipulative statements to others. By relating rules of the game and technical norms to preferences and values we find another reason why the case of a "value-free science" can easily be defended. Even if a person concedes that stipulative statements are norms, he can deny that they are value-loaded by referring to the distinction between values and norms. If he is not interested in studying the way stipulations are selected, he can easily uphold the doctrine of a value-free science by referring to the fact that stipulations are norms, no more and no less. Norms may direct behaviour but do not as such express values.

This is correct in spite of the fact that there is a relationship between norms and values (see the discussion by von Wright, 1963b, pp. 155ff.). In addition to the problem of the relationship between norms and values there is another problem: Which of them is more basic? Von Wright distinguishes between an *ethics of value*, assuming that values are fundamental and norms extracted from them, and an *ethics of duty*,

---

[1] An example of an anankastic statement is: "If the hut is to be made habitable, it ought to be heated." This is a *descriptive* proposition, expressing a logical necessity. The sentence "If you want to make the hut habitable, you ought to heat it" expresses a technical norm and is prescriptive.

which considers norms expressing duties as basic (ibid., p. 156). I do not wish and do not need to take a stand on this issue. However, if I were to do so my hypothesis would be that postulates are selected according to values and, when selected, reinforce them; thus a feedback relationship could exist between norms and values.

Using a common distinction between norms and values we may call norm concepts *deontological* and value concepts *axiological*. However, von Wright introduces a third category of interest to us: concepts which have to do with Man as an agent. They are related to norms and values and are called *praxeological* concepts (1968, p. 12). The relationship between praxeological concepts concerning Man as an agent or Man's nature on the one hand and value concepts on the other is not clear. If one wants to base ethics on a philosophical anthropology, one may consider praxeology as a "preliminary to or a preparation for the study of norms and values, or one can view it as a more comprehensive field of study of which axiology and deontology are two branches or off-shoots" (von Wright, 1968, prefers the second conception as being more fruitful).

This distinction is useful for our purposes. Our stipulations concern statements about Man as an agent, about Man's nature and the nature of society. They are therefore not only normative sentences but also may be classified as praxeological ones, i.e. as belonging to a philo-sophical anthropology preceding and founding the basis for empirical theories concerning Man and society. The normative expressions—formulated as rules of the games and technical norms—may then be perceived as being in one way or another inferred from broader philo-sophical anthropological conceptions. I would guess that statements containing such conceptions may often be confused with descriptive statements or statements expressing hypotheses of an empirical nature.

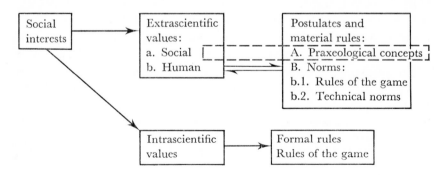

The fifth reason why the nature of postulates is not recognized may be due to the fact that a distinction between philosophical anthropology and a "general theory of action or human behaviour" is not upheld.

We can now represent in a diagrammatic way (see p. 180) our attempt at analysis.

5.2   VALUES AND INTERESTS

Stipulations and material rules are related to extra-scientific values of which there are two kinds. The first may be called *social values*. These concern the way a society is shaped, that is, if there is democratic rule, the way its institutions function, such as the existence of a "free market system" in the sphere of economy, and, finally, the goals which *ought* to be achieved, for example with regard to the distribution of goods which are scarce. The second class of values concerns either human abilities or characteristics which are conceived of as instrumental for the achievement of social goals which may be, or which for one reason or another are considered desirable "as such". These might properly be called "human values".

How are stipulations related to these values? Let us again use the previously quoted sentence by Parsons: "If a system is to constitute a persistent order or to undergo an orderly process of developmental change, certain functional prerequisites must be met." We can assume that this sentence states a technical norm or a directive. According to the previous analysis the antecedent states something which is wanted and the consequent conditions which ought to be or must be fulfilled. The question is whether it is possible to make inferences about certain values from analysing that which is wanted. What is wanted is a "social system in persistent order" or "an orderly process of developmental change". Depending on what is meant by "order", certain states seem to be rejected, e.g. states in which conflicts prevail. Therefore social control may be valued highly and that which is to be controlled, namely deviant behaviour, may be negatively valued.

If any of the stipulations in a theory can be formulated as technical norms, and if their antecedents state what is wanted, *values* can be derived from that which is wanted. This can be done either by spelling out the conditions which must be met to achieve that which is wanted or by clarifying what must be *excluded* as unwanted. The conditions which must be met may themselves express values or they may be related to values either causally or logically. That which is not wanted is in turn related to conditions which either in themselves may express negative values or may be causally or logically related to such values. (For a discussion of this problem see von Wright, 1963b, chapters 2 and 3.)

Now we can understand more easily how the dogmatic belief in a "value-free science" can be upheld. Values, according to our reasoning, do not enter directly into social scientific theories: they do so through their causal or logical relationship to stipulations. If one wants to uphold the doctrine of a value-free science one can either deny the relationship between values and stipulations, or deny the normative nature of stipulations and consider them to be descriptive statements. If the normative nature of stipulations is concealed it is easy to deny that they have to do with values. If, however, they are analysed as rules of the game and technical norms then their relations to values can easily be established.

We have said that social values are responsible for the selection of certain stipulations, which also implies that the acceptance of certain stipulations as a basis for empirical theories presupposes certain values standing in either a causal or logical relationship to these postulates.

In our diagram the box labelled "extrascientific values" is not the first one shown: it is preceded by another box labelled "social interests". The arrow between the boxes indicates that social and human values are determined by "social interests". Since this term is ambiguous (see Bergström (1970) who distinguishes between "subjective" and "objective", "normative" and "naturalistic" dimensions), it should be clarified. First, we will restrict the term to refer to "interests with regard to scientific activity"; and second, restrict it to the interests of those enacting solely the role of a scientist. Hence we may say that interests with regard to scientific activity are institutionalized strivings or aspirations determining the goal(s) of scientific activity. For example, an interest in scientific activity may be for the sake of acquiring knowledge, either "as such" or to obtain certain types of knowledge, e.g. empirical knowledge. Scientific activity may be carried out for the sake of being useful. Another instrumental goal may be to use scientific results as a means for social control or the control of nature; yet another might be to gain an "understanding" of phenomena, which may be the same as "getting an explanation" of what a phenomenon *means*. Finally, one goal, which is also instrumental, involves using science and its results in order to change society according to certain aims and values.

Institutionalized interests are therefore determined by social norms and values.

Habermas (1968a, 1968b) has developed a paradigm in which he relates societal conditions to "knowledge-guiding interests", types of research and research objectives. Without claiming to be faithful to Habermas I shall attempt to build upon his viewpoints in order to give my own interpretation of his paradigm. Habermas delineates three main social "media", namely *work*, *language* and *social power*. "Work" is to be construed in a very general way, in the broad sense in which Marx talks about the "basic process of material production". It comprises all those processes by which we produce the necessities of our life and by which we thus reproduce our life in a daily continuing process. The basic social process of work or production comprises "the manipulation of the environment, physical and social, including the manipulation of ourselves when we attempt to adjust to an immediate environment" (Radnitzki, 1970, vol. 2, p. 5). Instead of using the word "manipulation" in all its ambiguity, we can talk about attempts to transform "surrounding nature" into means of human need-satisfaction and the attempts in this process to exert control over resources and to rule men participating in this process.

Language as a means of communication and of understanding is the second medium. Language as the medium of symbolic interaction concerns actual communication as well as the transmission of traditional values, the products of past cultural activities (what Simmel calls "objectified culture", i.e. the products of cultural activities as written down and preserved). The goal of research activity concerned with "language" in this broad sense is twofold: (1) to mediate "understanding" and "making comprehensible" that which is "strange" (e.g. when analysing so-called "primitive societies" or when interpreting historical events as expressed in contemporary documents), which means trying to make comprehensible that which is "strange" and "different" by means of reflection leading to alternative interpretation; (2) to examine that which is understood and often considered as "natural" and "self-evident", that is to analyse the context of the "known environment" (Habermas, 1970), to question it by revealing it as not self-evident but much more problematical than we would accept from a first-hand impression.

5.3 A SHORT DIGRESSION ON LANGUAGE

Let us, with the object of making some analytical distinctions, return to the epistemological model described at the beginning of this chapter (p. 128).

We asserted that Marx's basic premiss is that Man creates his world in two ways: by theoretically constructing what he wishes to do and by realizing his ideas in work carried out, e.g. through complex tools and machines. Marx compares human work with activities carried out by animals, and asks what differentiates human work from the "work" performed by animals. His answer is briefly this: A spider carries out operations similar to a weaver's; and a bee is sometimes superior to a building contractor in its constructing activity. Nevertheless, in one aspect the worst building contractor is superior to the most excellent bee: the "cells" he builds have been previously envisaged in his mind. Therefore, at the end of the working process the result is equivalent (or similar) to the notions in the mind of the worker. Man first creates concepts of those objects which he thereafter constructs. ("Capital", vol. I, p. 193.)

We may add that a large part of Man's concepts are, however, not created in a new fashion but are learned and transmitted through tradition. Thus the concepts learned and transmitted as well as those which are new and original assign meaning to the words which they connote. Cognitive creation means constructing ideas and either applying them to reality, to give them meaning, or creating a reality in accordance with these ideas.

The material world and the world of social facts are accordingly created by Man in a dual way: through cognitive processes and through work. In human work Man's ideas are materialized or objectified, to use Marx's and Simmel's terms. Man, consequently, has to cope with the world of material objects partly created by himself and partly to be found as his natural habitat. Furthermore, he has to deal with the world of social facts, as exemplified by social institutions through which the basic work process or process of material production is regulated and controlled, i.e. the authority or the power structure of a society.

Man has notions and ideas about the material world as well as about the social world; these notions assign meaning to his material and social world and are expressed in his daily language. But theories about these phenomena, like the one illustrated in the diagram below, are formulated in a language which differs from everyday language. Therefore it is important to investigate the relationship between everyday language about the material and social world and the theoretical language of science dealing with the material and social world. One central hypothesis to be stated now is that everyday language has a *mediating function* between the material and the social world on the one hand and theories about these worlds on the other.

To make the picture more complete we can add a meta-language stating rules for the construction and use of a theoretical language. We will illustrate what has been said in a simple diagram.

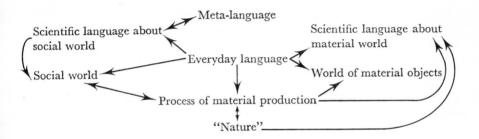

The process of material production does not only create the world of material objects, but also strongly influences the formation of the social world and is itself influenced by it. This social world, however, is at the same time constructed by means of the scientific language of the social sciences about the social world and through everyday language, by which this world acquires meaning. Moreover, everyday language has also an important mediating function for the development of a scientific language about the social world and of a scientific language about the world of material objects.

Scientific languages in turn are constructed with the help of meta-languages. In the present diagrammatic model there is one feature which ought to be emphasized. We have been talking about "constructing" the world. This term refers to two processes: (1) to the process of creation, of "bringing about", e.g. when a car is built in a factory or when a social institution is formed; (2) to the process by which meaning is conferred on material objects and social facts.

The scientific language about the material world is, on the one hand, about "nature", as in the language of theoretical physics. This language has a constructing function *only in the second use* of the term; thus "atoms"

G

are not "brought about" by the language of theoretical physics. On the other hand the scientific language about the material world is also about the process of material production by which "nature" is transformed into objects (and at the same time is affected through pollution for instance). This second type of language about the material world is the language of applied science, e.g. of technology. It has indirectly *a constructing function in the first sense* of the term because it provides the conceptual tools for the production process.

The scientific language about the social world, i.e. of the social sciences, has a constructing function in both senses in which the term is used. Consequently the technological function of "bringing about" the social world cannot be separated from the function of conferring meaning upon this world. Therefore the social sciences are always also a technology regardless of whether their representatives wish or intend it. Social scientific "technology" also concerns the aims of society and the means by which they are achieved. This is also one of the problems of ethics. Hence ethics and social science cannot be completely separated: neither can a theory of action be separated from a theory of change (for a discussion of this problem see p. 202).

This combined double constructing function of the social sciences, as compared to the separated constructing functions of the natural sciences, is the foundation for the basic difference between social and natural sciences.

By assigning to everyday language an important mediating function, the study of this language acquires a central importance for the social scientist. It helps him to understand the social world and his own role in it. Consequently, reflection about social reality and self-reflection about his own activity may lead to a transcendence of the limits set up by carrying out daily activities in an unreflected way, irrespectively of whether these activities consist of manual work or of mental effort in the literary, artistic, and scientific fields.

5.4 ON SOCIAL POWER

So far we have treated two media: *work* and *language*. Let us now briefly analyse a third medium, namely *social power*. Work is the means of production and reproduction of our daily lives; and language is the means of communication and understanding of the world in which this production occurs.

It is my contention that social power sets the goals for *work*, i.e. for the basic process of production by which we reproduce our lives. But it does not only set the goals; it also influences the formation of the institutional devices within which goals are strived for. "Institutional devices" refer to economic systems, for example those characterized by "free market" conditions versus planning and those characterized by private versus socialized ownership of means of production. Institutional devices refer also to different systems of political organization and of the distribution of various means of power, e.g. economic, political, military and ideological. Social power "involves the conscious drawing up, from an ethical base, plans, strategies and political lines and acting with these as guides in concrete situations" (Radnitzki, op. cit., p. 7). In this respect social science becomes a branch of ethics or at least becomes impregnated with ethical problems.[1] What does this mean? Does it mean that social science should aim at setting goals and trying to direct human behaviour towards these goals? A more realistic, and at the same time a more accurate, description would be that such a social science aims at the criticism of ideologies. By "ideology" I mean a scientific or quasi-scientific theory defending existing social conditions or by implication leading to such a defence. Social psychological and sociological theories are permeated with ideological elements as may have been shown in our previous discussion, partly because they are founded upon stipulative statements of which values form the basis. This means that they are indirectly and sometimes directly based upon certain values aiming at certain goals. It is the task of a critical social science dealing with the medium of social power to analyse ideologies and to reveal existing social objectives and their consequences. For example, take the nearly undisputed goal of highly industrialized societies with varying political systems to achieve constant and continuous economic growth. The task of a critical social science ought to be

---

[1] One may object to this assumption by referring to the accepted distinction between meta-ethics and normative ethics. One could then deny that social science *qua* science could deal with problems of normative ethics. However, I am not sure whether the distinction between meta-ethics and normative ethics is watertight. I accept von Wright's position (1963b). He asserts that enquiries into the meaning of ethical concepts lead to stipulative definitions and asks: "Is it in the 'stipulative' nature of their results that the affinity of these enquiries to 'normative' ethics consists"? (p. 5.) The conclusion he draws is: "I have not wanted to deny that there is an activity deserving the name 'meta-ethics' and another deserving the name 'normative ethics' . . . But I have wanted to say that there is also a philosophic pursuit deserving the name 'ethics', which shares with a common conception of 'meta-ethics' the feature of being a *conceptual investigation* and with a common conception of 'normative ethics' the feature of aiming at *directing our lives*." (p. 6.)

to make explicit such and other goals, and to indicate the social consequences of pursuing such goals both for the highly industrialized and
the less industrialized societies, while analysing the present consequences
and the future dangers which may arise. Such a social science ought
also to construct alternative social goals and think through and foresee
their consequences.

5.5   THE SUGGESTED MODEL

In Habermas' paradigm the three media of work, language and social
power correspond to three types of science: *a positivistic-empirical science*;
a historical and hermeneutic social science; and finally *a critical social science*.
These three types of science are built on three types of knowledge, which
Habermas labels "information", "interpretation" and "criticism".
Lastly, these three types of knowledge are related to three types of
research-guiding interests; that is, interests which determine the search
for knowledge and, what is equally important, the *type* of knowledge to
be sought. This type of knowledge in turn is due to the methodology
developed. The positivistic-empirical science is, according to Habermas,
mainly interested in theories explaining reality in such a way as to
ensure information about and control of activity, i.e. necessary for the
process of production. Its research-guiding interest is to acquire knowledge which is instrumental to technical control of the environment
(1968a, p. 157). This means developing an exact and precise science
based upon empirical knowledge forming the basis for technological
application. Its criterion of validity is pragmatic: successful application.
   Hermeneutic science is guided by a different research interest:
through reflection, self-reflection and interpretative activity to assign
"meaning" to reality and thereby to create an "understanding" of the
social world.
   A critical social science is guided by normative, ethical interests. It
tries to apply critical analysis and self-reflection to scientific procedures
as well as to the results of science. It aims at an increased awareness of
the world in which we live. Thence it may contribute to the development
of theoretical foundations for emancipation from existing dangers. The
research-guiding interest of a critical social science is therefore *emancipatory*.
   I do not share with Habermas the idea that it would be possible to
divide sharply the interests guiding the acquisition of knowledge by an

analysis of various types of sciences. I believe that there may be overlapping interests or at least more than one dominating interest for each type of science. But this is not the main point. It seems that Habermas' paradigm differentiates three types of interest in obtaining knowledge which do not necessarily correspond to private motivations of single

Model of the research process

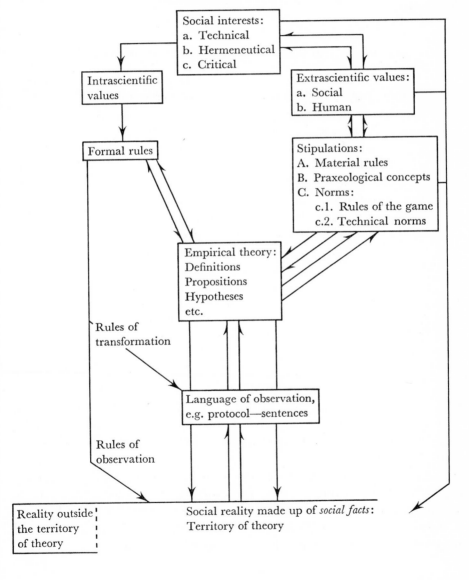

scientists, but are socially institutionalized motives for developing and supporting research. Interests which are technical—in a broad sense—as well as emancipatory, and those which aim at gaining understanding may each affect the selection of values, which in turn could affect the choice of stipulations.

Now, with the help of the new and more complete diagram shown on p. 189, we shall discuss the consequences of accepting the model which it depicts.

5.6 THE MODEL AND SOME OF ITS PROBLEMATIC FEATURES

We have now supplemented our model to include boxes referring to empirical theories and to the language of observation. We have also added rules of transformation and of observation. We do not need to elaborate these boxes and their content since they are well known to those who have been trained in the positivist-empirical tradition.

We have also indicated the territory of a theory or the world *about* and *in* which research is done. If we equalize the territory with "reality" we can, as we have done, divide reality roughly into two parts. One is the reality studied by the natural sciences, such as physics; the other is the reality studied by the social sciences. The territory of the social sciences is not closed: it has been left open deliberately. The reason is that social sciences studies *social* facts.

Before we elaborate upon the specific nature of social facts, let us make a short explication of what we mean by "facts". Following von Wright (1963a, pp. 255ff.), we distinguish between three classes of facts: *states of affairs, processes* and *events*. "Processes and events are things which happen, but unlike the happening of processes, the happening of events is *a taking place* and not a going on." (von Wright, ibid., p. 26.) In addition we may say that the beginning and the end of a process may both be regarded as events (ibid., p. 27): "The transition from an *initial* state of affairs ceases to be or *comes* to be. When a state continues to be, the world is unchanged with regard to this state." (von Wright, 1968, p. 39.)

Events imply changes occurring when there is a transition from one state of affairs to another. The transition may also occur from a state to a process or from a process to a state. Before we return to our subject we may introduce an additional distinction, that between *individual* and *generic* states. For example the state that the sun is shining is generic: it can occur at different places and at different times. When the sun shines now and here it is an individual state. Thus: "An individual state is a generic state instantiated." (von Wright, op. cit., 1968, p. 40.)

One important problem of our model—and I think one of the central problems of social science in general—concerns the territory of investigation. In the theoretical natural sciences, the world which is the object of research is clearly differentiated from the world of the scientist. In the social sciences the territory of research—the social world—is the reality to which the scientist belongs. He is inside that which he studies. And this is the first problematic feature.

However, there is still another and more complicated problem. In our model we have left the territory of the social sciences open, because we want to indicate that social facts also comprise values and interests. In fact they also comprise stipulations so far as they are identified as norms. Values are social facts in the sense of "states of affairs". They are *individual* as well as *generic* states.

As individual states they are the *object* of the study of empirical social research as is any other social fact. As with *generic* states, they *influence exactly the same empirical theories* as treat social facts, be they values, other states, events or processes. They influence empirical theories by being responsible for the selection of those stipulative statements which form the foundation of empirical theories. Thus the assertion that theories in the social sciences are value-laden means in the interpretation we are attempting (or it can at least mean) that values function as delimiting factors. Once chosen these delimit a scientist's possible action. His actions are in general limited in two ways: (1) with regard to his ability, which here does not mean only his professional qualifications but also refers to the limits imposed upon him by his social role as a scientist; (2) with regard to the goals "which science sets for itself". In other words he is limited by research-guiding interests prevalent in his culture. These interests are themselves mediated through values and stipulations and hence set limits to the content of the theory which is constructed. Thus scientific research is viewed as a constructing cognotive process.

This implies questioning the basis for accepting: (1) that *theories mirror or reflect social facts*; or (2) *the more primitive notion that social facts can be described without an organizing frame of a theoretical kind*. Empirical theories hence *partly* construct the social world. By "partly" we mean that they do not and cannot do so independently of the existing reality.

5.7 THE "CONSTRUCTIONAL" APPROACH

What is meant by the statement that empirical theories partly "construct" that which they deal with? Let us recollect the two senses in which we previously used the word "construction": that is *"conferring meaning"* and *"bringing about"*.

A theory of society "confers meaning" by the very fact that it precedes the collection of data,[1] and that it influences procedures of empirical science (e.g. observational methods) and thereby determines which data can be obtained. Furthermore, when data are "interpreted" and "scientific knowledge" is obtained, "meaning is conferred" again, but this time on the data collected. Only theories make data relevant. The interpreted data in turn affect and reorganize the original theory.

Those who cherish the notion that a theory "reflects" reality usually assume that reality "forces itself" in one way or another upon a theory and that organization, systematization or classification of data is "inherent in the nature" of reality. Consequently, they consider empirical data as influencing theory, but tend to reject the idea of the converse effect, i.e. that a theory should be able to affect reality.

The main problem of an empirical science thinking in terms of a theory "reflecting" or "mirroring" reality then becomes the development of reliable instruments and methods which would be able to "reflect" reality in a valid way.

In the "constructional" approach the relationship between theory and reality is *mutual*. Theories organize data; but only theories confer meaning upon them. Nevertheless data cannot be arbitrarily organized: theories have to take into account the "structure of reality". The concept of "structure", therefore, has a different place in the so-called reflectional approach than in the so-called constructional approach. There are at least two types of "reflectional" approach. In the first, it is not desired to say anything about the "nature of reality". True knowledge is considered to be the agreement between a judgement and data: no assumptions are made about the relationship between data and reality. "Structure", therefore, is something which characterizes a theory and has nothing to do with reality.

A second "reflectional" approach, e.g. the one characterizing a

---

[1] This is also the case even if theories are not explicitly formulated as in the type of empirical research which calls itself "purely descriptive". Implicit theoretical notions are always present, however primitive they may be.

vulgar interpretation of Marxism, assumes that "structure" is something inherent in and characterizing reality. This "structure of reality" is "mirrored" or reflected in the theory. However, it is not clear how this reflection occurs, since theory does not necessarily have a "structure" of its own.

Finally, in the "constructional" approach "structure" is considered to be something characterizing the theory as well as something inherent in reality. Thus, it is assumed that there exists an isomorphy between the "structure of a theory" and the "structure of reality". The function of a theory is not only to explain reality: it must also contribute to the creation of this reality, for example as a self-fulfilling prophecy. Therefore, one can truly talk about a mutual relationship between theory and reality.[1]

The "reflectional" and the "constructional" approach are also related to the analogy models used in social psychological and in sociological theories. The use of a mechanical model often implies a "reflectional" approach, and Duncan, in reviewing Parsons' theories, remarks that in these theories "actors are being moved by mechanical processes which are the expression of patterns in which norms are cathected" (1968, p. 16). This is not a parody, but a part of the approach in which " 'acts' are 'integrated', their patterns 'maintained' or their structure 'organized' " (ibid., p. 4). Duncan adds that when one examines closely how this organization occurs, one finds that the processes with which the theory deals cannot be demonstrated in social life: they can only be alleged to exist. Consequently, "construction" also occurs in the "reflectional" approach. But the word "construction" here acquires a *third meaning*, namely that of "making up". This in turn depends on the fact that "structure" is only "located" within the theory and not within social reality.

Another point to be stressed is the following. One main fallacy in the "reflectional" approach is the underlying assumption that data are considered to be objective in the sense of being independent of the subject collecting them. This illusion is upheld by the emphasis on "objective" methods of data collection. Although these methods may in some sense be "objective", the data collected by them are not

---

[1] In the structuralist approach as represented, for instance, by Lévi-Strauss, "structure", as I understand it, refers to linguistic rules establishing definite relations between elements. Such a structure, then, can be applied to social reality, to sub-systems within it, as well as to theories. Thus, "structure" seems to refer to a general organizing principle.

independent but dependent on theories. In addition, even if procedures are "objective", that which is collected by them may to a large extent be "constructed" in the sense of being "made up" by the procedures themselves: the answers received depend upon the questions asked.

The "constructionist" approach has consequences also for the debate concerning the value-freedom of science. What is the difference between the "constructionist" approach and the one advanced by Myrdal, for example, which asserts that values enter into the selection of research problems and the ways in which these problems are conceptualized and studied?

To answer this question and to clarify further the "constructionist" approach, let me present an example. Reissman and Halstead (1970) reviewed three major American sociological journals, looking for articles concerned with stratification. Sixty-eight per cent of the material found used "status" as a central concept, whereas only eight per cent used a "class" concept. The authors draw the following conclusion from their review:

> One might argue then that this distribution "provides" that status and not class *is* the dominant American *reality*. However, it is more proper to say that this heavy emphasis upon status is only the sociologist's choice for research convenience rather than a *valid reflection* of social reality [my italics].
>
> Ibid., pp. 297–298

This quotation expresses the idea that there exists a social reality which is *reflected* in existing theories, but that certain types of habitual behaviour like "research convenience" lead to an incorrect conceptualization.

This is an example of the "reflectional" position.

Reissman and Halstead desired to show that "class theories" in American sociology are neglected in favour of "status theories". They have endeavoured to explain this by referring to the scientist's "choice for research convenience". Although this expression is somewhat unclear, it can be interpreted in terms of values which influence the choice of research problems and the conceptualization of these problems. Their argument is in agreement with the Myrdal tradition. Marxists could say that the researchers were influenced by their class position to take a certain "ideological" stand. Therefore, their theories do not "reflect" scientific facts but values or ideologies, indicating that the researcher has a "false consciousness". Such an explanation takes for granted what it wants to prove, namely that classes are social facts and that society is a "class society" (which may be correct).

It is interesting how similar the two explanations are. But still they fail to realize a central point: one will find "status differences" if one conceptualizes them, and one will find "class differences" instead if these are the basis for conceptualization, since a theory can bring about exactly that which it pretends to have discovered.

The problem is consequently this: Is every type of conceptualization equally good? How can we choose between different types of theories, e.g. between "status theories" and "class theories"? This latter question will be discussed in the last section.

We can now summarize. For several reasons I wish to reject the notion of theories "reflecting" or "mirroring" reality. Theories not only organize and systematize data, but also interpret them. The moment we interpret data we must abandon the idea that they "mirror" or "reflect" reality. Consequently, I maintain that theories assign meaning to reality through the interpretation of data collected in social scientific enquiry. However, it is not only the social scientist who confers meaning upon social reality; other people do the same in their everyday life. Therefore one task of social science is to discover the meaning people assign to reality; but at the same time social scientists must be aware that when they try to interpret the meaning which people in general assign to social reality, they may confer a new meaning upon the meaning which social facts have acquired in daily language.

W. I. Thomas' well-known thesis states that if people define a situation as real, it will be real in its consequences. This applies to the activity of scientists as well as to those of people in their daily lives.

What are the consequences of the fact that meaning has been conferred upon social reality? The answer brings us to the second sense in which social science "constructs" reality, namely to the way in which it "brings it about". Let me take an example. Economics has traditionally considered air and water as utilities which can be used freely. Consequently the pollution of water and air has not been included when computing production costs. This has undoubtedly contributed to the immense social problem that pollution has become. Thus social science, by means of its concepts and theories, may "bring about" directly or indirectly, by influencing politics or the conceptions of people, the social world it studies.

There is a second sense in which the social sciences can "bring about" facts through their theories: by functioning as self-fulfilling prophecies, when the very prediction arrived at on the basis of theories concerning certain phenomena can create these phenomena or alternatively prevent their future existence.

We have often disregarded the role which reflecting about *our own scientific activities* plays in research. Instead attention has been concentrated on the content of the boxes in the lower half of the diagram presented on page 189, while to a large extent disregarding the upper half. We have usually been content with stopping at the level of "empirical theories," if we have not already let ourselves be satisfied with the mere collection of data and the computation of correlations between them. This emphasis on "low-level" activities has had its consequences. One of them is that theories have become "suspended in the air", since the preconditions on which they are founded have often been neglected. In order to overcome these shortcomings, the contents of the boxes in the upper half of our diagram must be included in the total research process. But that alone will not solve all the difficulties.

Another complicated problem is that values in themselves are social facts. I have pointed out that as individual states they may be the object of empirical research. As generic states they influence the formulation of social science theories. But as generic states they may in addition give rise to or bring about other social facts—especially events and processes—which social science studies.

Social facts, like events and processes, are historical facts in the sense that they occur due to specific historical conditions: they are not "eternal facts". The type of social organization we may find in a highly industrialized Western society and its institutions, as well as "the type of human nature" that exists now, are conditioned by a long process of development. They change and it is probable that they do so more rapidly now than before. If we adhere to the principle of methodological individualism as interpreted earlier in this paper, we have to accept that the world in which we live is "man-made", even if the institutions created by men may display their own conformity to laws. If we consider a society as a system, then Man is one of the elements in this system and he is affected by it even at the same time as he changes it.

Social values, and especially the values which are related to "social goals", belong to the most important factors determining the structure of society. Take as an example the existing sex-role differentiation. A social scientist will have not difficulty in finding a difference in income for the two sexes even if they carry out the same work. Sex-role differentiation and its consequent discrimination in income are social facts; they are historically conditioned social facts.

What is the meaning of the expression "historically conditioned"? One interpretation is that social facts are determined by certain social values and goals and by the social structure related to these goals. A majority of social facts—and this could be exemplified—are created under the influence of "generally" accepted values and goals.

The problems social science has to deal with accordingly are fourfold:
1. Scientists belong to the very same reality which they study and are influenced by it.
2. Social reality is constructed by social science theories in the double sense discussed on the previous pages. This problem is located in our model at the level of the box labelled "empirical theories".
3. Another process of construction concerns the empirical theories themselves. These are determined by stipulations which themselves depend on certain social facts, i.e. values, located higher up in our model. In this context we are mainly interested in how stipulations *delimit* the type of empirical theory used.
4. An additional process of construction is related to the notion that social reality itself is determined by certain social facts, for example by goals which are themselves a part of this social reality. This is indicated by the arrows in our diagram originating from the high-level boxes and directed towards the territory of the theory. Consequently, our model could be more adequately constructed so that everything located "above" the territory would be a part of this territory.

The social scientist is thus faced with the problems which arise in the analysis of a totality. He is himself part of a system in which certain elements generate other important elements and where the first mentioned elements at the same time delimit the theories which try to explain these elements and their functioning. Viewed in such a perspective the task of a social scientist is comparable to the well-known activity of lifting oneself by one's own boot-straps. To stop here would make the analysis self-defeating. For that reason I would like to indicate ways out of this meta-theoretical labyrinth.

6   Some tentative suggestions concerning the choice of stipulations and empirical theories

6.1   A DILEMMA PRODUCED BY THE MODEL

One solution of the problem posed which we want to suggest here can be sought at the level of the boxes labelled "stipulations" and "extra-scientific values". Accepting our model as the basis, we have to discuss the implication of the twofold generating or constructing role of values. It has been asserted that values bring about or generate social facts, as exemplified before, and that they have an important indirect influence on empirical theories by determining to a large extent the selection of stipulations. At the same time the acceptance of certain stipulations may have repercussions on the social values being accepted and thus affect the construction of social facts.

We must therefore ask: How can one as a social scientist select stipulations which, on the one hand, generate empirical theories of which we can expect that their structure has a satisfying correspondence to the structure of the social world, and which, on the other hand, affect the values which are partly responsible for the creation of social facts in a continuous process of change?

Before we can answer this question we have to deal with a rather disturbing condition. The model which was presented in the last section is not merely a meta-theoretical model. As such it presupposes a certain ontological position; it contains namely the inherent property of having been built upon certain stipulations about the "nature" of Man and society. In other words, the meta-theoretical model which we have suggested as a basis for social scientific research and which contains stipulations about Man and society as an important feature presupposes in itself the acceptance of certain stipulations. The case is still more complicated: the stipulations to which we have assigned in our previous discussion a certain preference and which we wish to use as alternatives to those in the traditional, "positivistic" social science are the ones which contribute to the generation of our model. If this reasoning is correct, the solution we suggest is of the following kind: In order to solve problems brought into the open by the model, we suggest the acceptance of certain stipulative assumptions which have played an important role in generating the model. A simple solution to our dilemma, therefore, may be to refute the model. If we do this, the problems which characterize social science when such a model is accepted may not arise when other models are used as a basis to work from. I myself would call such a procedure throwing out the child with the bath water. Those who repudiate the model may deny that there even has been a child.

How, then, can we solve the problem? It seems there are three possibilities: (1) one can assert that different models exist and no reasonable choice can be made between alternative models; (2) one can seek recourse to ultimate standards of justification to select one approach; (3) one can apply the approach of a critical theory.

The first position states that any approach may be viewed as being as good (or as bad) as any other. Therefore we cannot make rational choices between general models, between the stipulations one accepts or rejects and, in consequence, between competing empirical theories. Thus, we may end up in general scepticism; there is no rational choice possible. Another conclusion may be to attempt to seek refuge in certain ultimate standards, e.g. values, and let them determine which theoretical approach one may choose. However, it is doubtful whether, on the whole, one can *justify* a choice of a certain theory by reference to any ultimate standards.

W. W. Bartley analyses in an interesting essay on "rationality versus the theory of rationality" the "scepticist" solution as well as the solution seeking recourse to values or other non-rational standards. This approach he terms the "fideist". Both the "scepticist" and the "fideist" approach rest on the same claim, namely: *"From a rational point of view, the choice between competing beliefs and ways of life, whether scientific, mathematical, moral, religious, metaphysical, political, or other is arbitrary."* (1964, p. 5.) The problem is to show by means of rational arguments that it is logically impossible to make choices on rational grounds. Bartley refutes such a position. He asserts that choices have traditionally been justified by reference to some authority functioning as an ultimate standard. "Reason" or "empirical findings based upon sense experience", for example, have been invoked as authority-standards. Bartley, referring to Popper, shows that the authoritarian tradition to *justify* one's beliefs can be abandoned by accepting the notion of a critical theory or by exposing one's approach to criticism. Before I try to spell out this position, I want to treat shortly the empiricist-positivist claim that there exist *ultimate sources or standards of justification*. These standards are empirical facts. This position corresponds to the second approach.

Popper argues against this type of empiricism in the following way (1969, pp. 21ff.):

1. Most of our assertions are not based upon knowledge acquired through observations, but upon other sources of knowledge. To this an empiricist may answer that other types of knowledge are themselves based on observations if one only carries on one's enquiry sufficiently long. To this argument Popper retorts that it is logically impossible to trace back all knowledge to its ultimate source of observation, since it can be shown that such a procedure would lead to an infinite regression.

2. All observation involves interpretation of that which is observed based upon the theoretical knowledge we already have. Thus, observations are made with pre-notions (*Vorverständniss*).

3. The idea of appealing to ultimate sources or standards does not distinguish sufficiently between questions of origin and questions of validity: "In general we do not test the validity of an assertion or information by tracing its sources or its origins, but we test it much more directly by *a critical examination* [my italics] of what has been asserted—of the asserted facts themselves." (Op. cit., p. 25.) But that presupposes the neglect of the idea that there exist ultimate sources of knowledge, e.g. empirical observations, and the acceptance of the idea that "there are all kinds of sources of our knowledge; but *none has authority*" (ibid., p. 24). As a consequence the authoritarian reference to ultimate sources or standards must be substituted by the attempt to examine critically. This means that among other things the formulation of alternative theories and approaches, especially in the case when one approach—e.g. the empiricist-positivist—may become dogmatic. No rejection of empirical science is implied—as will be shown in the next section—but only the attempt to question its claims of monopoly of how science *ought* to be conducted. The consequence of this demand is "that some of the methods of modern empiricism which are introduced in the spirit of anti-dogmatism and progress are bound to lead to the establishment of a dogmatic metaphysics" (Feyerabend, 1968, p. 13). Though this charge is made against the development within natural sciences it applies, in my opinion, to the social sciences as well.

We shall now return to the problem raised at the beginning of this section. The model we have suggested presupposes the acceptance of some of the stipulations about Man and nature which are a part of the model. It therefore might seem that we are trying to justify our model *within* the scope of its own boundaries. Following a philosophical tradition we can maintain that a statement about our model does not belong to the class of statements which are a part of it. As a result we are left with two questions: (1) How do we justify our general model? (2) If we accept our model how can we choose between different theories? The first problem is—following the line of Popper's argument—a pseudo-problem. We really do not need to justify our general model, but we ought, all the same, to expose it to critical scrutiny. Such a scrutiny may have as *one* of its goals an exploration of the consequences for social scientific research of taking its points of departure in this general model. The second problem will be treated in the next section.

6.2   "WITHIN-CELL" AND "BETWEEN-CELL" DIFFERENCES

Before we can discuss problems of choice I will try to make clear my points by using a picture from statistical theory, more precisely from analysis of variance in which one differentiates between "within-cell" differences and "between-cell" differences. The application of this picture may be made clearer in the following way: Assume that when analysing the nature of society we have two social scientific theories, one based on a mechanistic analogy model and the other on a process-model. Both models consequently give rise to two different empirical theories. The first model may give rise to a consensus theory; the other may lead to the formulation of a conflict theory. The two analogy models and the empirical theories connected with them thus belong to the *class of empirical theories* about society. The differences between them, depending among other things on the different stipulations and assumptions preceding the formulation of the empirical theories presenting different points of departure and therefore alternative approaches, may be labelled "within-cell differences". This label underlines that the two theories can be subsumed under the same class of empirical social scientific theories.

Now let us differentiate between this class of *empirical theories* and a class of *critical theories*. The first class of empirical theories represents different and alternative theoretical approaches to the construction, study and explanation of the social reality. The other class of theories, those labelled "critical" (and there is not only one "critical theory"), does not deal with empirical problems at all; its main task is the analysis and examination of existing empirical theories including their stipulations and the formulation and presentation of alternatives on the basis of this criticism. Thus the differences between the class of critical theories and the class of empirical theories may be labelled "between-cell" differences.

Having made this distinction, I shall put forward the claim that a choice of a certain analogy model, its implicit stipulations and formal rules, e.g. those which may be labelled as "positivistic", and the empirical theory based upon such a foundation, may be questioned on rational grounds with the help of a critical theory. A critical theory, however, presupposes and can only function in relation to other theories, e.g. the empirical ones.

In a previous section I presented a general model including those conditions which may affect and delimit the formulation of an empirical theory, like social interests, values, normative stipulations. However, such a general model is also built upon certain assumptions and implies the preference for a certain type of empirical social scientific theory. The development of this general model has been based on a critical examination of predominant tendencies in current social science and ideas about how social science *ought* to be conducted.

There remain two problems to be discussed. One concerns which type of empirical social scientific theory is preferred as a consequence of the acceptance of the general model. What objectives are to be pursued by such an empirical social scientific theory? This problem is, therefore, concerned with "within-cell" problems, namely the consequences of the use of a certain type of empirical theory as compared to other ones. The second problem is concerned with the relationship between critical and empirical theories and is therefore a "between-cell" problem.

6.3   ACTION AND CHANGE

The previous analysis may have made clear my preferences and my aversions. These can be summarized in the following way. I have rejected traditional mechanistic models of Man and society as used by behaviouristic psychology and functionalistic sociology. The rejection is founded upon a basic ontological and epistemological position stressing the image of Man as an active creator of his own social world as well as being the result of the influences to which he as a member of this social world is exposed. This can be summarized by saying that Man is both a subject and an object. In behaviouristic psychology he is treated as an object only. The same holds true for those functionalistic sociological theories stressing consensus and conformity as pre-conditions for social integration, balance and stability. My ontological position is clearly based upon extra-scientific values about Man's role in a social world dominated by powerful social organizations. However, the criticized theories also build on extra-scientific values, though this is usually denied and concealed. In this context one can also criticize the neglect by "positivistic" science of a basic epistemological problem (e.g. the relationship between subject and object), which can be viewed as a consequence of certain meta-theoretical ideas stressing that knowledge is no more nor less than the outcome of scientific investigation. Therefore the problems of epistemology are transformed into those of scientific method.

Furthermore, mechanistic models do not explain social change. Since these usually treat social systems as closed systems, changes within the system can be explained, but changes of the system as such are not possible on the basis of such models and are therefore neglected. Another reason for the relative lack of interest in change is the "positivistic" disposition towards observation and analysing what is given now, i.e. concentration on positive facts.

I have previously given several reasons why it is desirable to place emphasis on change. Some of the arguments were of a heuristic type; others were a consequence of the meta-theoretical position taken. I would like to present a final reason which, it seems, is the most convincing one from a logical point of view. Throughout this analysis the role of stipulations for the formation of social scientific theories and of social reality itself has been emphasized. One central assumption has been that stipulations are normative statements, which means that they state rules for something which is obligatory, permitted, forbidden, etc. The "something" constitutes the *content* of norms. What then is the *content* of norms? I will give here an interesting analysis by von Wright (1968, pp. 38ff.).

He reasons that the content of norms is *action*. However, it is essential to distinguish between four separate types of action; furthermore, the distinctions must be made clear. Let us use the symbol O to refer to an "obligation" and the symbol p to stand for a certain state of affairs. The symbol Op then can be read as "one ought to act in such a manner that the state of affairs p is the result of one's action" (ibid., p. 37).

Now, the type of action in question necessarily depends on the existing state of affairs. Assume that p does not exist, then the norm states that one ought to *produce* p. Assume, however, that p exists; then the norm prescribes "*a forbearance* or *omission* of action" (ibid., p. 38).

Let us look at the symbol Ovp, standing for the normative expression which states: "One ought to act in such a manner that the state of affairs p is *not* the case." What type of action does this norm prescribe? Obviously again it depends on whether p or vp is the case. If the state of affairs is vp, the norm expressed by the symbol states one should not act so as to *destroy* vp and change it into p. In other words, one's action should be an omission. If, however, it is the case that p exists, i.e. that the state of p prevails, then once again the norm states that one should act to produce vp.

One question is forced upon us: What is action? Von Wright, asserting that we may not find an answer to cover all cases, gives the following definition: "To act is intentionally ('at will') to *bring about* or to *prevent* a change in the world (nature). By this definition to forbear (omit) action is either to *leave* something *unchanged* or to *let* something *happen*." (Ibid., p. 38.)[1]

We thus get two types of action, *productive* and *preventive*, and, correspondingly, two types of forbearance or omissions, leading to four elementary kinds of action.

The important conclusion which von Wright draws from this analysis is: "If action consists in the bringing about or preventing of changes, then in order to give an account of action, we must therefore give an

---

[1] This analysis throws some light on the consequences of the attitude taken by a majority of traditional social scientists. They claim that their position with regard to society is neutral, and that social science in the name of value-freedom should not participate in social action. In other words, far from their own claim that they do not take a normative stand, their position can be characterized by the norm not to act at all. In terms of the symbols used this can be depicted as $vOpVvp$, which means that one ought not to act in such a manner that the state of affairs is that p or vp is the result of one's action. In other words, a scientist ought not to act at all. Thus forbearance or omission is his normative position. But, since forbearance either means to "leave something unchanged" or "to let something happen", the representatives of this type of "positivistic" science either—willingly or not—support conservatism or become passive witnesses when things happen. To be conservative is to take a definite stand on matters of value. Therefore the "positivistic" accusation levelled against those rejecting this "positivistic" position, for not being value-free, becomes a boomerang. If, on the other hand, one "lets things happen", one makes oneself accessory in that which happens. This position is not less value-free than the one taken by those recommending an "emancipatory social science". The latter position seems to be preferable from a moral point of view.

account of change." (Ibid., p. 39.) In addition, one can assert that a theory of action presupposes a theory of change. In a certain sense, all social science is concerned with human action and therefore social scientific theory is or ought to be a "general theory of action"; so no social scientific theory which asserts to be "a theory of action" should neglect a theory of change.

What, then, is change? Change takes place, according to von Wright, when there is a transformation of a state of affairs. By this definition we have change when one state of affairs ceases and another begins. When a state continues the world is unchanged but only with regard to this particular state. Changes are brought about by agents. Assume, von Wright says, that we have a world characterized by p at a given time and by vp at a later point in time. Suppose, furthermore, that there is *one* agent in this world, and that we know that if he had not interfered but remained passive the transition from p to vp would not have taken place. In order to be able to describe action in terms of states and their transformation, i.e. in terms of change, three items are necessary: (1) we must know the state of the world just before action starts, i.e. the *initial state*; (2) we must know the state reached when action has been completed, i.e. the *end-state* or the result of action; (3) we must know the state in which the world would be had the agent remained passive (op. cit., p. 43).

States (1) and (3) together constitute the *acting-situation*, or, as von Wright also calls it, the *opportunity* of action; (2) is the result of action. States (1), (2) and (3) together "determine the *nature of action*. In other words, the nature of *action* is determined jointly by *opportunity* and *result*" (op. cit., p. 43).

Since, however, the state of affairs of the world is usually not changed by one agent alone but by several, any theory of action has to be transformed into a theory of *interaction* between agents, bringing about changes or transformations of states of affairs.

This short presentation of von Wright's analysis may furnish the argument for the necessity of including in social scientific theory a theory of change. If this is so, then postulative models which account for change should be preferred.

6.4 CRITICAL AND EMPIRICAL THEORY

The "initial state" of the social world can be described by an empirical social science which reflects about its preconditions, i.e. values and stipulations, and which describes the world "as it is now". Since, however, the acceptance of different preconditions will lead to different descriptions of the world "as it is now", it may well be that *one description* of the world "as it is now" is such that it is neither sufficient nor possible. Instead, different descriptions of initial states may be needed. The first step also includes the identification of the main, dominant or most powerful agents. Again, different alternatives can or may have to be pictured, so that the analysis must proceed to the description of one or several alternative end-states which we may wish to attain or fear and therefore wish to avoid. We must decide how this can best be done. The analysis here has to concentrate on the interference of, and interaction between, existing agents and on the assumption of alternative agents.

Agents are social groups or classes and there are values which are predominant in these groups or classes (this assertion is of a postulative kind). If predominant agents and their values are identified, alternative agents and their values can be postulated. I am trying to follow in this step a suggestion made by Adorno (1966) in his analysis of "negative dialectics".

In order to make this complicated analysis simple I will use a metaphor suggested by Skjervheim (1968). Assume one has been set the task of carrying out a content analysis of a newspaper. It should be possible to obtain two types of data: that which is printed and that which can be read between the lines or which is passed over in silence. Adorno defines that which can be "read" as "positive fact" and that which is passed over in silence as "negative fact". To use the terminology borrowed from von Wright, "positive facts" are states of affairs of the world "as it is now", including its predominant agents, while "negative facts" are facts which do not (yet) exist, but which can be thought to come into existence as the result of certain agents acting or others refraining or being prevented from acting. "Negative facts" or "probable end-states" can, according to Adorno, only be thought of— if one does not want to engage in fiction—in relation to "positive facts", i.e. initial states of the world "as it is now". The dialectical relation between positive and negative facts is, however, not only based on the condition that negative facts have to be related to positive ones as end-states to initial states. Assume that one could bring about a change by influencing dominant agents so that the imagined end-state is achieved. In this case the end-state becomes a positive fact or an existing state of affairs and at the same time—if one sees it as a process—the initial state for further change. Then new, negative facts must be considered.

In order to "construct" negative facts in the social world one has to develop a special social science *alternative* to an empirical or "positivistic" one. This can be labelled as a "critical social science" and has at its research-guiding interest the accomplishment of end-states which mean an emancipation from the world "as it is now". When it is here related to the sort of ethics which analyses concepts and tries to set standards to direct our lives, the nature of a critical social science becomes clear. In other words, the dialectical interplay between an empirical and a critical social science oriented towards ethics is one solution of the dilemma of social science. It presupposes, however, the acceptance of alternative values and goals and, related to them, alternative research-guiding interests.

The function of a critical theory is threefold. It can facilitate the choice between alternative approaches and models, i.e. help solve "within-cell" problems. By pointing out alternative models and theories it contributes to the criticism of an accepted theory, "which goes *beyond* the criticism provided by a comparison of that theory 'with the facts' " (Feyerabend, 1968, p. 15). One can add that the adequacy of a theory can often only be assessed "*after* it has been confronted with alternatives *whose invention and detailed development must therefore precede any final assertion of factual adequacy*" (ibid., p. 15).

The second reason for the development of a critical social science is therefore its anti-dogmatic function. It allows for a sharp criticism of *accepted* ideas, which often appear to be self-evident and are therefore no longer questioned. Thus, empirical theories and, in fact, the central thesis of empiricism, namely that knowledge is restricted to sense experience may, as discussed before, acquire such a strong dogmatic position that they prevent a "change of paradigms" (Kuhn, 1962). Whether an empirical theory acquires a dogmatic function or not depends on societal conditions, especially social and scientific institutions. Empirical science once functioned as a critical theory: during the Middle Ages when it opposed the dogmas of the church. Galileo and Giordano Bruno, to mention two names, represent the critical, anti-dogmatic tradition of empirical science.

Today, however, *empirical social* science is largely dogmatic. One of its convictions, that social science should not be concerned with future goals of a society, but only report observations and explain them, supports, as shown, conservatism. This ideological function of the social sciences can be made clear and disputed by a critical theory. Since, as I have tried to show, ethics and social science cannot be separated in a watertight way, the absence of a critical theory prevents self-reflection about the effects of social science and the activities of the scientists. The existence of a critical theory, on the other hand, may provide the means for an emancipatory social science, badly needed, but of value only if it itself remains undogmatic.

References

Addis, L. (1968). The individual and the Marxist philosophy of history. *In* "Readings in the Philosophy of Social Science" (Ed. M. Brodbeck). Macmillan, New York.

Adorno, T. W. (1966). "Negative Dialektik". Suhrkamp, Frankfurt.

Asplund, J. (1970). G. M. Mead. *In* "Sociologiska Teorier" (Ed. J. Asplund), 3rd ed. Almquist v Wiksell, Stockholm.

Allardt, E. (1970). Konflikt-och Konsensusteoretiker. *In* "Sociologiska Teorier" (Ed. J. Asplund), 3rd ed. Almquist & Wiksell, Stockholm.

Bartley, W. W., III (1964). Rationality versus the theory of rationality. *In* "The Critical Approach to Science and Philosophy" (Ed. M. Bunge). Collier-Macmillan, London.

Bauman, Z. (1969). Modern times, modern Marxism. *In* "Marxism and Sociology" (Ed. P. Berger). Appleton-Century-Crofts, New York.

Bergström, L. (1970). What is a conflict of interests? *Journal of Peace Research*, No. 3, 197–217.

Bertalanffy, L. von (1968). General system theory—a critical review. *In* "Modern Systems Research for the Behavioural Scientist" (Ed. W. Buckley). Aldine, Chicago.

Bertalanffy, L. von (1969). The theory of open systems in physics and biology. *In* "Systems Thinking" (Ed. F. E. Emery). Penguin Books, London.

Brodbeck, M. (1968). Methodological individualism: definition and reduction. *In* "Readings in the Philosophy of Social Sciences" (Ed. M. Brodbeck). Macmillan, New York.

Buckley, M. (1967). "Sociology and Modern Systems Theory". Prentice-Hall, Englewood Cliffs.

Buckley, M. (1968). Society as a complex adaptive system. *In* "Modern System Research for the Behavioural Scientist" (Ed. W. Buckley). Aldine, Chicago.

Carlson, G. (1962). Reflections on functionalism. *Acta Sociologica*, **V**, 201–224.

Churchman, C. W. and Ackoff, R. L. (1968). Purposive behaviour and cybernetics. *In* "Modern System Research for the Behavioural Scientist" (Ed. W. Buckley). Aldine, Chicago.

Cohen, R. S. (1963). Dialectical materialism and Carnap's logical empiricism. *In* "The Philosophy of Rudolf Carnap" (Ed. P. A. Schilpp). The Open Court Publishing Company, Chicago.

Copeland, J. W. (1964). Philosophy disguised as science. *Philosophy of Science*, **31**, 168–172.

Dahrendorf, R. (1958). Out of Utopia: towards a reorientation of sociological analysis. *American Journal of Sociology*, **64**, 115–127.

Dahrendorf, R. (1959). "Class and Class-conflict in an Industrial Society". Routledge & Kegan Paul, London.

Dahrendorf, R. (1967). "Homo Sociologicus". Westdeutscher Verlag, Köln.

Davis, K. (1949). "Human Society". Macmillan, New York.

Deutsch, K. (1966). "The Nerves of Government". The Free Press, New York.

Duncan, H. D. (1968). "Symbols in Society". Oxford University Press, New York.

Durkheim, E. (1966). "The Rules of Sociological Method". (Translated by S. A. Solovay and J. H. Mueller.) The Free Press, New York.

Easton, E. (1965). "A System Analysis of Political Life". John Wiley, New York.

Feyerabend, P. K. (1968). How to be a good empiricist—a plea for tolerance in matters epistemological. *In* "The Philosophy of Science" (Ed. P. H. Nidditch). Oxford University Press, London.

Furth, H. G. (1969). "Piaget and knowledge" (with a foreword by J. Piaget). Prentice-Hall, Engelwood Cliffs, N.J.

Gellner, E. (1968). Holism versus individualism. *In* "Readings in the Philosophy of Science" (Ed. M. Brodbeck). Macmillan, New York.

Goldman, L. (1959). "Recherches Dialectiques". Gallimard, Paris.

Goldstein, L. J. (1960). Review of Winch's "The Idea of a Social Science". *The Philosophical Review*, **69**, No. 4, 411–414.

Habermas, J. (1967). "Zur Logik der Sozialwissenschaften". J. B. C. Mohr, Tübingen.

Habermas, J. (1968a). "Erkentniss und Interesse". Suhrkamp, Frankfurt.

Habermas, J. (1968b). "Technik und Wissenschaft als Ideologie". Suhrkamp, Frankfurt.

Habermas, J. (1970). Der Universalitetsanspruch der Hermeneutik. *In* "Hermeneutik und Dialektik". J. B. C. Mohr, Tübingen.

Hartfiel, G. (1968). "Wirtschaftliche und soziale Rationalität". F. Enke Verlag, Stuttgart.

Hess, E. H. (1962). Ethology: an approach toward the complete analysis of behaviour. *In* "New Directions in Psychology". Holt, Rinehart & Winston, New York.

Hofman, W. (1961). "Gesellschaftslehre als Ordnungsmacht". Duncker & Humblot, Berlin.

Homans, G. C. (1961). "Social Behaviour: its Elementary Forms". Harcourt, Brace & World, New York.

Hook, S. (1953). Dialectic in society and history. *In* "Readings in the Philosophy of Science" (Eds H. Feigl and M. Brodbeck). Appleton-Century-Crofts, New York.

Inhelder, B. (1962). Some aspects of Piaget's genetic approach to cognition. *In* "Thought in the Young Child" (Eds W. Kessen and C. Kuhlman). Monographs of the Society for Research in Child Development, **27**, No. 2.

Israel, J. (1966. Problems of role-learning. *In* "Sociological Theories in Progress" (Eds J. Berger *et al.*). Houghton Mifflin, Boston.

Israel, J. (1969). Om behovet av en "multivarierad" sociologi. *Sociologisk Forskning*, **6**, 202–206.

Israel, J. (1971). "Alienation: From Marx to Modern Sociology". Allyn & Bacon, Boston.

Jordan, Z. A. (1967). "The Evolution of Dialectical Materialism". Macmillan, London.

Katz, D. and Kahn, R. L. (1966). "The Social Psychology of Organizations". John Wiley, New York.

Koch, S. (1965). Psychology and emerging conceptions of knowledge as unitary. *In* "Behaviourism and Phenomenology" (Ed. T. W. Wann). The University of Chicago Press, Chicago.

Koestler, A. (1970). "The Ghost in the Machine". Pan Books, London.

Kuhn, T. S. (1962). "The Structure of Scientific Revolution". The University of Chicago Press, Chicago.

Lenski, G. (1966). "Power and Privilege". McGraw-Hill, New York.

Lundberg, G. (1939). "Foundations of Sociology". Macmillan, New York.

Malcolm, N. (1965). Behaviourism as a philosophy of psychology. *In* "Behaviourism and Phenomenology" (Ed. T. W. Wann). The University of Chicago Press, Chicago.

Mandelbaum, M. (1957–58). Societal laws. *The British Journal for the philosophy of Science*, **8**, 211–224.

Marcuse, H. (1964). "One-dimensional Man". Beacon Press, Boston.

Marković, M. (1967). "Dialektik der Praxis". Suhrkamp, Frankfurt.

Marx, K. (1953). "Grundrisse der Kritik der politischen Ökonomie". (Rohentwurf). Dietz Verlag, Berlin.

Marx, K. (1964). "Selected Writings in Sociology and Social Philosophy" (Eds M. Bottomore and M. Rubel). McGraw-Hill, New York.

Marx, K. (1965). "Das Kapital". Dietz Verlag, Berlin.

Mead, G. H. (1956). "The Social Psychology of G. H. Mead" (Ed. A. Strauss). The University of Chicago Press, Chicago.

Moore, B. Jr. (1955). Sociological theory and contemporary politics. *American Journal of Sociology*, **61**, 107–115.

Moscovici, S. (1968). "Essai sur L'Histoire Humaine de la Nature". Flammarion, Paris.

Nadel, S. F. (1957). "The Theory of Social Structure". The Free Press, Glencoe.

Nagel, E. (1968). "The Structure of Science", 2nd impression. Routledge & Kegan Paul, London.

Parsons, T. (1952). "The Social System", 2nd ed. The Free Press, Glencoe.

Parsons, T. (1959). General theory in sociology. *In* "Sociology Today" (Eds R. K. Merton *et al.*). Basic Books, New York.

Parsons, T. (1961). An outline of the social system. *In* "Theories of Society". The Free Press, Glencoe.

Parsons, T. (1964). "Beiträge zur soziologischen Theorie". Luchterhand, Neuwied.

Parsons, T. and Shils, E. A. (ed.) (1951). "Toward a General Theory of Action". Harvard University Press, Cambridge, Mass.

Parsons, T. and Smelser, N. J. (1956). "Economy and society". The Free Press, Glencoe.

Peters, R. S. and Tajfel, H. (1957). Hobbes and Hull—metaphysicians of behaviour. *British Journal for the Philosophy of Science*, **8**, No. 29, 30–44.

Popper, K. (1968). "The Logic of Scientific Discovery", Rev. ed. Hutchinson, London.

Popper, K. (1969). "Conjectures and Refutations", 3rd ed. Routledge & Kegan Paul, London.

Radnitzki, G. (1970). "Contemporary Schools of Metascience", 2nd ed., Vols I and II. Akademiförlaget, Göteborg.

Rapoport, A. (1969). "Videnskab og Verdensopfattelse". Christian Eilers Forlag, Copenhagen.

Reissman, L. and Halstead, M. N. (1970). The subject is class. *Sociology and Social Research*, **54**, 293–305.

Rommetveit, R. (1954). "Social Norms and Roles". Universitetsforlaget, Oslo.

Scheff, T. (1966). "Being Mentally Ill". Aldine, Chicago.

Skinner, B. F. (1955–56). Freedom and the control of man. *American Scholar*, **25**, 47–65.

Skinner, B. F. (1965). Behaviourism at fifty. *In* "Behaviourism and Phenomenology" (Ed. T. W. Wann). The University of Chicago Press, Chicago.

Skyjervheim, H. (1968). "Det Liberale Dilemma". Johan Grundt Tanum Forlag, Oslo.

Sjöwall, T. (1968). Sex and human relations. *In* "Sex and Human Relations". Proceedings of the 4th Conference of the International Planned Parenthood Federation (Amsterdam), 1968.

Svalastoga, K. (1964). Social differentiation. *In* "Handbook of Modern Sociology" (Ed. R. E. Faris). Rand McNally, Chicago.

Tumin, M. (1953). Some principles of stratification. *The American Sociological Review*, **18**, 387–393.

Vickers, G. (1968). Is adaptability enough? *In* "Modern System Research for the Behavioral Scientist" (Ed. W. Buckley). Aldine, Chicago.

Washburn, S. L. and Howell, F. L. (1960). Human evolution and culture. *In* "The Evolution of Man" (Ed. S. Tax), Vol. 2. University of Chicago Press, Chicago.

Watkins, J. W. N. (1968). Methodological individualism and social tendencies. *In* "Readings in the Philosophy of Social Science" (Ed. M. Brodbeck). Macmillan, New York.

Wright, G. H. von (1963a). "Norm and Action". Routledge & Kegan Paul, London.

Wright, G. H. von (1963b). "The Varieties of Goodness". Routledge & Kegan Paul, London.

Wright, G. H. von (1968). An essay in deontic logic and the general theory of action. *Acta Philosophica Fennica*. Fasc. XXI.

Zigler, E. and Child, I. L. (1969). Socialization. *In* "The Handbook of Social Psychology" (Eds. G. Lindzey and E. Aronson), Vol. 3. Addison-Wesley, Reading, Mass.

5

Language Games, Syntactic Structures and Hermeneutics

In search of a preface to a conceptual framework for research on language and human communication

Ragnar Rommetveit

1 Introduction

Just as formerly there existed a movement for the physicalistic unity of science, so today we witness a legitimate request by the advocates of hermeneutic and dialectic positions for a more thorough explication of basic presuppositions underlying social scientific research. Such requests are usually accompanied by an appeal for subscription to some unitary philosophy of science, which may be a particular epistemology with its prescriptions concerning scientific methodology, or a "tradition of thought" with its unique set of ontological assumptions and definitions of knowledge. The novel hermeneutic-dialectic philosophy thus sets out to examine the social sciences in the broader context of an "anthropology of knowledge" (Apel, 1968), searching for the synthesis of *geisteswissenschaftliches Verstehen* and *naturwissenschaftliche Erklärung* ("understanding" and "explanation") by which social scientific research is to acquire its unique *emancipatory* function.

This chapter may be viewed as an empirically oriented psychologist's protest against the philosopher's persistent attempt to lure him into various traps inherent in monistic systems and views of the world. Such traps may be differently baited—by promises of an ultimate communion with the nuclear physicist in a future land of unity of science, or by the prospect of playing a significant political role in saving the world. An apparent intellectual simplicity and elegance of approach is usually achieved by singling out as *the* paradigm for social scientific research and mediation of knowledge, *particular* paradigms of research practice and knowledge mediation, such as the worshipped hypo-thetico-deductive method of the physicist or the psychoanalyst's "dialectic mediation of explanation and understanding". However, the philosophy-of-science version of how the physicist achieves his success may at times be so remote from his everyday professional experience that he himself refuses to subscribe to it; similarly, the psychoanalyst may well find himself unable to subscribe to the novel general paradigm of "dialectic mediation". Strangely enough, this does not appear to reduce the probability of support from researchers who are neither physicists nor psychoanalysts. We have witnessed psychologists confessing their faith in a hypothetico-deductive reductionism at a time when most physicists either ignored or rejected it; we may yet see sociologists subscribing to a "dialectic mediation of explanation and understanding" while psychoanalysts reject Apel's (1968) and Habermas' (1968) exegesis of their trade. It is tempting, therefore, to view the various unitary philosophy-of-science programmes as ideological superstructures or "false ideologies", i.e. as sets of ideas which primarily serve purposes other than explicating ontological premises, the essence of methods, and the ultimate goals of social scientific research. The gospel of an ultimate communion with the physicist, with its basis in the resemblance between social and natural sciences, had a particularly strong appeal for social scientists struggling for academic recognition and status to their young disciplines in a Western world committed to the blind pursuit of technological progress. The image of the social scientist as a therapist, which has its basis in humanistic understanding and engagement, helps us convey a *raison d'être* to a world in despair at the fruits of blind technological progress.

However, it is not my intention to attempt to refute Habernas' general theory of "objective interests" or his specific hypotheses concerning the relationship between capitalism and positivistic social science. Nor shall I argue that his novel hermeneutic-dialectic approach has its origins in an abrupt change in public relations programme in response to rapid changes in the world situation. I want to voice the suspicion, though, that we have little understanding of the relationship between largely inductively elaborated concepts of cognition, meaning and communication *within* social science and those apparently related philosophical concepts in which some of us are seeking support for a radical reorientation of our research. It thus seems probable that this reorientation may—like the presumably dominant positivistic orientation—merely serve to voice an ideology whose immediate emotive appeal contrasts strangely with its lack of unequivocal implications for our conceptualization of substantive issues and reflections on methodology. The lip service which psychologists pay to particular positivistic concepts has at times taken the form of puritan declarations of independence from "meaning". Skinner's programme for research on verbal behaviour (1957), for instance, represents an attempt at detaching himself as a scientist from his role as a participant in the games of everyday language. The futility of such an attempt has been cogently and eloquently demonstrated by Chomsky (1959) in his critique of Skinner. A tacit reliance upon "meaning" is also easily discovered as we examine behaviourist-associationist approaches to concept learning within the American tradition of research on verbal learning (Underwood and Richardson, 1956). Ease of learning is, for instance, in some experiments predicted as "response dominance" which is expressed in terms of the average frequency with which the "concept word" (e.g. "round") has been elicited in response to each of the "stimulus words" (e.g. "apple", "tomato", "collar", etc.). It is worth noticing, however, that a word such as "angular" is not included in the stimulus lists when the concept desired happens to be "round", even though the observed association linkage "angular-round" is very strong. Such *ad hoc* restrictions on choice of stimulus words for the concept reveal, of course, an exploitation of one's intuitive mastery of the language as a participant in language games, and *Vorverständigung* (presuppositions) of a nature quite different from the reported measures of associative strength. It is equally obvious, moreover, that such restrictions are a *sine qua non* for prediction of ease of learning from measures of associative strength (see Rommetveit, 1968a, p. 126). The *necessity* to transcend the role of the participant, however, is also pointed out with no less cogency, in a later work by Chomsky (1968, pp. 21–22 and 52). Referring to Wittgenstein's observations that the most important aspects of things are hidden because of their simplicity and familiarity, he states (ibid., p. 22): "We tend too easily to assume that explanations must be transparent and close to the surface. The greatest defect of classical philosophy of mind, both rationalist and empiricist, seems to me to be its unquestioned assumption that the properties and the content of the mind are accessible to introspection . . ." Despite his rejection of Skinner's particular strategy of *Verfremdung* (estrangement), Chomsky (ibid., p. 52) is thus clearly in agreement with Skinner concerning the necessity "to establish the appropriate physical distance [from the relevant phenomena] and to make them strange to ourselves . . ."

This paradox of futile necessity (or necessary futility) is a recurrent theme in social scientific and philosophical enquiries into language and human communication. Wittgenstein felt trapped inside the realm of what could be said because its premises could not be expressed. He insisted on silence rather than any metaphysical explication, however, arguing: "[All models or schemes of interpretation] will have a bottom level and there will be no such thing as an interpretation of that." (Wittgenstein, 1962, p. 739.)

Wittgenstein's attitude of resignation can thus be reconciled with the hermeneutic position that scientific knowledge presupposes "a certain understanding of the world publicly tested through interaction"[1] (Apel, 1965, p. 247), that acquisition of novel knowledge is preceded by *Vorverständnis* (agreement), and that "all objective knowledge presupposes intersubjective understanding" (Apel, 1968, p. 169). Wittgenstein might even have endorsed the assertion that "the constitution of every meaning refers back to a perspective which corresponds to a standpoint, i.e. a bodily engagement of the cognizing mind" (Apel, 1968, p. 39). He once remarked: "An utterance has meaning only in the stream of life." This comment struck Malcolm (1967, p. 93) as being especially noteworthy and as summing up a good deal of his philosophy.

The peculiar appeal of Apel's and Habermas' philosophy of social science seems to reside in their suggestions concerning the ways in which the social scientist—once he has realized his imprisonment—can *achieve freedom*. It seems to be the case, moreover, that their proposed road to freedom is paved with insights into "dialectic" and "complementary" relationships between "causes" and "rational reasons" (Apel, 1968, p. 46), between "analytic insight" and "misguided cultural

[1] This, and other original quotations in the text, have been translated by the editors.

process", and between presumably different modes of acquisition of knowledge such as "understanding" and "explaining". The famous "hermeneutic cycle" was described by Dilthey as a spiral, i.e. "[a structure] in which a rule which prompted the expression of another rule in an 'utterance' (*Ausdrück*) may itself be corrected by that subsequent rule . . ." (Apel, 1966, p. 86). Apel and Habermas appear to promise an expansion of the spiral from the realm of knowledge to that of human conduct: "[The prospect that] by reflecting about himself, Man can transform the language of psychological and sociological 'explanations' into the language of a deepened self-understanding . . . [and] . . . through self-consciousness he can transform into understandable actions those modes of behaviour which are amenable to causal explanation." (Apel, 1968, pp. 59 and 60.)

It is clearly the case, moreover, that the struggle towards emancipatory self-understanding is viewed as a continuous effort to understand the rules of the language games in which we participate. Habermas (1968, p. 237) speaks about "a grammar of language games", about "a world constituted by everyday language" (ibid., p. 239), and about "the grammar of the apprehension of the world and of action" (ibid., p. 241). And he states: "The grammar of everyday language regulates not only the context of symbols but also the intersection of the elements of language, of patterns of actions and of expressions." (Ibid., pp. 266–267.) Apel is equally seriously concerned with a grammar which is fundamental enough to cope with language as well as non-linguistic modes of human interaction. He writes: ". . . it is the mode of the sentence which expresses in the language game the interweaving between the way the language is used and the situational reference of the mode of life (*Lebensform*). Because of this, the 'deep grammar' of sentence modes cannot be restricted to those typical forms which are usually differentiated in the traditional grammar. Such a restriction is invalid, since it is contradicted by the fact that a sentence is initially endowed with meaning because it is placed in the context of a wider meaning which is composed of language and of the practice of living— i.e. precisely in the context of the 'language game'." (1966, p. 72.)

Those of us who are engaged in empirical enquiries into language and human communication are continually trapped within the games of our own everyday language, yet professionally obliged to disclose their mysteries by transcending them. And, being attracted to depth and fearing shallowness, we are also naturally attracted by the prospect of disclosing a grammar "deep" enough to account for verbal as well as non-verbal human interaction, and even for "schemata for the understanding of the world" (*Schemata der Wertauffassung*, Habermas, 1968, p. 237). I have argued elsewhere (Rommetveit, 1968a, pp. 217–218, and 1968b) that psycholinguists seeking depth only in "deep sentence structures" are bound to fail, and I shall try to demonstrate how Chomsky (1968), whose support they claim, is on the verge of expanding the scope of his search for deep syntactic structures beyond the utterance *in vacuo* and into complex patterns of communication.

A major object of this chapter is the examination of potentially fruitful novel orientations and paradigms for research on human communication across traditional academic boundaries. In surveying recent contributions in the fields of linguistics, psycholinguistics, cognitive psychology and social psychology, I shall attempt to explore underlying *philosophies of language* and positivistic or "hermeneutic-dialectic" *philosophies of science*. My attitude towards philosophical texts, however, is very different from that of the hermeneutic theologians towards the Bible at the time when the first version of the hermeneutic cycle was formulated in the context of "the authority of the Holy Scriptures". Even the fundamental notions of the novel hermeneutic-dialectic philosophy will be considered as symptoms of "false ideology" or, at best, suggestive metaphors, until their content can be elaborated in terms of precise relationships to current psychological concepts of cognition and communication and the particular implications (of rejection or acceptance) for the specific methods by which the empirically oriented social scientist of today tries to deepen his understanding of human cognition, communication and interaction.

The relationship between the philosopher (particularly the philosopher of science) and the social scientist is too often accepted as a relationship between master and servant: the social scientist is requested to clarify his tacit philosophical assumptions in a terminology dictated by the philosopher. My deliberate attempt at reversing this relationship is provoked by the suspicion that the proponent of novel hermeneutic-dialectic ideas may easily become insulated in a vicious hermeneutic triangle consisting of famous and "deep" philosophical forefathers, a straw-man of positivistic social science, and himself. I shall not try to refute the suggestion of Apel (1966) that Wittgenstein, by virtue of his later notions about "language games", may be counted among those famous forefathers; nor shall I question the potential depth of these

H

notions. It is worth remembering, however, that the idea of language as *games with words* struck Wittgenstein one day as he was passing a field where a game of football was in progress (Malcolm, 1967, p. 65). The potential depth of the idea, moreover, will hardly ever be reached if we consider the incident of its genesis as an instance of revelation.

What characterized Wittgenstein's own philosophy as *Praxis* was a programmatic disrespect for vague and indirect philosophical metaphors, not excluding those he had used himself. The best way of achieving further clarification of the ideas that occurred to Wittgenstein as a result of watching the football game is hence to attempt to relate them to notions emerging from our own research. The same applies to the main concepts of the novel hermeneutic-dialectic philosophy of social science. Their content and their relevance to social scientific research cannot be brought out by *werkimmanente Interpretation* of philosophical works only, but must be examined in the context of, for example, the recent linguistic search for universals of natural languages, reflections by sociologists and psychologists in connection with their empirical investigations of human cognition and communication, and even ideas which have been developed by psycholinguists while planning and watching the games known as psycholinguistic experiments.

2   Reference and deixis

The point of departure for any analysis of verbal communication is what might be called the *temporal-spatial-directional coordinates* of the act of communication. In the case of spoken language, these coordinates are defined in terms of the *time* at which the act of speech takes place, its *location*, and the reciprocal identification of *speaker* and *listener*. A social scientific analysis of the communication process, however, has to transcend the precise assessment of the *now*, and *here* and the *I-you* of the act of speech in terms of a physicalistically defined point-in-space and the proper names of speaker and listener. The intersubjectively established *now*, for instance, will have very different denotative extensions depending upon whether we are timing a sprinter at an athletic competition or engaged in a discussion of the history of Western philosophy. The *here* of the act of speech, moreover, may be tagged onto continental Europe or a particular corner of the conference room, depending upon whether we are oriented towards the issue of the relationship between American pragmatism and European hermeneutics or the issue of where coffee is going to be served. And the *I* of the act of speech has served as a pivot for perpetual philosophical and psychological disputes—including the issues of subjective experience versus public knowledge and the nature of and boundaries for Man's knowledge of Man.

All natural languages contain elements by which particulars of an intersubjectively presupposed and/or temporarily established shared and immediate *Lebenswelt* (life space) can be introduced into the process of verbal communication. They are the so-called *deictic* ("pointing") linguistic tools ("indicators") such as demonstratives, time and place pronouns, tense of verbs, etc. and deictic aspects of language may hence serve as an initial point of departure for a further clarification of the hermeneutic cycle. Apel states: "In order to achieve a constitution of meaning the mind must be fully engaged; that is, it must be genuinely engaged in the here-and-now. Every constitution of meaning refers back to an individual perspective, to a standpoint, or in other words to a bodily engagement (*Leibengagement*) of the cognizing mind." (1968, p. 39.) The role of bodily engagement and the dependence upon an individual perspective are revealed in a literal fashion in space and time deixis: the *here* versus *there* and the *now* versus *past* and *future* can play no role at all in the language game unless they are attached to an *I* as the centre of a *Lebenswelt*. That as a result of watching the football game is hence to attempt to relate active, subjective agent of speech and action, the *I*, which Mead (1950) considers inaccessible to introspection, has been described in subjective spatial-temporal terms as that which connects *behind* with *in front, to the left* with *to the right*, and *what has been* with *what is going to be* (Chein, 1944). The breakdown of such a basic spatial-temporal structuring of experience is, according to Koffka (1935, p. 323), the very clue to the understanding of his interesting case of "a behavioural world without an ego".

I shall return later to the issue of person deixis and the *I* as a "boundary of the world" (Wittgenstein, 1922, p. 631). What is suggested by the term *Leibengagement* (bodily engagement)—in addition to purely bodily position—is some sort of a vested interest, a state of drive or an intention on the part of any person seeking knowledge and participating in a communication process. Such a suggestion may be interpreted in different ways: as a claim that entirely disinterested cognition is as absurd a notion as subjective human experience without anchorage in a bodily defined here-and-now, as a recognition of hereditary sin, or as an insistence that human experience is pervaded by intentionality.

The first two interpretations are closely related. Both imply that human cognition is inherently constrained by subjective perspectives and somehow guided or affected by subjective desires. The latter may be described in existential terms, in terms of instinctive forces, or in terms of the necessarily instrumental nature of cognition by virtue of its intimate relationship to (technical) mastery of the world or of fellow human beings. What is required in order to attribute such an assumed state of affairs to hereditary sin is the postulate of one "good" or omniscient perspective and a notion of absolute unselfishness against which the individual's (and humanity's) shortcomings can be viewed.[1]

Leaving the issue of human intentionality for the moment, we are at this stage left with an apparent contradiction between *Leibengagement* and *intersubjektive Verständigung* ("intersubjective agreement"). Deictic words seem to be firmly anchored in a subjective perceptual-motivational perspective and bodily engagement in the world; yet they are entirely useless in the language game unless the participants in the communicative act are able to transcend their *Leibengagement* and establish a shared world. The deepest semantic content of *Leibengagement* thus implies an essential feature of *egocentrism* (Piaget, 1926). It is most clearly reflected in the child's incapacity to take the role of the other. Words such as *he* and *that* are often used by the small child in such a way that the listener is incapable of tagging them onto previously mentioned entities. Objects which are visible only to the child himself are talked about as if they belonged in a shared visual world. Erroneous inference concerning another child's preference ordering of toys, moreover, is diagnosed as a breakdown of a principle of transitivity due to a *breakthrough* of the egocentric child's own likes and dislikes (Smedslund, 1967). Furthermore, Werner and Kaplan state: "... early objects are defined almost entirely in conative-pragmatic terms, formed through the changing affective-sensory-motor patterns of the individual." (1963, p. 44.)

The child's mastery of deixis, however, is dependent upon aspects of cognitive growth which have been labelled *decentration* (Piaget, 1926) and *distancing* or *polarization* (Werner and Kaplan, 1963). The

---

[1] I have elsewhere (Rommetveit, 1960) discussed sin and potential criteria for rationality. Human irrationality, according to the criteria discussed in that essay, can be broken down into three S's: Sin, Stupidity and Sociability.

hermeneutic emphasis upon *Leibengagement* must hence, when extended beyond the egocentric child, be explained with reference to psychological observations and theories of cognitive development. It is a very important aspect of human existence that any effort to understand the world, oneself, and one's fellow human beings is embedded in a temporal-spatial-personal deictic frame. It is equally obvious, however, that the issue of imprisonment of thought in a bodily perceptual-motivational perspective represents very different issues, depending upon whether we study the inferences that Piaget made when he was four years old about another child's preference ordering of toys, or whether we consider his reflections, fifty years later, on the protocols derivable from such observations of egocentrism under carefully controlled conditions. Thus a strong and categorical denial of *Wertfreiheit* ("value-freedom") in social scientific research is, to a psychologist, entirely devoid of content unless such terms as *Leibengagement* and *Interesse* (Apel, 1968, p. 51; Habermas, 1968, p. 242) are clarified with reference to psychological observations and theories concerning decentration in the ontogenesis of human cognition.

Neither cognitive psychologists nor their physicalistic colleagues (if such creatures exist) can deny the fact that Piaget was "engaged in the world" in both the instances referred to above. But some cognitive psychologists—among them, Piaget—have adopted the attitude that the issues of the nature and potential transcendence of bodily engagement and individual perspectives cannot be adequately explored within the framework of a traditional philosophical dialogue about *a priori* boundaries of human cognition; and this is clearly reflected in their *Praxis* as researchers. Piaget's reflections have become a psychological contribution not because he has rejected the general philosophical topic of basic human conditions of knowledge, but because of his decision to invite fellow human beings who are *not* professional philosophers to enter the dialogue, his deliberate attempt to break well-established hermeneutic cycles by exploring human cognition at such an early stage of ontogenetic development that the transcendence of the *Interpretations-gemeinschaft* ("community of interpretation") of philosophers becomes essential, and so does his strategy of systematic experimental variations of *conditions of cognition*. Despite the "prediction and control" implicit in them, experiments on cognition are primarily means of expanding the observational basis for reflection beyond the speculative philosopher's restricted reserve of pertinent incidents from everyday life and his unlimited, but somewhat more dubious, collection of imagined states of affairs. It is puzzling, therefore, that a theory of science which is explicitly formulated within the context of an anthropology of knowledge as opposed to a "logic of science" (Apel, 1968, p. 37) should be outlined in the terminology of Kant, Fichte, Hegel, Marx and Dilthey, as if psychological enquiries during the last fifty years into the acquisition of knowledge and ontogenetic development had added nothing to our insight into the anthropological problems raised by Kant.[1]

Let us return briefly to the problem of *Wertfreiheit* and Habermas' notion of *Erkenntnisinteresse*.[2] Habermas writes: "Interests which guide knowledge (*Erkenntnisleitende Interessen*) mediate between the natural history of the human species and the logic of its process of creation. By interests I mean the basic orientations which relate to the fundamental conditions that enable Mankind to reproduce and organize itself. These conditions are work and interaction." (1968, p. 242.) He also claims: ". . . knowledge is not purely an instrument for the adaptation of the organism to changing environment; nor is it an act of a purely rational being, a contemplation divorced from the context of life." (Ibid., p. 242.) It is difficult to decide what is implied by "the logic of the process of creation of the human species" in this context— unless one is willing to subscribe to Hegel's metaphysics. If we try to relate "interests which guide knowledge" to the notion of the "bodily engagement of the apprehending mind", however, we are immediately faced with the issue of emancipation of thought from perceptual-

---

[1] Kant's programme for a philosophy *in sensu cosmico* was characterized by four fundamental questions: (1) What can I know? (2) What ought I to do? (3) What may I hope? (4) What is Man? He considered the fourth question *the anthropological problem* ,and, since the first three questions are intimately related to the last, all four problem areas are "anthropological". The first question, however, was considered the basis for metaphysics, the second one the core of ethics, whereas the answer to the third question was to be sought in religion (cf. Buber, 1962, p. 689.)

[2] It is interesting to notice how an *evolutionary perspective* pervades Habermas' reflections on *Interessen*. His assertion that such interests *bemessen sich allein an jenen objektiv gestellten Problemen des Lebenserhaltung* (1968, p. 242) reminds one of the basic evolutionary perspective on human cognition adopted by the prominent American behaviourist Clark L. Hull, whose "Principles of Behaviour" (1943) is replete with references to survival and whose hypothetico-deductive style bears the unequivocal marks of 'Principia Mathematica" on the writing desk of the author. Habermas' *Lebenserhaltung* is clearly expanded so as to comprise *continuation of cultural life*. But this does not relieve him from making very difficult decisions concerning two types of knowledge, namely knowledge about what cannot be changed and "emancipatory knowledge".

motivational imprisonment which Piaget, as a professor of child psychology *and* of the history of scientific thought, has discussed in his genetic epistemology (Piaget, 1950). The constructive and adjustive aspects of cognition have been thoroughly discussed in connection with his concepts of "assimilation" and "accommodation". Also, his empirical enquiries into cognitive achievement at successive age levels have been summarized in an elaborate theory of (dialectic?) stages of egocentrism, pre-operational and concrete operational thinking, and genuinely abstract thought, a theory according to which decentered scientific reflection about the world and the conditions and potentialities of human knowledge emerges as the negation of—and final emancipation from—the stage of entirely drive-and-stimulus bound *Leibengagement* of the newborn child.

The capacity for decentering implies, amongst other things, that a scientist or a philosopher can reflectively and systematically counteract any vested interest in the outcome of his research and reflections *once such an interest has been diagnosed and clearly identified*. And the most complete emancipation of acquisition of knowledge from "world and interaction" and immediate *Leibengagement* is encountered in the role of the professional truth-seeker, e.g. in Wittgenstein's philosophy and reflection and Piaget's enquiries as a professor of child psychology and of the history of scientific thought. It is hence very difficult to refute a weak thesis of *Wertfreiheit* of social science, i.e. that the social scientist is able to take presumably efficient precautions against potential "sources of errors" ranging from self-fulfilling prophesies in experimentation (Rosenthal, 1966) to ideological compliance with the demands of a capitalistic society (Habermas, 1968). A strong thesis of *Wertfreiheit*, on the other hand, would imply that the social scientist should be able to counteract constraining and biasing conditions *before such conditions are identified*, and such a thesis is therefore meaningful if and only if we dare at this stage to claim revelation of an omniscient perspective and absolute truth.

Consider, for instance, Habermas' hypothesis concerning the relationship between capitalism and positivism in social science. The image of the positivistic psychologist and sociologist emerging from his analysis (Habermas, 1968) and from Skjervheim's discussion (Skjervheim, 1959) is a horror image of a person eagerly trying to manipulate, control and predict his fellow human beings as "objects", taking care to write down what he finds out in terms of causal laws which are *comprehensible* only within the *Interpretations-gemeinschaft* ("community of interpretation") of his positivistic colleagues and *useful* only to those who have power to exploit others. What has been omitted from this image is, among other things, the basic epistemological and methodological rationale for Man's dependence upon other fellow human beings in his struggle towards self-understanding. Malcolm (1964, p. 154) has aptly summed up behaviourism's shortcoming as a philosophy of psychology (*not* as a theory of evidence) by saying that it regards Man as *solely* an *object*. The other horn of the dilemma is to regard Man *solely* as a *subject*, implying an imprisonment of Man's knowledge of Man inside the active *I* which constitutes the *origo* of the deictic temporal-spatial-personal coordinates of individual human experience and action. This *I* is "a boundary of the world" because it is in principle inaccessible to introspection. I have argued elsewhere (Rommetveit, 1960), partly on the basis of experiments on cognitive achievement, that the "double intentionality" of cognizing and reflecting upon the act of cognizing (Husserl, 1964, p. 157) is bound to result in an oscillation between an active *I* of immediate cognition followed by another active *I* reflecting upon the first *I as a passive "me"*, *in retrospect*; there is then a third active *I* engaged in a cognitive activity *which has been modified* by the intervening activity of retrospection and reflection, and so on. Resort to other human beings as subjects in experiments[1] is hence a *sine qua non* when one wishes to acquire knowledge about one's own cognition under conditions in which it is not being self-supervised and guided by the characteristic double intentionality of the introspective philosopher and psychologist.

Embedded in empirical psychological research as *Praxis* are thus various detour strategies of getting at the active *I* of actions, cognitions, and acts of speech. What is known as "deception" in social psychological experiments, for instance, must be interpreted as an antidote against the self-deception inherent in introspection. Treating fellow human beings as "objects" in an experiment and either withholding from them completely the purpose of the experiment or giving them distorted information about it, cannot truly be regarded as an instance of tacit positivistic metaphysics of causation and denial of human intentionality. On the contrary, such detour strategies testify to a clear recognition of the crucial role of human intentionality and of Man's capacity

---

[1] This implies, according to the terminology of Skjervheim (1959), treating them as "objects".

for self-reflection and self-control. Thus they should be viewed and evaluated as serious attempts at transcending a *Verstehen* constrained by the tradition of an aristocracy of philosophers whose empirical basis for insight into conditions of human knowledge has consisted of their own reflections, introspection (sometimes raised to the second and even third power), and selected anecdotes.

It must immediately be admitted that the social psychological experiment is a very dubious antidote for self-deception when ingenuity of experimental design is combined with a behaviouristic attempt at emancipation from "meaning". What in published form takes on the appearance of tests of "behavioural laws", phrased in terms of concepts equally applicable to Man and to the rat in the Skinner box, may, upon a closer examination, turn out to be something else. Success at predicting behaviour in the experimental situation may be shown to be intimately related to the experimenter's familiarity with the subject's *Lebenswelt* and his interpretation of the experimental situation. Failure to replicate the outcome in different cultural settings indicates that the "variables" or "laws" may have been strongly infected by tacit surplus meaning of the kind hermeneutic philosophers emphasize. Successful prediction in the familiar setting may thus actually reveal more about the extent to which the experimenter and his subject share a *Lebenswelt* than about the "laws" as formulated in published papers. A programmatic declaration of independence from meaning prohibits the experimenter from exploiting such failures of replication for the purpose of gaining deeper insight into the processes he wants to understand. It is possible, however, to subject this issue of subject-experimenter relationship to theoretical and empirical investigations. (See chapters by Tajfel and Flament in this book.) I shall thus not for a moment deny that some psychologists—and in particular those who have openly confessed to a behaviouristic philosophy—have at times been so absorbed in the study of Man as a *He* that their efforts can hardly be defended as methodologically sophisticated detours aiming at an *I*. But a careful analysis of particular contributions, from the inception of the main ideas to the publication of the findings, very often reveals quite intriguing relationships, such as those existing between the researcher's own *Lebenswelt* and subjective reflections on basic human condition and *the published reports* which lead a hermeneutic philosopher of science to assign the researcher to the class of predicting (and predictable), controlling (and controlled), manipulating (and manipulated) social scientists. For instance, published "quasi-causal" theories of affiliation motives may, upon closer examination, turn out to be more appropriately interpreted as a social psychologist's reflections about his own loneliness and about Man's dependence upon others as part of the "basic human condition". The reason why an underlying humanistic orientation is concealed in the published report may in such cases often be sought in an imitation of natural scientific style and terminology (Koch, 1959). There is always the temptation in a novel field of empirical enquiry to establish some contact with the ideas developed within different and more highly advanced fields by means of analogies. Psychologists will thus sometimes feel that talking about "valences" may promote their insight into interpersonal relationships, whereas the chemist feels that little is gained by talking about love between atoms. The psychologist studying affiliation will also, of course, try to transcend his subjective and idiosyncratic notions by anchoring his concepts in observations accessible to a more inclusive "community of interpretation". The necessary resort to other human beings as subjects in his experiments, *and*, possibly, the positivistic ideological superstructure to which he has been exposed in his experience with editors of journals, may at the same time seem to promote communication of results, and serve to conceal underlying existential and humanistic orientations.

Suppose that Habermas' description of American society were essentially correct and even confirmed by thorough empirical studies and critical theoretical analysis. If Skjervheim and Habermas examined modern American social science with less of an attitude of estrangement (and more "hermeneutic understanding"), they might even encounter latent patterns of subtle protection beneath the surface of historical co-occurrence of capitalism and positivism. A positivistic superstructure may at times serve as a camouflage and protective device which allows the "egghead"—the sensitive intellectual who feels alienated in a society presumably pervaded by competition and a striving towards technical mastery of the world and fellow human beings—to be paid by that society for pursuing his explorations of those very issues which Kant tried to formulate as "the anthropological problem" (see footnote 1, p. 222). And a psychology of Man in the third person would not be abolished once and for all the moment the inadequacy of a physicalistic philosophy of psychology had been proved. The issues of understanding "the mind of the other person" and the futility of self-observation as the only avenue towards understanding the self must reappear in terms of intricate problems of epistemology, methodology and ethics in any serious novel philosophy of social science.

Let us at this stage comment briefly upon some ethical issues. The goal of deepened and emancipatory self-understanding and the paradigm of "dialectic mediation of explanation and understanding" seem to imply an oscillation between Man as subject and object, between the *I* and a *He* of person deixis. The request for emancipatory self-understanding, however, may be translated in terms of more specific and quite severe constraints upon social scientific research. There is first a potential constraint upon choice of problem area and conceptualization which may be expressed in the novel commandment: *Thou shalt not seek knowledge about thine Brother that cannot be converted into self-insight in Him.* This means, more specifically, that some pre-knowledge concerning possible implementation via communication of the researcher's insight into the "naive" fellow human being must be available in advance: we should thus pursue issues which allow for such implementation and abstain from pursuing those whose solutions are unlikely ever to be converted into genuine self-insight. Practical application of social scientific knowledge in pursuance of issues in this forbidden latter category might imply circumvention of the other person's self-reflection and control and hence *manipulation* of some sort.

It is worth noticing that ethical issues such as those suggested above seem to be very salient in current theoretical and methodological reflections upon research on decision-making and management. Soelberg (1970), for instance, wants to elaborate a model of decision-making with a one-to-one correspondence (if not *identity* between model constructs and the symbolic entities used by subjects in their own thinking. This request is in part based upon an explicitly stated programme of establishing the necessary conditions for a dialogue between the social scientists studying decision-making and those who are continually and professionally engaged in making decisions without any professional obligation to reflect upon intuitive strategies and tacit presuppositions inherent in their choice behaviour. Choice of empirical approach and conceptualization (such as inviting the "naive" decision-maker to "think aloud" and trying to capture what is happening in concepts fitting the perspective of the decision-maker as an *I*, or observing specific conditions and outcomes of decisions in order to test "quasi-causal" hypotheses derived from simple hedonistic or utilitarian models of Man) may thus affect the prospect of potential emancipatory self-understanding in crucial ways.

Neither of these approaches seems to possess any inherent emancipatory political value, *irrespective of potential practical implementations*. A well-fitting quasi-causal model, for example, might very well become useful to workers trying to predict the behaviour of a powerful management; it would be especially useful if they were to have a long-range perspective of taking over the management of the firm. The "thinking-aloud" approach may, on the other hand, be successfully exploited by a powerful management trying to improve its control and exploitation of the workers.

It is nevertheless important to keep in mind, as Israel points out in this book, that the social scientist is able to transcend what appears to be given and present novel potential alternatives of action and future outcomes. However, none of those imagined states of affairs may be real alternatives in the sense that they would be chosen, assuming specific criteria for rational choice. If the "naive" person includes them in his visualization of futures in the form of a regret matrix, his rational choice among "real" alternatives may still be affected: his visualization of imagined (including unrealistic) futures will thus under some conditions affect the course of action which *determines* his future (see Rommetveit, 1960). On the other hand, whether subsequent plans of action are going to be successful may in turn be highly dependent upon knowledge of biological constraints (see chapter by von Cranach). Hence, in "action research" we are often forced to adopt an eclectic position of "combined voluntarism and determinism" (see Wiberg's chapter).

The psychologist's services to his fellow human beings are very often called upon when these fellow human beings have already been defined by society as outside the "community of communication" of ordinary social life. His attempts at understanding mental retardation and behavioural disorders of various varieties and degrees start, as a rule, at that very locus of interpersonal intercourse at which a hermeneutic cycle has been broken. The possibility of being able to convert his insight into his fellow human being into emancipatory self-insight *in the other*, moreover, may be very slim in many such cases.

Consider, for example, the diagnosis of various cognitive disorders such as failure to cope with abstract ideas, or speech and reading disorders varying from severe aphasia to various forms of dyslexia.

Faced with such problems, we are immediately forced to realize that we are on our own. Our philosophical forefathers—however profound their ideas might have been—were reflecting upon the human mind within hermeneutic cycles of "normal" (and even particularly gifted) human beings. Their understanding of the world, tacitly preserved within their own community, did not imply being with others whose individual human conditions were, in some important respects, at variance with those of the philosophizing *I*. Their *Verstehen* of cognition and speech, for instance, was therefore never seriously challenged beyond its plausibility as a description of presumed universals or culturally defined "normal" or "ideal" models of functioning.

The challenge of cognitive dysfunctions to psychology may illuminate some of the ambiguities inherent in the novel hermeneutic-dialectic programme for social scientific research. The request for conversion of knowledge of "the other" into emancipatory self-insight in him appears palpably absurd in research on mental retardation. What may be achieved, however, on certain occasions, is a somewhat different and more thorough self-insight *on the part of the researcher*, a self-insight which in turn may contribute to empathy with the deviant. This may possibly be accomplished by a systematic oscillation between the attitudes of estrangement and empathy. The aphasic's strange behaviour is "explained" by careful experimental analysis of perceptual and ideational achievements in a variety of specific conditions, and his globally perceived acts of cognition and communication are broken down into hypothetical, interrelated functions and sub-functions. The purpose of such a procedure is to try to identify the locus (or loci) of the dysfunction within a complex architecture of cognitive and sensory-motor activities. An unequivocal identification, moreover, paves the way for a more appropriate empathic understanding. The psychologist can now ponder: "How would *I* experience the world if I were not capable of performing that particular function?" But he is most likely to achieve through this reflection an expansion of knowledge which is purely unilateral and not of a kind that can be converted into self-insight in the handicapped person. It may nevertheless enable the handicapped person to see ways in which particular rearrangements of immediate material conditions may help him circumvent his handicap in everyday life, and may indirectly improve his condition by unilateral dissemination of the psychological knowledge to "significant others" surrounding him.

In what sense, then, is such a case[1] an instance of "dialectic mediation of explanation and understanding"?

Apel may be interpreted as claiming that a functional analysis of the other person is necessarily "causal" (or "quasi-causal"), whereas self-insight is devoid of such "causal" or "quasi-causal" components. Such a claim may appear plausible against the intangible background of physicalistic psychologists, but blatantly implausible against the more real background of modern cognitive psychology. A survey of important psychological contributions within the latter field, across subfields as diverse as Piaget's early developmental psychology (1926), Heider's psychology of interpersonal relations (1958) and Miller's enquiries into hierarchically organized processes (Miller *et al.*, 1960), leaves us with an unequivocal impression of a common acceptance of, and concern with, the fact of human intentionality. The various proponents of this quite complex and very heterogeneous psychological research tradition might indeed express an essential aspect of their underlying philosophy of science by a collective endorsement of Brentano's definition of psychological phenomena as "those phenomena which contain within themselves an intentional object"[2] (Brentano, 1874, p. 116).

This implies that cognitive dysfunctions in the other person are always explored as contained in a matrix of intentionality and more or less successful self-control. It implies *eo ipso* that the cognitive psychologist is entirely—and reflectively—unwilling to alternate between a "causal" analysis of "the other" and a "non-causal" analysis of self. According to this basic outlook on the historical origin of the discipline and the legitimate practical demands upon it, psychology must develop as an expansion of that "understanding in the human sciences" (and, of course, as the correction of "misunderstanding") that philosophers established before the first psychological laboratory was built. A

---

[1] An abundance of specific cases conforming to this general paradigm are available in research on aphasia, and on schizophrenic thought and speech, etc.

[2] Strangely enough, some of the most interesting explications of this definition are currently being formulated in connection with laboratory experiments on the role of efference in perception (Festinger and Canon, 1965). Philosophers who fight against physicalism and *for* explicit recognition of human intentionality in social scientific research may thus stumble upon their most powerful evidence in psychological laboratories which they enter with the expectation of finding psychologists studying persons solely as objects with instruments resembling those of the well-equipped laboratory of natural science. Such visits, combined with, perhaps, a careful study of Michotte's (1954) experimental analysis of perception of causation, may open their eyes to some very thought-provoking *empirical* games with human conditions and potentialities beyond the conditions of everyday life.

functional analysis of the other person is an absolutely necessary detour, however, if we are ever going to transcend the self-insight into cognition and speech of that stage of knowledge. And one test of transcendence is encountered when we are called upon to deal with dysfunctions.

My thesis is that Apel's paradigm of "dialectic mediation of explanation and understanding" is not applicable in such a situation. The paradigm presupposes, amongst other things, a kind of psychological knowledge of causal or quasi-causal textures of cognition and speech which does not exist.[1] Even Skinner, the lonely defender of a behaviouristic philosophy of psychology, appears to withdraw—or at least qualify—his declaration of independence from "meaning" (Skinner, 1964). And some sort of a synthesis of *naturwissenschaftliche Erklärung* and *geisteswissenschaftliches Verstehen* appears already to be a characteristic feature of an empirical cognitive psychology of language, thought and communication, including the novel and rapidly expanding field of psycho- and sociolinguistics. The salient feature of this synthesis is *not* an amalgamation of two distinctively different modes of acquiring knowledge, but rather an adaptation and application of some abstract rules for documentation of knowledge, developed within natural sciences, to problem areas in which progress has been hampered because of an unfortunate tradition of heavy reliance upon subjective and intuitive verification procedures.[2]

To clarify this issue let us examine in detail some acts of speech. We may then, with Merleau-Ponty (1962, pp. 174–199), reflect upon the intentionality of the body, the *Leibengagement* of the *I* of the act of speech, the perceived unity of thought and word, and the immediate expression and comprehension of "meanings" which appear and exist externally as segments of speech. Merleau-Ponty's insistence that acts of speech and comprehension are rooted in social action and social life, moreover, is in agreement with Wittgenstein's notion of language games and emphasis upon the *use* as opposed to the *meaning* of words. Merleau-Ponty's unique perspective, however, is consistently and solely that of *Man as a subject*, the *I* of speaking and listening. His phenomenology of speech and speech perception is thus in a way an attempt at explicating

[1] My subsidiary thesis, which will be elaborated in somewhat more detail later, is that research on "causal connections" with no recognition of intentionality would be bound to fail.

[2] The intersubjective agreement achieved under such conditions may, of course, in turn, be partly due to ideological uniformity within the *Interpretationsgemeinschaft*, and hence serve to sustain prejudices against, for example, racial and ethnic groups whose access to higher education has been prohibited by economic and political barriers.

what Wittgenstein left undefined but called "a boundary of the world".[1]

I shall not try to refute Merleau-Ponty's phenomenology,[2] but shall attempt to show that there is no such thing as a plausible anti-thesis of causal explanation, which, in conjunction with Merleau-Ponty's thesis, provides the required conditions for a synthesis of "explanation" and "understanding". My thesis is that the essential components of Merleau-Ponty's subjectivistic philosophy of language—inherent intentionality, some sort of unity or complementarity of thought and speech, and the idea that speech has its origin in social action and life— are (*and have to be*) preserved even when attempting to expand our enquiries (by detour to other speakers and hearers) into those automatized and intuitive aspects we have to understand in order to diagnose and eventually cure speech disorders.

Some details of the proof of this thesis have been presented elsewhere (Rommetveit, 1971). We will now consider briefly the issue of subcomponents of speech, for example, words, morphemes, phonemes and single speech sounds. A physicalistic definition of such entities would have to resort to articulatory motor activities and acoustic sound patterns. Merleau-Ponty seems to deny the psychological existence of such entities. Suppose, however, that we follow a natural scientific approach and try to interpret them by adopting an attitude of "estrangement", that is by listening to (and "measuring") speech sounds as if they were not phases of acts of speech, in the way in which we might

[1] This is clearly the case in his analysis of authentic speech and speech comprehension, when he refers to comprehension as "a synchronizing change of my own existence, a transformation of my being" (Merleau-Ponty, 1962, p. 184). Authentic speech appears *by definition* to be unitary, devoid of the duality of "symbolic activity" and "natural sign". The discovery of such a duality in ordinary verbal communication cannot be made by the engaged speaker or listener as an active *I*. A third person is required in order to disentangle what is intentionally made known from what is (involuntarily) mediated by, for example, paralinguistic means. The significance of the distinction, however, is often clearly revealed when the speaker is called upon to assume (public) responsibility for what has been said. He will then (hopefully) assume responsibility for the message conveyed by the narrowly defined linguistic medium, but hardly for subtle "surplus" aspects mediated by shifts of tone of voice, concomitant facial expressions, etc. Authenticity can then be re-established as a normative notion. We may publicly subscribe to an ethical code according to which perfect unity of (or harmony between) linguistic and concomitant paralinguistic aspects is considered good and desirable.

[2] Thorough phenomenological enquiries into the "tip of the tongue" phenomenon and experience of groping for appropriate words, as well as experimental studies of "coding stations" along the temporal axis of an utterance (Rommetveit, 1968a, p. 218), however, seem to call for important modifications of his metaphors dealing with thought and speech and his approach to temporal organization.

study an entirely unknown and esoteric spoken language. Such a physicalistic description would, if feasible, in turn serve as an anti-thesis to Merleau-Ponty's humanistic and phenomenological approach.

The identification of segments of speech *qua* sound, with no reference to its *embeddedness* in acts of communication and its *subordination* to the intentions of communication is, according to the central ideas of modern linguistics and psycholinguistics, an utterly futile task. It contradicts an idea which serves as a common denominator for all varieties of structuralism, namely the assumption that "a structure is sufficient unto itself and does not require that, in order to grasp it, one resorts to all kinds of elements which are alien to its nature" (Piaget, 1968, p. 6). This implies, in the case of speech, that a purely physicalistic description of the speech sound is blatantly inadequate, and even if it were *possible* for some classes of speech sounds it would be extraneous to any structuralistic description of acts of speech and speech comprehension.

What, then, is implied by the relationship between embeddedness and subordination suggested above? Let us, first of all, make an excursion into the laboratory studies of the psychophysics of speech sounds. A reasonable minimal requirement for a physicalistic anti-thesis to Merleau-Ponty's thesis seems to be a rough one-to-one correspondence between the acoustic shape of the speech sound (defined in terms of a spectrographic pattern) and experienced quality. This means, more specifically, that a given acoustic pattern such as the one that is experienced as the phoneme /d/ in the acoustic context /di/ should preserve its experienced quality of /d/ across different contexts such as /de/, /du/, and /da/. Liberman and his co-workers at the Haskins laboratories (Liberman *et al.*, 1967) have shown that this is definitely not the case. The same acoustic pattern is experienced as distinctly different speech sound categories (phonemes) in different contexts. Continuous variation of one sound pattern along a given acoustic dimension, moreover, is responded to by discontinuous experience (e.g. from /b/ via /d/ to /g/).

An impressive series of experimental studies of the psychophysics of speech sounds has thus provided conclusive evidence that there can never be such a thing as simple psychophysics of speech sound in terms of specific invariant relationships between physically defined sound patterns on the one hand and experienced qualities (or categorization) on the other. The investigators have suggested, however, that invariance is reached as we go beyond the acoustic shape, via the act of articulation, and towards the "neural signals" by which the speaker initiates and controls his articulation. And, translated in more mentalistic terms, this means an approximation to a one-to-one correspondence between the quality experienced by the hearer and the articulatory intention of the speaker.

I have argued elsewhere (Rommetveit, 1968a, p. 43) that encoding implies anticipatory decoding, and that decoding implies a retrieval of the intention inherent in the act of encoding. The Haskins studies may be interpreted as a literal confirmation of such a thesis of complementarity; they indicate that we do not hear the sound pattern produced by the speaker but his "intention to speak".[1] The highly automatized component of anticipatory decoding in speech, moreover, is revealed in the unreflected and spontaneous switch from one language to another of the multi-lingual person in accordance with the requirements of the "you" of the deictic frame in which his speech is contained. We can thus consider the minimal segments of speech as Chinese boxes contained within successively larger boxes until we reach the utterance contained within the more inclusive pattern of interpersonal interaction; ultimately we find patterns of interactions that are embedded in a *Kommunikationsgemeinschaft*.

What is entirely lost in such an analogy is the dynamic aspect of subordination, i.e. the fact that the very identity of any such "box" is determined by the box in which it is contained.[2] This may be exemplified by one of Chomsky's instances of syntactic ambiguities (Rommetveit, 1968a, p. 77). The "are" in the utterance "They are flying planes" is either the copula (i.e. a mode of assertion) or a constituent of the progressive form ("are flying"), depending upon whether something is being said about pilots or about not-yet-identified objects appearing in the clouds. What is being said is, in turn, determined by the situation in which it is said (including such things as a convergence of attention or intention on pilots or objects in the air on the part of the speaker and the hearer).

---

[1] All these studies may hence be viewed as empirical explications and confirmations of the basic ideas of symbolic interactionism (see chapter by Asplund).

[2] Simon's (1962) "architecture of complexity" is thus, as far as I can see, hardly appropriate as a description of the patterns of part-whole relationships and the interdependences involved. All instances he refers to as examples of "nearly decomposable systems" (p. 99), seem to consist of sub-systems whose identity is preserved across inclusion in different more inclusive systems. The notion of embeddedness as used in the present context is thus clearly something other than *membership* in the logic of classes and *inclusion* in set theory.

The phenomenon of subordination has also been explored under highly artificial experimental conditions of reading (Rommetveit *et al.*, 1968; Rommetveit and Kleiven, 1968; Kleiven, 1969; Kleiven and Rommetveit, 1970). Two letters may compete for the same position in the visual field. The two letters *r* and *g*, for instance, may be binocular rivals in non-word strings of letters such as *sog* (to the left eye) or *sor* (to the right eye), or they may compete for the last position in two Norwegian words such as *sug* ("suck") and *sur* ("sour"). What is seen under such conditions of brief exposure to binocular rivalry depends to a significant extent upon which solution of the conflict yields a word. The rivals *sog* and *sor* are thus often seen as the Norwegian word *sorg* (meaning "grief"), whereas *sug* and *sur* are seen as either *sug* or *sur*. These studies are only a few of numerous similar investigations demonstrating how sensory-motor processes in the acts of speaking, writing, listening and reading are intrinsically controlled by more inclusive and at the same time *higher-order* processes in which they are embedded.

The intuitive, spontaneous, and automatized nature of speech and speech comprehension prohibits conversion of such insights into emancipatory self-understanding of the kind Habermas refers to in his resort to psychoanalytic therapy as a model for applied social research. Speech therapy and educational programmes for the teaching of reading must as a rule be based upon quite different principles. The vicious circle in stammering, for instance, will become only more vicious if the therapist forces his patient to reflect even more than before, and in psycholinguistic terms, upon his speech disorder. According to many researchers it is precisely a reflective interference in acts of speech that keeps the stammerer imprisoned in a vicious circle: his situation resembles that of the centipede who started reflecting upon which foot to put forward first.

Very similar difficulties arise in connection with other problems of speech and communication. Hardly anyone—unless he is programmatically committed to protest against analytic thinking and empirical research—would deny that speech often has the dual character of behaviour (or "natural sign") *and* symbolic activity. My voice may on one occasion involuntarily betray my state of depression while conveying a message that is entirely unrelated to my mood; on another occasion it may reveal engagement and devotion to the cause I am talking about. Enquiries into such subtle interrelationships between linguistic and paralinguistic aspects of speech have already yielded insight transcending our present intuitive knowledge; such insight, moreover, may be (and has been) converted to self-insight and implemented in rhetoric.

This insight itself is, in some important respects, "value-free". It can be deliberately disregarded on the ethical grounds that we do not want to add any more faked components to our verbal communication than those which have already been involved. It can even—at least temporarily and in some cases—make for a reflective interference producing centipedian speechlessness. It can, on the other hand, be used in a deliberately manipulatory fashion to promote causes which themselves may be subject to ethical judgement. It may, finally, also help members of the audience to discover the manipulatory manoeuvres of the person promoting a good or a bad cause, and thus serve as an antidote against demagogic persuasion of any kind. It is difficult to see, however, which *Interesse* is involved in such psycholinguistic research in the first place, and which particular emancipatory power is contained in the resultant knowledge—beyond the potentialities of increased self-control and control of others which are embedded in any novel insight into conditions of human existence and interaction.

These excursions have led us far away from the problem of deixis in the more restricted, purely linguistic sense. We have discussed *Leibengagement* as related to the *I* of the act of speech, the various detours that psychologists resort to in order to capture that *I* when it is not in a state of self-supervision, Merleau-Ponty's phenomenological reflections on the inherent intentionality of speech, and the futility of a dialectically opposed physicalistic approach. Most of these issues, and in particular the recurrent themes of *Vorverständnis* and the fact that the act of speech has its basis in social interaction, are bound to arise once we expand our enquiries into deixis beyond the strictly linguistic domain; they are at the same time central issues in a hermeneutic analysis of language. The point of departure for such analysis is, according to Apel (1968a, p. 47), that "it is only those human behaviour patterns (*Verhaltensreaktionen*) which can be made understandable as intentional structures related to speech which are endowed with the property of 'understanding' ".

It is not very easy to decide precisely what is implied by "the property of understanding" when attributed to *Verhaltensreaktionen*. It is quite obvious, though, that an act of pointing cannot serve a deictic function unless it is being performed *and* perceived as a gesture of communication. The entity pointed to, moreover, is by no means automatically identified immediately the gesture is understood by both participants in the act of communication.[1] Successful deixis presupposes both a "grammar of pointing" and *Vorverständnis* (presuppositions) with respect to the target of the gesture. Acts of pointing or purely deictic words such as "this" and "that" cannot, therefore, via ostensible definitions, serve as the pivot for linguistic reference. This is clearly demonstrated in the *Philosophische Untersuchungen* of Wittgenstein and constitutes one of the most significant points of convergence between his late philosophy and a hermeneutic philosophy of language.

A researcher approaching these issues from recent studies of linguistics and psychological enquiries into verbal communication would find it particularly interesting to examine how different monistic philosophies of language have achieved their unitary nature by elevating different universal functions or aspects of usage to the status of the primary or essential function. A consistent hermeneutic philosophy is, by virtue of its foregrounding of *Liebengagement*, *Vorverständnis* and embeddedness of speech in social life and action, primarily a philosophy of deixis. The picture theory of Russell and Wittgenstein's *Tractatus*, on the other hand, make predication and reference the essence of language. Wittgenstein's later refutation of the theory and his insistence upon investigations of use instead of search for meaning should hence be interpreted as a plea for careful social scientific studies of the ways in which deictic, referential and as yet not appropriately identified aspects of use are called into action as language enters into different and sometimes quite complex and composite games of human interaction.

In every natural language reference is achieved by some linkage between linguistic signs and non-linguistic events. This linkage allows the *I* of the act of speech to transcend the *here* and *now* of the immediate deictic frame. One can inform the hearer about past events and state one's beliefs about states of affairs beyond that shared perceptual world which constitutes the immediate matrix for deictic functions. Reference is thus a prerequisite for deception, and hence a *sine qua non*

---

[1] I have elsewhere (Rommetveit, 1968a, pp. 188–190) tried to clarify this issue by the example of two persons watching a football game. One of them is thoroughly familiar with the rules and all the subtleties of the game, but the other has never watched a football game before. A "that" uttered by the former in the sense of "that pass" or "that tackling" is hardly intelligible at all to the person beside him who is watching football for the first time in his life.

for so-called empirical verification of statements. Utterances may accordingly be viewed not only as further explications of a pre-linguistically established *Vorverständindung*, but as devices depicting "facts" or as "elementary sentences" which in turn can be checked against observation or "sense data". As we then focus upon problems of predication and representation as *the* issues of human language, we leave the grammar of deixis in favour of *the syntax of assertion and the semantics of the content word*.

The more complex issue of predication will be discussed in the next section; I shall therefore restrict my present exploration of reference to a few comments about the role of content words or "designators" ("general terms") in predication. It is obvious that we need linguistic signs which have reference when we use language in games of seeking or giving information; and it is equally obvious that the process of reference is very subtle, and that a linkage between given signs and corresponding classes of objects or events in itself does not provide the necessary condition for predication. Take any psychological theory of reference: a theory of representation of the object via the word which triggers "the idea" of it; an orthodox behaviouristic theory of object-word substitution;[1] a neo-behaviourist theory of covert and mediating stimulus-response patterns;[2] or a cognitive-psychological approach emphasizing active categorization.[3] What any such theory can account for—if successful—is the process by which (or the conditions under which) some non-linguistic entity may be made psychologically salient to a hearer via the utterance of the word for that entity. Combination of such content words may in turn account via endocentric linguistic constructions (Miller and Ervin, 1964) for "representation" of more complex entities. The noun "triangle" and the adjective "equi-angular", for example, may, in the combination "equi-angular triangle", provide the basis for reference to a class of geometrical entities denotatively defined as the intersection of all triangles and all equi-angular subsets of planes. Such a reference is then extensionally defined in terms of a subset of the extension of each of the designators entering the construction.

Any assertion, however, transcends the purely combinatorial reference of the content elements that enter into it. A search for the

[1] See, for instance, Russell (1940, p. 82).
[2] See Morris (1946 and 1964) and Osgood (1952).
[3] See Rommetveit (1968a, pp. 112–127).

"composite reference" of utterances such as "Man is mortal", "the triangle is equi-angular" in terms of the intersection of all men and all mortal beings, and the intersection of a given triangle and all equi-angular entities, is thus utterly futile. What is achieved by such linguistic constructions appears to be a description of particular states of affairs (*Tatsachen*) which is exocentric in relation to the reference of constituent words. The reference of content words is thus a necessary, but insufficient, condition for predication. The inadequacy of a purely extensional approach to reference of content words, moreover, is clearly illustrated by the example of Husserl's "equi-angular triangle" and "equilateral triangle".[1] What is easily lost sight of as we switch from deixis to reference, however, is the subtle interplay of deictic linguistic elements and content elements in natural language. Consider once again the sentence "The triangle is equi-angular". The definite article serves as *eine Als-bekannt-setzung* (Reichling, 1963): the attribute of equi-angularity is ascribed to some entity towards which the speaker and hearer are already oriented during the act of speech, or an entity which the speaker *is going to* make known to the hearer. Alternatively, consider the simple utterance: "He went home." "He" is in this case— apart from the sex content—entirely dependent upon a temporarily established deictic frame; "home" is in turn dependent upon "He", and "went" contains, in addition to its reference to an act of going, a temporal determination relative to the "now" of the act of speech. Articles and mixed deictic-designative elements thus ordinarily work jointly when language is used in games of exchange of information as well as for other purposes. Pure content words, moreover, will vary with respect to reference, depending upon their linguistic and extra-linguistic context.[2]

This subtle interplay of tacit presuppositions, deixis and reference in verbal communication prohibits the invention of any simple formula by which the reference of complex utterances can be assessed. Wittgenstein's picture theory of language, which he refuted in *Philosophische Untersuchungen*, has therefore very little to offer in terms of specific rules for verification. The validity of his *Tatsache* is, by definition, assessable by observation (Wittgenstein, 1922, 4.024). The proposition and the

---

[1] See Rommetveit (1968a, p. 121.)

[2] Systematic variations have been dealt with by linguists in terms of "selection restrictions". The impact of extra-linguistic factors upon reference of content words has been discussed elsewhere (Rommetveit, 1968a, pp. 185–193).

state of affairs it depicts are said to have a common form. Also, utterances conveying false beliefs do so because they arrange "names" in ways in which objects are *not* arranged. Wittgenstein's and Russell's philosophy of reference is thus geared away from the issue of reference of content words and endocentric constructions towards isomorphy between complex assertions and composite states of affairs.

3   Towards a grammar of human communication

The search for *forms* common to complex sentences and composite states of affairs has been pursued relatively independently by logicians developing calculi of propositions and relations and by linguists explicating syntactic relationships within the framework of categorial grammar. The confounding of symbolic logic and structural linguistics will be discussed later on: here we will comment briefly upon the ways in which *sentences* may be said to depict *events* according to the traditional categorial definitions of constituents of sentences.

The basic principle may be illuminated by considering simple active, declarative sentences such as "John hit the ball". "John" is the *subject*, "hit" the *predicate*, and "the ball" the *direct object*; and the sentence may be said to depict an event which may be appropriately described as an agent acting upon some (acted upon) element. There is thus a one-to-one correspondence between constituents of the sentence and components (or aspects) of the event. The *agent* of the event enters the slot of the *subject*, the *activity* that of the *predicate*, and the *acted-upon element* that of the *direct object*. There is even, in this case, a temporal or quasi-logical isomorphy: an agent exists prior to the activity he engages in, and that activity is required in order that some object can be acted upon. This order reappears in the left-to-right concatenation of subject-predicate-direct object.

Chomsky's redefinition of syntactic surface structure (Chomsky, 1957) represents an entirely different principle of sentence decomposition. Constituents are, in his generative grammar, defined in terms of the sequence of decomposition (or, if we adopt the point of view of sentence formation, in terms of the sequence of sentence derivation). What in categorial grammar was labelled *subject* appears as the *main noun phrase* of the sentence, defined as NP in the formation rule (1) S→NP+VP. The predicate, moreover, appears as the *main verb*, defined as V in (2) VP→V+NP. The direct object finally reappears as the NP in (2). What remains of syntactic categories must hence, in addition to their loci in a process of derivation, be explicated in terms of *parts of speech* ("word classes") now devoid of the semantic constraints imposed upon them by a one-to-one correspondence to agents, action, and acted-upon elements of non-linguistic states of affairs. The numerous exceptions to the simple rules of categorial grammar therefore constitute no problem at all when constituents are defined in terms of their loci in a sequential derivation. The verb "ignored" in "John ignored the ball" is clearly *the main verb* of that sentence and "the ball" is the direct object (as NP in $VP \rightarrow V+NP$), despite the fact that we would hesitate to consider "ignored" a name of activity and "the ball" the name of the acted-upon element of the event. Chomsky's description of syntactic surface structure may hence, for the lack of a more appropriate label, be described as a *technical-derivational approach* to grammar.

The issue of isomorphy between sentence and event structures reappears, however, in Chomsky's search for deep syntactic structures. Consider, for instance, his analysis of the sentence: "What disturbed John was being regarded as stupid." (Chomsky, 1965, p. 70). "John" is in this case said to be the object of "disturbed" and "regarded" but the subject of "stupid". This inference concerning deep structure is arrived at via a two-step procedure of (1) breaking down the complex sentence into more atomic sentences contained within it, and (2) analysing the resultant, more atomic sentences in terms of their structure according to the principles of categorial grammar *and* the logic of predication. The constituent more "atomic" sentences must be of the form (A) "X disturbed John", (B) "Y regarded John", and (C) "John . . . stupid". "John" is then clearly the acted-upon element of (A) and (B); and "John" is *the subject of a proposition* in (C).

Another example is provided by the following sentences: (1) "I expected John to be examined by a specialist." (2) "I persuaded John to be examined by a specialist." The deep structure of sentence (1) is explicated in terms of *a derivational history* as follows:

$$S_1 \longrightarrow NP_1 + VP_1 \qquad\qquad S_2 \longrightarrow NP_2 + VP_2$$
$$\longrightarrow NP_1 + V_1 + S_2 \qquad\qquad \longrightarrow NP_2 + V_2 + NP_3$$

S_1 is then to be interpreted as "I expected S_2" and
S_2 as "a specialist will examine John".

Chomsky, 1965, p. 221

---

[1] It is interesting to observe that Chomsky, in his preliminary explication of the deep structure of this sentence, does not even mention the *normative expectation* interpretation of the verb

The derivational history of (2), on the other hand, is portrayed in the following way:

$$S_1 \longrightarrow NP_1 + VP_1 \qquad\qquad S_2 \longrightarrow NP_3 + VP_2$$
$$\longrightarrow NP_1 + V_1 + NP_2 \qquad\qquad \longrightarrow NP_3 + V_2 + NP_2$$

S_1 is to be interpreted as "I persuaded John" and S_2 as "a specialist will examine John". "John" appears therefore in the deep syntactic structure in two separate capacities, as the direct object of "persuaded" and as the direct object of "examine".

Similar procedures have repeatedly been applied by psycholinguists who have tried to explore how deep syntactic structure affects learning and mnemonic organization of sentences. Blumenthal (1967) and Blumenthal and Boakes (1967) have studied prompted recall of superficially similar sentences such as "John is eager to please" versus "John is easy to please" in which "John" is said to be *the logical subject* of the former and *the logical object* of the latter sentence. The finding that "John" serves as a better prompt word for recall of sentences in which it is *the logical subject* is then interpreted as evidence for the "psychological reality" of deep structure relationships as operationally defined by Chomsky's procedures for assessment of such structures.

A closer examination of these procedures reveals considerable ambiguity with respect to underlying principles. The procedures are, in some respects, *ad hoc* procedures for assessing "event structures" encoded in the complex utterance, and may accordingly be interpreted as evidence for an underlying picture theory of language like that put forward in Wittgenstein's earlier works. The decomposition of the composite sentence into more simple sentences resembles the decomposition of complex propositional expressions into simple propositions. The interrelationships between the inferred more simple sentences, however, are left largely unexplored by Chomsky. Nothing is said, for instance, about the way in which the two constituent

---

"expected". Notice, moreover, that the "descriptive expectation" interpretation can be fairly easily fitted into a model for depicting future states of affairs, whereas the "normative expectation" alternative requires some explication of impact of present language use upon those future states of affairs. The more complex alternative of a dual intention of conveying a belief about the future *and* contributing to its verification can hardly be explicated at all within the framework of an underlying picture theory of language. The issue of normative aspects of descriptive sentences, however, is a central problem in enquiries into social norms and roles (Rommetveit, 1969, p. 22) as well as in current discussions of self-fulfilling "prognoses" concerning future social conditions.

sentences "I persuaded John" and "a specialist will examine John" are related in the deep structure of "I persuaded John to be examined by a specialist."[1]

The structure of the constituent sentences, moreover, is described in a terminology which testifies to a confounding of the logic of propositions and categorial grammar. This seems definitely to be the case in the analysis of "What disturbed John was being regarded as stupid". The inferred sentence "John . . . stupid" is analysed as a proposition, and "stupid" is obviously interpreted as *a logical predicate*. When "John" is considered the object of "disturbed" and "regarded", on the other hand, we are apparently dealing with the direct object of categorial grammar. The confounding of logic and categorial grammar is also revealed in terms like *logical subject* and *logical object* (for "John" in "John is eager to deceive" and "John is easy to deceive").[2]

Even if we move slightly from Chomsky's linguistic procedures for assessing deep sentence structures towards the cognitive capacity for comprehending such structures we will find that the clue to the depth in some cases must be sought in the individual's capacity for "polarization" of composite non-linguistic events into, for example, attributes of *persons* and *tasks*. The difference (with respect to deep structure) between "John is easy to deceive" and "John is eager to deceive" is unintelligible until the child has learned to attribute *easiness* to *tasks*, but *capacity* and *eagerness* to *persons*. Mastery of the deep grammar of sentences about interpersonal relations presupposes therefore mastery of a "grammar" of interpersonal relations such as that of Fritz Heider

---

[1] More detailed comments on this particular sentence have been presented elsewhere (Rommetveit, 1968, p. 213 and pp. 216–217). There is nothing in Chomsky's tentative explications corresponding to the operators of the propositional calculus. Empirical investigations of children's mastery of English words such as "and", "or", "if-then", etc. indicate a strong interrelationship between use of such words and a variety of other cognitive achievements. The syntactic competence required in dealing with syllogisms can thus hardly be disentangled from mastery of particular *abstract operations* as defined by Piaget (Gardiner, 1965).

[2] A logistic frame of reference with an implicit underlying picture theory of language is particularly transparent in Katz and Fodor's early attempts at developing a semantic theory as an expansion of Chomsky's first version of his theory of syntax. Their relegation of sentences such as "my spinster aunt is an infant" from the set of ordinary, legitimate English sentences can only be defended by reference to combinatorial rules prohibiting arrangements of words which are at variance with the arrangements of objects (or states of affairs) depicted by those arrangements of words (Katz and Fodor, 1963, p. 200). The prohibition is made possible only by very strict conventions concerning the reference of such words as "spinster" and "infant".

(1958).[1] The linguistic competence revealed in the comprehension of some deep syntactic structures can hardly be disentangled from general cognitive competence, a competence which Habermas seems to have in mind when he talks about *eine umgangssprachlich konstituierte Welt* and *grammatische Regeln der Konstituierung dieser Welt* (see p. 216).

Let us now return to the issue of the confounding of logic and linguistics in recent structural linguistics and the ambiguities inherent in Chomsky's structural analysis. Summarizing what has been said so far, we may roughly distinguish between three different approaches to the problem of the form of sentences. The first approach is what has been labelled the technical-derivational approach (see p. 241). This approach is adopted in the assessment of *surface structure*: it defines constituents of sentences in terms of their roles and loci in some inferred process of *sentence formation*, and it is devoid of assumptions concerning isomorphy between sentences on the one hand and states of affairs to be depicted by those sentences on the other.

Secondly, we have the approach adopted in identification of deep syntactic structures of sentences. This approach is, as indicated above, very similar to that of traditional categorial grammar. Constituents are *not* defined in terms of their loci in the process of sentence formation but rather by a matching of the sentence against some state of affairs it is assumed to portray. Let us therefore label it *the picture approach*.

Finally, we encounter an attempt to identify which tacit assertions are conveyed by *the sentence*. This approach may in many cases be impossible to distinguish from the picture approach, since the latter also may be interpreted as portraying beliefs concerning possible states of affairs. The underlying principles, however, are in one case inherited from categorial grammar, whereas in the other case they are borrowed from the logic of predication. The inferred "John . . . stupid" in "What disturbed John was being regarded as stupid", for instance, must be interpreted as *a proposition*, i.e. "stupid" is being considered the *logical predicate* of "John" (as distinguished from the *activity predicate status* of "regarded" and "disturbed" according to which "John" becomes the acted-upon element of those two verbs in the deep structure of the composite sentence). We may label this attempt—which in Chomsky's analysis is adopted in combination with the picture approach—as *the communication approach*.

---

[1] One interesting expansion of Heider's approach, of particular relevance to psycholinguistics, is Abelson and Reich's attempt at extracting "implicational molecules" from discourse (Abelson and Reich, 1969).

Let us approach the sentences "John is easy to deceive" and "John is eager to deceive" from all three, presumably different, angles. The *technical-derivational procedure* yields identical structures in the two cases: "John" is clearly the main noun phrase in both sentences. *The picture approach*, however, reveals an underlying structure according to which "John" is the victim of an act of deception in the first sentence and the agent of deception in the second.

The communication approach, on the other hand, does not allow for any unequivocal solution in the present case. We may, arbitrarily, decide to consider the phrases "easy to deceive" and "eager to deceive" as composite logical predicates. But in doing so we would ignore the fact that predication is a *semiotic*, and not a narrowly defined linguistic form, or, as Wittgenstein describes it, "a form complete in itself" (1961, p. 18). What is required, in order to borrow principles from the logic of predication, is hence an expansion of the scope of the analysis from the sentence *in vacuo* to the utterance in its specific setting of inter-personal communication.

What should be considered the logical predicate in the sentence "John is easy to deceive" will obviously vary across different com-munication settings, depending upon what is already known or pre-supposed and which novel elements are conveyed by the utterance. The topic of deception may already be presupposed, and the utterance may then be made in response to the question: "Is John difficult or easy to deceive?" If so, we may perhaps consider "easy" as conveying the logical predicate. What is known beforehand may in another situation be that somebody is easy to deceive, and the question then becomes "Who is that person?"

I do not claim that "logical predicates" can be determined by any simple formula such as inferring *the question* to which the utterance is an answer.[1] But I do claim that the only plausible expansion of the logic of predication to verbal communication appears to be an exploration of

---

[1] One of the many intricate problems we encounter as we proceed from a logic of predication to a grammar of communication has to do with modes and gradation of novelty, that is, with which beliefs, categorizations or states of uncertainty exist in the hearer *before* something ("the logical predicate") is made known by the act of speech. Some of these problems can be illuminated by case analysis of "redundancy", using the Shannon guessing game techniques (see Rommetveit, 1968a, pp. 66–70, and 1971). Achievement in the guessing game may, from one point of view, be interpreted as a measure of *Vorverständigung*. Another related problem has to do with subtle mixtures and gradations of *assertive and interrogative communications* (Rommetveit, 1968a, pp. 62–64).

what is being asserted, claimed, or made known when something is said, and that such an exploration is entirely futile unless we transcend the utterance as such and examine it "in the stream of life", i.e. in the more inclusive semiotic matrix of human interaction. If we want to study language employed in games of information exchange, construction and modification of social realities, and social influence, we must—as Habermas and Apel seem to suggest—start searching for a grammar of communication deep and comprehensive enough to cope with deictic aspects of speech and tacit presuppositions involved in the act of communication as well as those aspects of message transmission which are mediated by speech sounds. The line of demarcation between what is being transmitted via intentional acts of communication and via "natural signs" does not coincide with that between *speech* and *non-verbal behaviour*. The current tendency of specialization in terms of, for example, studies of non-verbal communication and searching for the deep structures of sentences *in vacuo* as entirely separate autonomous social scientific fields of research are, viewed in such a perspective, entirely irrational and only comprehensible as symptoms of the modern academician's need for personal security within a narrow field of personal competence and his institution's docile acceptance and encouragement of such needs.

There are, however, some definite symptoms of expansion of scope and cooperation across traditional boundaries between academic disciplines: Chomsky's structural analysis has thus had a peculiar appeal to cognitive psychologists. What will emerge out of the resultant psycholinguistic research tradition once—and if—the scope is expanded from *individual cognitive structures* to *communication*, is yet to be seen. There are signs in Chomsky's more recent work (1968) that his own search for depth may take the direction of a grammar of communication.

His recent work on linguistic transformations is clearly geared towards disclosure of principles of universal grammar, and his examples from English phonology and syntax are introduced in order to illuminate such potentially universal principles. The specific rules for formation of wh- questions (and also relative clauses) in English are thus tentatively explicated as manifestations of a general "A-over-A principle", which states: ". . . if a transformation applies to a structure of the form [S . . . [A . . .] A] . . .] S for any category A, then it must be so interpreted as to apply to the maximal phrase of type A." (1968, p. 43.)

The sentence

(1A) "He saw the picture of Bill",

will thus in interrogative form appear as

(1B) "What did he see?"

whereas the form

(1C) "Whom did he see the picture of?"

is prohibited by the A-over-A principle (1968, p. 46).

The sentence

(2A) "John kept the car in *the garage*",

on the other hand, is ambiguous. It can mean "the car in the garage was kept by John", or "the car was kept in the garage by John" (1968, p. 43). In the first case, the italicized phrase is part of a noun phrase, "the car in the garage"; in the latter case it is not.

The interrogative

(2B) "What (garage) did John keep the car in?"

presupposes an interpretation in which the italicized phrase is *not* part of a noun phrase.

There are, however, numerous violations of the A-over-A principle. The sentence

(1A′) "He saw a picture of Bill"

can thus be transformed into the question

(1C′) "Whom did he see a picture of?"

In order to account for the cases in which the transformation can be applied to a noun phrase which itself is a part of a noun phrase, Chomsky is hence led to suggest a rule stating the conditions under which the maximal noun phrase is *transparent*: "It seems that what is involved is indefiniteness of the dominating noun phrase; if so, then for certain dialects there is a rule assigning transparency to a noun phrase of the form

$$\begin{bmatrix} & \text{indefinite} \ldots \text{NP} \\ \text{NP} & \end{bmatrix} \text{NP"} \quad (1968, \text{p. 46})$$

What is implied by "indefiniteness of the dominating noun phrase" in the above context seems to be something more than strictly linguistic indefiniteness (as defined by the English indefinite article). Consider, for instance, the following sentences:

(1A″) "He saw the picture of that man"

(1A″′) "He saw the picture of that particular man"

The dominating noun phrase ("the *picture*") is in each of these cases definite, but the corresponding wh- question may still be

(1C″) "Whom did he see the picture of?"

This is definitely the case with the Norwegian equivalents

(for 1A″) "*Han såg biletet av den mannen*" and

(for 1A″ ′) "*Han såg biletet av den spesielle mannen*"

The grammatically fully acceptable—and even most plausible—
"kv- question" for those sentences in Norwegian is

(equivalent to 1C) "*Kven såg han biletet av?*"

Transparency is thus assigned in spite of the fact that the dominating noun phrase ("*the* picture", "bilet*et*") is definite. The rule assigning transparency may hence have to be rephrased in terms of *which entity* (*picture* or *man*) is most unequivocally identified. The deictic identification ("that man") and the strengthened deictic identification ("that particular man") override, in a way, the *Als-bekannt-setzung* mediated by the definite article of the dominating noun phrase. The issue of indefiniteness versus definiteness thus becomes an issue of nesting of interrelated elements of the message, that is, *which entity is presupposed when the other is mentioned*. The constructions "that picture of something" and "a picture of that" represent very different patterns of nesting as far as "picture" is concerned. What has already been unequivocally identified in the first case is *a particular picture*, and information concerning its content is dependent upon a joint attention or intention toward that picture on the part of the speaker and the hearer. What is presupposed in the other case is some deictically identified entity ("that") which is "transparent" or "free" (Henry, 1971). It is *not* contained within the preceding "a picture" and can hence freely appear in the wh- slot of the interrogative form. Chomsky's "A-over-A principle" may thus be interpreted as an attempt at analysing how the speaker himself imposes a particular structure upon the event the moment he has to make that event known to others (and himself?) by means of verbalization; this is an instance of transition to a "communication approach" to grammar.

The more subtle aspects of such an analysis, which are potentially very significant, may perhaps become clearer if we reflect upon the notion of nesting of message elements as compared to a simple picture theory of language. The latter approach puts the speaker, in a sense, in the role of a photographer. The notion of nesting, on the other hand, provides him with considerable freedom and opportunity for productivity, even in a situation in which he uses language to inform another person "truthfully" about events and states of affairs which he did not know about before. In addition to the productivity inherent in the openness of the semantic system,[1] he has the freedom of choosing what to presuppose as "background information", which aspects of the complex states of affairs to introduce as *fair accompli* and, in a way, prerequisites for other aspects. Two persons observing exactly the same sequence of events may thus structure their "true" stories about that sequence in such a way that quite different *social* realities are mediated in the two cases.[2]

A consistent communication approach also implies a somewhat different attitude towards problems of structural ambiguity. Sentences such as "I disapprove of John's drinking" (Chomsky, 1968, p. 27) may be *genuinely ambiguous* in the sense that the speaker is encoding a diffuse approval whose target has not yet been unequivocally identified. His omission of disambiguating elements (such as either "excessive" in front of or "beer" immediately after "drinking") may even be deliberate, serving as a provocation and an introduction to a discussion of the issue of whether John should stop drinking altogether or merely should be advised to reduce his consumption considerably. The ambiguity may hence reveal a *shallow intention* on the part of the speaker (Naess, 1953) or an intended duality of the assertion conveyed by his utterance.

Chomsky's attitude toward Wittgenstein's *Philosophische Unter-suchungen* may indeed be interpreted as revealing either some shallow-ness of intention or a deliberate ambiguity. He claims: "If we hope to understand human language and the psychological capacities on which it rests, we must first ask what it is, not how or for what purposes it is

---

[1] This has been discussed elsewhere (see footnote, p. 238). The freedom to describe a given complex event by words contained within entirely different semantic-associative networks *and*, at the same time, within socially defined very different deictic frames, is exercised intentionally and successfully in political mass media. The strike of miners in Kiruna in Sweden, for instance, may be described in terms of the traditional terminology of trade union negotiations, salaries, and productivity, or in terms of alienation and the imprisonment of underprivileged human beings in a capitalist society. I have elsewhere (Rommetveit, 1970) tried to show how institutions planning information campaigns on drug and drug abuse even in their choice of vocabulary to be used are forced to clarify their position with respect to ideologically controversial issues, such as drug and alcoholism legislation.

[2] This, by the way, is involved in the very definition of "social" as opposed to "physical reality" (Festinger, 1954). Whether a belief is anchored primarily in a social reality or not is thus determined not by the topic, that is by the issue of whether the belief concerns such things as interpersonal relations or astronomy. Anchorage in social reality is defined in terms of dependence upon other human beings (*eine Interpretationsgemeinschaft*).

I

used." (1968, p. 62.) It is very difficult, however, to see how he can define "indefiniteness" in connection with the A-over-A principle and transparency of embedded noun phrases without resorting to language use and, more specifically, to nesting of message elements as related to an extralinguistic matrix of shared presuppositions on the part of the speaker and the hearer. The linguistic competence required in such nesting, moreover, has to be of the kind Chomsky has in mind as an instance of "the most characteristic and normal constructions of human intelligence" (1968, p. 53), and *not* the innate structure which "appears to be a species-specific capacity that is essentially independent of intelligence" (1968, p. 68). The latter notion is more consistent with what has previously been referred to as "a technical-derivational approach" to grammar, and to psychological enquiries into the sense (and ways) in which Man can be said to be "pre-programmed for language" (Lenneberg, 1967).

The programmatic decision to find out what language *is* before raising questions of purpose and use is thus very problematic. The transition from surface to deep structures is clearly not only characterized by increased depth, but also, as suggested above, by resort to an underlying picture theory of language use. Also, the principles adopted in recent analysis (as exemplified by the A-over-A principle) seem to indicate a necessary modification of assumptions concerning use—in the direction of the philosophy of the late Wittgenstein.

The problems of nesting, of patterns of dependency between what is *seen* and what is said, of "free" and "tied" information, etc., have been pursued in recent psychological investigations.[1] The shared

---

[1] A number of such rather exploratory experimental and theoretical enquiries have been published in "Social Contexts of Messages" (Eds Carswell and Rommetveit, 1971). The notion of nesting may be illuminated by comparing the two sentences: (A) "The old professor is stupid" and (B) "The professor is old and stupid". Chomsky's analysis of deep syntactic structures, which has also been adopted by Osgood (1963), leads to the conclusion that both sentences contain the following assertions ("propositions"): (1) "The professor is old", and (2) "The professor is stupid". The word "old" in sentence (A), however, may most often provide *specification* or *identification*, i.e. contribute to a convergence of orientations onto the same person in a deictically structured and shared world. Stupidity is, by sentence (A), attributed by the speaker to the "free" (i.e. presupposed) entity "the old professor". "Old" in sentence (A) has hence *not* the status of "logical predicate", irrespective of the situational frame of the utterance. If the two participants in the discourse share the beliefs that there are two professors, one being young and the other old, and that only one of them is stupid, then, of course, "old" will convey the only element of novel information. Which elements are "free" (presupposed) and which are "tied" (i.e. belonging to presupposed elements) can hence never be determined for the utterance *in vacuo*.

perceptual world which constitutes the stage for an utterance may sometimes provide specific presuppositions without which comprehension of what is said appears to be impossible. What is being said, may, on the other hand, at times impose a definite structure upon *what is seen* or upon *the situation in which it is being said* (Rommetveit *et al.*, 1971). I may be told, for instance, as I am watching a large and derelict building: "There was not enough profit from the production." What I am not told at all—but yet am forced to assume in order to make sense of what I hear—is that the building in front of me is a factory or a business building of some sort.

The interdependence between parts of messages has also been studied in connection with intra-linguistic contextual arrangements such as *pre versus post position of adjectives* in noun+adjective combinations (Wold, 1971; Jaspars *et al.*, 1971; Skjerve, 1971). The nesting of the adjective (as attribute) and the noun is revealed in retrieval of such adjective+noun combinations: the recall is approximately twice as good when the adjective *follows* the noun (post position), i.e. the condition under which the contextually appropriate reference of the adjective can be determined immediately because the noun to which it refers is already known. The problem of nesting has been explored, moreover, in attempts at assessing the syntax of connected discourse and its "conditions of production" (Pêcheux, 1969), and in enquiries into the ways in which referents are *constructed* and imposed upon *eine Interpretationsgemeinschaft* in ideologically loaded discourse (Henry 1971).

What is emerging as the common denominator of these studies is not yet sufficient for the formulation of a theory; but it provides the beginning of a preface to a theory in which irrational and traditional boundaries between linguistics and a social psychology of communication tend to disappear. There is already considerable evidence indicating that utterances are decoded, stored and retrieved in markedly different ways, depending upon whether they are experienced in experimental contexts resembling natural communication settings or *in vacuo*, i.e. as stimuli for rote learning only. The problem of what language *processing* is can hence no longer be safely approached with the underlying assumption that modes of comprehension, retention and retrieval remain essentially invariant across the whole range of possible conditions of use. What language is in a typical laboratory rote learning situation may actually bear a rather moderate resemblance to what it may be in some other laboratory situations and in games of communication in every day life.[1]

Hermeneutic-dialectic philosophers seem to emphasize that speech has its origin in human action and interaction, the subtle interplay between *Vorverständigung* (presuppositions) and what is being said; and this has thus already been made the topic of theoretical and experimental enquiries. Meanwhile we are becoming more and more convinced that metaphors and armchair philosophies are at best only first approximations to an understanding of some aspects of language. What Wittgenstein had in mind when talking about language games may possibly be somewhat further clarified as we examine in an exploratory, yet systematic, way the very complex patterns of articulation between linguistic and non-linguistic aspects of human interaction. Acts of human communication may—in accordance with Wittgenstein's outlook in *Philosophische Untersuchungen*—be explored as extremely intricate equations. The loci of the unknown entities may vary, depending upon which kind of game is being played.

Even if, in our analysis of verbal communication, we remain within the present, very restricted frame of games of information exchange, we have to engage in an extremely intricate analysis. For example, what is being said may sometimes reveal significant and previously unknown aspects of the speaker's social identity (see Uhlenbeck, 1967)—his identification with some collectivity on whose behalf he is acting in the given situation, his assumed power or authority relative to the "you" toward which his speech is being addressed, etc. Such (and other) important aspects may be revealed by a variety of different and ordinarily intimately interacting means. We may have to identify particular tacit presuppositions underlying what is being said, notice which segments of speech have their basis in, for example, stress and intonation, examine which aspects of composite events are being encoded as "free information" and dealt with as pre-conditions for other aspects, etc.

Whatever "grammar of communication" will emerge from such analysis will put a very heavy strain upon our reflective capacities. Whether emancipatory implementation is within the realm of possibility or beyond it will depend upon our interpretation *and* how far

---

[1] Exploratory studies by Rommetveit *et al.* (1971) have thus been replicated and expanded (Blakar and Rommetveit, 1971), and results not yet published reveal very interesting differences with respect to *mode of recall* in the two types of situations.

we pursue our enquiries. If we demand implementation in the form of reflective choice of tacit presuppositions, deliberate planning of nesting of information, etc. *during discourse*, we are clearly once more up against the problems of the inaccessibility of the "active I" and there is a very high risk of centipedian speechlessness. But if our emancipatory efforts are focused solely on ourselves and our fellow human beings as *listeners*, we are faced with at least two problems. The first concerns the feasibility of converting our wisdom to "school grammars of communication" which might enable the man in the street to achieve a deeper reflective understanding (of, for example, tacit presuppositions) when listening to others. This may turn out to be primarily an issue of overloading public programmes of general education. The other problem has to do with potentially undesirable components of *reflective interference* and *psychologizing* in the trained and reflective listener; it would arise if dissemination of such insight into language games became possible on a large scale.

It is hard to see, therefore, in what sense the problem of emancipatory application in such cases can be clarified in terms of the substantive issues, conceptual framework, and research paradigms involved; that is, in terms of inherent value orientations rather than policies of technical implementation and dissemination of knowledge, which, in certain important respects, in itself must be considered "value-free". The commandment prohibiting knowledge about our brothers that cannot be converted into emancipatory self-insight in them may then perhaps be rephrased in rules by which the investment in the seeking of new knowledge is proportioned and paced in accordance with estimates of immediate and large-scale dissemination of emancipatory results.

A categorical request for emancipatory and *only* emancipatory goals may thus very easily lead to the conclusion that social scientists should not use too much of their current talents and resources in a search for a grammar of communication of the kind suggested above. From all reports it seems that what has been achieved so far by experimental studies may not be worthy of *werkimmanente Interpretation*; *at best* it has provided tentative insights which may serve to encourage and guide future dialectic efforts to deepen our understanding of human communication. Nevertheless these efforts will continue through reflections upon everyday experience and attempts at expanding our observational basis for self-understanding by playing the games of psychological experiments. The prospects of progress may be slim. But it is hard to see how they can be improved by adopting a philosophy of social science prohibiting penetration of the rules of language games beyond the point at which knowledge no longer can be mediated as emancipatory self-insight via "school grammars of communication".

References

Abelson, R. P. and Reich, C. M. (1969). Implicational molecules: a method for extracting meaning from input sentences. Paper read at International Joint Conference on Artificial Intelligence, Washington, D.C.

Apel, K. O. (1965). Die Entfaltung der "sprachanalytischen" Philosophie und das Problem der "Geisteswissenschaften". *Philosophisches Jahrbuch*, **72**, 239–289.

Apel, K. O. (1966). Wittgenstein und das Problem des hermeneutischem Verstehen. *Zeitschrift für Theologie und Kirche*, **63**, 49–87.

Apel, K. O. (1968). Die erkenntnisanthropologische Funktion der Kommunikationsgemeinschaft und die Grundlagen der Hermeneutik. *In* "Information und Kommunikation" (Ed. S. Moser), pp. 163–171. R. Oldenburg, München, Wien.

Apel, K. O. (1968a). Szientifik, Hermeneutik, Ideologie-Kritik: Entwurf einer Wissenschaftslehre in erkenntnisanthropologischer Sicht. *Man and the World*, **1**, 37–63.

Blakar, R. M. and Rommetveit, R. (1971). Processing of utterances in contexts versus rote learning of sentences: some pilot studies and a design for an experiment. *In* "Social Contexts of Messages". (Eds E. A. Carswell and R. Rommetveit). Academic Press, London and New York.

Blumenthal, A. L. (1967). Prompted recall of sentences. *Journal of Verbal Learning and Verbal Behaviour*, **6**, 203–206.

Blumenthal, A. L. and Boakes, R. (1967). Prompted recall of sentences. *Journal of Verbal Learning and Verbal Behaviour*, **6**, 674–676.

Brentano, F. (1874). "Psychologie vom Empirischen Standpunkte". Leipzig.

Buber, M. (1962). What is Man? *In* "Philosophy in the Twentieth Century" (Eds W. Barrett and H. E. Aiken), Vol. 4, pp. 688–719. Random House, New York.

Carswell, E. A. and Rommetveit, R. (eds.) (1971). "Social Contexts of Messages". Academic Press, London and New York.

Chein, I. (1944). The awareness of the self and the structure of the ego. *Psychological Review*, **51**, 5.

Chomsky, N. (1957). "Syntactic Structures". Mouton, The Hague.

Chomsky, N. (1959). A review of *Verbal Behaviour* by B. F. Skinner. *Language*, **35**, 26–58.

Chomsky, N. (1965). "Aspects of a Theory of Syntax". M.I.T. Press, Cambridge, Mass.

Chomsky, N. (1968). "Language and Mind". Harcourt, Brace & World. New York.

Festinger, L. (1954). A theory of social comparison processes. *Human Relations*, **7**, 117–140.

Festinger, L. and Canon, L. K. (1965). Information about spatial location based on knowledge about efference. *Psychological Review*, **72**, 373–384.

Gardiner, W. L. (1965). An investigation of understanding the meaning of the logical operators in propositional reasoning. Unpublished doctoral dissertation, Cornell University.

Habermas, J. (1968). "Erkenntnis und Interesse". Suhrkamp, Frankfurt.

Heider, F. (1958). "The Psychology of Interpersonal Relations". John Wiley, New York.

Henry, P. (1971). On processing of language in context and referents of messages. *In* "Social Contexts of Messages" (Eds E. A. Carswell and R. Rommetveit). Academic Press, London and New York.

Hull, C. L. (1943). "Principles of Behaviour". Appleton-Century-Crofts, New York.

Husserl, E. (1964). "The Phenomenology of Internal Time Consciousness". Martinus Nijhoff, The Hague.

Jaspars, J., Rommetveit, R., Cook, M., Havelka, N., Henry, P., Herkner, W., Pêcheux, M. and Peters, G. (1971). Order effects in impression formation. A psycholinguistic approach. *In* "Social Contexts of Messages" (Eds E. A. Carswell and R. Rommetveit). Academic Press, London and New York.

Katz, J. J. and Fodor, F. A. (1963). The structure of a semantic theory. *Language*, **39**, 170–210.

Kleiven, J. (1969). Om frekvens og mening ved binokular rivalisering. Unpublished thesis. Institute of Psychology, University of Oslo.

Kleiven, J. and Rommetveit, R. (1970). Meaning and frequency in a binocular rivalry situation. *Scandinavian Journal of Psychology*, **II**, 17–20.

Koch, S. (1959). Epilogue. *In* "Psychology: A Study of a Science" (Ed. S. Koch), 729–788). McGraw-Hill, New York.

Koffa, K. (1935). "Principles of Gestalt Psychology". Harcourt, Brace & World, New York.

Lenneberg, E. H. (1967). "Biological Foundations of Language". John Wiley, New York.

Liberman, A. M., Cooper, F. S., Shankwelier, D. P. and Studdert-Kennedy, M. (1967). Perception of the speech code. *Psychological Review*, **74**, 431–461.

Malcolm, N. (1965). Behaviourism as a philosophy of psychology. *In* "Behaviourism and Phenomenology" (Ed T. W. Wann), pp. 141–154. University of Chicago Press, Chicago.

Malcolm, N. (1967). "Ludwig Wittgenstein. A Memoir". Oxford University Press, London.

Mead, G. H. (1950). "Mind, Self and Society from the Standpoint of a Behaviourist" (Ed. C. W. Morris). University of Chicago Press, Chicago.

Merleau-Ponty, M. (1962). "Phenomenology of Perception". Routledge & Kegan Paul, London.

Michotte, A. (1954). "La Perception de la Causalité" (2nd edition). Publications Universitaires de Louvain, Louvain.

Miller, G. A., Galanter, E. and Pribram, K. H. (1960). "Plans and the Structure of Behaviour". Holt, Rinehart & Winston, New York.

Miller, W. and Ervin, S. M. (1964). The development of grammar in child language. *Monographs of the Society for Research in Child Development*, **29**, 9–34.

Morris, C. (1946). "Signs, Language and Behavior". Prentice-Hall, New York.

Morris, C. (1964). "Signification and Significance". M.I.T. Press, Cambridge, Mass.

Naess, A. (1953). "Interpretation and Preciseness". Jacob Dybwad, Oslo.

Osgood, C. E. (1952). The nature and measurement of meaning. *Psychological Bulletin*, **49**, 197–237.

Osgood, C. E. (1963). On understanding and creating sentences. *American Psychologist*, **18**, 735–751.

Pêcheux, M. (1969). "Vers L'Analyse Automatique du Discours". Dunod, Paris.

Piaget, J. (1926). "The Language and Thought of the Child". Harcourt, Brace & World, New York.

Piaget, J. (1950). "Introduction à L'Epistémologie Génétique". Presses Universitaires France, Paris.

Piaget, J. (1968). "Le Structuralisme". Presses Universitaires de France, Paris.

Reichling, A. (1963). Das Problem der Bedeutung in der Sprachwissenschaft. *Innsbrucker Beiträge zur Kulturwissenschaft*. Sonderheft 19, Innsbruck.

Rommetveit, R. (1960). "Action and Ideation". Munkgaard, København.

Rommetveit, R. (1968a). "Words, Meanings and Messages". Academic Press, New York, and Oslo University Press, Oslo.

Rommetveit, R. (1968b). Review of J. Lyons and R. J. Wales (eds): Psycholinguistic Papers. *Lingua*, **19**, 305–311.

Rommetveit, R. (1969). "Social Norms and Roles" (2nd edition). Oslo University Press, Oslo.

Rommetveit R. (1970). Verbal communication and social influence. *In* "Communication and Drug Abuse" (Eds. R. J. Wittenborn, J. P. Smith and S. A. Wittenborn). Charles C. Thomas, Springfield.

Rommetveit R. (1971). On concepts of hierarchical structures and micro-analysis of language and thought. *In* "Hierarchical Models in the Study of Cognition" (Ed. G. Eckblad). University of Bergen.

Rommetveit, R. and Kleiven, J. (1968). Word generation: a replication. *Scandinavian Journal of Psychology*, **9**, 277–281.

Rommetveit, R., Berkley, M. and Brøgger, J. (1968). Generation of words from stereoscopically presented non-word strings of letters. *Scandinavian Journal of Psychology*, **9**, 150–156.

Rommetveit, R., Cook, M., Havelka, N., Henry, P., Herkner, W., Pêcheux, M. and Peters, G. (1971). Processing of utterances in context. *In* "Social Contexts of Messages". (Eds E. A. Carswell and R. Rommetveit). Academic Press, London and New York.

Rosenthal, R. (1966). "Experimenter Effects in Behavioural Research". Appleton-Century-Crofts, New York.

Russell, B. (1940). "Inquiry into Meaning and Truth". Allen & Unwin, London.

Shannon, C. E. (1951). Prediction and entropy of printed English. *Bell System Technical Journal*, **30**, 50–64.

Simon, H. (1962). The architecture of complicity. *Proceedings of the American Philosophical Society*, **106**, 467–482.

Skinner, B. F. (1957). "Verbal Behaviour". Appleton-Century-Crofts, New York.

Skinner, B. F. (1964). Behaviourism at fifty. *In* "Behaviourism and Phenomenology" (Ed. T. W. Wann), 79–96. University of Chicago Press, Chicago and London.

Skjerve, J. (1971). Word sequence and recall. *In* "Social Contexts of Messages" (Eds E. A. Carswell and R. Rommetveit). Academic Press, London and New York.

Skjervheim, H. (1959). "Objectivism and the Study of Man". Universitetsforlaget, Oslo.

Smedslund, J. (1967). "Psykologi". Universitetsforlaget, Oslo.

Soelberg, P. (1970). "A Study of Decision Making: Job Choice". M.I.T. Press, Cambridge, Mass.

Uhlenbeck, E. M. (1967). Language in action. *In* "To Honour Roman Jakobson", pp. 2060–2066. Mouton, The Hague.

Underwood, B. J. and Richardson, J. (1956). Verbal concept learning as a function of instructions and dominance level. *Journal of Experimental Psychology*, **51**, 229–238.

Weinreich, U. (1963). On the semantic structure of language. *In* "Universals of Language" (Ed. J. H. Greenberg). M.I.T. Press, Cambridge, Mass.

Weinrich, U. (1966). Explorations in semantic theory. *In* "Theoretical Foundations" (Ed. T. A. Sebeok), pp. 395–477. Vol. 3 of "Current Trends in Linguistics". Mouton, The Hague.

Werner, H. and Kaplan, B. (1963). "Symbol Formation". John Wiley, New York.

Wittgenstein, L. (1922). "Tractatus Logico-Philosophicus". Routledge & Kegan Paul, London.

Wittgenstein, L. (1961). "Note Books" (Eds G. H. von Wright and G. E. M. Anscombe). Harper & Row, New York.

Wittgenstein, L. (1962). The Blue Book. *In* "Philosophy in the Twentieth Century" (Eds W. Barrett and H. D. Aiken), vol. 2, pp. 710–774. Random House, New York.

Wittgenstein, L. (1968). "Philosophische Untersuchungen—Philosophical Investigations" (Ed. G. E. M. Anscombe). Blackwell, Oxford.

Wold, A. H. (1971). Impression formation. A psycholinguistic approach. *In* "Social Contexts of Messages" (Eds E. A. Carswell and R. Rommetveit). Academic Press, London and New York.

6

On the Concept of Value Relevance

Johan Asplund

For a very long time social scientists have been engaged in a dialogue with the classics in their field, a dialogue which is impressive both in extent and intensity. The writings of Tocqueville, Marx, Tönnies, Weber, Simmel, Pareto, Durkheim and many others have been re-discovered and exploited anew time and again. This is a remarkable feature which social science certainly does not share with natural science, and consequently it has been a source of encouragement to some of us and a source of embarrassment to others. Whether this feature is a sign of profundity or immaturity, it must be realized that no source of ideas can be inexhaustible; thus for some time now it has been clear that we must eventually break away from the founders of social science. For example, modern conflict theory is not only more precise and more firmly anchored in hard data than is Simmel's *Der Streit*; it is also more *subtle*. If this is so then Simmel has at last become outdated. However, at a time when classical social enquiry seems to have become irrevocably *aufgehoben* a change of climate in modern social science has occurred which may force us to return once more to the classics. I may be mistaken about the nature of this change, but the indications are that there will be a move to look again at the texts.

If I am right, nineteenth century social science must possess a singular facet as yet scarcely exploited; furthermore, it must be a facet that modern social science has not before considered a *proper* subject of study. There is one feature common to all the classics which stands out clearly. But it has not been considered as a source of ideas until recently; instead it has been thought of as a totally unscientific aspect which had to be stripped away if anything at all useful was to be gained.

The French apologist for violence, Georges Sorel, was obviously a *moralist* as well as a sociologist. And clearly there can be no question of "stripping away" the moral facet from his various works: very little of what Sorel had maintained would remain. If it were possible to enter into a dialogue with Sorel, whether to refute his apology for violence or not, the discourse would have to be of Sorel's own kind; that is to say moral issues would be basic to the argument. After all, Sorel's problem was whether violence was *right* or *wrong* (cf. Sorel, 1961).

He was as conspicuous a moralist as Frantz Fanon, the author of *Les Damnés de la Terre* (1968). Nobody would dare to suggest that the moral facet of this formidable book must be extracted before we can draw from it in any respectable way. One can argue that Durkheim, Pareto and Weber, for example, were moralists as well as sociologists, although perhaps less conspicuously so than Sorel. This has probably been recognized for fifty years, and it comes out very clearly in Raymond Aron's book on these three thinkers; it can even be said that the blend of ethics and sociology in Durkheim, Pareto and Weber is the basic theme of Aron's book (Aron, 1970). All three thinkers were deeply concerned with the problem of maintaining social stability, and with the problem of what could take the place of traditional religion, which they saw wither away in three different corners of Europe. Durkheim was, according to Aron, a "sober optimist", Pareto an "ironic pessimist" and Weber a "bitter observer". These are, of course, just labels for three different and exceedingly complex webs of ethics and sociology.

There is nothing new about the recognition of the fact that classical sociology is not *wertfrei*; what may be new is the attitude to this fact. One has to be very careful in guessing about the nature of such an attitude change. The following is a fairly conservative assumption: we now consider it as a fact of *interest* that the writers of the classics in the field of sociology were both moralists and social scientists; we thus no longer find it necessary to ignore the moral facet of their writings and can study them in their entirety, unpurged, as it were, of their morality.

To describe the attitude change in this way still reflects a drastic change in outlook; certainly until recently the moral content of the classics has been thought of as the scandal of nineteenth century social science.

The root of the problem is that in the classics moral discourse and descriptive matter merge, so that it is impossible to remove the moral factor without distorting the meaning and changing the nature and quality of the text. We are confident of our ability to handle either a purely moral discourse or a purely descriptive one, but are at a loss when confronted with a discourse which is *both* moral and descriptive. It may even strike us as paradoxical. Can a discourse be both these things simultaneously?

In philosophy we distinguish between *normative ethics* which decides what things are good and bad and tells us where our moral duties lie, and *meta-ethics* which concerns the meaning of "good" and "bad" and "duty", but neither evaluates nor prescribes. The Finnish philosopher, von Wright, observes that the idea of a sharp distinction between normative ethics and meta-ethics is an off-shoot of the more general idea of a sharp distinction between norm and fact, that is between the "ought" and the "is". And another off-shoot of this general idea is, according to von Wright, the concept of *die Wertfreiheit der Wissenschaften*. He writes: "Anyone who thinks that a sharp distinction can be maintained between meta-ethics and normative ethics is invited to consider the nature of such works as Aristotle's 'Nicomachean Ethics', Kant's *Grundlegung zur Methaphysik der Sitten*, or John Stuart Mill's 'Utilitarianism'. Is their contents meta-ethics or normative ethics? Some, I think, would answer that the works mentioned contain elements of both types of ethics and perhaps deplore that their authors did not distinguish more sharply between the two. My own inclination would rather be to say that the difficulties in classification here show the artificiality of the distinction." (von Wright, 1963, pp. 3–4.) Von Wright's thesis is that there is a legitimate philosophic pursuit "which shares with a common conception of 'meta-ethics' the feature of being a *conceptual investigation* and with a common conception of 'normative ethics' the feature of aiming at *directing our lives*" (ibid., p. 6.)

The existence of such a branch of ethics might justify the defence of the combination of moral discourse and empirical investigation found in nineteenth century social science.

Consider again the approach of Georges Sorel. In "The Illusions of Progress" (1969) he tried to ascertain whether or not society had *objectively* changed towards a "better state". However, he was also trying to define *what* progress was; and this is something which certainly cannot be done in a detached or objective manner.

Borrowing some expressions from von Wright's treatise, Sorel's efforts might be described in the following way. Possibly he was bewildered about the meaning of the word "progress". He tried to discover what criteria could be used in deciding whether a certain process was "progressive". He did not seem to be seeking an *existing meaning* of "progress"; rather he attempted to *mould* the concept of progress and in doing so was acting both as a moralist *and* a sociologist.

Analogously, Durkheim's intentions could be analysed as follows: For him the concept of *social cohesion* required definition; instead of endeavouring to uncover an existing meaning he *moulded* this concept. Therefore he too was as much a moralist as a sociologist.

To mould an unmoulded concept (the phrase is von Wright's) might, in the Kantian sense, be regarded as a "practical" activity. Certainly it is an activity which brings into existence things which were not there before; for example, normative *and* descriptive meanings of "violence", "progress", "social cohesion" or "Protestant ethics". I believe we are here fairly close to the fundamentals of classical social enquiry. Whereas modern positivistic social science has tried to keep theory and practice apart, classical social science was both theoretical and practical.

The foregoing argument does not amount to a denial of the possibility of a sharp distinction between "ought" and "is"; neither is it a rejection of the possibility of a value-free social science or the existence of regularities and "laws" of social behaviour. However, it is an affirmation that a *value-relevant* social science may be both possible and legitimate, whether the distinction between "ought" and "is" is artificial or not.

Consider the type of theory discussed so intensively in books on the philosophy of science. Such theories are, in one aspect, purely formal; thus theoretical work partly consists in manipulating certain symbols in accordance with the rules of logic. But if the theory is to be empirical, it must be interpreted, that is at least some of the symbols must relate to so-called observables. Is it conceivable that a theory of this kind, for instance, can be value relevant?

It is certainly *conceivable* that a theory of this kind might be value relevant. Even a theory of this kind has aspects which are inherently vulnerable; there is, for instance, always some risk in the interpretation of the formal structure. Furthermore, one can argue that however value free the theory *per se* may seem, it can always be *used* in realms into which normative considerations enter.

However, I wish to distinguish between theories which attempt to meet the venerated requirement of being value free (whether or not they succeed) and those which make no such attempt. The writers of the classics did not make any secret of their values and norms. They cannot have been unaware of the fact that their work had the character of moral investigation as much as that of conceptual and/or empirical investigation. I shall thus use the concept of value relevance only in connection with theories which are *recognized* to aim at directing our lives. There will therefore be no need to quarrel with the defenders of value-free theories, nor yet with those who maintain that value-free theories are impossible, since only cases in which the absence of *Wertfreiheit* is obvious and freely admitted will be considered.

I have argued that the moral facet of classical works may be *inseparable* from the other facets. As already explained, this does not indicate a contention that the distinction between "ought "and "is" is untenable *in principle*; it means that I believe in *some* cases this distinction may be artificial or even impossible to make. A decision to omit from, say, the works of Durkheim, everything with a moral flavour would be almost as odd as leaving out the moral content in Tolstoy's novels.

However, not everything in the works of Durkheim, Pareto, or Weber, is tinged with morality: there are statements of fact and attempts at explaining facts as well as normative statements. It must then be admitted that to some extent the moral aspect of classical works is separable from the other facets of their content; but it seems that these works contain certain statements which cannot, except in an artificial and distorted way, be described as either normative or descriptive. I shall therefore argue from the position that the value relevance of some social theories is due to their containing statements which are neither purely normative nor purely descriptive.

It cannot be said that the value relevance of some social theories is due to the occurrence of *normative* statements in these theories; this would probably be a tautology. However, if one were to think of "Some social theories are value relevant" as a *critical* statement, it could be interpreted to mean that one had not yet realized the extensiveness of the moral facet of some social theories. Statements which are really normative have been *mistakenly* thought of as statements of fact or as attempts at explaining facts. Whether or not there are good reasons for engaging in this kind of "unmasking", there would be no point in doing so here. Thus I must return to the position discussed above, that is end up tying the the concept of value relevance to a particular kind of statement, not yet identified. It seems probable that the *moulding* of concepts takes place at the level of this particular kind of statement.

Let us consider some existing structures of values and/or norms. For example, a certain group of people may at a given time think that phenomena of the kind A are *good*, whereas phenomena of the kind B are *bad*. They may also believe that a certain x is of the kind A and hence think of x as good. Suppose that someone maintains that there are good reasons for believing that x is not of the kind A, but is instead of the kind B. What will happen? If it is accepted that x is of the kind B we get the practical syllogism: phenomena of the kind B are bad; x is of the kind B; hence x is bad. That is, the evaluation of x has *changed*.

There is no need to concern ourselves with the logical validity of the practical syllogism, or about the logical validity of the change of the evaluation. It is sufficient to observe that people behave *as if* the drawing of the conclusion in the syllogism, and the change of the evaluation, were fully justified.

Clearly the values and norms which are attached to x are not independent of the conception of *what x is*; thus a change in the conception of what x is may bring about a change in the values and norms attached to it. One could now simply let the concept of value relevance refer to these features. A *theory* about x naturally contains some conception of what x is. It could then be said that a certain theory about x has been proved to possess value relevance when it has been demonstrated that the values or norms which *one* person attaches to x have to some extent been changed by the conception originally contained in the theory of what x is. This would mean that it is *empirically possible* that *all* theories are value relevant. Such is no doubt the case, but then this statement is probably also completely trivial.

It has already been proposed that the classics brought into existence things which did not exist before. It is probable that they tried to create a conception of what x is (where x might stand for "violence", "social cohesion", etc); they *also* tried to create a moral conception of x, *and* to create a connection between the two. I shall use the word "value relevance" to denote this complex task. That is, a theory which puts forward a *new combination* of factual and moral conception of a certain phenomenon will be regarded as value relevant.

In a classical work, the construction of a new combination may continue steadily from the first page to the last. But in some works there are certain points where the construction or *moulding* of a new compound is particularly conspicuous—points where striking glimpses are given of the overall concept or, on the contrary, where reference to the compound is extremely elliptical. There occur at these points statements about the "essence" or "true nature" of phenomena: *ontological* statements, for want of a better term.

Let us proceed as if the change in outlook in social science has been such that the ontological statements in the classics are no longer regarded as the scandal of nineteenth century social science.

Before pursuing this "ontological" theme further, let us return to the fact that the values and norms attached to x are not independent of beliefs concerning the nature of x. I do not intend to define "value relevance" solely in these terms but, as the classical writers moved in the realm of more or less explicitly stated practical syllogisms, a few examples are in order.

Some social scientists may assert that a particular kind of behaviour can be classified as "learned"; others may insist that this same behaviour is "instinctive". Similarly, some believe that social behaviour is always reducible to individual behaviour (Homans), while others deny that this is so (Durkheim).

Assume that our evaluation of a certain kind of behaviour is strongly *positive*, and that we more or less consciously believe that it has a specific character. Also suppose that our almost tacit conception is that the behaviour in question is learned or acquired. If now a new theory is put forward which maintains that this kind of behaviour is really *not* acquired and that instead it is of an instinctive or genetically determined character, then it is possible that our positive evaluation of the behaviour in question may be endangered; it may seem unwarranted or untenable if the new theory is accepted. Probably ethological treatises often have a profound effect of this sort, transforming those aspects of human conduct which we glory in into mere "animal" behaviour. A book like "The Naked Ape" has a distinctly *moral* impact (Morris, 1967). In this and many other cases the impact has admittedly been fairly shallow, but even so it cannot be denied that it has got something to do with morality.

We are as familiar with the effect new theories can have when a supposedly acquired behaviour is initially *negatively* evaluated. For instance, new theories of criminology have, time and again, radically changed our attitude towards crime. Again ethology provides us with pertinent examples. For instance, even the title of the much discussed book *Das Sogenannte Böse* by Konrad Lorenz (1963) reveals that it is *intended* to have a moral impact. But this impact is not unambiguous. The main premiss of the book, that aggressive behaviour is instinctive behaviour, may lessen our disquiet about violence and war, but the moral consequence may also be quite different; that is our sense of responsibility and of urgency may become a hundred times magnified. It thus seems that Lorenz is engaged in the *classical* type of social enquiry. He has certainly tried to *mould* the concept of aggression. And it would be very odd to try to "unmask" Lorenz's reasoning by attempting to show that it is not at all value free. It is clearly not value free. He has affirmed the *reality* of aggression, for, in a sense, nothing can be more real than instinct; simultaneously he has maintained that instinctive aggression is a formidable threat against mankind, perhaps *the* threat against mankind.

In *Les Règles de la Méthode Sociologique* (Durkheim, 1895) Durkheim made clear his methodological—or really *ontological*—standpoint. He explained that society is a reality *sui generis*, and that sociology is not a corollary of psychology. This well-known sociologistic dictum may seem rather empty, but it has been the basis for some remarkable results, in this book as well as in Durkheim's later works. Our understanding of suicidal behaviour, for example, is almost entirely due to Durkheim's way of thinking.

Homans holds the opposite view. He maintains that a few *psychological* postulates would suffice to explain vast amounts of data about elementary social behaviour, and that it should not be necessary to formulate *sociological* propositions for this purpose. In a footnote he states: "In saying this I necessarily reject Durkheim's view that sociology is *not* a corollary of psychology." (Homans, 1961, p. 12.)

Homans evidently thinks that the "reductionist" approach is superior; he must mean that it makes possible a better explanation of social phenomena than the approach favoured by Durkheim. Yet it has become increasingly clear that Homans' "Social Behavior—Its Elementary Forms" is both barren and confused. There can be no doubt that, for instance, *Le suicide* (Durkheim, 1897) is a much better book.

In the rest of this chapter, I shall not only be trying to give examples of sociological reasoning at the level of ontological assumptions; I shall also commit myself to a particular ontological position, and will attack opposite positions. It is fully possible that this will not make my views any clearer.

It may be worth pointing out that it is not at all strange to draw comparisons between Homans' recent works and Durkheim's books written at the turn of the century. On the contrary, Homans and Durkheim are, in one respect, theoreticians of the same kind. Homans shows as little interest as Durkheim in establishing rules for social behaviour by fiat. Instead, *both* have a strong ontological bent; and both want to lay bare the "true nature" of social behaviour. They do not ask how social behaviour can be conventionally described; they ask what it is. The fact that there is a world of difference between their respective *answers* does not alter this. Thus Homans too engages in the classical type of enquiry. On page 6 he even states: "At the level of elementary social behaviour there is neither Jew nor Gentile, Greek nor barbarian, but only Man."

Let us now turn to Homans' fifth proposition. First he lays down the "rule of distributive justice", according to which the net rewards, or profits, of each man should be proportional to his investments. Then comes the fifth proposition: "The more to a man's disadvantage the rule of distributive justice fails of realization, the more likely he is to display the emotional behaviour we call anger." (Op. cit., p. 75.) There is no doubt that this is an important generalization based on innumerable observations. The curious thing is, however, that this proposition, according to Homans, is a *psychological* law.

The rule of distributive justice was by no means invented by Homans. One comes across it in a great many classical treatises. Malinowski, for example, dealt with it extensively; he termed it "the principle of give and take" (Malinowski, 1926). More recently Lévi-Strauss (1949) has immersed himself in this theme which he calls *le principe de reciprocité*.

For Malinowski and Lévi-Strauss the justice proposition is a proposition about *social structure*, not about individual dispositions. Their paradigm can be crudely rendered in this way: Anger displayed by human beings in certain situations becomes intelligible when one realizes that "the principle of give and take" or *le principe de reciprocité* is a characteristic of the social structure of which these human beings are parts. Homans' version is quite different: Anger displayed by human beings in certain situations becomes intelligible when one thinks of how a pigeon reacts when the psychologist, who has fed it regularly under certain conditions, suddenly stops feeding it under these same conditions. And this is no distortion of Homans' position (cf. pp. 27–28).

Malinowski and Lévi-Strauss use the justice proposition, in its *sociological* sense, to illuminate, among other things, the incest taboo. What could Homans with his psychological proposition say about such a phenomenon? Perhaps only this: The communal anger against a person who has committed incest is of the same kind as the "anger" which a pigeon displays when it does not get fed although it "expects" to be fed. *This* may certainly be a distortion; in any case it is not an *explanation*.

It might, however, be described as a *metaphor*. But then it is a very peculiar kind of metaphor. Alternatively, take a proposition like "society is an organism". The concept of an organism is not, of course, metaphorical in biology where it has a literal meaning. A society can be said to be an organism only in a metaphorical sense, but the concept "organism" is not itself metaphorical. If we return to Homans' proposition, we may say that "anger" and "expectation" are not metaphorical in sociology: they have a literal meaning when they refer to human social behaviour. These concepts become metaphorical, however, if applied to behaviour displayed by pigeons in Skinner boxes. Thus one may say, that if one were to identify human anger with a pigeon's "anger" some understanding might be gained of the pigeon's "anger" but one would learn nothing about human anger.

We have here two conflicting views: that the individual is prior to society (Homans), and that the society is prior to the individual (Durkheim). Neither can be conclusively proved, or conclusively disproved. Yet these views are certainly not void of descriptive meaning; neither are they value-free. My reasons for preferring Durkheim's view to that of Homans are, at least in part, moral reasons. What is good or bad, right or wrong in Homans' universe is different from what is good or bad, right or wrong in Durkheim's universe. This is a somewhat dogmatic statement, but I have not been able to form any *clear picture* of what is good or bad, right or wrong in the two cases. About certain features, particularly in Homans' writings, there can be no doubt at all; for instance, Homans' conviction that the individual is prior to society means, primarily, that the profit-seeking tendency is an individual attribute which pertains in all circumstances, that is, *independently* of society. I find this concept of Man difficult to accept. On the other hand one can argue that few things stand out so clearly in Durkheim's works. He would certainly have denied that a profit-seeking tendency in Man could exist independently of society. However, in the works of both authors there is a vast territory of ethics *and* sociology which I have only been able to explore in a very superficial way. I lean *tentatively* towards Durkheim's position, but at the same time am aware that Durkheim's and Homans' positions are not the only alternatives.

The classical discourse, in which the distinction between "ought" and "is" may become blurred or even seem quite pointless, may be very difficult to follow; but it is nevertheless intelligible. One may have to read Durkheim's essay on democracy ten times over before understanding it, but understand it one can. The positivistic philosophy of science, which attempts to impose its decrees on social science, has had the effect of impairing our trust in the intelligibility of the classics. If, according to some criterion or other, the classical type of discourse is "meaningless", then it seems that there can be *nothing to understand*. It may be that the views of, for example, logical empiricists, do not *logically imply* that the classical works are unintelligible; yet such a conclusion has been drawn many times. But it would be an immense vulgarity to try to get rid of Karl Marx or Sigmund Freud simply by formulating a requirement of *Prüfbarkeit* or *Bewährung*. Here, the Society for the Prevention of Cruelty to Dead Horses (the expression is Arthur Koestler's) might like to intervene. None the less, in the past fifty years we have seen one road after another closed, and as a result, each has subsequently deteriorated. But one could argue that the task of philosophy should be to open up new roads and at the same time to encourage traffic on as many roads as possible.

To regard the classical compounds of norm and fact, of "ought" and "is", as intelligible, does not entail an *endorsement* of these compounds. Even if one understands Durkheim's views on democracy, one need not share them. Entering into a dialogue with him must entail making moral judgements, since he was concerned with what truly constituted the *good* institution of democracy, for he was trying to discover the *essence* of democracy.

I shall now confine myself to a discussion of one particular school in classical social theory, namely, *symbolic interactionism*. An effort has been made to prepare the ground for the interpretation of this theory. Again, it may be necessary to state the case rather too dogmatically. An endeavour will be made to show that the moral point of view inherent in symbolic interactionism is a *resource*; although I shall not be able to define the *precise* nature of this point of view.

Charles Horton Cooley's methodological, or really ontological, standpoint was this: "I myself and the other person do not exist as mutually exclusive social facts." (Cooley, 1902, p. 126.) He goes on to say that a human being is like a point of intersection between an indefinite number of circles which represent social groups, and there pass through him as many arcs of circles as there are different groups.

This dictum which has a strong and, to my knowledge, unexplored resemblance to Durkheim's ideas, may seem surprisingly "modern", since a circle model of this kind is often employed by modern social psychologists. Yet it is easy to overlook the boldness of Cooley's view. It is doubtful that Cooley intended the passage just quoted as a metaphor. Of course, "point of intersection", "circles" and "arcs" are similes, but man's dependence on social groups was asserted by Cooley in a quite literal sense.

Both Cooley and Mead maintained that the separate individual was an abstraction—he did not exist—and that consequently mental phenomena, mind and self are social products. Social interaction precedes mind and self, or mental phenomena arise in interaction.

Through taking the role of another person, B, A becomes conscious of his own self, and, in the same way, B becomes conscious of his self when he takes the role of A. When taking the role of the other one sees oneself with the eyes of the other. In this way one can become the object of one's own perception. Consciousness thus emerges in social interaction (Mead, 1934). "We must be others if we are to be ourselves." (Mead, 1932, p. 194.)

We must risk reading Cooley and Mead literally. They did not say that the relation between the individual and society was *as if* the one presupposes the other: they said that the separate individual did not exist—as unicorns do not exist.

Symbolic interactionism may seem a highly familiar theory. One comes across its main thesis in a great many contexts. Of course one can argue that popular belief contains elements of symbolic interactionism in embryonic form. It is also true that the themes of numerous works of fiction could have been constructed by Cooley and Mead. But "symbolic interactionsim" spreads far beyond proverbs and novels. There is a profound similarity between the teachings of Martin Buber, on the one hand, and the American classics on the other; indeed, a book has been written about this similarity (Pfuetze, 1954). Some aphorisms by Friedrich Nietzsche provide another example: he maintained that *Das Du ist älter als das Ich* and that *Jeder ist sich selbst der fernste*. Again, if we once more turn to a contrasting context, some of T. S. Eliot's observations on the relation between identity and language sound like direct quotations from Cooley or Mead. A good summary of one of the main points made by Cooley and Mead can be found in a science fiction novel, "The Day of the Triffids" by John Wyndham. To quote: "To deprive a gregarious creature of companionship is to maim it, to outrage its nature. The prisoner and the cenobite are aware that the herd exists beyond their exile; they are an aspect of it. But when the herd no longer exists there is, for the herd creature, no longer entity. He is part of no whole; a freak without a place. If he cannot hold on to his reason, then he is lost indeed; most utterly, most fearfully lost, so that he becomes no more than the twitch in the limb of a corpse." (Wyndham, 1965, pp. 208–209.) This is exactly the tone and style of Cooley. There is indeed a quality of *déjà vu* about symbolic inter-actionism. One could say that symbolic interactionism is a kind of *terminal* in social thought—an important characteristic not to be confused with triviality.

The central thesis in symbolic interactionism could then be that the separate individual is an abstraction, or a fictional entity, and, since the individual, his mind and self are social products, one should not say that the individual is "affected by", "worked upon" or "swayed by" society; one should not choose verbs which implicitly state that there might be some part of the individual which is *not* social.

Symbolic interactionism may thus seem "metaphysical". While admitting this it would be very rash to conclude from such an admission that we need no longer ask the question: What is the *point* or *meaning* of symbolic interactionism?

According to common sense, deviant behaviour is something which is displayed by individuals. When we talk about criminality, alcoholism or mental illness what *kind* of phenomena are we discussing? It seems obvious that generally we are speaking about characteristics, qualities or traits of individuals; we do *not* think of varieties of deviant behaviour as relations between people.

We certainly do not consider deviant behaviour as *social* behaviour. Instead, we darkly imagine some characteristics, qualities or traits "within" the individual, which account for his deviant behaviour. Deviant behaviour is not social behaviour; on the contrary, it is *asocial* behaviour.

We hope to cure or reform the deviant individual; but we do not try to cure or reform relations between people, or a social structure. Our way of thinking in this respect is individualistic to such an extent that the expression "to cure a social structure" seems very peculiar. It is always *individuals* who are *sick*, never relations or structure.

Symbolic interactionism maintains that the ordinary way of thinking about deviant behaviour must be turned upside down (the central thesis in symbolic interactionism even *implies* this). *All* behaviour is social. Thus if we cure some characteristics, qualities or traits which we think the deviant person possesses, we are curing not causes but effects; indeed, it may be that we are not curing anything at all.

The separate individual is a fictional entity. In so far as the individual is real, he is wholly social; so the concept "asocial" is an *impossible* concept. To break the law is as social as to obey the law. The alcoholic is as much a social creature as the teetotaller. Mental illness is no more individual, and no less social, than so-called mental health. If one admits all this, then the world, or the *moral order*, is no longer quite the same.

Suppose we were asked to explain an idea which we knew a certain person had. In order to make this idea intelligible, we would have to ask the question: *With whom* did this person think when his idea first occurred to him? It might sometimes be better to ask the question first suggested to me by Stefan Dagler: *Against whom* did the person think. It is possible to dissent as well as to consent. Symbolic interactionism certainly makes us understand better what it is *to agree*; at the same time it does not rule out the possibility of disagreement. In both cases the fundamental point is that we always think socially or relationally. Therefore human thought must be understood in "dialectical" terms.

Suppose the idea in question is a neurotic or psychotic idea. If we believe, contrary to Cooley and Mead, that thinking is an *individual* activity, we may "logically" say that the *idea* or *person* is deluded, sick, or even dangerous, and that the idea must be eradicated. And it can be eradicated if we isolate the person, make him work hard with gardening or basketry, and make him take various drugs. If all else fails we can always resort to brain surgery. And then when the person no longer entertains the idea we can consider him *normal* again.

For the symbolic interactionist, however, the idea is a social product; the person must have acquired it in some kind of interaction. It is no longer "logical" or "natural" to think of the *idea* or the *person* as deluded, sick or dangerous. Instead, the idea may be a wholly intelligible, rational or healthy reaction to social relationships that have somehow gone wrong; it must therefore be the *relationships* that are sick or dangerous.

The idea in question is not to be found "within" the individual; rather it is to be found "between" the individual and other people. When you appeal to him to abandon his idea or try to make him "see reason" your efforts are misdirected, for the idea, or the unreason, is not where you think it is. It is not possible to make him see reason since he never was unreasonable. He cannot be cured because he was never sick.

This is not to say that mental illness and mental health are synonymous. It is to suggest that the locus or reference of "mental illness" should be changed, so that our moral reaction can be directed against the social order rather than against the individuals. Mental illness would still be regarded as wrong but we ourselves would have to assume some responsibility for it.

My aim here is not primarily to put forward a new approach to mental illness *per se*; the views expressed have already been far better presented by, for one, Ronald Laing (1959 and 1967). Similar conclusions to those presented above have been drawn by others. Thus David Cooper has explicitly denied the existence of individuals as "schizophrenics"; instead he defines the disease as a *micro-social* crisis, that is a process involving several people and the relations between them. Cooper's frame of reference is, however, inspired by Sartre, and not by symbolic interactionism (Cooper, 1967). For comments on the affinity between existentialism and symbolic interactionism see, for example, Berger and Luckmann (1966). In a recent book by Hugh Duncan we read: "The locus of psychobiological events is not in the soma of the individual but in a nexus of persons and their relations. Neuroses and some of the psychoses are not a characteristic peculiarity of some 'fraudulently isolated patients', but the result of malfunctioning of relationships within the group. We thus enter a new realm of medicine, the 'socio-somatic'." (1968, p. 216.)

What I have tried to show is that the above account reveals something of the value-relevant meaning of symbolic interactionism. However vague and groping it may be, this account still tries to *mould* the concept of mental illness.

Advertising is another social phenomenon, or social problem, which can be illuminated—or perhaps affected—by symbolic interactionism. Few would deny that advertising is a problematic social phenomenon. Even those who defend or profit from it seem to admit that it *could* be dangerous; but in reality they probably believe that it is only potentially dangerous, and not actually so. Others think that advertising could never become dangerous because the consumer possesses some kind of defence mechanisms against it, or, alternatively, has some kind of *integrity* which makes it possible for him to take a detached view and therefore resist all that is abominable in it.

This implies thinking of "integrity" as a simple individual attribute. According to symbolic interactionism it should, instead, be thought of in terms of social relations. If integrity is something real, it must emerge from interaction between people, or it must *be* a certain kind of relationships between people. Advertisers assume that integrity is something which exists among the consumers, that it is a characteristic, quality or trait that individuals are endowed with; also they believe that it is static or lasting. To a symbolic interactionist integrity is something corruptible and transient, something which is wholly dependent on the existence of certain kinds of social relationships.

Advertisers take integrity *for granted*. If advertising is to be wholly acceptable or "harmless", it must in itself be an interaction of the kind from which integrity can emerge. But can we claim that advertising can be classed as an interaction of this type?

We do not have one unique identity which is permanent and static. We have as many identities as there are different roles for us to take. An increasing proportion of our repertoire of roles is now supplied through the mass media, and it cannot be assumed that we can take the roles offered in advertisements, commercials, etc. without some degree of identification. Symbolic interactionism maintains that to take the role of the other and to achieve an identity is *the same thing*.

Hugh Duncan says: "If a holy day is turned over to businessmen who create a community drama of purchased gift exchange, it matters little what we tell children in our schools about the Pilgrims, the founding fathers, or the cavalier. The trader controls our community because he controls communication. The community drama he mounts is a drama of buying and selling, and soon we are spending our way to heaven." He continues: "In America there are daily and hourly enactments of earning and spending money. In print, film, radio, and television, thousands of actors spend vicariously for millions who yearn to spend properly and thus become successful Americans . . . We use such symbolic expressions not to 'define' or to 'celebrate' already existing social bonds, but to *create* them." (1962, pp. 264–265.)

Man has a remarkable capacity of taking the role of the other. His humanity resides in just this capacity. One might describe advertising as a fantastic *perversion* of this capacity.

I have not attempted an original criticism of advertising, nor have I attempted to make any profound statements about the corruptible and chameleonic nature of Man. The case has been far better put by, for example, the Polish dramatist Witold Gombrowicz. None the less, I have tried to show that criticism of advertising can be anchored in symbolic interactionism.

Symbolic interactionism has now and again been used in discussions of various social problems. Cooley's thesis of the looking-glass self has been repeatedly quoted in analyses of race relations in America. Some contend that the self-evaluation of American Negroes has been strongly negative due to the looking-glass image of the white people's discriminatory attitude. The latter has seemed legitimate even to the Negroes themselves.

The race revolution is now also a revolution in self-evaluation. Negro leaders are fully aware of this fact. They know that equality cannot be obtained until the black people's self-evaluation is drastically raised.

The looking-glass concept is, however, a comparatively weak thesis within symbolic interactionism. It presupposes that one can conceive of the black people's self-evaluation as "affected by", "worked upon" or "swayed by" the attitude of white society without at the same time being *at the mercy of* white society. If this were so the black people's self-evaluation could be easily and rapidly raised. What is it that stands in the way of the American Negroes beginning to think more highly of themselves? Whatever difficulties exist must be due to the Negroes themselves—perhaps because of some quality of sluggishness or incorrigibility.

The central thesis of symbolic interactionism implies that a high self-evaluation is not easily acquired; and it also implies that a high self-evaluation is not an attribute which, once acquired, cannot be lost. Indeed, "self-evaluation" is not an individual "attribute" at all and it cannot be "acquired" as, say, wealth can be acquired. A positive self-evaluation is a relation between people, and if it is to be lasting the relation has to be of a permanent kind.

A Negro incantation like "I am black and beautiful" is often thought of as revealing an *improper self-esteem*. If self-assertions of this kind are repeated by someone in all kinds of situations our reaction is that the person making these assertions is suffering from megalomania or that he is coarsely joking with his audience. Consider the public image of Cassius Clay. We do not know whether Clay intended to mock his audience or not but his utterances ("I'm the greatest", etc.) could be interpreted as a cryptic and brutal mockery of the American public. He seemed to *invite* his audience to think of him as a villain. His reign as heavyweight champion certainly was an intriguing and disturbing episode. Possibly the concept of "dramatism", which can be regarded as a branch of symbolic interactionism (see Burke, 1962), might be most relevant to the analysis of this episode; but whatever approach is used one can reasonably expect a closer analysis to yield important knowledge about the "depth structure" of American society.

"Sluggish" and "incorrigible" as well as "black" and "beautiful" are *social* words. From an individualistic standpoint they either become misinterpreted or remain wholly unintelligible. It goes without saying that "I am black and beautiful" cannot be an expression of an improperly high self-esteem. It is not reasonable either to say the opposite, that it is an expression of an extremely low self-esteem. "I am black and beautiful" is an expression of a *social structure*. When someone says "I am black and beautiful" it is not the statement of an isolated individual. According to symbolic interactionism, there is no such thing as an isolated individual.

Yet our moral doctrines presuppose the existence of the isolated individual. Hence symbolic interactionism is potentially revolutionary. A great many concepts, including "mental illness", "advertising" and "self-evaluation", emerge as new compounds of norm and fact, of "ought" and "is".

In a purely trivial sense it is clearly false to say that Man is *wholly* social. He is *also* a physical entity, a biological entity, and a psychological entity. One might say that this fact severely *constrains* his social nature. In every conceivable society Man has to eat, sleep, breathe and eventually die. In a somewhat less trivial sense, it can be said that psychological laws exist (about the child's acquisition of language for instance) which pertain universally and cannot anywhere be transcended.

One could conceive an exhaustive list of all the words which might be used to describe Man. It could then be claimed that the concept of Man as being wholly social is meaningful only in terms of a certain *subset* in the list of words compiled to describe him.

The fact of having brown eyes is *not* a social product. Eye colour does not result from interaction. Instead, it precedes all social encounters; it is an individual attribute neither created nor changed by society.

However, the *significance*, if any, of the colour of one's eyes is a social product. The significance or meaning of individual attributes of various kinds clearly belongs to the subset of words which permit one to conceive of Man as wholly social. But this does not change the fact that there *are* individual attributes—physical, biological, and psychological.

It can therefore be said that Cooley's and Mead's concept of Man becomes *reasonable* only if it is *restricted*. But by restricting their concept of Man there is a danger of completely changing it. In a sense their concept was *unrestricted* as, surely, ontological propositions always are because they encompass the total list and not merely the subset.

From this point it is difficult to develop the argument. The statement "Man is *wholly* social" can always be countered by the reply "no, he is *partly* social". From then on the discussion becomes meaningless, since to think of the *essence* of Man as *partly* social is ridiculous.

● Symbolic interactionism is therefore probably best thought of as a very elaborate thought experiment in that branch of social science which is neither purely normative nor purely descriptive and/or analytical. (I do not know whether this is in agreement with the views expressed by Louch in "Explanation and Human Action", 1969.) If we *suppose* that man is *wholly* social how may we, in the light of such an assumption, direct our lives? At first this may seem a naive question rather than a remarkable one; besides, it may seem logically odd. Yet symbolic interactionism conceived of in this way has some startling effects. Within its context the items in the vocabulary of social science can undergo profound changes in meaning, or they may become moulded in a different way. Ego and Alter no longer meet to reward or punish each other, thereafter either forming a lasting association or parting. Now they must be seen as *creating each other*. Surely a world in which Ego and Alter create each other would be very different from a world in which they merely interact fairly frequently.

Suppose instead that *all* elementary behaviour could be explained by Homans' five postulates, and that at this level of behaviour, in terms of Homans' conception of it, there is neither Jew nor Gentile, Greek nor barbarian. How would we then direct our lives? What is wrong and what is right in Homans' world? It is at this dilemma that theory and practice meet.

References

Aron, R. (1970). "Main Currents in Sociological Thought", Vol. 2. Penguin Books, Harmondsworth.

Berger, P. L. and Luckmann, T. (1966). "The Social Construction of Reality". Doubleday Anchor Books, New York.

Burke, K. (1962). "A Grammar of Motives" and "A Rhetoric of Motives" (in one volume). The World Publishing Company and Meridian Books, New York.

Cooley, C. H. (1902). "Human Nature and the Social Order". Scribner's, New York.

Cooper, D. (1967). "Psychiatry and Anti-Psychiatry". Tavistock Publications, London.

Duncan, H. D. (1962). "Communication and the Social Order". Bedminster Press. New Jersey.

Duncan, H. D. (1968). "Symbols in Society". Oxford University Press, New York.

Durkheim, E. (1895). "Les Règles de la Méthode Sociologique". Alcan, Paris.

Durkheim, E. (1897). "Le Suicide". Alcan, Paris.

Fanon, F. (1968). "Les Damnés de la Terre". Libraire François Maspero Editeur, Paris.

Homans, G. C. (1961). "Social Behavior—Its Elementary Forms". Harcourt, Brace & World, New York.

Laing, R. D. (1959). "The Divided Self". Tavistock Publications, London.

Laing, R. D. (1967). "The Politics of Experience and The Bird of Paradise". Penguin Books, Harmondsworth.

Lévi-Strauss, C. (1949). "Les Structures Élémentaires de la Parenté". Presses Universitaires de France, Paris.

Lorenz, K. (1963). "Das Sogenannte Böse". Borotha-Schoeler Verlag, Wien.

Louch, A. R. (1969). "Explanation and Human Action". University of California Press, Berkeley and Los Angeles.

Malinowski, B. (1926). "Crime and Custom in Savage Society". Routledge & Kegan Paul, London.

Mead, G. H. (1932). "The Philosophy of the Present". University of Chicago Press, Chicago.

Mead, G. H. (1934). "Mind, Self and Society". University of Chicago Press, Chicago.

Morris, D. (1967). "The Naked Ape". Corgi Books, London.

Pfuetze, P. E. (1954). "The Social Self". Bookman Associates, New York.

Sorel, G. (1961). "Reflexions on Violence". Collier Books, New York.

Sorel, G. (1969). "The Illusions of Progress". University of California Press, Berkeley and Los Angeles.

von Wright, G. H. (1963). "The Varieties of Goodness". Routledge & Kegan Paul, London.

Wyndham, J. (1965). "The Day of the Triffids". Penguin Books, Harmondsworth.

7

On the Marxian Concept of *Praxis*

Jaromír Janoušek

Our civilization is a human product. The social changes in the relations between people, which in our time can be observed so distinctly, are also, to a great extent, the product of the activity of people themselves. A clear understanding of this state of affairs is important for effective socio-psychological research. My aim is to indicate the theoretical and methodological possibilities which the Marxist conception of *Praxis* may provide in this respect.

The concept of *Praxis* in Marxism refers to the activity of Man which aims at transforming the world as well as aiding his own self-development. Man is not a passive product of external influences, but instead participates, through his own practical activity, in shaping the conditions for his existence. It is through these conditions that his personality is formed. The transformed environment does not cease to have the character of an objective reality, while it simultaneously develops and is changed through the activities of human generations. It does not lose its determining influence on Man, even though it is at the same time the expression of his activity in the socio-historical process of self development. Thus, practical transformation of the world includes shaping as well as *changing human mind and consciousness*.

The theoretical starting point for an explanation of these relations by Marxism had already been provided by German classical idealistic philosophy. Of great significance in this respect is Hegel's *Phänomenologie des Geistes*. The young Marx understood the rational nucleus in Hegel's phenomenology and accepted the idea developed by Hegel that Man is created by himself in a continuous process as the result of his own work (Marx, 1932). At the same time, he objected to the fact that Hegel analysed the problem only on an abstract level, and that he considered Man the expression of "the world spirit". Instead, Marx moved *real Man* into the foreground, stressing that his creative and transforming activity, which determines his relation to his world, is called forth by *natural needs*.

Needs as the source of Man's activities have, since that time, been included as an integral part of the Marxist conception of *Praxis*. In the first place the fact that Man has needs means that there is a scarcity of objects which are indispensable to his life. These objects may be things in his immediate environment. But it is impossible for him to acquire them. When in need of something Man *lacks* the basic necessities for life. In this sense, needs refer to the *passive dependence* of Man on the surrounding material world. At the same time, however, Man's need for indispensable objects of which he is deprived mobilizes him in an endeavour to overcome the existing scarcity. Thus, needs can be conceived simultaneously in two ways. They are: (1) a state of tension which creates *activity*, aimed at obtaining necessary objects in the objective world; and (2) an indication of Man's dependence on his world.

The development of the theory of needs as a source of human activity, and problems connected with it, were tackled by materialist philosophers even before Marx. For example, Ludwig Feuerbach criticized Hegel's idealistic system because, among other things, it does not recognize the needs and passions of the subject, who is thereby transformed into a purely spiritual object. In Feuerbach's conception, the subject is living Man, not just an object of our cognition. The fact that the subject is a living human being allows Feuerbach in one of his basic assumptions to assert the unity of the subject and the object. Due to Man's bodily existence, the *I* is not only a subjective *I*, but also an object. To have a physical existence means to be incorporated into the world. The basis of the unity of subject and object is therefore assumed to be Man himself, who combines in himself thinking as well as being in the sense of acting. The essential characteristics of Man are his needs. Existence without needs is useless existence.

Feuerbach tried to find a solution of the basic ontological problem in the concept of *Praxis*. The question of being, according to him, is only a pra ical question. But Feuerbach's *Praxis* is entirely subordinated to needs; when needs are satisfied, *Praxis* stops.

Marx critically analysed Feuerbach's conception of *Praxis* in his

"Eleven Theses about Feuerbach" and in "German Ideology". Marx wrote in "German Ideology" that Feuerbach remained "a theoretician" in spite of his emphasis on *Praxis* and that his main interest was in Man's striving for correct knowledge about existing reality. "The Practical Materialist" (Marx and Engels, 1958, p. 42), on the other hand, attempts to change the world. Marx's conception of *Praxis* results in the general claim that continuous revolutionary change of the world is indispensable.

To be able to reach this objective a collective change of Man is required, a change which can only be achieved through *practical activity of a revolutionary kind*. In contrast to abstract speculations about activity in general, the Marxist conception of *Praxis* is in principle concrete. It understands *Praxis* as a concrete totality of interconnected activities in which *socially productive activity*, or *productive work*, are the point of departure. Other varieties of practical activity arise as a consequence of productive activity, and are always dependent upon it. There exists, therefore, a mutual interdependence of these different kinds of activities.

The analysis of the social character of production makes it possible to understand the relationship between *Praxis*, consciousness, and needs in a broader and deeper context. Marx's "Introduction to Criticism of Political Economy" may serve as the starting point for such an analysis. The social nature of production is revealed in the relationship between the producing activity and the product of this activity.

Since the process of production is social in its character, mediating processes between the producer and the product, between production and consumption, develop. One of these processes is the *distribution* of products. It is this social factor which determines how big a share the producer can obtain in the consumption of what he has produced. The process of sharing the products of the production is in turn dependent on other factors. The distribution of goods depends on the distribution of means of production and on relations of ownership. It also depends on the existing social division of labour in the various sectors of the production process. Finally, it depends on definite relations of production. The process of distribution is central to the total social process of production. Productive activity is a totality, the sum of all activities and the sum of all products created. The individual producer alone cannot achieve much. He can only achieve something in interaction with all those who are engaged in the total process of production. This distribution is the internal aspect of production. It does not mean that

K

productive activity is realized by an individual, nor that the individual producer is the essential factor in production, but that producing activity is realized by the sum of the producers and their interrelations.

Another social factor mediating between the producer and products is *exchange*, which is a logical consequence of the process of distribution. Besides the exchange of finished products, one has to consider the exchange of activities and abilities which occurs in the process of distribution. In this sense, exchange is a necessary internal aspect of production. The social character of production is reflected in the mutual exchange of various activities and abilities. If the process of distribution expresses the necessary social involvement of practically active, producing individuals, then the exchange process expresses the way in which the social involvement of producers is exploited by themselves. In other words, in the exchange process, the subjective factor comes more into the foreground than it does in the distribution process. At the same time, exchange invariably presumes distribution as a preceding process. Exchange is only possible as a consequence of the existing distribution process, especially the distribution of activities in the production process.

We can say that both these factors express the character of Man's productive activity as being socially determined. The process of distribution refers especially to objective aspects of this determination: the inclusion of individual subjects into socio-economic relations, independently of their consciousness and volition. In the exchange process, on the other hand, the subjective factor (the conscious social activity of people) comes more into the foreground. The differentiation between subjective and objective factors is nevertheless only relative. Social determination, and the proper place of people in this determining process, pass through various stages of development, with the development of types of ownership and of the corresponding class structures.

Marx refers to the interaction occurring between people in the basic process of production as "intercourse" or "communication" (*Verkehr*). Along with the processes of production and reproduction, this mutual social intercourse constitutes an essential element of the social life process. It characterizes two fundamental spheres of human life, the production process and family life, and as society becomes more and more differentiated social intercourse is extended to other spheres, such as business, culture, etc.

According to Marx, social intercourse can be analysed and differentiated according to several of its intrinsic aspects. One aspect of social intercourse is *structural,* and he refers to it as the "type of intercourse" (*Verkehrsform*) or "manner of intercourse" (*Verkehrsweise*); and defines it as comprising mutual relations of people in the basic process of production. Another important aspect of social intercourse is that concerned with the process as such. Mutual social intercourse must be regarded as the "moulding" of Man by Man (*die Bearbeitung der Menschen durch die Menschen*), as distinguished from Man's transformation and reshaping of nature in the process of production. This aspect also includes mental social intercourse (*geistiger Verkehr*), which is developed and made possible through the mediation of language, and which occurs within the framework of the social intercourse that takes place during the process of material production.

Besides the broader concept of social intercourse, in certain contexts Marx also refers to "social contact" (*gesellschaftlicher Kontakt*). For example, he points out that social intercourse, within the sphere of practical exchange, makes possible the social contact of private producers, that is producers who are otherwise separated from each other (Marx, *Das Kapital,* 1962, pp. 78–88).

This means that "social contact" is understood in two ways: as an aspect of mutual intercourse on the one hand, and as the *result* of the process of mutual intercourse on the other. At the same time, social contact has an important psychological impact. Marx illustrates this in his analysis of the process of cooperation. He points out that co-operation in the process of production is identical to the mutual inter-dependence of those who work side by side or with each other. The force which is created in cooperative work, when defined in this way, is greater than the sum total of the same number of workers working in isolation. But he makes an additional point: though social contact is a consequence of cooperative work, it leads to competition between those who cooperate. This competition, in turn, functions as a stimulus to mobilize energy, thus resulting in increased individual performance (Marx, ibid., p. 345).

Marx's notion of social intercourse thus comprises a number of aspects which relate to some of the significant problems of social psychology. Among them are the following: problems of mutual interaction, mutual communication, mutual social contact, and finally problems concerning the facilitation of performance under certain social conditions, or social facilitation.

The content of the socio-historical process comprises production, reproduction and the associated changes in relations between people. The activities and relations in the process of production and reproduction are the result of the activities dependent on intrinsic characteristics of the individual. As the process of production develops, these activities become more and more independent of the individual's personality. The more the activity of the individual becomes independent of his individual characteristics, the more it gains *social character*. In other words, it becomes the expression of *social roles*. For example, if we take the relationship between a buyer and a seller in the process of capitalistic production, we will find, according to Marx, that in this relationship the purely individual character of the persons involved is expressed only to a very small degree. This is due to the fact that the buyer as well as the seller enter this relation by means of their work performance. The seller sells his working power, which is treated as a commodity by the buyer and is exchanged for money. Thus, working power is abstracted from the person who owns and sells it. The buyer's and the seller's social characteristics are not permanent social states of human individuality, but are influenced by a given mode of production. However, this does not imply that such relationships mean the total abolition of this individuality. According to Marx they represent the ways individuality is necessarily expressed at a given level of development of the basic process of social production.

The social nature of the process of production results necessarily in the social nature of Man. This is due to the fact that the needs of a certain person may be satisfied by the products produced by another one and vice versa. One person may be able to produce an object which creates a need in a second person, and the second person may be the owner of an object needed by a third person, and so forth. All this indicates that Man not only acts to satisfy his own special needs, but also exceeds his own needs by producing for others. This lays the foundation for the idea of people acting towards each other as human beings. Therefore, according to Marx, the very fact of the basically social nature of the process of production helps to realize Man's social nature. This social nature is what characterizes the human species (Marx, 1953, p. 154).

The relevance of the Marxist notion of *Praxis* for the theoretical foundation of social psychology is contained in the analysis of the role of social production, as it develops in the historical process, in mediating the relationship between Man and Man. We shall compare the Marxist approach with other approaches to the basic problems of social psychology.

One classical approach to the socio-psychological problem of establishing one's self through interaction with others is outlined in the writings of Mead (1934, 1938). Mead also takes as his starting point the social character of Man's activities. He believes that the primary act is the collective social act, which comprises cooperation and interaction between a large number of individuals. The activity of an individual is only a fragment of such a social act. For that reason, the performance of the social act necessarily requires mutual communication. On the other hand, communication can take place only when collective activities are performed. The meaning of such communication must necessarily be common. It is not sufficient for the individual to interpret the meaning of the vocal "gesture" of the acting other; he must be able to interpret the meaning of his own vocal "gesture". That is to say, the individual must be able to evoke implicitly in himself the response which his gesture explicitly will evoke in the other, and then use the response of the other to check upon his own behaviour. Vocal "gestures" become significant symbols when their meaning becomes conscious.

In Mead's conception, Man's mind, i.e. his consciousness, is developed by the internalization of meaningful symbols which in turn are transmitted from certain social situations by means of communication. At the same time the individual's self is formed, that is, the individual becomes a subject through his characteristic ability to perceive himself as an object. The essential factor in the formation of the subject (his self) is the ability to take over the attitudes and roles of other people, especially those of the "significant others".

Mead distinguishes between two stages in the evolution of the subject. First there is a period where the child takes over one role after another, as one person after another appears in his life. The second stage is characterized by the generalization of role-taking. It is in this context that Mead writes about the "generalized other". His idea is that it is not only certain persons but also a whole group or a community that may function as the generalized other. The conditions for the formation of the subject (the self) include not only the taking over of attitudes of other persons towards himself, but also taking over the attitudes which others have towards various phases of the collective act. Another condition for the development of the individual subject, according to Mead, is the adoption of attitudes of an organized group in which the individual is a member, attitudes concerned with the organized social activity performed by the group.

Mead's conception of the generalized other is an important contribution to the analysis of social interaction. I do not wish to deny that taking the role of others, which can, for example, be witnessed in certain children's games, is a necessary evolutionary phase in the formation of the subject. Likewise, attitudes towards other people are generalized in the sense that the image one has of others is an important element in the adjustment of interpersonal behaviour. The better a Man's ability to consider his behaviour in a social situation, not only from his own point of view but also through the eyes of others, the more successfully will he be integrated into social relationships and the more effective will be his social interaction.

Nevertheless, it is impossible to explain in a satisfactory way either the development of the self or the individual's involvement in the social situation on the basis of taking the role of the "generalized other". The process of adapting to others is, no doubt, a factor in a subject's activity, but to restrict this activity to taking the role of others means eliminating other types of activity.

Mead tried to avoid this extreme position. In his theory of the subject he distinguishes two components. One consists of all the attitudes and roles of the other which are taken over by the individual. In addition to this adaptive component, which he denotes as *me*, he also considers the *I*, which is the self's creative component. The *I* is the acting part of the self and is evident, for example, when an individual responds to others' attitudes by presenting his own attitude towards them. Although the attitude he assumes towards others appears to be that which he has taken over from them in his experience of interaction, his response also includes another element: the *I* creates a feeling of freedom and initiative, and this leads to the concept that society not only creates the subject, but that the subject also participates in creating society.

Nevertheless, the problem of the subject remains unsolved in Mead's theories. The two components, the *I* and the *me*, remain separated. The subject's social evolution is reduced to taking the roles of others. We learn its meaning *ex post facto*, in reminiscence. The idea of future action will, according to Mead, not appear in our experience while activity remains unrealized. Social creativity does not include in Mead's conception the anticipation of the future, which is indispensable for the subject and his present social activity. The activity of the subject is, no doubt, conscious with regard to the accepted meanings of the "generalized other". With regard to the future, however, this activity is impulsive, even in the fully developed processes of communication.

What help can Marx's idea of "finding oneself in the other" be in this context? In contrast to Mead, for whom taking the role of the other is central, Marx assumes that Man becomes conscious of the common generic substance, and thus also of himself as a human being, through the mediating role played by his relations to others. The subject does not disintegrate into two parts, one in his relation to others and one in relation to himself. The subject is related to himself as a subject through the mediation brought about by his relations to others. It is, therefore, possible to generalize what is common to the actual subject and to other people, to separate oneself from one's social surroundings and thus to create aims for future activity. Marx's conception of *Praxis* as a creative revolutionary activity suggests a possible synthesis.

Another type of social activity is the interaction within the framework of market relations existing between people. This type of interaction is concerned with the *mutual exchange* of activities, judged from the point of view of their advantage to participants in the interaction. Homans (1961) writes about the values of activity and its costs (which at the same time are the lost values of alternative activities), psychological profit and investment. He formulates a number of proposals concerning the relationships of these variables. The secret of human exchange, in Homans' view, is the possibility that an actor can offer the other person behaviour which is more valuable to him than costly to the actor, and obtain from him behaviour which is more valuable to the actor than costly to the other person. Homans emphasizes the fact that the exchange does not concern commodities but activities, the value of which varies with regard to quality and quantity. This makes anticipation of results more difficult. The difficulty is increased still more by the fact that at the same time prestige, pride, and other altruistic and selfish values can constitute rewards.

It is evident that some characteristics of social interaction are expressed in the exchange of activities. To "calculate" one's own behaviour, and to compare it with the behaviour of others from the point of view of its value or the rewards and punishments involved, is indisputably a widespread socio-psychological phenomenon. Bargaining and negotiating behaviour have been the topic of numerous investigations, as, for example, in the experimental studies of games. Generally speaking, such an approach yields only one type of result. The activity exchanged is considered mainly from the point of view of its usefulness to others, while the course of this activity and its structure is regarded as less significant.

It is not possible to enter here into a general discussion of the reasons why the promotion of abstractly conceived exchange as the principle for interpreting interaction does not allow the understanding of concrete social and psychological factors of interaction. But one of the main reasons is that free exchange is illusory even in a highly developed system of exchange. It appears free only as long as it is abstracted from the existing social conditions and relations which in reality determine the shape that exchange will assume.

In order to solve this problem, it is essential to know to what extent contact influences the mutual development of subjects, the finding of oneself in the other. This influence is to be found in the fact that individual interests are expressed in market relations; this makes it possible to understand an existing common relation. In the framework of abstractly-conceived exchange, however, there exists no difference between the subjects. "It is impossible to trace any difference or even contradiction between them." (Marx, 1953, p. 152.)

The general nature of a market relationship, however, reduces considerably the process of taking the partner's attitudes and roles as well as the process of self-expression. It is characteristic of research making use of experimental games that the rational choice of strategies does not enable one to analyse adequately the covert motives. Therefore, experimental games are usually supplemented by the use of questionnaires, even though questionnaires are external to the game. I believe that one of the main reasons for the inadequacy of the experimental-game approach is that we are not fully aware of the model of Man underlying the idea of abstract exchange relationships. The private exchanging producer remains concealed by the game.

In Marx's *Grundrisse* we find an idea directly related to this problem. In an exchange relationship common interests between the participating individuals exist. These common interests are due to the mutual dependence of partners in a relation of exchange. The common interests, which may even be acknowledged, *appear* as the motive for the act of exchange. But, since the individuals involved in a market relationship are indifferent to each other, common interest does not *function* as a motive:

the interests of one individual are often perceived as being in contradiction to the interests of the other.

The differentiation which Marx makes between the consciously acknowledged common interest and the actual motivation for common activity provides a basis for a more adequate analysis of mental processes occurring within the framework of abstract exchange relationships. Thus, one has to look beyond the common interests which are a consequence of mutual interdependence in order to find the confrontation of special individual interests and motivations. In addition, Marx's differentation points to a concrete historical delimitation of the abstract exchange relationship itself.

From our point of view, this means that social activities always take place within concrete social conditions and relationships. These conditions and relationships are not something external to social activities but an integral part of them. They enter as a *means* of mutual influence, and then reproduce themselves also as internal meanings, norms, and values.

The psychological significance of such mediation has been emphasized by Vygotskij, who took as the starting point of his theories about mental development the decisive significance of both work activity and interaction between people. Work has a mediating character because tools for handling the environment are used during the course of work activity; and, in their interaction, people use various means provided by culture, such as language, numbers, codes, etc.

Even the higher mental functions of men acquire, according to Vygotskij, a mediated character as a consequence of using tools. Mediation of higher mental functions occurs because Man uses cultural phenomena for controlling his own mental processes. Vygotskij investigated from this point of view especially the function of words as means for creating meaning (see Vygotskij, 1962). He attributed, however, a broader historical meaning to this process of mediation. Taking as a point of departure his notion that words can be used to create meaning, he analysed some rudimentary mental functions which presented typical "petrified" memories from former phases of development, such as making knots to prevent forgetting, finger counting, etc.

It is important from our point of view that Vygotskij relates mediation of higher psychological functions to the interaction of people. He distinguishes between immediate and conditioned relations. Immediate relations are based upon various types of expressive movements and acts which have an "instructive" function. The contact between the instructing and the instructed persons is brought about by these expressive aspects of behaviour. Relationships mediated by signs have a more highly developed character.

Vygotskij accepts the so-called basic rule of psychology, already formulated by Janet, that a child gradually applies to himself the types of behaviour that others have applied to him. With regard to a sign, this means that if it previously served as a means for influencing others, it is only afterwards that it becomes the means of self-influence. Vygotskij's formulations stress the transference of social environment into the subject, although in general he emphasizes the activity of the subject and of his tasks in determining himself. A pointing gesture, for example, is at first simply an unsuccessful grasping movement. The hand of the child remains in the air in the direction of the object which he cannot reach. In the second phase, the unsuccessful movement evokes another person's reactions, usually a response by the mother. This response provides a new meaning for the child's movement. Against the background of this new situation, caused by the intervention of another person, the child learns to understand his movement as "pointing". From being a gesture interpreted by others, the gesture becomes one which the child himself interprets. The movement, however, had a certain direction. This means that internalization cannot take place without the activity of the subject himself.

A similar situation, according to Vygotskij, helps to create volition. At first the child obeys an order by an adult who points at an object and instructs the child to do something. The child learns gradually to express the same verbal instruction and to direct it towards himself. The significant event is that the child, having started as the performer of another person's intentions, becomes the performer of his own purpose. Vygotskij generalizes this transformation thus: "A personality becomes what he is for himself through what he is for others." Vygotskij's theory lays the foundation for a conception of finding oneself in other persons. The subject's activity in interaction with others is the precondition as well as the consequence of his self-development.

Let me return to our problem on a more general level. Interpreting Marx's concept of *Praxis* and re-examining some of the basic types of sociopsychological relations, I took as a starting point the fact that the practical activity of a subject, operating upon an objective environment, comprises the interaction between people and the self-development of the subject. It is now necessary to examine the relationship mediating between *Praxis* and social interaction.

The development of the subject against the background of practical activity and in interaction with other people, that is his forming a certain self-conception and a certain degree and type of self-realization, is determined by the subject's *social role*. This is expressed in relationships with other people and with himself. This fact does not represent the end of social intercourse or social interaction, but merely its beginning.

After he has achieved certain results by his practical activity, the subject develops his social interaction further by means of roles. It is here that social interaction and *Praxis* are typically *mediated* through social roles. A role, therefore, has two functions: an establishing function and an operating one. The individual is usually incorporated in the social structure by a number of roles. He cannot, however, perform them all at the same time. Therefore he activates these roles *alternatively*, or keeps them in a latent state, depending on the situation in which he finds himself (see Linton, 1945, p. 77).

The founders of Marxism pointed out that capitalism, in connection with personal independence, made it possible for a subject to have a certain freedom in choosing his activities and to move from one activity to another. But the negative aspect of this freedom was the accompanying indifference towards these same activities, from which Man becomes alienated. Reversals of roles which occur during this alienation process are inauthentic from the point of view of the individual. The same is true of the new form of contemporary capitalism in which changes within the structure of productive activities take place with an increasing speed and mobility characteristic of modern life. In spite of the apparent dynamic vigour inherent in these changes, they imply for the subject his withdrawal from active participation in social life.

An interesting confrontation of viewpoints took place between two representatives of neo-psychoanalysis in their attempts to analyse this problem. Sullivan (1953) considered the experience of inauthenticity and the experience of the disappearance of oneself as an active subject integrated into the process as a natural adaptation to new circumstances. He contended that the subject is constituted by roles which he enacts in his social intercourse with others, and the function of these roles is to make agreement between interacting people possible, thus avoiding disagreement and the resulting anxiety. Fromm (1955), on the other hand, pointed out that the disappearance of the subject's experience of himself as an active being is a pathological phenomenon. It has to be compensated for by substituted experiences, such as the subject's considering himself successful, useful, pleasant, etc., from the point of view of others, in order to avoid the damage which the inauthenticity could otherwise cause. Fromm regarded direct participation in decision-making, and in directive processes which influence Man's life as an essential, and not compensatory, way of recovering from the state of inauthenticity. Mental balance can be reached, he considered, only by adapting society to the basic, existential needs of Man which result from his productive orientation: needs for love, creativity, brotherhood, freedom, objectivity, reason and identity with himself. Thus, mental balance must be defined in terms of society's adaptation to Man's needs, and not in terms of Man's adaptation to society. Fromm asserted that the goal of adapting society to Man's needs serves basic human values. In Fromm's theories the entire process of mental self-realization becomes an abstract postulate which is all the more abstract because the matrix of basic needs is taken out of the context of the socio-historical process.

Socialism creates preconditions for the mental self-realization of Man. It abandons private ownership of means of production and transfers them into the hands of society in order to create new living conditions. The development of consciousness in accordance with the new social existence necessarily carries with it inner limits, since the new being provides at first a rather narrow framework for the formation of new psychic structures and must itself be developed. Therefore it is important to stress class consciousness, not only in the sense of adaptation to the new social conditions, but above all in the development of new productive activities.

The perspective of the socialist variant of the scientific-technological revolution helps to transcend these limits. It takes into account the full development of the processes in which the development of the human subject is necessarily a component of the realization of the social changes themselves. In this way it includes the changes in the relationship between Man and society. One does not *assume* Man's adaptation to society or society's adaptation to Man, but instead one postulates the coincidence of the development of Man's human qualities, and the reshaping of society as a permanent, progressive process. In other words, Man is to be determined by that social reality which he is actually designing and creating himself in according with basic human qualities.

The prospect of such a development puts new demands on social psychology, demands of which social psychologists are not yet sufficiently aware. The increased speed in changes in civilization may lead to a disappearance of earlier stereotypes and to a loss of various low-level activities, such as aggressive and escapist actions.

The perspective of the socialist scientific-technological revolution, and the formation of a new awareness connected with it, place education, understood as the conscious self-development of Man, in the centre of human efforts. One of the reasons for the strategic importance of education is the fact that Man is a complex entity functioning at various levels of biological and historical development, some of which may contradict the aims of education. This difficulty sometimes leads towards the radical concept that education, as we know it now, must be completely replaced by the discovery and planning of the new Man who will not turn against himself, but will make full use of his ability for self-modification and self-regulation in order to achieve a full realization of the self. In this process, psychology may play a dominant role (see Hacker, 1969).

The feasibility of such a project can be questioned. A more practical orientation for social-psychological research would seem to consist of investigating present human activities to find out which of these tend to lead towards development of the new awareness, and which do not. The Marxist conception of *Praxis* is an important clue to the solution of this problem.

References

Fromm, E. (1955). "The Sane Society". Rinehart, New York.

Hacker, F. J. (1969). Human implications. *In* "Mankind 2000" (Eds F. Jungkand and J. Galtung). Akademisk Forlag, Oslo.

Homans, G. C. (1961). "Social Behaviour: Its Elementary Forms". Harcourt, Brace & World, New York.

Linton, B. (1945). "The Cultural Background of Personality". Appleton-Century-Crofts, New York.

Marx, K. (1932). Ökonomisch-Philosophische Manuskripte. *In* "Mega", 1.3. Marx-Engels Verlag, Berlin.

Marx, K. (1953). "Grundrisse zur Kritik der politischen Ökonomie (Rohentwirf)". Dietz Verlag, Berlin.

Marx, K. (1962). "Das Kapital". *In* "Werke" (Eds K. Marx and F. Engels), Vol. 23. Dietz Verlag, Berlin.

Marx, K. and Engels, F. (1958). Deutsche Ideologie. *In* "Werks" (Eds K. Marx and F. Engels), Vol. 3. Dietz Verlag, Berlin.

Mead, G. H. (1934). "Mind, Self, Society" (Ed. Charles Morris). University of Chicago Press, Chicago.

Mead, G. H. (1938). "The Philosophy of the Act". University of Chicago Press, Chicago.

Sullivan, H. S. (1953). "The Interpersonal Theory of Psychiatry". Norton, New York.

Vygotskij, L. S. (1962). "Thought and Language". M.I.T. Press, Cambridge, Mass.

PART 3

Methods and Models

8

Rational and Non-Rational Models of Man

Håkan Wiberg

1   Statement of the problem

Our intention is to review some rational and non-rational models in order to try to clarify the following issues:

What is meant and presupposed when describing a model as rational or non-rational?

What presuppositions are made in the different models, and to what extent are these presuppositions tenable?

What are the main problems implied by the different models?

2   Weber: a classical model

One way of summarizing Weber's writings on modern society is to state that his main thesis is that society is becoming increasingly

297

rational in different respects. This, however, applies to a number of more or less connected themes, such as ethics becoming more rational, institutions and organizations becoming more rational, and social action becoming more rational. Roughly, we have to deal with a rational model of society and a rational model of Man, which are connected by Weber's typology of social action. We will shortly come back to the relations between models of society and models of Man. At present, it should be noted that Weber makes two different types of distinction between different senses of rationality.

On the one hand, concerning rationality as a property of societies, he makes a distinction between what he calls *formal* rationality and *substantive* rationality. The meaning of "formal rationality" can be inferred from passages such as the following:

> Rational commerce is the field in which quantitative reckoning first appeared, to become dominant finally over the whole extent of economic life.
>
> Weber, 1966a, p. 170

> The term "formal rationality of economic action" will be used to designate the extent of quantitative calculation or accounting which is technically possible and which is actually applied. The "substantive rationality", on the other hand, is the degree in which a given group of persons, no matter how it is delimited, is or could be adequately provided with goods by means of an economically oriented course of social action. This course of action will be interpreted in terms of a given set of ultimate values no matter what they may be. There is a variety of different possibilities.
>
> Weber, 1966b, pp. 185–6

But he also notes that "formal rationality" is unambiguous, at least in the sense that expression in money terms yields the highest degree of formal calculability. The concept of substantive rationality, on the other hand, is "full of difficulties", which stem from its *relative* character. An economy is substantively rational only relative to some given standard of value, often including some standard of distribution of goods. And, in principle, there is an indefinite number of possible standards of value that are "rational" in this sense. Furthermore, there is a tension between the two kinds of rationality, as Parsons pointed out (Weber, 1966b, p. 35), even if they tend to coincide under certain conditions (ibid., p. 212).

In any case, Weber's substantive rationality refers to *collective* action. At present we shall only note that one way of formalizing this is in terms of welfare functions, to which we shall return later. Instead, let us concentrate on the characteristics of *individual* social action.

Social action, like other forms of action, may be classified in the following four types according to its mode of orientation:

(1) in terms of rational orientation to a system of discrete individual ends (*Zweckrational*) . . .

(2) in terms of rational orientation to an absolute value (*Wertrational*) involving a conscious belief in the absolute value of some ethical, aesthetic, religious, or other form of behaviour, entirely for its own sake . . .

(3) in terms of affectual orientation, especially emotional . . .

(4) traditionally oriented, through the habituation of long practice.

Weber, 1966b, p. 115

As Weber points out, here too there is a tension between *Zweckrationalität* and *Wertrationalität*. For, since *Zweckrationalität* is concerned with the end, while the means and the secondary results are all taken into account rationally and weighed, the more *Wertrational* action is the less *Zweckrational* it will become.

The following essential points need to be mentioned here:

a. Weber distinguishes four different types of *orientation* in this context, whereas both he and many of his followers later refer more precisely to *purposes* or *ends* of actions (see, for example, Becker, 1950, pp. 22–32 and 199–201).

b. Weber distinguishes four different *types*. In individual actions, these types may coexist or not in a fairly complicated pattern. Roughly, (2) above is incompatible with (3) and (4), (4) shades over into (1), (1) and (2) are negatively correlated, etc.

c. Although Weber makes a distinction between two different senses of rationality, he is not very clear (beyond the obvious) as to what it is that they have in common to make them both rational. As we shall see later, it is very difficult to give a precise notion of rationality, in the sense which would closely correspond to *Zweckrationalität*.

Therefore, even before trying to give a more precise notion of rationality, it is important to note that we are faced with a set of different *explananda* in "rational" and "rationality". Before going further, we shall try to disentangle this set of *explananda*.

3 Different explananda in "rational" and in "rationality"

In his exploration of the meaning of "rationality", Bennett (1964) started with a kind of behaviour which was not rational in order to see what had to be added to it in order for it to be accounted rational.

After a thorough discussion, which we will not include here, he arrives at the following conclusion: "The idea of rationality is that of the ability, given certain present and particular data, to unite and relate them with other data in certain appropriate ways." (Bennett, 1964, p. 85.)

This, therefore, provides us with a start: What are these ways that are appropriate, relative to presumed needs or wants?

3.1 TYPE OF ACTOR

In principle, it would be satisfactory to be able to speak of actors in general whose actions could be categorized. For many purposes, however, this may not be appropriate. Thus, Heiskanen, discussing different approaches in organizational and administrative research, writes:

> The inherent strain in the idea of applying the decision making scheme . . . : the problem is to cope with both individual and organizational (collective) decision making and still use the theoretical concepts of the scheme persistently in the same meaning. The easiest way out seems to be to follow the old tradition and assume that organizations and organized and administered activities in general are based solely on cooperation, whereby objective or organized action and those of the participating individuals become assimilated.
>
> Heiskanen, 1967, pp. 74–75

He goes on to indicate that this coping has not yet been successfully done (ibid., p. 84). Johnsen (1968, pp. 222ff.), though he has a more favourable opinion of the possibility of using individual properties ("rationality") in the analysis of organizations, still concedes that they have to be refined for each specific organization analysed.

Therefore, we shall initially restrict our *explanandum* "rationality" to some property of individuals or individual actions in order to introduce later some of the additional complications that arise when more persons are involved.

3.2 TYPE OF DECISIONS

In the discussion of Weber above, *Zweckrationalität* was found to be closely connected to means-end reasoning. This is not the only type of connection. Thus, Eckhoff and Jacobsen (1966, p. 9) write:

> When "rational" is defined as suggested here, several types of decision-models will satisfy the requirements of rationality. On the one hand, we have the *means-end*

models according to which the decision-maker outlines the consequences attached to the various alternatives of choice, calculating the probability of each consequence, and chooses the alternatives which have the greatest utility value. On the other hand, we have several models where the consequences of the decision are irrelevant or of minor importance, and where the emphasis is on the correct subsumption under given categories.

Again, we will restrict the *explanandum*. Means-end models and subsumption models are, no doubt, related to each other. Thus, in some versions, the rules are made by the actor for the actor, and in such cases the difference becomes fairly slight. In other cases the rules are made by some collective decision-maker or some decision-maker on behalf of a collective; but consideration of this would entangle us prematurely in the problems concerning collective decisions.

3.3 SOME SUGGESTIONS FROM THE LITERATURE

In this section we quote a collection of statements from various authors on the definition of, or conditions for, rationality.

Third is "rationality". This concept is, as has been shown, a difficult one in Weber's work. What he means here includes above all two things. On the one hand tradition is radically devalued . . . On the other hand it means the systematization of conduct according to rational norms. No single act can stand by itself or be valued on its own merits alone, but only terms of its bearing on a whole system of rational conduct.

Parsons on Weber in Weber, 1966b, p. 80

The rationality of behaviour does not consist in the principle of selection of the first choice, which is a formal principle . . . The distinction between rational and irrational behaviour must be found in the content of the image either of the field or of the value ordering. Thus, behaviour is irrational if it is based on a false image of the world or on a bad system of value ordering. The exact meaning of "false" and "bad" we leave to a fairly distant future.

Boulding, 1963, p. 9

Williamson . . . claims that rational behaviour requires that the individual discriminate in his attempts to achieve need satisfaction: in one environment he will seek satisfaction for one group of needs, in another environment for a second group, and so forth.

Johnsen, 1968, p. 239

Scott, discussing international attitudes, declares that we are all both rational and irrational; he defines irrationality as the intervention of (1) personality mechanisms and (2) extracognitive factors such as social norms . . . Scott further defines rationality as cognitive consistency plus empirical validity.

Converse, 1968, p. 509

The distinction between rational and irrational lies in the degree of self-consciousness and the stability of the images rather than in any distinction of the principle of the optimum.

Boulding, 1963, p. 151

Another usual characteristic attached to this set of rational characteristics is that decisions be made coolly, with a clear head. Essentially, this derives from the requirement of accurate calculations. It does not specify that the individual must avoid emotional involvement in the outcome or experience no emotion during the process of deliberation. Whether or not he does so is irrelevant as long as his calculations are not affected by his emotion . . .

Verba in Knorr and Verba, 1965, p. 108

Decision-makers are not simply distributed along a one-dimensional scale that stretches from complete rationality at one hand to complete irrationality on the other. Rationality is a collection of attributes, and departures from complete rationality may be in different directions. Irrationality can imply a disorderly or inconsistent value system, faulty calculation, an inability to receive messages or communicate efficiently; it can imply random or haphazard influence in the reaching of decisions or the transmission of them, or in the receipt or conveyance of information; and it sometimes merely reflects the collective nature of a decision among individuals who do not have identical value systems and whose organizational arrangements and communication system do not cause them to act like a single entity.

Schelling, 1963, p. 16

What the rational political man wants, I believe, is to win, a much more specific and specifiable motive than the desire for power. Furthermore, the desire to win differentiates some men from others. Unquestionably, there are guilt-ridden and shame-conscious men who do not desire to win, who in fact desire to lose. These are the irrational ones in politics.

Riker, 1962, p. 22

Each player is assumed to be "rational" in the sense that, given two alternatives, he will always choose the one he prefers, i.e. the one with the larger utility.

Luce and Raiffa, 1958, p. 55

Game theory . . . is concerned with *rational* ways of playing and this means only one thing: to get as much as possible in terms of utilities.

Rapoport, 1966, p. 29

3.4   CONCLUSIONS FROM SECTION 3.3

The first impression that might be gained from this series of quotations is that the various authors have different (sometimes very different) views about the precise meaning we should attach to rationality. But they start from rather different *explananda* and it is thus not surprising that they should arrive at different *explanantia*.

To sort out the picture, let us assume the existence of an actor who has some *picture of the world*, and some *value system*, and who makes a *decision* leading to an *action*. First of all, we need only take *either* the decision *or* the action into consideration in this context if we assume the decision to be equivalent to what would happen if it were carried out. In the quotations at least the following *explananda* can be found "rational":

a. Rationality as a property of a world picture.
b. Rationality as a property of a value system.
c. Rationality as a relation between a world picture, a value system, and a decision.
d. Any combination of a–c.

Clearly more can be found than these, but perhaps they are the most interesting. So the next set of questions to answer will be:

a. What, if any, qualities should a world picture or, in general, a system of assumptions have in order to be described as "rational"?
b. What, if any, qualities should a value system have in order to be described as "rational"?
c. What relations should exist between the given world picture, the given value system, and the decision (or action) in order for us to describe the decision (or action) as "rational"?

And we could add a fourth question to sum up the first three:

d. What combination of rationality in the first, second, and third sense of "rationality" should a man exhibit in order for us to describe *him* as "rational"?

3.5 RATIONALITY OF A WORLD PICTURE

It would seem that there are two main types of criteria offered in the literature, more often than not by implication rather than explicitly. The first type is expressed in criteria of what this totality of assumptions should *look like*. In this category belong the various logical criteria. Instead of going into detail I would prefer to summarize them as follows:

A world picture should satisfy the rules of formal logic (if it is to be considered as rational).

But this is certainly not a sufficient criterion. In addition to those formal rules, all of which could be vaguely summarized by saying that contradiction is irrational (though a coherent system need not necessarily be rational), we often find a set of more or less tacit rules defining what assumptions a rational world picture must *not* contain. Usually these assumptions contradict some of the latest findings of science or of common sense. Let S be the set of propositions that are taken to be "true" (in the sense just stated). In such a case we could, still in a very abstract manner, formulate the first formal (but also to some extent material) version of the criterion of rationality for world pictures. *If S is the set of "true" propositions, then, for a world picture W to be considered as rational, the conjunction "S and W" should satisfy the rules of formal logic.* (If S is empty, we must return to the original version.)

Since this is not a treatise in formal logic let us stop here, having noted this version simply for the sake of being systematic. The second type of criteria of world pictures seems to be much more central to this discussion. These are criteria concerning the ways in which the picture is acquired, about the owner's title to it as it were. This would mean that two people could entertain exactly the same assumption about some aspect of reality but we would reject one of the pictures as irrational *since it was acquired in the wrong way.* This would seem sufficient to convey the idea of criteria of acquisition. A little more generally, the claimant to rational knowledge should either be able to give a satisfactory account of its acquisition or be able to defend satisfactorily the proposition claimed as knowledge. Since we are discussing epistemology rather than psychology, these two conditions tend to amount to the same. (For a discussion of the meaning of knowledge, see, for example, Ayer, 1961, pp. 31–35 and pp. 68–75). Assuming this, we might formulate the second epistemological version of a criterion of rationality of world pictures thus:

In order that a set of assumptions can be called rational, they should have been acquired in accordance with the rules of sound scientific methodology, or at least not deviate too far from them.

This, of course, is intentionally very vague. The point is not to be precise but to indicate a problem area that is connected with one of the senses of rationality. Discussions of how it could be made more precise could be found in a large number of textbooks. (For a lucid exposition we refer the reader to, for example, Ackoff *et al.*, 1965.)

3.6   RATIONALITY OF A VALUE SYSTEM

While it is clearly possible to state both a set of rules of formal logic and at least some methodological principles which express widespread agreement between logicians and methodologists, to do something similar for a value system appears much more difficult, if at all possible. In consequence, to try to state some more precise criteria for rationality of value systems appears to be a hard task.

There are, however, some restrictions we can make in order to render the task slightly less complicated. First, we can restrict the ambiguous word "value" to mean "preference", which appears to be the most relevant sense in the present context. Second, we may cut short the discussion concerning the interpretation of value judgements by accepting the position that one may formulate a logic for such judgements irrespective of whether they are to be interpreted as theoretical or not. We would therefore be inclined to formulate a first, formal, criterion for rationality of an individual value system thus:

In order for a system of preferences to be rational it has to conform to the axioms of a logic of preference.

That this does not get us very far is indicated by the expression "a logic of preference". Several such logics have been proposed, for example by Halldén (1957) and von Wright (1963). After the critical review by Hansson (1970), only very few complicated axioms remain as well founded in intuition.

Again, when we say that a value system is rational we usually mean more than this. Thus, after leaving the exact meaning of "false" and "bad" to "a fairly distant future", Boulding goes on to state that it is clear that schizophrenic behaviour is based on an image of the world that is at least false enough to occasion sanctions imposed by those who have power to do so, and explains that criminal behaviour is based on a value ordering that is false in much the same sense. If we let V stand for a conjunction of value judgements that is "true" in the sense Boulding hints at, we can formulate another criterion for value systems analogous to that for a world picture:

For a value system S to be regarded as rational, the conjunction "V and S" has to conform to the axioms of a preference of logic.

Again, of course, V varies between societies and generations. Even so, this formulation may seem a bit doubtful; one way to defend it is to assume that the negative impact of the anticipated sanctions is somehow incorporated into V.

And, finally, in many cases we will also find professed criteria of rationality parallel to the third theoretical case: in order for a value system to be regarded as rational, it has to be acquired, or (and this applies also to theoretical case) defensible in a certain way. Now, there appears to be much less unanimity about what is a reasonable way of acquiring or defending value beliefs than there is concerning theoretical beliefs. Therefore, in order to avoid controversies, I shall use the following rather vague summary:

For a value system to be regarded as rational it should either have a special genetic history involving certain logical operations ("logical" in a wide sense), or it should be defensible in a certain way (e.g. the person holding the value system should be willing to generalize value judgements according to certain rules).

As pointed out, there are strong reasons for leaving the formulation vague, since there is a considerable difference of opinion among the philosophers of ethics as to what are the logical operations, rules of generalization, etc.

4 Rational Decisions

Under section 3 we have attempted to cover most of the interesting *explananda* "rational"; but we have omitted the crucial one. This might be formulated as follows:

Given an individual with a world picture W and a value system V, who is in a situation S with a set of alternatives for action A_1, A_2, . . ., what should be the relation between A_j, W and V in order for us to describe A_j as a rational action, or the decision to do A_j as a rational decision?

The intuitive answer to this question would be some statement to the effect that the alternative chosen should lead to at least as much value as any other alternative, given the assumptions in the world picture.

Essential problems arise, however, when we try to formulate this more precisely. In order to get a systematic overall view of these problems, we shall structure the discussion according to the type of situation in the following order:

a. Decisions under certainty.
b. Decisions under known probabilities (risk).
c. Decisions whose results essentially depend on at least one other decision maker (games).
d. Decisions under uncertainty.

Before entering the discussion case by case, some general points should be made. First all of them are ideal cases: they are models for decision. As we shall see when the presuppositions made in these models are spelt out, they are (probably) never fulfilled. The point is rather to outline some comparatively simple assumptions and to present what are essentially prescriptive models based on these assumptions in order to discuss: (1) how the concept of rationality can be made more precise by reference to the models; and (2) how fruitful these models are as starting points for empirical research at various levels.

The order of exposition is traditional in many treatises on the topic of decisions and games. The case of decision under certainty is the simplest one. When one proceeds to decisions under risk some complications are added to the problems of case (a). The notion of expected utility derived from the discussion on decisions under risk is essential in discussing strategic decisions and games. Finally, the reason for treating decisions under uncertainty after games is that some of the solutions proposed originate from the theory of games.

4.1 DECISIONS UNDER CERTAINTY

In a discussion of explanations in human sciences, Kmita and Nowak (1970) point out that many proposed explanations have the following logical structure:

(1) The end of the action C (or the property C of the product of the relevant action) has been for X the realization of the state S.

(2) X believed that by undertaking C (or by making his product have the property C) he would realize the state S.

(3) X did undertake the action C, or

(3') The product of X's activity has the property C.

They also point out that the conjunction (1) and (2) does not logically imply (3) or (3'), so that some additional premise has to be added in order to make the explanation a deductively valid one. Essentially, three types of additional premises have been proposed. These are: (a) a set of psychological laws; (b) assumptions of some kind of intuition peculiar to human studies (and different from extraspection and introspection); or (c) what the authors call the rationality assumption. They formulate this rationality assumption for the case of decisions under certainty. Slightly rephrased, it runs as follows: If (at the moment t) X has to undertake one of the actions $C_1, \ldots, C_n$, which to his knowledge at t are mutually exclusive and jointly exhaustive and unfailingly lead to the results $S_1, \ldots, S_m$ respectively ($m \leq n$), and if $S_1, \ldots S_m$ are ordered by a relation of preference characteristic for X at t, then X will undertake an action C_i leading to a most preferred result S_j.

For our purposes, this is a fairly clarifying formulation. Let us now analyse it in terms of its different elements. It is to be noted that Kmita and Nowak are not concerned with rationality as a predicate of a world picture. The only thing that is assumed about the *world picture* is the standard supposition for decisions under certainty, i.e. to each possible action is tied one well-defined consequence only.

As for the *value system*, a fairly weak assumption is made. It is supposed that all the consequences under consideration are comparable, that is that the preference relation defined on the set of pairs of consequences is complete. Although this is not explicitly stated, we may take it that this relation is thought to define an ordinal scale. (Less would not be sufficient and more would not be necessary in this context.) In other words, preference is assumed to be at least a total preordering relation. (For the properties of such relations, we refer to Debreu, 1962, pp. 7–10.)

The rationality of the decision, finally, is the one referred to in the quotations from Rapoport and from Luce and Raiffa in section 3.3. It should only be noted that the formulation above refers to rationality as a relation between an action, a *subjective* world picture, and subjective preferences.

Several criticisms have been made of this model, both as a descriptive model and as a prescriptive model; and some of these criticisms have led to suggested reformulations of the model.

The interesting question concerning the assumptions made about the world picture is not so much whether it is realistic but whether it is so grossly unrealistic that it makes the model untenable as a descriptive model, whatever its prescriptive merits may be. The assumption of certainty is rarely, if ever, fulfilled. There is another difficulty which is common to all the different cases of decision: if we want to know what choice has been made by an actor, we have to know amongst what alternatives that choice has been made. Luce (1959) states:

> Actually, in practice, it is extremely difficult to know, and much experimental technique is devoted to arranging matters so that the organism and the experimenter are (thought to be) in agreement about what the alternatives are. All of our procedures for data collection and analysis require the experimenters to make explicit decisions about whether a certain action did or did not occur, and all of our choice theories . . . begin with the assumption that we have a mathematically well-defined set, the elements of which can be identified with the choice alternatives . . . More than any other single thing, in my opinion, this Achilles' heel has limited the

applicability of current theories of choice: it certainly has been a significant stumbling block in the use of information theory in psychology, it has limited learning theory experiments to a rather special class of phenomena typified by T-maze experiments etc.

pp. 3–4

The assumption made about the value system was a fairly weak one. Nevertheless, many authors have argued that it is still too strong to be realistic. Thus, Hansson (1970, p. 12) points out that it is quite consistent to say that one cannot have a preference for catching a bad cold over losing $20.00, nor the reverse, without admitting that the two alternatives are, at least in a positive sense, equally good. He further points out that this has consequences for the axiom of transitivity which is necessary to make from preference even a weak total order relation. For, repeating the above argument and substituting $21.00 for $20.00, it would follow from the axiom of transitivity and the two arguments that one could not strictly prefer losing $20.00 to losing $21.00.

When it is not a single individual but a group making decisions by a majority vote the axiom of transitivity is also challenged. The "voting paradox" states that if we have three alternatives and three persons who order the alternatives thus:

A	B	C
x	y	z
y	z	x
z	x	y

then the majority rule implies that x is preferred to y, y to z, and z to x (Luce and Raiffa, 1958, p. 333).

Several different modifications of the assumptions are possible. (We shall leave the group decision case for the present.) Hansson points out that a set of alternatives with only partial comparability would always contain maximal subsets with total comparability, but goes on to opine that even if this were so it would be possible to find counter-instances.

We may keep the axioms of transitivity and reflexivity defining a preordering but drop the axiom of comparability. We will thus get a partial preordering.

Even if the objections to transitivity were not valid, a partial preordering would allow only a trivial mathematical treatment. One way of rendering it mathematically tractable is to add the axiom of symmetry, stating that no two alternatives can be equally good, and another axiom saying that any two objects have a least upper bound and a greatest lower bound. Then we would have enough to warrant a mathematical theory for deducing non-trivial consequences, that is the theory of *lattices* (see, e.g. Rutherford, 1965), but the axiom of anti-symmetry is no doubt too strong to lead to an empirically applicable model.

Another way of avoiding the problem of incomparability is to define pay-offs as vectors. This is what Simon (1957) suggests in the case of "an individual . . . trying to implement a number of *values that do not have a common denominator*—e.g. he compares two jobs in terms of salary, climate, pleasantness of work, prestige, etc." (p. 251). This appears intuitively satisfactory but in a way only pushes the problem one step further on since it is very difficult to compare vectors without reducing them to scalars. The only simple way of comparison would be that of dominance. We say that one vector pay-off $(x_1, x_2, \ldots, x_n)$ (weakly) dominates another $(y_1, y_2, \ldots, y_n)$ if there is one or more j such that x_j is better than y_j, while, for all other i, x_i is at least as good as y_i. It is easily seen that, out of two vectors, one rarely dominates the other. Furthermore, these are the trivial cases since the problem of choice becomes interesting only when comparing two jobs, out of which one has better salary but lower prestige. This, then, becomes the problem of finding an indifference curve describing how people trade off one value against another. At least on the individual level, the empirical problems connected with this issue appear to be still unsolved. Thus, Johnsen (1968, p. 361), after considering different psychologists' treatment of utility by experiments, concludes that we "find no answer to the trade-off question".

Finally, *time* has to enter our considerations in two ways at least. One is connected with the world picture W. If W has at least a minimal degree of sophistication, it includes something about the consequences at *various* time points after the action. This means at least two things. First, at least some actions have consequences at several time points, and each action is evaluated with respect to all these consequences. Second, these *consequences* of the action under consideration are *situations* for later actions.

Furthermore, as pointed out by Shubik (1963), in the case of game theory the value system must somehow be able to cope with *time preference,* i.e. inter-temporal comparisons. If I prefer an apple now to a banana now, what about a banana now compared to an apple tomorrow? In economics, this problem is often taken care of by assuming individuals to have *discount rates.* The general assumption behind this is that later enjoyment of something is seen as less valuable than enjoying that same thing now. This appears reasonable in many, if not all, situations, even if one can have doubts concerning the specific functions that are used to describe these discount rates.

This problem has been treated by Fishburn (1968), who discusses seven different cases: impatience, extreme impatience, eventual impatience, time perspective, no time preference, persistence, and variety. Let us, however, simplify the discussion by making the assumption that the preference relation is strong enough to allow for representation by a function (see, for example, Debreu, 1954), and that the preference over time can be represented by a discount rate.

Then, at least in principle, it is possible to use fairly simple technical devices. Generally speaking, if we substitute the sum of the discounted values of all the consequences in the track of an action for the value of the single consequences considered before, we can use exactly the same criterion.

When it comes to the fact that the consequence of one action is a situation for another action we are confronted with a more complicated problem. For, assume that I am now taking a decision concerning my *last* action, i.e. I will survive for some time to enjoy the consequences of it, but can never intervene again in the course of nature. Then we are left in the previous situation, and the criterion of rationality will pick out one or more actions which are best in the sense defined by the criterion. If, however, I am to engage in further actions in addition to the one I am presently considering, then picking the best action now may entail changing the future in such a way that my best action the next time I am to decide on one will be less good than the action that would have been best if I had chosen another action now.

(Let us take an imaginary, but concrete, example. Imagine a game in which I may be able to get three cents in the first move, but this restricts my choices in the second move to give me maximally two cents; or I may get two cents in the first move and have an option to choose four cents in the second move. Assuming no discount rate, it would not be reasonable to take the maximal pay-off in the first move.)

The solution to this difficulty is to generalize the discourse to discuss strategies rather than actions. We need not include as yet the full complexity of the strategy concept involved in game theory. Let us, therefore, call a "strategy" a series of decisions concerning all one's actions from the present one to the last one. We can then say that a *strategy is rational* (with respect to V) if it leads to at least as good a sum-total of all consequences (predicted by W) as any other strategy, and that an *action now* is rational, if it belongs to a rational strategy.

4.2 DECISIONS UNDER RISK

Let us now change our assumptions about W so that, instead of assuming that only one consequence is ordered to every action alternative, we assume that there exists a set of possible consequences, C_1, $\ldots C_p$, such that for every alternative A_i it is known with what probability p_{ij} the consequence C_j will occur. We may then represent the underlying W for a decision in a matrix:

$$
\begin{array}{cccc}
 & C_1 & C_2 \ldots C_p \\
A_1 & p_{11} & p_{12} \ldots p_{1p} \\
\cdot \\
\cdot \\
\cdot \\
A_n & p_{n1} & p_{n2} \ldots p_{np}
\end{array}
$$

Let us assume initially that $C_1, \ldots C_p$ are amounts of money in some game. What is the rational decision in this situation?

We define the *mathematical expectation* of alternative A_j as

$$E(A_j) = p_{j1}C_1 + p_{j2}C_2 + \ldots + p_{jp}C_p.$$

The classical idea is that the rational choice is to take the action whose mathematical expectation is the highest, and the traditional justification for that idea is that this will, in the long run, lead to the highest pay-offs. This means that if the same game is repeated over and over again a gambler sticking to this principle will, eventually, become better off than any other gambler.

The oldest counter-arguments were developed in the early eighteenth century by Daniel Bernouilli (see Savage, 1954, pp. 91–104); they are: Why do prudent people buy insurance policies although they know that this increases the expected wealth of the insurance company and decreases their own? How can the St. Petersburg paradox be solved?

We will now formulate the St. Petersburg paradox. Assume that one is offered a game with a fair coin and the following rules: if, in the first toss, heads come up, one wins nothing and the game ends; if tails come up, one is given two dollars and a second toss takes place; if heads come up, one gets nothing more and the game is over; if tails come up, one wins another four dollars and a new toss, and so on. Generally, if tails come up in the nth toss, one receives 2^n dollars and is allowed another toss. As can easily be verified, the mathematical expectation is

$$\tfrac{1}{2} \times 2 + (\tfrac{1}{2})^2 \times 2^2 + \ldots + (\tfrac{1}{2})^n \times 2^n + \ldots = 1 + 1 + \ldots + 1 + \ldots,$$

i.e. greater than any infinite number. According to the principle of mathematical expectation, a gambler should be willing to pay any sum of money to take part in this game. But he will not.

Bernouilli's solution is to disregard the cash value and look at what he calls the *moral worth* of the cash value. This moral worth, or, using a more modern term, utility, is then assumed to be a concave function of money, i.e. the marginal utility of money is assumed to be decreasing. Bernouilli proposes the logarithm. But in order to solve all versions of the paradox one also has to assume a finite upper limit for utility.) In his account, Savage goes on to add that so far nobody has suggested a better prototype for Everyman's utility function.

The law of decreasing marginal utility does not, however, solve the trade-off problem already referred to. Furthermore, if this is our only assumption, any monotonically increasing function of one utility is another utility. In order to avoid this difficulty, von Neumann and Morgenstern have developed a stricter notion of utility in the presentation of which I shall follow Luce and Raiffa (1958, pp. 23–30; this differs slightly from the original).

Assume that one prefers an apple to an orange to a banana, or, in general, A to B to C. This can be expressed by writing

$$V(A) = 0, \ V(B) = 3, \ V(C) = 7.$$

It can also be expressed by any other strictly monotonic transformation of these values. Even if we norm the values so that the least preferred alternative is given value 0 and the most preferred one value 1, any number between 0 and 1 will do for the alternative in the middle. This is rather awkward when it comes to expressing the idea that one very much prefers A to B, and prefers B to C only slightly, or, more generally, expressing how much more one prefers A to B than B to C.

The essential idea in the notion of utility put forward by von Neumann and Morgenstern and later authors is that utility is defined by a *lottery*.

To be more precise, assume that one is given the choice between either the certainty of getting B or taking part in a lottery where one gets A with probability p and C with probability 1-p. If p is very close to 1, the lottery is to be preferred, but if p is very close to 0, getting B for sure will be the best alternative. It is now assumed that there is precisely one p value such that there is indifference between B and the lottery. This p value is therefore defined as the utility of B, so that

$$V(A) = a \times 1 + b, \quad V(B) = a \times p + b, \quad V(C) = a \times O \, \psi + \; b = b,] \quad \text{[where } a \text{ is positive.}$$

This is tantamount to saying that utility is measured on an *interval scale*.

Usually, if we solve some problems we uncover others in the process. A number of objections have been raised and discussed in connection with the concept of utility introduced by von Neumann and Morgenstern (see Savage, loc. cit.). Most of them concern the empirical aspect of the theory rather than its normative aspect. Some of these empirical problems are mentioned below.

First, there is an axiom of transitivity underlying the theory; the objections to that axiom have already been reviewed.

Second, the theory requires an interval scale; and, as we know, such a scale is a *rara avis* in psychology and sociology. We are confronted here with a familiar dilemma. For, if we insist on an interval scale, the theory is mathematically powerful, and therefore useful in many different contexts, but its empirical foundation is weak. If, on the other hand, we are satisfied with the ordinal scale that we can easily produce, at least in principle, then we are back in the position where any strictly monotonic transformation of a utility is a utility. The obvious solution is to try to find scales that are strong enough to warrant as much as possible of the mathematical properties of the theory, but not so strong as to be impossible to construct.

Instead of trying to measure utility on an interval scale (as, for example, Davidson, Siegel and Suppes, 1957), experiments have been designed to measure utility on ordered metric scales and higher-ordered metric scales, which are stronger than ordinal scales but weaker than interval scales (Siegel, 1964, chapters 4 and 7).

The principle of the proof of the pudding being in the eating means, in this case, that one should be able to predict choices better from the utility functions measured on the scales constructed than from the objective quantities of money or similar commodities. This is also found in the work of Davidson, Siegel and Suppes (1955), Siegel (1956) and Siegel (1964, chapter 4). Another way of putting this is to say that utility is not a linear function of money (the classical experiment is given by Mosteller and Nogee, 1951) or of cigarettes (Siegel, 1964). To my knowledge, however, the successful construction of strong scales (not to mention prediction from them) has so far been limited to fairly elaborate laboratory conditions.

4.2.1 Utility and probability

Theoretically, the most interesting thing about the modern utility concept is that it links utility with probability. But this creates new problems. For, if starting from the matrix given above we redefine the quantity to be maximized according to the rationality criterion to

$$U(A_j) = p_{j1}U(C_1) + \cdots + p_{jp}U(C_p),$$

know the probabilities and have measured the utilities, then we can test the rationality assumption by seeing whether the subject does in fact maximize his expected utility. And, inversely, if we know the probabilities, assume rationality (i.e. maximizing expected utility) and observe the choices, we can infer the utilities. (This was, as described above, the essential idea in the modern utility concept.) But both measurement and predictions presuppose that we know the probabilities involved. Do we?

Kyburg and Smokler (1964, Introduction) review the three different principal ways of interpreting the notion of probability. One way, developed by von Mises (1957), is to interpret a probability statement as empirical: to say that the probability that an *A* is a *B* is *p means* that the limit of relative frequency of *B*'s among *A*'s (as the number of observations is increased without bound) is *p*. A probability statement, then, becomes a statistical hypothesis.

Another view, held by Keynes (1921) and Carnap (1962), maintains that probability statements are *logical* statements, which are either logically true or logically false. The essential characteristic of this view is that, given a statement, and given a set of evidence statements, there is precisely one degree of probability that the statement may have relative to the given evidence.

From the subjectivistic view (of which there are many versions) probability represents a relation between a statement and a body of evidence, but not a purely logical relation: a given statement may have any probability between 0 and 1, on given evidence, according to the inclination of the person whose degree of belief the probability represents. Again, it is not purely psychological, since its subject is *coherent* behaviour, so the fact that people sometimes violate the laws of probability does not invalidate them. Whether behaviour is coherent or not therefore depends on how well an individual can be expected to do in various wagers. Thus, the subjectivistic notion of probability is (often) linked to the notion of preference, for example in Savage (1954).

Since the subjectivistic conception of probability tends to be dominant among modern writers on utility, things become a bit complicated. On the one hand, the notion of probability is derived from, *inter alia*, preferences; on the other hand, the notion of utility is built on preferences and probability. This would seem to lead to very difficult problems when it comes to measurement, prediction, and testing.

Davidson, Suppes and Siegel (1957) have tried to cope with this. They have separated the subjective probability and utility problems by working with events having subjective probability $\frac{1}{2}$ (dice with meaningless letter combinations instead of dots). This means that certain equations arising from the expected-utility hypothesis can be reduced to equations involving only utilities, and, once the utilities are ascertained, the subjective probabilities of other events can be calculated from the expected-utility hypothesis.

But even with this problem solved, there still remains the problem of the extent to which subjective probability and utility contaminate each other empirically. Edwards (1962) reviews two assumptions about this. One may expect that an outcome which has a low probability will, by virtue of its low probability, have a higher utility than the same outcome would have had if it had a high probability (the grass is greener on the other side of the fence). Also, one might, like Irwin (1953), expect that people will overestimate the likelihood of desirable events and underestimate the likelihood of undesirable ones. Edwards reports empirical support for the second assumption, and points out that the first assumption has two possible interpretations: one making it a proposition about the environment (things get scarce if many people want them), and the other, for which no very convincing evidence exists, stating that people value the same object more highly when it is scarce.

Edwards, however, also points to one additional difficulty with the subjective expected utility model (assuming that people maximize the subjective expected utilities with the subjective probabilities used in the equation). Most of the experiments based on the model use fairly long series of repeated choices. It appears that, in addition to the utility of the reward or loss used in the experiments, people have a marginal utility for varying their responses. If this is so, the model is not very useful in predicting choices, unless this marginal utility is separately measured. (Such measurement has been proposed in Siegel (1964), chapter 11.) Not only does this preference for variance disturb ordinary choice experiments, but Ofshe and Ofshe (1970, p. 23) have also argued that it would disturb game experiments with coalition formation.

4.3 STRATEGIES UNDER RISK

If we treat the case of strategies rather than simple choices, one difference between decision under certainty and decision under risk should be noted. In the case of certainty, there is in principle no difficulty in defining an optimal strategy, given the assumptions stated. Furthermore, having picked an optimal strategy, there is no reason for regret, unless either the world picture or the preference order is changed. But in the case of decisions under risk, we may find ourselves in the following situation:

First, Subject presses a red button R or a black button B. Next, Chance switches on a white W or a green G light. If R was pressed, then the probability for W is $\frac{1}{4}$ and for G $\frac{3}{4}$; if B was pressed, they are $\frac{1}{2}$-$\frac{1}{2}$. Finally, Subject presses one of the buttons again. The pay-off is as follows:

$$RWR = 64 \qquad BWR = 0$$
$$RWB = 0 \qquad BWB = 6$$
$$RGR = 4 \qquad BGR = 2$$
$$RGB = 8 \qquad BGB = 4$$

Let us now assume that Subject has to make both his decisions before the start. Then he has four possible strategies, and it is easily verified that their expected utility values are RR = 19, RB = 6, BR = 1, BB = 5. So, according to the rule of expected utility, he should choose RR, the expected utility of which is 19; this will, in fact, give him either 64 or 4.

If he does so, and if G comes up, he will wish that he had been able to alter his choice, or to define conditional strategies from the beginning, since his second R will only give him 4, whereas a change to B would have given him 8.

Thus, in decisions under risk involving more than one action, the actor is better off if he can either (a) take one decision at a time (cross the bridge when he comes to it), or (b) make his initial decision conditional, saying, for example, "First R; then R if W, and B if G" (look before you leap).

5 Games

Until now, we have discussed types of decisions in which no interaction with other people's decisions has been (explicitly) assumed. The decisions have taken place in an inanimate environment, some properties of which were known. We have an essentially new situation when the outcomes or pay-offs of Ego's decisions depend not only on his own choices but also on the choices of Alter, and vice versa. In this case we are considering *games*. In order to have something precise to discuss, we will start from the definition of a game used by Luce and Raiffa (1958, chapter 3). A game in its so-called normal form consists of:

a. A set of n players.

b. n sets of pure strategies, S_i, one for each player. A pure strategy is a recipe saying what to do in every possible case. Let us, for example, imagine a truncated chess game where the players have only one move each. Then White's strategy set must coincide with the set of his possible moves. This set contains 20 elements. A strategy of Black, however, is a rule saying, for example: "If a3, then a6; if a4, then e5; . . .". Thus, a Black strategy must specify what Black is to do for every possible move by White. And, since for every White move Black has 20 options, it follows that Black has $20^{20} = 104\ 857\ 600\ 000\ 000\ 000\ 000\ 000\ 000$ possible strategies.

c. n linear pay-off functions, M_i, one for each player, whose values depend on the strategy choices of all the players. That the pay-off function is linear means, roughly, that the expected utility hypothesis is true for all choices between lotteries. This has the consequence that if we change a game by making a positive linear transformation of one player's utility function, the new game is strategically equivalent to the old one, and in this sense it is the *same* game. From this follows that a theorem in game theory must be true for all games that are strategically equivalent, or for none of them.

d. Each player is assumed to have full knowledge of the game in its normal form, i.e. he knows who are the players, and he knows all strategy sets, and all pay-off functions.

e. Each player is assumed to be "rational" in the sense that, given two alternatives, he always chooses the one he prefers, i.e. the one with the larger utility.

In order to simplify the argument, we are mainly going to discuss the simplest case: two players who have two strategies each. Rapoport and Guyer (1966) have shown that there exist exactly 78 such games, or equivalence classes of games.

The general matrix for two-person 2×2 games is shown below.

Column

		A	B
Row	A	y_{11} / x_{11}	y_{12} / x_{12}
	B	y_{21} / x_{21}	y_{22} / x_{22}

The x's denote the pay-offs to the Row player (the player who controls which row they move into), and the y's the pay-offs to the Column player.

Obviously, the preference orders of the two players can be related to each other in many different ways, notably 78. Some cases are mathematically trivial, as when the preference orders strictly coincide, or at least the most preferred outcome coincides. (That does not mean that they are psychologically trivial, as we shall see later.) In such cases the obvious solution is that both players choose their strategies in order to arrive at the jointly preferred outcome.

The opposite of this situation is one in which the preferences of the players are strictly opposed. These games are referred to as strictly competitive or zero-sum games. The name zero-sum derives from the fact that if one player wins what the other loses the sum in every box is zero, i.e. $x_{11} + y_{11} = 0$, etc. It is customary to write zero-sum games in the simplified form:

Column

A   B

Row

	A	B
A	x_{11}	x_{12}
B	x_{21}	x_{22}

where the x's stand for what Column loses to Row. Consider the games

A B

	A	B
A	1	2
B	3	4

(I)

A B

	A	B
A	1	4
B	3	2

(II)

In game I, if Row chooses A, the worst thing that can happen is for
him only to get 1; and if he chooses B he can do no worse than to get 3.
Since the minimum in B is maximal among the minima, B is called a
minimax strategy. If Column chooses A, he may have to pay 3, and if
he chooses B he may have to pay 4. Thus, A is his minimax strategy. If
both players use their minimax strategies, they arrive at (B, A), where
Column has to pay 3 to Row. This combination has the property
that the pay-off is greatest in its column and least in its row. Such a
point is called a saddle point, or an equilibrium point. If the players
have reached this point, the fact that it is greatest in its column means
that Row can only lose from changing strategy if Column keeps his;
and the fact that it is least in its row means that Column will have to
pay more, if he changes strategy while Row keeps his. The classical
result in game theory, which is valid not only for 2×2 games, but for
any two-person zero-sum game with a finite matrix, is that *if a game
has saddle points, then the best each player can do (assuming both to be rational)
is to choose the strategy which contains a saddle point.* This is called the minimax
principle.

However, not all zero-sum games have saddle points; for example,
game II has not. Here, if the players arrive at (B, B), which is the
combination of their minimax strategies, Row will prefer to switch to A,
since this will give him 4 instead of 2. If A switches, they arrive at
(A, B), and Column will prefer to switch his choice from B to A, since
that reduces what he has to pay from 4 to 1. But then Row will want to
go back to B, because this will give him 3 instead of 1, and then, finally,
Column will switch again to take a loss of 2 rather than 3. So we are
back where we started and can go round again.

Here, the notion of a mixed strategy is introduced. A mixed strategy, e.g. ($\frac{1}{2}$A, $\frac{1}{2}$B), means that instead of choosing a pure strategy the player hands the choice over to some random mechanism with determined probabilities (in this case $\frac{1}{2}$, $\frac{1}{2}$).

Another classical theorem in game theory, which is an extension of the minimax theorem, states that each player in a zero-sum game without saddle point has one probability distribution which is minimax in a generalized sense, and that the combination of the two mixed strategies thus defined is in equilibrium. It is also possible to compute the solutions.

The two-person zero-sum game is thus solved in the sense that there exists a well-defined prescription concerning what two rational players facing each other should do. Furthermore, this prescription is derived from the assumptions defining a game and is intuitively reasonable. (For details, see Rapoport 1966.)

When one moves from mathematical theory to experimental reality, things look a bit different. Messick (1967) summarized thus the experiments concerning the minimax theorem:

This theory has also led to a number of experimental studies designed to evaluate the famous minimax theorem as a descriptive model for human behaviour (e.g., Lieberman, 1962; Kaufman and Becker, 1961; Suppes and Atkinson, 1960; Morin, 1960; Brayer, 1964). The results of these investigations suggest that the minimax theorem provides a descriptive statement of human behaviour only in games having saddle-points (Lieberman, 1960). Even this statement must be qualified since humans do not use a minimax strategy in games with saddle points if the other person does not (Brayer, 1964). At best the minimax theorem provides a poor descriptive theory.

p. 33

5.1 NON-ZERO-SUM GAMES

In most games the preferences of the players for the different outcomes do not coincide, nor are they strictly opposed. Such games are referred to as mixed-motive games, or non-zero-sum games (to be precise, the latter term also includes coincidence.) To the extent that games model real social interaction, the mixed-motive case would appear to be the typical one, since even parties in war typically have at least some interests in common.

The fact that game theory in its infancy was most interested in zero-sum games might derive from the early theorists' interest in modelling "parlour" games, which are typically set up in the fashion that one side wins what the other one loses.

Rapoport and Chammah (1965, p. 11) argue that the mixed-motive games are the psychologically interesting ones, precisely because of the mixed motives. The mixed-motive game that has attracted most interest, both theoretically and empirically, is the so-called Prisoner's Dilemma. It is theoretically discussed by, amongst others, Luce and Raiffa (1958), Rapoport (1966), and Midgaard (1965). Reviews of empirical findings are given in, for example, Rapoport and Chammah (1965), Lumsden (1968) and Gallo and McClintock (1965). Any game described by a matrix

	C	D
C	R ⟍ R	T ⟍ S
D	S ⟍ T	P ⟍ P

where $S<P<R<T$ and $2R>S+T$

is a Prisoner's Dilemma; thus, games III and IV are examples of it.

	C	D
C	3 ⟍ 3	4 ⟍ 1
D	1 ⟍ 4	2 ⟍ 2

(III)

	C	D
C	1 ⟍ 1	10 ⟍ −10
D	−10 ⟍ 10	−1 ⟍ −1

(IV)

Since any PD game is strategically equivalent to any other PD game, we can take any PD as a starting point for our theoretical discussion. Let us take game IV.

In the discussions of non-zero-sum games two additional assumptions are often found in the literature. The first assumption is that there can be no communication between the players, and thus no negotiations or agreements. Such games are referred to as non-cooperative or non-negotiable games. The other assumption is that the players can negotiate and make binding and enforceable agreements before the game (in the strict sense) starts. These games are referred to as cooperative or negotiable.

If a PD game is played as a negotiable game, the rational solution appears obvious, at least as long as the game is symmetric: the players should agree that both play C. Therefore, it is the non-negotiable version of PD that has attracted interest. Here one can argue from many different principles and all of the traditional ones point to (D, D) as the solution. This, however, means that, if both players are rational, they both get worse off than if neither is (C, C). This is what is referred to as the Prisoner's Dilemma paradox.

Let us briefly review some of the arguments. If the minimax principle is extended to non-zero-sum games, it would prescribe (D, D), since both players have D as minimax strategy (the worst possible outcome of D is –1, that of C is –10), and furthermore (D, D) is in equilibrium in the sense that neither player will prefer to depart from it, as long as the other one sticks to it. (It is also the only equilibrium point.) If the sure-thing principle is applied to the case of games, it states that if one strategy dominates another, then it should be preferred to the other one. Concretely: if Column plays C, Row is better off playing D than playing C; if Column plays D, then Row is also better off playing D; therefore, Row should play D. Since the game is symmetric, the parallel argument is also valid for Column who should therefore also play D.

Various efforts have been made at resolving the paradox. Shubik (1970) maintains that there is no paradox, since the behaviour prescribed by the theory would seem quite explicable. His main argument is that the interaction aspect is missed, and, more generally, that in empirical situations the game-theoretic assumptions are not satisfied. Howard (1966) has constructed a more complex game (metagame) based on the PD, and derived (C, C) as solution to the original game from the solution of the metagame.

Rapoport (1966) has argued that, in the case of the Prisoner's Dilemma, the notion of rationality bifurcates into what he calls individualistic rationality (the one assumed in game theory, at least in Luce and Raiffa) and collectivistic rationality, which is defined by leading to the *joint* pay-off being maximized. As Midgaard (1965, pp. 127–128) has pointed out, one should not confuse individualistic rationality with egoism (except in the trivial and irrefutable sense), since a PD situation may very well arise from both players being more concerned about the other player's health than about their own.

The notion of joint pay-off must be carefully used, lest the axioms of the game be violated, since they do not allow for addition of different persons' utilities. Thus, improving the joint pay-off must mean that both players are moved up in their respective preference order, or that one is moved up without the other one being moved down. Thus, collectivistic rationality, if viewed as normative, prescribes that the players find some solution that is optimal in Pareto's sense, unless cardinal utilities are assumed.

The discussion of the normative validity of the theory may therefore lead to the more general version of non-zero-sum games, the negotiable version. The starting point can be found in reconsidering the essential difference between zero-sum games and non-zero-sum games. In the former type, there is no reason whatsoever for negotiations because there is nothing to negotiate about. Nevertheless in the latter type it may be favourable for both players to be able to negotiate and make agreements. In some situations, this may be not only strategically but also physically necessary for the players in order that they may arrive at some jointly preferred outcome. (If the players have one mixed strategy each, they may in fact arrive at outcomes that neither of them wants, whereas this could be avoided by playing a joint mixed strategy. See, for example, Braithwaite, 1963, p. 34) How, then, is the "surplus" obtainable by negotiated agreements to be divided?

There are two ways of putting this question. The first is "What solution will two rational players reach by bargaining?" The second is "What solution will an equitable arbiter prescribe?" It has been held by Harsanyi (1962a) that these are two quite different questions, because arbitration makes use of some principles of equity while bargaining does not. On the other hand, Rapoport (1966, pp. 210–212) argues that the difference is not sharp, since both cases presuppose some principle of rationality; but as soon as we leave the zero-sum case notions of what is rational are in any case *socially* determined.

In order to enter this discussion, we would have to present a survey of the different solutions proposed to the two problems. (For this, see Luce and Raiffa, 1958, chapter 6). Instead, let us simply note that one essential distinction among such solutions is whether interpersonal comparisons of utility are assumed to be meaningful or not.

Some authors, like Raiffa (1953) and Braithwaite (1963), assume interpersonal comparisons of utility to be meaningful in presenting some of their suggestions for solutions. Since interpersonal comparisons of utility require or imply some judgements of an ethical nature (Graaff, 1963), this means that such solutions are normative not only in the sense of being (technically) prescriptive but also in the sense of presupposing definite ethical judgements.

Thus Raiffa's solution constructs interpersonal comparability by equating the value of the best outcome to 1, for both players, and the value of the worst outcome to 0, for both players. So far, this is only a consequence of the notion of utility. He then goes on to let this establish an interpersonal comparison of utility (conceding that there is no adequate rationale for doing so). However, quite independently of whether there does or does not exist any theoretical argument for doing so, we maintain that this implies an ethical judgement. For if the best possible outcome for one of the players is getting two cakes, and the worst possible outcome is getting one cake, whereas the best possible outcome for the other player is to get the princess and half the kindgom and the worst one to be beheaded, then clearly it is an ethical judgement to say that these two best-worst differences are to be seen as equally important, or should be given equal weight.

5.2 EMPIRICAL APPLICATIONS OF GAMES

The literature on empirical applications of game theory has been growing very rapidly during the last two decades. Furthermore, many of the applications are applications of games of other kinds than those presented here; for example, there are n-person games involving varying assumptions about the structure of the pay-offs. Two main types of literature can be distinguished, namely reports on laboratory experiments and discussions on how the theory can, could or should be applied in the case of real-life social interaction, often on macro-level. Here, we shall mainly discuss the former, since experiments allow for a more detailed comparison between theory and data. In the latter category, the writings of Shubik (1964), Schelling (1963), Riker (1962), Midgaard (1965), and Rapaport (1960, 1964) should be mentioned.

One fairly general experimental finding is that, in most cases, players do not play as they should according to the formal theory. To take one striking example of seeming irrationality, consider the following game:

		B	R
B	4	4	3
			1
R	3	1	0
			0

(V)

Here, by any game-theoretical argument, all players should choose B. Still, Scodel (1962) reports that 47 per cent of the choices were R.

A great number of factors have been shown to correlate with behaviour in game experiments. These tend to be factors describing the game, factors describing the subjects and factors describing social interaction.

Degree of cooperation in PD games has been related to the P,R,S,T parameters (Rapoport and Chammah, 1965), and to various indices based on them, for instance to a measure of the degree of conflict in the game structure (Axelrod, 1967).

How behaviour is related to the kind and size of the pay-offs appears to vary between games (Lumsden, 1968).

Behaviour also appears to be related to sex, race, and various personality factors. Summing up the findings on various such factors, Lumsden concludes that, taken together, they seem to indicate that *socialization* towards cooperative and competitive behaviour, as it differentially affects age-groups, sexes, classes, races, friends, unknowns and enemies, is a major factor determining the cognitive processes behind game-playing behaviour.

Social interaction appears to be a major factor. Thus, Rapoport and Chammah (1965, p. 59) report that when the same game is played several hundred times and the subjects see the game matrix, the average product-moment correlation between the frequencies of cooperative responses of paired players is 0·96. Most authors also find that when one of the players is replaced by a stooge playing according to preprogrammed strategies, variations in stooge strategy affect the behaviour of the *bona fide* player, often in a somewhat complicated but explainable way. Thus, in PD, a stooge who just repeats what the other player did in the preceding move (tit-for-tat) leads to more co-operation than with stooges who always play C or always play D.

Summarizing the experimental record, Lumsden suggests: ". . . it seems to show that human subjects do act in logical and consistent fashions in PD and other such situations, but the *logic is not that of game theory* . . . Since in many cases each player will be less than completely rational (in the game theory sense), and will be unlikely to credit the other player with a greater degree of rationality, each will be faced with the additional problem of making some assessment of what *kind of person* the other player is. A strategic choice is much easier to make if the nature and capabilities of the other player are known." (Op. cit., 16.)

6 Decisions under uncertainty

Before summarizing our comments on rational models, let us consider one more type of situation, i.e. decisions under uncertainty, be they individual or collective. The reason why this case of decisions was not discussed in the context of decisions under certainty and decisions under risk is that, for decisions under uncertainty, two-person game theory is often presupposed; as a matter of fact, several of the solutions to decisions under uncertainty are directly applied from solutions to games.

It stands to reason that this is so. In the case of decision under certainty we know everything relevant about Nature; all we have to do is to make up our minds which set of consequences we prefer and choose the course of action leading to them; and in the case of decision under risk, Nature is seen as a Monte Carlo game, although the odds may depend on which course of action the decision-maker takes. Decision under uncertainty is quite different from this. All we know is that various consequences *may* occur but we have no idea as to how probable they are, nor do we know whether any concept of probability applies here at all.

As a matter of fact, it is just this which is a point of ramification. Among the four main types of criteria that appear in the literature three can be seen as in some sense modelling the situation as a game; but at least two of them make the concept of probability irrelevant, whereas the fourth is based on the idea of trying to estimate probabilities and then using the criterion of maximizing the expected value.

To be more concrete, the minimax criterion is taken over from two-person game theory. To take an example, I may have the strategies of bringing my umbrella or not, and Nature may have the strategy of raining or not. The situation may then be the following:

		Nature		Minimum in row
		Rain	No rain	
Person	Umbrella	1	2	1
	No umbrella	0	3	0

The minimax criterion then prescribes that I should bring my umbrella since the worst possible outcome of bringing it is better than the worst possible outcome of not bringing it.

This criterion is highly conservative, as it says "Take no risks". One way of rationalizing it would be to assume Nature to be spirited and malevolent. This would, however, contradict the underlying assumption that the decision is under *uncertainty*. It is also possible to give examples that cast doubt over the criterion. Thus, if the value of walking in the sunshine without an umbrella was very much higher, say 3000 instead of 3, the criterion would still prescribe bringing the umbrella, which appears counter-intuitive.

Next, the *minimax regret* criterion is based on the idea that, for a given state of nature, one (or more) of my available strategies is best. If I choose some other strategy my *regret* is the difference between what I get from my best strategy and what I actually get, given this state of Nature. Thus, my regret from a given outcome (a combination of one strategy of Nature's and one of mine) depends both on my choice and of the state of Nature. Different regret values are associated with each of my strategies (two values in the umbrella case), and at least one of these is maximal. The criterion requires me to choose a strategy of which the maximal regret is not higher than the maximal regret of any other strategy. So the umbrella matrix becomes transformed into the following regret matrix:

| | | Nature | | Minimum regret in row |
		Rain	No rain	
Person	Umbrella	0	1	1
	No umbrella	1	0	1

Here one strategy would be just as good as the other because the minimax regret value, 1, occurs in both rows. From an intuitive point of view, this criterion has the same weakness that it may involve missing the possibility of a great gain in order to avoid a small loss. (Luce and Raiffa, p. 281.)

Hurwicz's *pessimism–optimism criterion* can be described as follows: for each of a set of strategies, S_1, the best possible outcome is M_i, and the worst is α. Let m be a fixed number between 0 and 1. For each strategy the magnitude $\alpha \times m_i + (1-\alpha) \times M_i$ is defined. This is called the α-index of the strategy. The criterion prescribes the strategy with the highest α-index. If we take $\alpha = \frac{2}{3}$, the umbrella cases give $\frac{2}{3} \times 1 + \frac{1}{3} \times 2 = \frac{4}{3}$ as the α-index of the umbrella strategy, and $\frac{2}{3} \times 0 + \frac{1}{3} \times 3 = 1$

as the α-index of the no-umbrella strategy. It would be best to bring the umbrella. (Hurwicz 1951a, after Luce and Raiffa, op. cit., pp. 282ff.)

If $\alpha = 1$ (maximal pessimism), then we are back in the minimax case. If $\alpha = 0$ (maximal optimism), we get a maximax criterion. The main weakness is that the criterion may define two strategies as equally good, even if one dominates the other as for example in the following case:

		State of Nature					
		1	2	3	4	5	6
Person's choice	1	0	1	1	1	1	1
	2	0	0	0	0	0	1

Finally, *the principle of insufficient reasons* states that if one is completely ignorant of the probabilities one should regard all states of Nature as being equally probable. Having done this, one should maximize the expected value of a strategy. In the umbrella case, where Nature has precisely two options, this is the same as using the Hurwicz criterion with $\alpha = \frac{1}{2}$; where nature has more than two options, however, it differs from the Hurwicz criterion by taking all possible outcomes into account, whereas the former only takes the best and the worst into account. In the umbrella case, the expected value of bringing the umbrella becomes $\frac{1}{2} \times 2 + \frac{1}{2} \times 1 = \frac{3}{2}$ and the expected value of not bringing the umbrella becomes $\frac{1}{2} \times 0 + \frac{1}{2} \times 3 = \frac{3}{2}$, so the strategies are equally good.

One main weakness of this criterion is that it is dependent on how we prefer to categorize the possible states of nature; this appears counter-intuitive.

How, therefore, is one to choose between the different criteria for choosing? The problem is obviously there, because, as we have seen, the different criteria give different solutions to the same problem, even if that problem is as simple as our umbrella case. One way of carrying out such a meta-choice is to try to fractionate the problem by stating what axioms a reasonable criterion should satisfy, and then proceed to throw out those criteria which are unsuitable. A great number of axioms have been suggested and any treatment of this aspect in depth would inevitably become highly technical. Such a treatment can be found in, for example, Luce and Raiffa. Let us just summarize the axioms suggested, as well as some of the essential results. Luce and Raiffa (op. cit., pp. 287ff.) discuss the following *desiderata* (and some other versions of them, here deleted):

1. Each problem of decision can be solved, i.e. one or more of the possible alternatives should be chosen as *the best*.
2. The solution does not depend on the specific choice made of zero point and unit in the utility scale used. This obviously follows from the utility functions being defined as invariant under positive linear transformations.
3. The solution does not depend on how the different alternatives have been labelled or alphabetically ordered.
4. If A′ is a solution and A″ gives the same utility as A′ in each state of Nature, or A″ gives higher utility in at least one state of Nature and at least as much utility as A′ in all the other states of Nature, then A″ is also a solution.
5. If A is given, and if there exists some A′ such that A′ gives more utility than A for some state of nature, and at least as much utility for all other states of nature, then A is not a solution.
6. If, to a problem of decision under uncertainty, we add a new alternative act A, and there exists some A′ in the original problem such that A′ is equivalent to A or better than A for some states of nature and exactly as good for the others, the optimal acts in the original problem remain optimal, and the non-optimal acts remain non-optimal.
7. If an act is non-optimal for a problem, then it cannot become optimal by the addition of some new act.
8. Let A and B be problems. In B the pay-offs do not depend on the act chosen. Let C be the following problem: A occurs with probability p and B with $1-p$, and we must find a solution before knowing which one comes up. The solutions to C are then precisely the same as the solutions to A.
9. If A′ and A″ are both solutions to a problem a mechanism choosing A′ with (the arbitrary) probability p and A″ with $1-p$ is also a solution.
10. The set of solutions to a problem should not depend on how the states of nature are labelled.
11. If two states of nature are equivalent concerning pay-offs, then one of the states can be deleted from the problem without the set of solutions being changed.

Some of these criteria appear fairly obvious while others require some lengthy discussion for their foundation. Similarly, while some of them are more substantive, others have rather the status of assumptions made in order to simplify the mathematical treatment of the topic. Finally, axioms 10 and 11 are those which define what should be meant by saying that a decision problem is a problem under complete uncertainty.

To summarize the results briefly, none of our four criteria satisfies all the axioms. The minimax regret criterion violates axiom 7, the maximin and all the Hurwicz criteria violate 8, Hurwicz violates 9. The principle of insufficient reason, finally, is the only one that satisfies 1–10, but it violates 11.

We will attempt to show what these violations mean. For axiom 7 the example can be taken from Luce and Raiffa:

DOCTOR: Well, Nurse, that's the evidence. Since I must decide whether or not he is tubercular, I'll diagnose tubercular.

NURSE: But, Doctor, you do not have to decide one way or the other, you can say you are undecided.

DOCTOR: That's true, isn't it? In that case, mark him not tubercular.

NURSE: Please repeat that!

(Note, however, that this conversation is not necessarily absurd in all conceivable situations. For, in the first case, the doctor may be led to assume that it is extremely important that all suspect cases are picked out, whereas in the second he may conclude that it is not so important, preferring then to declare the person healthy—his suspicion was extremely slight, anyhow—to giving them both some additional trouble. This, however, means that additional information has been brought into the problem, which violates the assumptions for the problem.)

It should also be noted that axiom 7, a version of the principle of independence of irrelevant alternatives, is similar to the axiom that is seen as the villain in Arrow's paradox for group decisions. (See Hansson, pp. 14–19.)

A violation of axiom 8 would, in our umbrella case, take the following form:

PEDESTRIAN: I am not going to bring my umbrella.

WIFE: If it rains today we can collect £100 on our insurance.

PEDESTRIAN: I did not know that. If that is the case I shall bring my umbrella.

A violation of 9 would be:

PEDESTRIAN 1: We'll come to Rome whether we take the right or the left path. After all, we decided that we preferred Rome to Florence.

PEDESTRIAN 2: All right, so let's toss a coin.

PEDESTRIAN 1: No, we had better go to Florence.

Finally, a violation of 11 might go like this:

PEDESTRIAN: Either it rains or it doesn't. My only reason for taking an umbrella is that I hate to get wet, so having considered the matter carefully, I have decided not to take it.

WIFE: Have you considered that it might rain once or even more than once?

PEDESTRIAN: I would get just as wet however many times it rained, so it would make no difference. Nevertheless, having considered this point, I have made up my mind to bring my umbrella.

How are we to make our choice in this complicated situation? Various suggestions have been made. Thus, Milnor (1954) has suggested that the assumption that the player has absolutely no information about Nature may seem too restrictive, although he keeps its counterparts in his own efforts at constructing a new criterion that does not violate any "obvious" axiom. His result turns out to be a modification of the minimax regret principle, although he concedes that "these criteria are probably too difficult computationally to be of any practical interest". It would therefore seem appropriate to summarize the discussion of decisions under uncertainty with a quotation from Suppes (1961):

> Recent work in decision theory has shown in similar fashion that there is no simple coherent set of principles capable of precise statement that corresponds to naïve ideas of rationality. Just as research in this century in the foundations of mathematics has shown that we do not yet know exactly what mathematics is, so the work in decision theory shows that we do not yet understand what we mean by rationality. I mean by this not merely that we have no adequate general definition of rationality, but that, even for highly restricted circumstances, it turns out to be extremely difficult to characterize what we intuitively would mean by a rational choice among alternative courses of action.   p. 607.

7 Rational models: criticisms and suggestions

As a way of structuring the discussion, let us start from the definition of a game given above in order to provide an overall view of the criticisms that have been launched.

i. *A set of n players.* In experiments this has usually been unproblematic. The experiments have been set up in such a way as to make it clear to the subjects how many players there are.

In many other situations, however, this element becomes problematic. Different participants in a conflict may have different (open or hidden) assumptions concerning *who* the parties in the conflict are. The war between the USA and Vietnam is an instructive example. For a long time the USA refused (at least officially) to regard the NLF of South Vietnam as an independent participant; likewise the NLF and DRV have traditionally refused to regard the Saigon administration as an independent participant. Even at this point an analyst trying to model the situation as a game would have great difficulties.

ii. *To each player, a set of strategies.* Again, the problems involved here are usually not apparent in experiments as they are set up in such a way as to make this unambiguous. As pointed out in the preceding discussion, in order to know what action an actor performs, it is essential to know what were his (conceived) possible choices.

As Midgaard (1968, p. 112) points out, there is an infinite number of things a person can do in any situation. One way of coping with this problem is to attempt to lay down some criteria for what should be regarded as the *same* strategy, for instance by saying that two (almost) strategically equivalent lines of action should be counted as variants of the same strategy. But this presupposes that we already know the actors' preferences over the outcomes, and, before that, their perceptions of what the outcomes will be.

Another possibility, suggested by, *inter alia*, Shubik (1963), is that we should extend the strategy sets to be infinite, or even continuous. Such games have been treated mathematically (see bibliography in Luce and Raiffa), and experiments based on continuous generalizations of PD and other games have been suggested by, for example, Hamburger, (1969).

Speaking in terms of game theory, the problem is complicated even more by the fact that a *strategy* in a strict sense *is not* simply a line of action, but rather a catalogue of prescriptions concerning what to do for everything the other party or parties may do, etc. Generally we have no such elaborate strategic plans.

iii. *A pay-off function for each player.* This assumption consists of different parts. It says that the actors have a one-dimensional preference ordering, that this preference ordering is over all possible outcomes, and that it satisfies the axioms defining utility (in the modern sense).

All these assumptions become problematic when confronted with empirical evidence. The problem of dimensionality has already been discussed. Here, the general problem is that we mostly evaluate objects or events according to several different values. If we are to lump these different evaluations together in a one-dimensional utility, we must know how the actors "trade-off" one value against the other, and this problem can only be solved in special cases. Rationality is consistent with maximizing other things as well as monetary profits (Johnsen, 1968, p. 111); and it does not even necessitate maximization of monetary profits, since it is an empirical question whether they contribute to a person's utility (although they usually do). Boulding (1963) states: ". . . for a true understanding of conflict, we also have to examine love, affection, empathy, and community of feeling. These are concepts alien to game theory." (p. 57.) But he is wrong as regards game theory as defined above, for the notion of utility is assumed to take care of all this.

In the review of game experiments it was noted that, in many cases, the behaviour of the players was *seemingly* irrational in the sense that they did not maximize the monetary pay-off even in situations where it was quite clear how to do it. In the experimenters' discussion of the results (Scodel *et al.*, 1959; Scodel, 1962; Minas *et al.*, 1960), it was suggested that this might be explained by assuming that the subjects valued *both* monetary pay-off *and* maximizing the difference between themselves and the other player, *and* also variety. If maximizing difference is most important, then playing R in game V is the rational choice. The authors quoted also discussed how these values influencing behaviour might change over time, for instance by the difference maximizing motive becoming dominant when the players had already collected so much money that the marginal utility of money had decreased. In general, one speaks of *utility function confounding* when the utility for outcome A is less than the utility for outcome B, although the real reward for A is greater than that for B. Various attempts have been made to deal with this problem, at least in the case of utility deriving from two motives. Conrath and Deci (1969) have proposed a way of scaling a bivariate utility function in the case of monetary pay-off and maximizing differences. Siegel (1964, chapter 11) has developed a method of predicting choices in the two-value case by means of the (empirically derivable) quotient of the marginal utilities of the two values, and Ofshe and Ofshe (1970) have applied Siegel's idea in successfully predicting choices in coalition games.

But even if utility can be measured independently of the behaviour to be explained in some limited cases (laboratory experiments with two values essentially contributing to the utility function), this often is not so in real life situations outside the laboratory. Abrahamsson (1970) has pointed out the difficulties encountered by the exchange paradigm developed by Homans ad inspired by game theory, noting that this paradigm has the same weakness as the old hedonistic theory: anything can be a reward, so the explanatory value of the paradigm is low (cf. Tajfel's chapter). This argument is supported by Abrahamsson's citing several pairs of cases, where Homans assumes one thing to be a reward in one explanation and the opposite thing to be a reward in another explanation.

This is, in general, a traditional objection both to hedonism and to the theory of utility underlying the version of game theory presented here. But it is difficult to see when the objection becomes mortal. As Savage (1954, p. 101) describes it:

In general, the reinterpretation needed to reconcile various sorts of behaviour with the utility theory is sometimes quite acceptable and sometimes so strained as to lay whoever proposes it open to the charge of trying to save the theory by rendering it tautological. The same sort of thing arises in connection with many theories, and I think there is general agreement that no hard-and-fast rule can be laid down as to when it becomes inappropriate to make the necessary reinterpretations.

There is, however, another problem with references and utility functions which has been suggested by several authors (for example, H. W. Kuhn, 1962; Shubik, 1963). Preferences change over time. The point is not that one prefers an apple now to an apple tomorrow (that can be taken care of by, for example, rates of discount), but that, even if today one prefers an apple tomorrow to a banana tomorrow, it is possible that one may change one's mind tomorrow and prefer a banana to an apple.

This change can be brought about in different ways, for instance by the parties' mutual adjustment in a negotiation (Harsanyi, 1962b).

Midgaard (1965) discusses the German Schlieffen plan in World War I and points out that German strategy failed because the Germans lost their nerve when the Russians entered East Prussia, although this was foreseen by the plan. Having changed their preferences from those underlying the plan, they weakened the offensive in France by sending several divisions from there to East Prussia. He also discusses another case of change, which he refers to as dialectically conditioned. This is the case where a player who is to take part in a PD situation, having reflected over it, is stuck by the stupidity of ending in a DD situation; his preferences are therefore so changed that this becomes the worst outcome instead of the next to worst.

iv. *Each player is assumed to have full knowledge of the game.* This is what Luce and Raiffa themselves see as "the real source of unreality in the model" (op. cit., p. 55). Since (i)–(iii) are so difficult to ascertain for the researcher, it must, in general, be even more difficult to know what they are for the other players in the game.

Most attention has tended to be drawn to the knowledge of the other players' utility functions. There are even more arguments than those reviewed under (iii) why (iv) should, in general, not be satisfied. Thus, Ikle and Leites (1962) point out that one of the objectives of a participant in a negotiation is to modify the other participants' estimates of what he is minimally willing to accept, and, concurrently, Rapoport (1966) writes that parties to a conflict often have reasons for keeping secret what *is* their repertoire of considered strategies. Furthermore, Schelling (1963) states:

> ... certain elements in a bargaining game are *inherently unknowable* for some of the participants, except when there are special conditions. How can we know how badly the Russians would dislike an all-out war in which both sides were annihilated? We cannot; and the reason we cannot is *not* solely that the Russians are necessarily unwilling that we should know. On the contrary, circumstances may arise in which they are desperate that we should know the truth. But how can they make us know it? How can they make us believe that what they tell us is true?
>
> p. 115

Thus, if a game-theoretical approach to conflicts and bargaining (and, for that matter, cooperation) is to be more fruitful, it must somehow be capable of taking into account that the actors misconceive, or are ignorant about, each others' utility functions. Several authors have tackled this problem, more often by indicating what should be done than by doing it (the present author being no exception). Harsanyi (1962b) suggests that much of the actors' estimates of the relevant utility functions is due to what he calls "stereotype utility functions". This means that people belonging to certain groups are culturally expected to have certain preferences (believed to be) common to their class, sex, age, etc. Midgaard (1965) has treated situations where the players are uncertain about the other players' preference structures in a game-theoretical framework. Generalizing Schelling's approach, he points out the importance of what he calls "structural" clues which may give the players hints about the preference structures of the other players, their way of modelling the situation as a game (whether they call it so or not), their way of analysing the game, etc. Lumsden (1968) has applied the Semantic Differential as an instrument for determining how ethnic groups in conflict see their opponents and their goals, and has discussed how this affects strategic thinking.

Here, as before, it is only in the laboratory, if at all, that any stricter tests of the theory can be made. Several studies have been made of how the degree of information about the pay-offs in the game affects behaviour, and most have been concerned with how it affects cooperative behaviour (see, for instance, Rapoport and Chammah, 1965; Gallo and McClintock, 1965; Swensson, 1967; Guyer and Rapoport, 1960). These studies heavily support the assumption that information plays a crucial role. Thus, Rapoport and Chammah, studying PD games, varied the experimental conditions so that some of the pairs of subjects had the game matrix in front of them, whereas others merely had the pay-offs to both sides announced after each play. In the former case, cooperation was, on the average, twice as high as in the latter.

v. *The players are assumed to be rational in the sense of always choosing the alternative with the larger utility.* This is perhaps the most interesting assumption in the present context, since it is common to all the cases of decisions so far discussed. Roughly, the criticisms of this assumption belong to three different types: the argument that it is meaningless, the contention that it is empirically false (and so false that it kills the model), and the belief that this is not the point of interest about rational models.

We have already reviewed several findings to the effect that players in game experiments do not behave rationally. The objection to this interpretation was that it presupposes, for instance, that people only play for money; we have shown that this presupposition is empirically false. In the experiments where the utility functions of the subjects were ascertained empirically and independently rather than assumed, the subjects behaved much more rationally (in the sense of (v)), i.e. prediction of behaviour from utility functions was considerably more successful.

There is, however, another obection to (v) which is stronger. March and Simon (1963) state: "Most human decision-making, whether individual or organizational, is concerned with the discovery and selection of satisfactory alternatives; only in exceptional cases is it concerned with the discovery and selection of optimal alternatives." (pp. 140–141.)

This is by no means primarily a criticism of (v) in itself, but rather of the fundamental assumptions of the whole model, mainly of its perception of all the alternatives of choice as "given". March and Simon emphasize the *search process* in non-routine situations. This process, in general, does not lead to, and is not intended to lead to, alternatives that are preferred to all other alternatives, but to those alternatives that meet the criteria of what is a minimally satisfactory alternative.

Consider, for example, the situation described in section 4.3, and assume that it takes some time and effort to gain information as to the consequences of different strategies, and that the subject regards 4 as minimally satisfactory. March and Simon would then predict that an actor would choose BB, if that was the alternative he considered first, whereas the criterion of expected utility would predict RR, and the minimax criterion BB *or* RR (or, if supplemented with the principle of domination, only RR), the latter criteria assuming that he chooses between *all* the alternatives.

As already stated, it is here not (v) *in itself* that is challenged. March and Simon mention the possibility of including the cost of information in the calculus and going back to the maximizing model, although they doubt whether this would be a fruitful model in very many situations. Simon (1957) suggests other alternatives for formal treatment, such as operating with a simplified utility function (with values 0, 1 or –1, 0, 1), or using a vector pay-off with one minimum standard for each vector component. The former approach is compatible with maximization (by redefinition) but for the latter which is not, the problem of translating a vector pay-off to a one-dimensional function is eliminated.

There are two main versions of the type of criticism describing (v) as meaningless. On the one hand, we have already quoted some authors who have pointed out that it is simply not clear what (v) should mean for some kinds of non-zero-sum games or decisions under uncertainty. On the other hand, (v) is sometimes criticized for being tautologous; but it is doubtful whether this is a meaningful criticism.

Luce and Raiffa themselves freely concede the point, writing: "Although this assumption of rationality in game theory is often subjected to ridicule, logically it is not really an assumption but a tautology [p. 55] . . . in the sense that the postulate does not describe behaviour but it does describe the word 'preference' [p. 50.]"

Now the point in the "tautology" type of criticism has not so much been that (v) in itself is tautologous but that the combination of (iii) and (v) becomes tautologous in the weaker sense of being non-testable. Again, Luce and Raiffa themselves point out that treating rationality as tautological creates serious experimental difficulties.

This tautology can be removed by making substantive assumptions about the utility functions. Ofshe and Ofshe (1970) point out that one of their objectives in assessing utilities independently of behaviour has been to free the expected-utility approach from tautological overtones (p. 4). Riker (1962) makes the substantive assumption quoted in section 3.3; by means of von Neumann and Morgenstern's theory of *n*-person games he deduces that political coalitions will tend to be minimally winning, since forming more than a minimal winning coalition entails having more people to share the gains with. He goes on to show (a) that this "size principle" is non-tautologous because it clashes with the theory of Downs (1957) according to which political parties seek to maximize votes, and (b) that the principle can be used to explain what happened, for example, to the Republican party in the USA in the early nineteenth century, the modern Congress party in India, and to the grand coalitions following the Napoleonic wars or World War I.

The third type of criticism, exemplified by the quotations from Boulding in section 3.3, is the most interesting one. It can be put in various ways; for instance we can say that we must include something more than maximizing in the concept of rationality, or that an adequate model must account for processes of selecting goals and setting standards, of searching for information, of finding out or deciding *what* game one is involved in, etc.

These criticisms have usually not been offered as arguments for the abandonment of game-theoretical, or, more generally, rational models, but rather have been thought of as stating how the models must be extended and supplemented in order to work. Roughly, the outcome of the objections to classical game theory has been that, on the one hand, some of its assumptions are now thought to be too strong to be compatible with our body of psychological and sociological knowledge, and, on the other hand, the model must be fed with more of substantive psychological and sociological assumptions in order to produce empirically interesting results.

We have already dealt with the assumptions concerning *knowledge* and *preference*. A third factor that must be accounted for and brought into the model is *social interaction* and the way it affects, among other things, both knowledge and preferences. As Schelling and Midgaard and many others have pointed out, there are the phenomena of *tacit communication*, of *threats and promises*, and of *commitments*, out of which the first is not at all taken care of and the others only partly accounted for by classical game theory. These phenomena are interesting for several reasons. It is by means of them that the actors *learn* about each other in different relevant aspects, such as preferences, psychological make-up etc., and likewise *teach* each other, veridically or otherwise. Furthermore, they have the effect of changing the actors' preferences. (As shown in the classical experiment by Deutsch and Krauss (1962), it is not necessarily an advantage to obtain access to a unilateral threat, since it might cause the opponent to become even tougher.)

However, instead of trying to make a more definite summary on rational models here, we will first review some non-rational models in order to make the profile of the rational models clearer by stating the compatibilities and contradictions between rational and non-rational models.

8   Non-rational models of Man

Let us now turn to the opposite extreme in models of man, those we have styled "non-rational". First of all, we must find an adequate means of defining rational and non-rational models. When earlier we discussed rational models, the word "rational" was taken to qualify *models* rather than *men*. Thus certain predicates and relations were singled out as important ones to be included in the model; certain assumptions were made concerning these predicates and their interrelations; and the consequences of these assumptions were derived, including some which were verifiable. The "test" of the model was then to compare the predictions from the model with actual observations. Clearly, it is extremely difficult—if it is at all possible—to state the rules for comparisons explicitly and abstractly. Here, as with other models, several things may happen when the predictions do not agree with the observations made.

Rarely, if ever, is a model dismissed solely on the grounds that some single observation or even a whole set of observations disagree with it. Let us turn to physics for a clear-cut illustration. Galileo, inspired by Nicolaus Oresmius and others, stated that a falling body would fall $\frac{1}{2}gt^2$ units of length after t units of time. Here, g was assumed to be a constant, depending only on the units chosen and not on the mass of the falling object. At the time this was considered a fairly bold assumption, principally because it stated that the mass did not matter. Not only was this in disagreement with the Aristotelian tradition, but it was also at variance with common sense: our everyday experience of falling bodies is that small and light bodies take longer to fall to the ground than big and heavy bodies. Now to the point: since Galileo, physicists have been undisturbed by this common-sense fact which they have explained by saying that the conditions for measurement have not been fulfilled so that our everyday experiences cannot really test the model. In order to test it it was necessary to eliminate the presumably disturbing factor of air friction. When this was done by arranging the falls in vacuum tubes, the agreement between prediction and data became very much better. (This narrative is not strictly historical, nor is it intended to be.) But some difficulties remained. Using more refined methods of measurement, it was found that *g* was *not* constant but somewhat higher at the poles and somewhat lower at the equator. Thus the model had to be changed by abandoning the assumption of constancy. It was, however, not abandoned just like that; there were careful predictions about *how g* would vary. These predictions were derived from Newton's general law of gravitation which could then be used to explain Galileo's law.

Still, happiness is not complete. It is easy to arrange experiments in a vacuum tube where different bodies fall with different speeds. Such experiments are not taken to demonstrate that Galileo was wrong but rather that there is an electromagnetic field in the tube and that this field affects various materials differently.

Let us summarize the logic of this. If we have a model, *in which we believe*, then disagreements between predictions and data are explained away in different ways. In some cases, they are explained away by assuming or showing errors in measurement. In other cases, they are explained away by including some *ceteris paribus* clause which refers to the model ("*if* the distance to the centre of the earth is the same") or which refers to the occurrence of phenomena extraneous to the model ("*unless* there is an electromagnetic field"). It is only when all possible explanations have been tried that we (possibly) decide to abandon the model.

So far this has only been a *descriptive* statement about what happens to models. For a fuller treatment we refer to Kuhn's "The Structure of Scientific Revolutions" and Quine's "From a Logical Point of View". We do not intend to enter a normative discussion for the moment. Some points should, however, be made. We have already quoted Savage's saying that there are no hard-and-fast rules for when a reinterpretation of a model should be seen as legitimate and when it should not. Clearly, we have extreme cases. On the one hand, it is just the explaining away of discrepancies that may lead to the discovery of more general laws, or even of new phenomena and their properties. On the other hand, the plethora of auxiliary interpretations may lead to the model's assuming an entirely tautologous character, in the sense that it is virtually impossible to state what *would* constitute a definite counter-instance to the model.

We have already seen this process of explanation in the case of rational models. In some instances it was simply maintained that the measurement (or lack of measurement) of utility had been erroneous, and it was shown that a more refined measurement considerably decreased the separation between prediction and data. In others, it was pointed out that the assumptions contained in the model had to be revised with respect to constancy (of preferences), or otherwise substantively (the assumptions on knowledge and the search process). When we come to the question of assuming factors extraneous to the model, we have a starting point for discussing non-rational models.

But first we will briefly discuss the (perhaps hypothetical) case where the data consistently *agree* with the predictions from the model. Does this *prove* that the assumptions in the model are true so that we can start thinking of *man* and his true properties rather than a *model of man?* From a (normatively) logical point of view we certainly cannot! This means precisely that the joint set of the assumptions, and thus every one of them, is *compatible* with what we have observed of reality. When we go further, we are transferring from proof to belief. Of course, it must be conceded that such beliefs can be more or less justifiable; but this would lead us into the normative discussion which we would like to avoid for the moment.

Saying that we are dealing with a rational model of man means that the model is such that any man satisfying all the assumptions in the model would be an extremely self-conscious, deliberating, and rational man (not to speak of his other features, such as that of being virtually omniscient). Showing that a rational model of man nicely fits the data from controlled experiments therefore does not mean that we have found any rational men; it means, at most, that we have found men who, in very specific situations, act as rational men *would* act. Furthermore, it does not even show that the men we have observed have *actually* made all the deliberations, calculations and considerations consciously, but only that they behave *as if* they had done so.

In the same vein, saying that a model is *non-rational* means precisely that the *model* is non-rational, i.e. that the properties and relationships considered in the model do *not* refer to deliberation and conscious calculation, and that the assumptions made in the model are *not*, or are only marginally, assumptions such that we would describe somebody satisfying them as rational. Rather, the advocates of such models mostly concede that men do deliberate and calculate; but they maintain that this is an inadequate basis for a model, since these deliberations may be epiphenomenal, and since, in any case, the more important aspects of human behaviour are better explained from other assumptions. This, of course, refers to the more sophisticated proponents of non-rational models; the less sophisticated ones tend to confuse the model with reality and go on to derive conclusions which *do* presuppose that man is irrational.

There is, however, one thing that can already be said in their defence. Confusing the model and reality is much easier in the case of non-rational models than it is for rational models, because the latter are much less "model-like". By this I mean that, whereas the rational models are often mathematical or simulational models, stating explicitly the model assumptions in axiomatic and often mathematized form, the non-rational models are merely verbal and not even systematized. (Much of learning theory does, of course, provide very clear exceptions to this, as do some other theories.) This means, among other things, that the distance between model assumption and testable consequence tends to be rather great in rational models; it is, in general, much smaller in non-rational ones. To some extent the assumptions may even be directly testable, or at least thought to be so.

The logic of the exposition is as follows: first, we present the essential logic in different non-rational models; then we proceed to give some substance to the different logics by discussing the cases of aggression and war as *explananda;* and finally we try to compare rational and non-rational models in various respects.

8.1 NON-RATIONAL MODELS: WHAT IS BEHAVIOUR?

The first problems that arise when discussing non-rational behaviour are the semantic ones. To start with, the term "behaviour" may often be ambiguous. One way of using the term is to make it refer to sequences of physically observable events, and just that. This means that two sequences of events are said to represent the same behaviour if they have identical physical properties, or, from a slightly less strict point of view, if they show remarkable and describable physical similarities. According to another way of using the term, two sequences of events are said to represent the same behaviour, if they are *intended* the same way, i.e. if they constitute the *same action*. In this usage, a physical description is not enough to define (specific) behaviour (it may even be irrelevant), but the actor's interpretation of the event must be known. To be more precise, this is usually not enough either as we have to include the interpretation of some other person (the receiver, we might call him, or just Alter), the actor's intentions as to or expectations of the other's interpretation, and so on. The essential thing here is not what precisely we mean by an action, but that somehow somebody's interpretation must be included in the definition in addition to, or instead of, the physical description.

As can readily be seen, we have used here a logical trick. Instead of trying to give definitions of the term "behaviour" or the term "action" we have attempted to lay down definitions of what should be meant by "the same behaviour", or "the same action", this being in general a more fruitful way of entering problems of definition while avoiding scholastic questions. Clearly, the two definitions suggested so far differ in many instances, in the sense that two sequences that are counted as the same according to one definition are not so counted according to the other. Thus, instead of asking, with Wittgenstein, what would remain if one's arm going up were subtracted from raising one's arm, we should ask: What properties should two events have in order to be counted as the same? Consider the following four situations:

1. I raise my arm to greet a friend.
2. I raise my arm to attract the waiter's attention.
3. I clap my hands to attract the waiter's attention.
4. I clap my hands to express my admiration.

According to our first definition of "same behaviour", there are two classes of behaviour involved here.

A. 1 and 2 belong to the class of arm raising.

B. 3 and 4 belong to the class of hand clapping.

According to one version of our second definition we have three classes:

A'. 1 belongs to the class of greeting a friend.

B'. 2 and 3 belong to the class of calling a waiter.

C'. 4 belongs to the class of applauding.

Our only excuse for stating this triviality is to point out that not only do we have two different means of classification but that they are in some cases incompatible.

In order to begin our discussion on how to qualify behaviour, we must introduce a third way of defining sameness. Here, two sequences of events coincide if they are functionally equivalent, or if they have the same consequences (according to some criterion for determining sameness of consequences). Certainly the first formulation here may be teleological (although this is not the only possible interpretation), whereas the other is not. In any case we speak of consequences, and possibly of some *telos* in addition; the exact physical similarity is not immediately essential, nor is anything assumed (explicitly) about anybody's (conscious) interpretations.

The semantics of "behaviour" would not occupy us here if it were not for the fact that they become essential in discussing different ways of classifying behaviour as rational or non-rational. For, in the scientific parlance about what is called "behaviour", we encounter a multitude of more or less precise expressions, such as "instinct", "drive", "instinctual drive", "reflex", "motive", "motivation", "habit", etc. It appears clear that, as usual: (a) different authors sometimes use the same term with different connotations; (b) different authors sometimes use different terms to express the same connotation.

In order to reach some clarification, let us consider a few of the various definitions or explications of some of the concepts:

Instinct, or instinctive behaviour: Innate tendencies to respond in *particular*, usually adaptive, ways to *particular* internal and/or external conditions.

Berelson and Steiner, 1964, p. 38

. . . some "intelligent" acts are innate. The simplest of these are the reflexes, e.g., the sucking reflex of the sibling. Others are more complex, e.g. birds' tendency to avoid human beings without any previous experience of them. These more complex acts were called instincts . . . [Unfortunately it was necessary to translate back from a Swedish translation.]

Murray, 1964, chapter 1

An instinct is a hierarchically organized nervous mechanism that is receptive for certain activating, releasing, and directing impulses of both external and internal origin, and which reacts to these impulses with co-ordinating movements which contribute to the survival of the individual and the species. [The author cites this as Tinbergen's definition.] [My translation.]

Fabricius, 1961, pp. 112–113

. . . "drive" . . . simply denotes states of activation in certain central nervous mechanisms.

Ibid., p. 112

Two phrases will constantly reoccur throughout the course of this discussion: *instigated response sequences* and *drives*. The former phrase more clearly implies an ongoing activity (which, however, may be internal to the organism), but both are intended to be synonymous here. [Later (p. 32) he writes about the *emotion* anger as a drive.]

Berkowitz, 1962, p. 27

Instincts (innate behaviour) . . . [The author gives no definition.]

Lorenz, 1967, Index

M

... das Es; sein Inhalt is alles, was ererbt, bei Geburt mitgebracht, konstitutionell festgelegt ist, vor allem also die aus der Körperorganisation stammenden Triebe ... Die Kräfte, die wir hinter den Bedürfnisspannungen des Es annehmen, heissen wir *Triebe*. ... the Id; its content is everything that is inherited, innate, constitutionally determined, mainly the drives originating from the structure of the body ... The forces that we assume behind the tensions between needs are called *drives*. [My translation.]

Freud, 1946, pp. 70–72

Motivation: the general term that we will use to refer to all those inner striving conditions variously described as wishes, desires, needs, drives, and the like ... Formally, then, a motive is an inner state that energizes, activates, and moves (hence "motivation"), and that directs or channels behaviour towards goals ... In short, a motive results in and hence can be inferred from purposive means-end behaviour.

Berelson and Steiner, 1964, pp. 239–240

These will do for the time being. (We shall return to the more critical writers later.) The point of the quotations is not to show that different authors use the same term in different ways, but rather to get a first notion of what distinctions appear to be essential because they underlie the definitions that are proposed.

Many authors use the term "innate" to describe behaviour, or behaviour tendencies. In general, such behaviour is called instinctual. (It should be noted that the German *Trieb* can be translated both as "drive" and as "instinct"; in our translation we should perhaps have used the latter.) To say that behaviour is instinctive, then, is to say something about its *cause*. Another distinction is sometimes made between "simple" and "complex", behaviour. Behaviour of the former type is referred to as "reflex", whereas only the latter qualifies as "instinctive".

When behaviour is described with respect to its causes, more or less explicit assumptions are made as to the mechanism of the cause. One of the definitions above included a fairly detailed description of such a mechanism, whereas other definitions that can be found may simply refer to "biological inheritance", "genetic information", or the like. This also applies to behaviour styled as instinctive. The matter stands somewhat differently with drives. First of all, it should be noted that, in general, drive is not a behavioural category; rather, it somehow characterizes an inner state of the organism. It is often left open whether this state is, or is not, innate in some sense; sometimes this distinction is used to distinguish primary from secondary drives.

Furthermore, and this is a crucial point, different distinctions are made on the basis of whether behaviour is conscious or not. Here, the problems tend to get rather tricky. Consider the sentence "X was not conscious of what he did." Clearly, what this means depends, amongst other things, on what we mean by "the same behaviour". Thus, it may mean:

1. X was not aware that he made certain physical movements;
2. X was not aware that he performed a certain (intentional) action;
3. X was not aware of the consequences of his action;
4. X was not aware of the functions of his action;
5. X was not aware of the causes of his action;
6. X was not aware of the motive of his action.

Several questions now arise. How are the interpretations (1)–(6) related to each other? How are they related to explanations of behaviour from motives and from instincts? What theories should be termed "rational" and what theories "non-rational"?

First, (6) is crucial here. The term "motive" is sometimes used to blur the differences between cause and end. That is, sometimes (6) is used as a synonym for (2) or (4), and sometimes it is used as a synonym for (5). When it is said that a motive results in purposive means-end behaviour, it would appear that this would characterize a motive explanation of behaviour as a rational model; but, again, this does not appear to be the way that "means-end" and "purposive" is used in this context. One of the points in many instinct and motive theories is that people often are not conscious of their motives or instincts, or have erroneous ideas about their own motives, and it is precisely this that makes such theories "non-rational".

It might be tempting to extend this discussion into a treatise on the problem of "free will". We shall, however, refrain from that. Instead, in order to introduce some systematic element into the following discussion we shall propose two definitions which are to some extent arbitrary.

a. We shall refer to a theory as an instinct theory if the theory attempts to explain some classes of behaviour as the effect of innate tendencies or dispositions.

b. We shall refer to a theory as a motive theory, or drive theory, if the theory attempts to explain some classes of behaviour as the effect of an inner state of the organism.

Some conclusions from this usage should be pointed out immediately. First, it does not imply a contradiction between instinct and drive;

on the contrary, some theories are at the same time instinct and drive theories by virtue of explaining behaviour as the result of an inner state of the organism, which state in its turn is assumed to be the result of inheritance rather than learning (adopting, for the moment, this distinction). Second, it appears difficult to reconcile instinct theories with rational models (unless one assumes utility functions to be innate). Therefore, instinct theories will (provisionally) be included in the class of non-rational models. Third, motive theories may, or may not, be rational models, depending on how they are spelt out in detail. We shall discuss later what theories should be put where.

8.2 INSTINCT THEORIES

There is general agreement that some behavioural elements in human behaviour are instinctive in the sense that they are ubiquitous and innate. Thus, human babies start to smile spontaneously during their first month. From their second month they also smile as a reaction to physical stimuli. In the third month an oval and two dots is enough to elicit a smile. Gradually the stimulus has to be more and more detailed, until after about eight months mother is necessary to elicit the smile (Hinde, 1968, p. 361; Ploog, 1967, pp. 320–329).

There is also general agreement that some other behavioural elements in babies are instinctive, such as sucking (Hinde, op. cit., p. 395), clutching certain objects (Ploog, op. cit., pp. 312–314), avoiding visual cliffs (Hinde, op. cit., p. 346), etc.

These elements are physically well defined and stereotyped, and they *normally* lose these characteristics fairly early (Ploog, op. cit., pp. 311ff.). Sucking behaviour is modified by the first experiences connected with it (Hinde, op. cit., p. 395).

We shall not try to make here a complete list of such elements. Some more could be mentioned; but the longer one makes the list the less general agreement there is about it (e.g. fear of snakes). Using "instinct" as here defined, there does not even seem to be general agreement as to whether any instinctive movements survive until the mature age. Fabricius (1961, p. 93) states that there are very few fixed action patterns, and Berelson and Steiner (1964, p. 41) are of the same opinion.

There is a great number of behaviour elements and behaviour inhibitions, about which there are controversies as to whether they are or are not innate.

This means that theories attempting to explain parts of or all human behaviour as instinctive are controversial (as most theories are). Despite a tradition dating from ancient Greece, in modern times it is only from the turn of the century that instinct theories of human behaviour have been current; and they had their heyday in the first quarter of the century (Murray, 1964, chapter 1). Amongst the most prominent proponents, Freud, James, and McDougall are usually mentioned; Pareto might be included too. These theorists are, in our terminology, typical motive theorists as well. What they try to explain is not so much behaviour in the simplest physical sense but actions (which require for their definition also something about interpretation); and these actions are seen as results of motives which are, in their turn, innate.

The *explananda* as well as the number and the definitions of the instincts vary considerably. If we take Pareto's residues as instincts, we have six; McDougall, in 1908, counted twelve. How many instincts should be ascribed to an author depends on whether we are considering instincts in general, or fundamental instincts from which the others are assumed to be derived. Thus, while Freud is generally credited with describing two instincts, first Ego and sexuality, and later Eros and Thanatos, these were *basic* instincts. Freud himself states that one can distinguish an indefinite number of instincts (*Triebe*), but that the important question becomes whether it is possible to derive these from some few fundamental instincts; and, after long hesitation and vacillation, he made up his mind to assume only two such instincts, Eros and the Death instinct (Thanatos). (Freud, 1946, pp. 70–71.)

The list of assumed instincts very soon expanded. Bernard found almost 6000 urges that had been counted as instinctive until the 1920's (Berkowitz, 1962, p. 14). Among the instinct theorists, however, there are some areas of human behaviour that tend to be central for the location of instincts. These areas include sexuality, aggression, acquisition, and territorial behaviour. We have chosen aggression as an instructive example, and shall return to the general logic and the current criticisms of instinct theories in general after a review of the instinct theories of aggression.

8.3 MOTIVE THEORIES

If we define motive theories as theories of behaviour that attempt to explain it by reference to inner states channelling it towards some goal, then the definition of goal becomes crucial. For example, a hungry man can be said to seek (a) food, (b) to eat, and (c) satiation. In part the distinction is empirical as well as semantic. (Berelson and Steiner, 1964, p. 240.) To put it very roughly, food-related behaviour and eating typically appear as *explananda*. Eating is often included in the explanation as the goal response in the sense of Dollard *et al.* (1963, p. 6); and the satiation as the intermediary link between the goal response and the (temporary) reduction of the motive.

Motive theories vary considerably, both with regard to the motives assumed and their characteristics and with regard to the logic of explanation. A distinction is frequently made between primary, or physiological, motives (which are sometimes assumed to be innate) and secondary, or learned, or social motives. Berelson and Steiner include the following in the primary category:

(a) Positive or supply motives: these result from deficiency and produce seeking and consumption of the needed substance.

(b) Negative or avoidance motives: these result from the presence of harmful or potentially harmful stimulation and produce flight or avoidance.

(c) Species-maintaining motives: these result from the nature of the reproductive system and produce mating, children, and nurturant behaviour.

This classification is clearly based on biological function or consequence, not on subjective goal.   1964, p. 242

The fact that the classification is based on biological functions does not necessarily mean that some of the motives cannot be conscious subjective goals; but this is an empirical question.

One of the main arguments put forward for motive theories as superior alternatives to rational models is the fact that, in many cases, people do not know their own motives. This can be so for several reasons: the goal and means can be so habitual as to escape awareness; or the motives may be so (psychologically and/or socially) unacceptable as to be unrecognized by the actor. Therefore, the actor's behaviour may be non-rational, or even irrational, *if judged by the subjective standards of the actor*. This may appear to be a similar case to that of the seemingly irrational players; but there is one essential difference. The players seemed irrational because the experimenter *did not know* what their utility functions were; but presumably (although not necessarily) the players did know them, and might even have told the experimenter, if he had cared to ask them. In the present case the behaviour is deemed irrational in the sense that it is not optimal, or satisfactory, in relation to the actor's conscious goals; and furthermore, the goals in relation to which the behaviour is optimal, or satisfactory, are *not* known and are sometimes even actively denied by the actor.

Among motive theories, too, we have chosen to look closer at agression, saving the exposition of the logic till later.

9 The case of aggression and wars

Amongst the traits making up the "nature of man", sex and aggression belong to the most popular. A multitude of authors have attempted to explain aggression on different levels and in very different ways, into which we are now going to enquire.

The first problem when trying to give an exposition of explanations of aggression is to define the *explanandum*. As pointed out by, for instance, Lyon (1970), here we already face serious difficulties. The word "aggression" is used to denote behaviour, character traits (disposition to aggressive behaviour), motives, instincts, etc. (For a thorough discussion of definitions, see Kaufmann, 1970, chapter 1.) We shall discuss the term "aggression" as used to denote *behaviour*, using other words to refer to these other phenomena.

But this does not solve the problem; it merely delimits it a little. For even when it seems that only some classes of behaviour are defined as "aggression", and that the definition is a "pure" description of behaviour (in the physical sense), one finds that often one or more of the following are somehow included in that definition:

1. the consequences of the behaviour;
2. the intended consequences of the behaviour;
3. the interpretation by Alter, and intentions related to it;
4. some hypothesis about the cause or origin of the behaviour.

In their classical monograph of 1939, "Frustration and Aggression", Dollard *et al.* (1963, pp. 10–11) give two definitions of the term "aggression". The first, which they call dependent, is of type 1. It is as follows: "Aggression is that reponse which follows frustration, reduces only the secondary, frustration-produced instigation, and leaves the strength of the original instigation unaffected." They also give a definition intended to be independent of the frustration–aggression hypothesis, and which appears to be of type 2, viz. "Aggression is . . . an act whose goal-response is injury to an organism (or organism-surrogate)."

There are two terms that are crucial in this definition. "Injury to an organism" (or, as Berkowitz, 1962, p. 1, puts it, "injury to an object") has a fairly wide field of denotation. This is recognized by the authors, who state: "In fact, the aggression may be undirected towards any object—a man swears after striking his thumb with a hammer—when the action would cause pain if it were directed towards a person." (Dollard *et al.*, op. cit., p. 10.) So, whatever its other merits, it appears that the definition was intended to be inclusive (i.e. it includes *any* behaviour that could possibly be deemed as "aggressive" in everyday language) rather than exclusive.

Moreover, the term "injury" is also problematic as it appears to imply some kind of value judgement originating from the target of the behaviour; the actor does not automatically know what hurts the object. Dollard *et al.* try to take care of this objection by pointing out that "every member of a society learns by experience what categories of behaviour are defined by that society as aggressive" (op. cit., p. 77). Given this, we may be in doubt when asked to classify an instance of behaviour whether to apply (a) the standards of the society (assuming that the actor has learnt them), or (b) what we are able to find out about the actor's theory of Alter's values.

What put the definition in type 2, however, is the use of the phrase "goal-response" (Berkowitz uses "aimed at"). The term was intended to help to avoid the difficulty of subjectively conscious intentions by using instead the strictly behavioural "goal-response". In doing so it runs into another difficulty; for, from a strict point of view, the goal-response of an action can only be observed by seeing whether the act really terminates the behavioural sequence whose goal-response it is assumed to be.

Bandura and Walters (1963, pp. 112ff.) do not feel that intentionality has been satisfactorily eliminated from Dollard's formulation. On the other hand, they recognize that it is difficult to define aggression in such a way as to exclude the concept of intent and at the same time avoid placing in this category responses that, on the basis of common-sense criteria, would certainly not be regarded as aggressive. Their own suggestion is to define aggression as "responses that *could* injure or damage *if* aimed at a vulnerable object" (ibid., p. 114). This definition, however, still makes us dependent on our knowledge of the values of some (possibly unspecified) Alter.

This is more or less unavoidable: the values of the (possibly hypothetical) object of the behaviour *must* be taken into account in order to make the term "aggression" refer to something meaningful (by our everyday standards). One way to simplify the problems would be, of course, to assume value homogeneity in large-scale social groups, or even, in the case of animals, in whole species. Physical injury will serve as a good example of this. (But remember the classical cartoon dialogue:

SADIST: Now I am going to beat you!

MASOCHIST: Yes, please!

SADIST: No!)

9.1 INSTINCT THEORIES OF AGGRESSION

The above discussion of the definition of the term "aggression" has different relevance in different contexts. When it comes to instinct theories the relevance is fairly low, for in such theories the behaviour to be explained tends to be either left undefined or is very generally defined in terms of, for example, "destruction".

In order to see more clearly the crucial points in various kinds of explanations, let us work with logical reconstruction rather than with historical exposition. From a logical point of view, the simplest prototype of an instinct explanation would be as follows:

There exists an innate instinct which we call the aggressive instinct. Aggression is the product of this instinct.

In order to arrive at more precise formulations that can be identified with various authors, some decisions have to be made. Is this instinct assumed to be fundamental, or is it derived from some other instinct? Is the instinct conceived as an instinct relating to spontaneous behaviour, or is it conceived as a response to certain stimuli, or both?

Case 1: Fundamental instinct, spontaneous behaviour.

Provided that "spontaneous" does not exclude response we may put Lorenz into this category, since he insists both that aggression is a fundamental instinct, one of the "big drives" (op. cit., p. 85), and that it may be spontaneous (op. cit., chapter 4), if only in the sense that it may become spontaneous if the normal stimuli have been absent for a while.

It may also be taken to represent the psychoanalytic theory of Hartman, Kris and Leowenstein (Berkowitz 1962, pp. 11ff.), with the same proviso as for Lorenz. Common to both is the idea of aggression as some kind of a basic energy. Phenomena such as danger or frustration do not *cause* aggressive behaviour, they only serve as releasers for the aggressive instinct, which may manifest itself even without the normal releasers.

Case 2: Derived instinct, spontaneous behaviour.

> Here we include Freud (after about 1920). He postulated an aggressive instinct, but saw it as derived from a more basic Death instinct. In this period, he no longer conceived frustration as a necessary source for aggressive behaviour. He thought that the aggressive instinct itself accounted for tensions and demanded their reduction.

Case 3: Fundamental instinct, behavioural response.

> One could marshal arguments for putting the theory of Dollard *et al.* here, since they maintain that the connection between frustration and aggression is innate (as does the early Freud). However, since that position was quickly changed (Miller, who was a member of the group, even in 1941 preferred to leave the question open, according to Berkowitz, 1969, p. 3), we prefer not to treat them under this heading.

Case 4: Derived instinct, behavioural response.

> Ardrey (1967) may be seen as an exponent of this version because he states both that the aggressive instinct is derived from what he calls the territorial instinct and that aggression will need a stimulus to occur. This stimulus will typically, but not always, consist of seeing or hearing something that resembles a male of the same species.

After this listing of cases, we may start to deal with some of the problems connected with explanations, taking *Case 1* as an example. But before doing so, we should point out that it was not our purpose to leave the impression that the theories listed above were simplistic, nor should the present discussion of problems be seen as a polemic with the authors in question, unless this is explicitly stated. As we shall see later, the theories referred to above typically do contain answers to at least some of the problems posed.

Theories of the type described will have to solve at least two problems. They will have to offer some evidence for the existence of the instinct invoked, and they will have to explain why it is that, in general, men do *not* behave aggressively. Thus, speaking of "aggressive instincts", Barnett (1967, p. 41) states: "If these phrases are defined in terms of overt behaviour, then they are names. But if they are supposed to refer to internal processes, of which the behaviour is an expression, they may seem to be explanations when none has been achieved." Various types of arguments have been marshalled for the existence of a biologically inherited aggressive instinct. Thus, Dilger (1962) states that increased aggressivity can be inbred in, for example, the Siamese fighting fish, fighting cocks, mice and dogs. So far, no such evidence has been produced concerning Man.

Instead of using genetics, one may try neurophysiology. Thus, some researchers have been able to find loci in the amygdala of cats which, when electrically stimulated, cause the cat to adopt a threat posture. Again, it appears that little evidence is available concerning Man. (Some is found in Mark and Ervin, 1970, chapter 7.)

A third type of argument will follow the evolutionary history of Man, and contend that, since aggressiveness is likely to have benefited Man some time ago (while conceding that it does not now), Man is likely to have acquired it, and since it takes a long time to change the genetic structure of a species, Man is likely still to have this instinct. Such evolutionary histories can be found, for example, in Freeman (1964), Lorenz (1966), and Corning (1971). Certainly, Lorenz does not present this as a proof for the existence of an aggressive instinct in Man, arguing himself along the same lines as Barnett (Lorenz, 1967, p. 82). Quite apart from the point raised by Lorenz and Barnett, the functional reasoning just cited would seem to commit what Berkowitz (1962, p. 8) calls the teleological error of mistaking the end-state of a process for its cause.

Finally, one may ask whether it is legitimate or not to infer instincts from behaviour. If a model predicts certain behaviour, and this behaviour is found, and if it also predicts successfully other behaviour, then we would seem to have a non-trivial explanation, even if it is not very well founded. It appears as if most evidence cited for the existence of an innate aggressive instinct in Man is based on observations of human behaviour; but the observations providing evidence and the observations providing *explananda* are, in general, not kept apart; so even this type of evidence would not appear too strong, especially since observations of human behaviour are adapted with great difficulty to arguments for the existence of *innate* instincts.

The second problem for models of the type discussed was to explain why so little aggression occurs after all. This may, in principle, be solved in two ways. If the theory is of the response type it may argue that the relevant stimuli are rare. In addition, whether the theory is of one type or the other, it may postulate some inhibitory drive or instinct released by some other stimulus. This is what Lorenz does in several instances.

In this context, he argues that such inhibitions are innate in animals, but learned in man (op. cit., pp. 218ff.), contrary to Ploog (op. cit., p. 334), who sees them as innate in man.

Lorenz produces some evidence for the existence of such inhibitions in animals. As concerns man, however, one may argue that both an aggressive instinct and an inhibitory instinct would sin against Occam's razor unless one could produce independent evidence for each. Since this is a problem common to several different theories of aggression we shall return to it later.

9.2 MOTIVE THEORIES OF AGGRESSION

There are several ways of dealing with aggression that do not assume it to be an innate instinct of some kind. Some psychoanalytic writers prefer to leave open the question of its innate or learned character. This also applies to most of the modern writers who adopt the frustration–aggression hypothesis. Aggression is included in Murray's list of social motives. Likewise, Bandura and Walters (1963) regard aggression as learned behaviour, and even in 1959 discussed such ways of learning it as receiving encouragement (1959, pp. 127–128), having inconsistent parents (1959, pp. 88–94), and subcultural imitation (1959, pp. 356–358).

The theories commonly referred to as the frustration–aggression hypothesis are, at least in their original form, a halfway house between drive theories and learning theories (Lyon, 1970). Actually, one can distinguish two different kinds of such theories: one that sees early frustration as the cause of a persistent aggressive motive, and another which, by and large, sees individual frustrations as sources of a temporary motive for aggression (there are, of course, many intermediary forms). We shall follow here the lucid exposition by Berkowitz (1962) of the different modifications that have had to be made in the course of a critical evaluation of the original version of the theory.

In the original version, the theory stated that all frustration leads to aggression, and that all aggression is a result of frustration. But as early as 1941 Miller suggested the reformulation that "frustration produces instigations to a number of different responses, one of which is an instigation to some form of aggression" (Berkowitz, 1962, p. 37).

Furthermore, not all aggression is the result of frustration. *Instrumental* aggression need have no relation to frustration (ibid., p. 31).

Psychological attacks, insecurity, anxiety and fear may also cause aggression (Lyon, 1970). Whether these should be seen as counter-examples to the F-A hypothesis does, of course, depend on what frustration means. In the original statement the definition of frustration was "that condition which exists when a goal-response suffers inter-ference" (Dollard et al., 1963, p. 11). If this definition is to be taken as it stands, it is difficult to draw a borderline between the cases where it is reasonable to construe a deprivation, absolute or relative, as a frustra-tion, and those where doing so would render this part of the hypothesis tautologous. What objective events do or do not constitute a frustration also depends on the actor's cognitive interpretation of the situation: what constitutes a frustration for one man may not do so for another man (Berkowitz, 1962, p. 41.) Thus, it matters whether a frustration is seen as arbitrary or not: non-arbitrary frustrations may result in the ending of the goal-directed activity rather than in frustration. The finding that expected frustrations cause less aggression than unexpected ones may be interpreted in the light of this (expected frustration lowers goal instigation), or by introducing the notion of contrast effect (Berkowitz, 1962, p. 70).

Summing up so far, there is a considerable difference between the original version, which defines frustration as interference in a goal-directed activity, and the more refined versions taking the actor's cognitive system and value system, as well as changes in both, into account. Berkowitz (1969, p. 7) concludes that many failures to confirm the hypothesis have been due to the vagueness of the term "frustration". This may be so, but it may not.

But the notion of frustration, or in any case the antecedent of the F-A hypothesis, has been generalized even further to include, for example, Davies' (1962) theory of revolutions as results of an A-shaped develop-ment of rewards over time, giving rise to rising expectations and, in consequence, to relative deprivation. And Galtung (1964) takes rank disequilibrium as antecedent in his theory of aggression.

Berkowitz (1962) suggests that frustration and the resulting anger may not be enough to elicit aggression: some kind of releasing cue may also be important. Such a cue may, in some cases, be similar to, or otherwise associated with, the perceived frustrator. Further support for this is given in Berkowitz (1969, pp. 17ff.).

In the F-A hypothesis, as well as in the instinct theories, the notion of inhibition has been introduced. In addition to the anticipated punishment for an aggressive act mentioned in the original version, Berkowitz (1962, pp. 90ff.) discusses the role of internalized norms. One essential problem that has already been mentioned is that it is difficult to keep aggression and inhibition apart, since both may be activated by the same stimulus. Thus, a person with high aggression and high inhibition may behave like a person low on both. If one wants to test the theory by comparing behaviour in a test situation and behaviour in a real situation, the difficulty is that the relative strength of aggression and inhibition as activated by the test situation may differ from the relative strength in the "real" situation.

This problem has recently been studied by Olweus (1970). Working with habitual and activitated tendencies of both kinds, he was able to isolate an independent measure for habitual inhibitory variables. When aggression in the test situation was correlated with overt aggression in the "real" situation, no connection between the two was observed. When the groups differentiated according to the inhibition test were separately considered, it was found that: (a) in the low-inhibition group, the correlation between the test rates of aggression and the rate of overt aggression was positive and significant, whereas it was negative and significant in the high-inhibition group; and (b) that among those who had been low on aggression in the test, the high-inhibition group was more overtly aggressive than the low-inhibition group. Thus, this model, which operates with both aggression and inhibition, does not have the weaknesses mentioned above.

9.3   WARS

It has previously been pointed out that, in the case of rational models, behaviour of social units on the macro-level was particularly difficult to deal with; for instance, Rapoport's conclusion is that game theory is useless as a strategic theory for the behaviour of states. In spite of this, many unwarranted generalizations have been made from the individual level.

The situation appears to be the same in the case of non-rational models. Many authors on aggression have gone on from their findings to conclusions or speculations about how to explain wars or how to get rid of them. Several problems arise when such attempts are made. As Nicholson (1970, pp. 23ff.) has pointed out, "aggression" used as a term denoting behaviour of states means something rather different from the term used to denote individual behaviour or biological properties. Thus, the former term has clearly a normative connotation, implying that aggression is illegitimate. (Though this is also the case with some definitions of the latter term, as shown by Lyon, 1970.)

This is one reason why conclusions between levels are unwarranted. But there are also empirical reasons. Ardrey, for example, proposes the idea that the territorial instinct accounts for wars, at least in the sense that wars are results of territorial intrusion. A tentative idea of the validity of this suggestion can be obtained by looking at the statistics collected by Richardson (1960a), which include 83 major wars between 1820 and 1949. Only in a minority of the wars do territorial factors (according to Richardson's tentative classification) play a role, and even in the majority of these territory has been an issue for reasons of trade rather than for straightforward "territorial" reasons.

Another popular notion has been that wars are related to people being aggressive, and that the distribution of aggressiveness is different in different countries; hence, some countries are more warlike than others (and we all know which). Again, this assumption does not fit in very well with the data. The data collected by Wright (1942) indicate that, during the last five hundred years, every major European power has, in at least one of the ten periods of fifty years, had the distinction of being involved in the greatest number of wars. Therefore, this theory can be saved only if one makes auxiliary assumptions, such as, for example, that the degree of aggressiveness in a nation fluctuates fairly rapidly.

So far, the most successful non-rational model for wars is that for arms races proposed by Richardson (1960b). He starts with some simple assumptions concerning the interaction between the armament levels of any two neighbouring states, expresses these assumptions as differential equations, solves them, and is reasonably successful in describing the arms race preceding World War I. (In other cases, the model has been less successful.)

10   Rational and non-rational models. An attempt at summary and synthesis

In this section we shall summarize the logic and criticisms of non-rational models, discuss the divergencies and convergencies between the different types of models, and finally speculate about both models from the perspective of sociology of knowledge.

10.1   THE LOGIC OF NON-RATIONAL MODELS

Some suggestions concerning non-rational models in general may be derived from the discussion of the case of aggression. ("Suggestion" is the strongest word that can be justifiably be used here.) In doing this, we follow the distinction made between instinct and motive (drive) theories, and, having done that, criticize the distinction itself.

Descriptively, the general logic of instinct models of human behaviour appears to be the following. It is postulated that man has one or more instincts, which are innate and inherited. These instincts are assumed to direct behaviour either in general or in more or less specified situational contexts. Hence, when certain behaviour is found to have certain characteristics this fact is explained by reference to the postulated instincts. Evidence for the models is typically given by showing that the predicted behaviour does in fact occur. In this case, showing that a certain type of behaviour is universal and hence occurs in all men, or at least in all cultures, is taken to be the most convincing evidence. In a few cases, evidence is provided by correlating behaviour with the genetic structure, for example, by showing that men with additional male chromosomes tend to be more violent than other men. (Mark and Ervin, 1970, chapter 4.)

Another type of evidence consists in showing that some instincts appear in many other species, especially in primates, and going on to argue that *Homo sapiens* is not fundamentally different (in this respect).

Various types of criticisms have been made of instinct models. It has been argued that such models are tautological. This type of criticism is valid in the case where the only evidence offered for the instinct is the occurrence of the very behaviour that the instinct is invoked to explain. In other cases, it is not necessarily valid. Thus, if more than one kind of behaviour, or behaviour in more than one situation, is predicted from the model, then there should be a positive correlation between the different instances of behaviour; and if such correlations are found, then, according to the logic in use concerning models in general, this would lend some support to the model, even if, from the point of view of formal logic, it is not permissible to conclude the truth of the antecedent in a conditional statement from the truth of the consequent.

The accusation of tautology also applies to the more sophisticated versions of instinct theories, such as those that operate with a balance between instinct and (instinctive, or sometimes learned) inhibition. In order to allow for a reasonable degree of testability, fairly sophisticated designs must be used; and these in turn presuppose precise theoretical statements as to how the different factors are assumed to operate and interact. For non-rational models this appears to have been the exception rather than the rule.

Next, the validity of universality as a proof for innate character has been challenged. It has been pointed out already by Rousseau that we never observe men except in a cultural context, so difficulties arise in ascertaining what elements of behaviour are what. In addition, the substantive objection is often made that the assumption of universality is empirically false, and that, in any case, it has only been tested in selected populations (e.g. the famous American freshmen in psychology classes).

Several authors have pointed out the risks involved in generalizations between species. To the extent that certain knowledge exists about animals (otherwise there would be nothing to generalize from), it is about fixed action patterns, that is sets of physically well-defined movements that are elicited by physically well-defined stimuli and, in some cases, shown to have a well-defined neurophysiological substratum or to be affected by selective breeding. It is generally agreed that the higher organisms have increasingly complex patterns of this type, and that this increasing complexity is a consequence of the patterns being more and more flexible in various respects. Since, in general, the instinct theories want to explain more than just movements, analogies become highly problematical.

If we are to take the strict view of Hinde that "evidence that a difference in behaviour is to be ascribed to genetic differences must come ultimately from the rearing of animals, known to differ genetically, in similar environments" (op. cit., p. 319), then the obstacles to showing the existence of genetically determined instincts in Man must appear insuperable, if only for the reason that it is extremely difficult to define what should be regarded as the "same environment" in the case of Man.

Some of the criticisms above have been used as arguments for abandoning instinct theories of Man and explaining behaviour by reference to drives or motives instead. Thus, at least in the case of the physiological motives and some of the social motives, tautology is avoided by having independent measures of the drive (for example, number of hours without food, concentration of adrenalin, etc.) and of behaviour. In addition, as the question of origin is left open, there is no need to be particularly concerned by the fairly sterile question of innate versus learned.

It should be noted, however, that this applies only to drive theories in the fairly narrow sense we have adopted here in defining drive as an internal state. Otherwise, there is a considerable confusion between different authors as regards the use of the term "drive"; it can be used to denote the stimulus, the response, mathematical intervening variables, etc. But, also in the case of the narrower definition, severe conceptual difficulties tend to occur, as, for example, when one wants to explain the correlation between two types of behaviour, or between one external and one behavioural variable, by reference to some specific drive. The essential difficulty is the definition of the stimulus. As we have shown in the case of aggression, it is, in general, impossible to define the "same stimulus" as the "same external conditions", since (a) the number of variables that *can* be used to describe a condition is indefinite, unless we *assume* that only some specific variables are relevant, and (b) different people have different ways of perceiving a situation, due to differences in cognitive structures and in value systems.

The "same stimulus" is difficult to define (and to measure), but this is also true of the "same behaviour". In most cases this must be taken to refer not to the "same physical behaviour", but rather to "behaviour with the same intentions", or "behaviour with the same functions". Hence, we need information either about the intentions of the actor, or about the objective consequences of his behaviour, whether those are changes in internal states, in future behaviour, or in other people.

The Danish philosopher Alf Ross has suggested that the legal notion of property is meaningless, in the sense that it has no independent meaning. His argument is that this notion has a stenographic character. If, in a legal system, we have ten different ways of acquiring a title to some object, and twenty different legal consequences of having a title to something, then the law could be codified without ever referring to the notion of property by the following series of statements: Way 1 will have the consequences 1, 2, . . ., 20; . . . way 10 will have the consequences 1, 2, . . ., 20. This would involve 200 sentences, whereas introducing the term "property" would reduce the number to $20 + 10 = 30$ sentences.

The same treatment of the notion of "drive" has been suggested. (Hinde, pp. 141ff.) In this interpretation the term "drive" is introduced for reasons of economy when expressing the fact that a number of conditions may have any one of a number of behavioural consequences.

10.2 RATIONAL AND NON-RATIONAL MODELS

At this stage it may be interesting to look for parallels between the developments of the expected-utility model and the frustration–aggression model. Both had a fairly simple first version. As results of logical criticism and experimental confrontation, both have developed into fairly sophisticated and complex models. To a large extent, the roads of sophistication have been rather similar. Thus, both had to take into account cognitive factors. Our orientation towards the external world is an orientation towards what we believe about it, for example about the consequences that our behaviour will have. Likewise, both have had to take into account that our evaluation of events does not necessarily stand in any simple relation to any objective measures of these events. What is a utility for me is not necessarily a frustration to you. Also, both theories have had to take into account that we have some ideas about other people's values; and that we somehow learn about these values, usually by means of social interaction of various kinds.

It would be rash to make the assumption on the basis of this parallel that the models tend to converge. It is, however, possible to give more examples of convergence. Thus, Rapoport and Chammah (1965) try to incorporate models from learning theory into their theory of the Prisoner's Dilemma game. Simon (1957, chapter 16) shows that, in the light-guessing experiment, Estes' learning model leads to exactly the same predictions as would a model of the guesser based on his attempts to "minimax" his regret. Erik Moberg has shown that Richardson's non-rational model for arms races (which Richardson describes by saying that "this is what is going to happen, unless somebody stops to think") can be derived from a simple strategic model.

The cases just cited are, nevertheless, rather special, since learning theory is similar to the rational models, at least in those aspects that deal explicitly and mathematically with probabilities and, in some cases, with utilities.

While there is no sufficient basis for making any predictions about the eventual convergence of rational and non-rational models in general, some more specific points can be made about possible developments.

Thus, both types of models point to the importance of acquiring more knowledge about cognitive processes and their social basis. This is more than a matter of perception or attitudes, since studies of perception usually emphasize perception of physical objects, and attitude studies usually deal with "simple" attitudes, i.e. in general they do not treat such components as causal beliefs and more complicated beliefs about other people. (The question "What do you believe other people think about?" is usually employed as a masked question to find out what the person himself thinks. The theoretical basis for this is quite interesting although not very much developed.)

The need for a decent theory of value is also (explicitly or implicitly) emphasized by both types of models. In order to avoid confusion, it should be pointed out immediately that we mean "theory of what objects (in a very wide sense) are valuable to men". What we have so far is a formal theory of preference, which is still rather meagre, and a model for utility, which until now has hardly been applied outside the laboratory (although some attempts have been made, for instance in operations research); and, of course, a lot of research on consumer behaviour, seriously limited, however, in its choice of objects. In the case of rational models, we shall also need a normative theory of value because the concept of rationality applied to more complicated cases appears to require such a theory; the same is true of the interpersonal comparisons of value which seem essential for the development of various kinds of theories of group decision and for a (normative) welfare theory.

An essential limitation in both types of theories, at least in the cases discussed here, is that they are both individual theories rather than social theories, in so far as they have reached the stage of explicit models. The neglect of social interaction has already been pointed out in the case of rational models; but this also applies to several of the non-rational models, especially those of the instinct type. Having a theory of Man often entails lacking a theory of men. (See chapters by Moscovici, Tajfel, Israel and Asplund.) This deficiency is underlined by the indiscriminate use of both kinds of models for drawing conclusions about groups and societies.

References

Abrahamsson, B. (1970). Homans on exchange. *American Journal of Sociology*, **76,** 273–85.

Ackoff, R. L., Gupta, S. K. and Minas, J. S. (1965). "Scientific Method: Optimizing Applied Research Decisions". John Wiley, New York.

Ardrey, R. (1967). "The Territorial Imperative". Collins, London.

Axelrod, R. (1967). Conflict of interest: an axiomatic approach. *Journal of Conflict Resolution*, **H11**, no. 1, 87–99.

Ayer, A. J. (1961). "The Problem of Knowledge". Penguin Books, Edinburgh.

Bandura, A. and Walters, R. H. (1959). "Adolescent Aggression". Ronald Press, New York.

Bandura, A. and Walters, R. H. (1963). "Social Learning and Personality Development". Holt, Rinehart & Winston, New York.

Barnett, S. A. (1967). Attack and defense in animal societies. *In* "Aggression and Defense" (Eds C. D. Clemente and Lindsley, D. B.). University of California Press, Berkeley.

Becker, H. (1950). "Through Values to Social Interpretation". Duke University Press, Durham.

Bennett, J. (1964). "Rationality". Routledge & Kegan Paul, London.

Berelson, B. and Steiner, G. A. (1964). "Human Behaviour. An Inventory of Scientific Findings". Harcourt, Brace & World, New York.

Berkowitz, L. (1962). "Aggression: A Social Psychological Analysis". McGraw-Hill, New York.

Berkowitz, L. (Ed.) (1969). "Roots of Aggression. A Re-examination of the Frustration-Aggression Hypothesis". Atherton, New York.

Bliss, E. L. (Ed.) (1962). "Roots of Behavior". Harper, New York.

Boulding, K. (1963). "Conflict and Defense". Harper, New York.

Boulding, K. (March 1967). Am I Man or Mouse — or Both? War/Peace Report.

Braithwaite, R. B. (1963). "Theory of Games as a Tool for the Moral Philosopher". Cambridge University Press, London.

Brayer, A. R. (1964). An experimental analysis of some variables of minimax theory. *Behavioral Science*, **9,** no. 1, 33–44.

Carnap, R. (1962). "Logical Foundations of Probability". University of Chicago Press, Chicago.

Carthy, J. D. and Ebling, F. J. (Eds) (1964). "The Natural History of Aggression". Academic Press, London and New York.

Conrath, D. W. and Deci, E. L. (1969). The determination and scaling of a bivariate utility function. *Behavioral Science*, **14,** no. 4, 316–327.

Converse, Elizabeth (1968). The war of all against all: a review of the Journal of Conflict Resolution, 1957–68. *Journal of Conflict Resolution*, **12,** no. 4, 471–532.

Corning, P. A. (1971). The biological bases of behavior and some implications for political science. *World Politics*, **23,** no. 3, 321–70.

Criswell, J. H., Solomon, H. and Suppes, P. (Eds) (1962). "Mathematical Methods in Small Group Processes". Stanford University Press, Stanford.

Davidson, D., Siegel, S. and Suppes, P. (1955). Some Experiments and Related Theory in the Measurement of Utility and Subjective Probability. Rep. No. 4, Stanford Value Theory Project.

Davidson, D., Suppes, P. and Siegel, S. (1957). "Decision Making". Stanford University Press, Stanford.

Davies, J. C. (1962). Toward a theory of revolution. *American Sociological Review*, **27,** 5–19.

Debreu, G. (1954). Representation of a preference ordering by a numerical function. In "Decision Processes" (Eds R. M. Thrall, C. H. Coombs and R. L. Davis), John Wiley, New York, pp. 159–166.

Debreu, G. (1962). "Theory of Value". John Wiley, New York.

Deutsch, M. and Krauss, R. M. (1962). Studies in interpersonal bargaining. *Journal of Conflict Resolution*, **6**, no. 1, 52–76.

Dilger, J. (1962). Behavior and genetics. In "Roots of Behavior" (Ed. E. L. Bliss). pp. 35–47. Harper, New York.

Dollard, J., Doob, L. W., Miller, N. E., Mowrer, O. H. and Sears, R. S. (1963). "Frustration and Aggression". (1st ed. 1939). Yale University Press, New Haven.

Downs, A. (1957). "An Economic Theory of Democracy". Harper, New York.

Eckhoff, T. and Jacobsen, K. D. (1966). "Rationality and Responsibility". Munksgaard, Copenhagen.

Edwards, W. (1962). Utility, subjective probability, their interaction, and variance preferences. *Journal of Conflict Resolution*, **6**, no. 1, 42–51.

Fabricius, E. (1961). "Etologi". Bonniers, Stockholm.

Fishburn, P. C. (1968). Utility theory. *Management Science*, Theory Series, **14**, no. 5, 335–378.

Freeman, D. (1964). Human aggression in anthropological perspective. *In* "The Natural History of Aggression" (Eds J. D. Carthy and F. J. Ebling). Academic Press, London and New York.

Freud, S. (1946). Abriss der Psychoanalyse. *In* "Gesammelte Werke", no. 17, Imago, London.

Gallo, P. S. and McClintock, C. G. (1965). Cooperative and competitive behavior in mixed-motive games. *Journal of Conflict Resolution*, **9**, no. 1, 68–78.

Galtung, J. (1964). A structural theory of aggression. *Journal of Peace Research*, **2**, 95–119.

Graaff, J. de V. (1963). "Theoretical Welfare Economics". Cambridge University Press, London.

Guyer, M. and Rapoport, A. (1969). Information effects in two mixed-motive games. *Behavioral Science*, **14**, no. 6, 467–482.

Halldén, S. (1957). "On the Logic of Better". Gleerup, Lund.

Hamburger, H. (1969). Separable games. *Behavioral Science*, **14**, no. 2, 121–132.

Hansson, B. (1970). "Preference Logic: Philosophical Foundations and Applications in the Philosophy of Science". Studentlitteratur, Lund.

Harsanyi, J. C. (1962a). Rationality postulates for bargaining solutions in co-operative and non-cooperative games. *Management Science*, **9**, 141–153.

Harsanyi, J. C. (1962b). Bargaining in ignorance of the opponent's utility function. *Journal of Conflict Resolution*, **6**, no. 1, 179–196.

Heiskanen, I. (1967). "Theoretical Approaches and Scientific Strategies in Administrative and Organizational Research". Commentationes Humanarum Litterarum, Helsinki.

Hinde, R. A. (1968). *Animal Behaviour*, McGraw-Hill, London.

Howard, N. (1966). The theory of meta-games. *General Systems*, **11**, 167–186.

Iklé, F. C. and Leites, N. (1962). Political negotiation as a process of modifying utilities. *Journal of Conflict Resolution*, **6**, no. 1, 19–28.

Irwin, F. W. (1953). Stated expectations as functions of probability and desirability of outcomes, *Journal of Personality*, **21**, 329–35.

Johnsen, E. (1968). "Studies in Multiobjective Decision Models". Studentlitteratur, Lund.

Kaufman, H. and Becker, G. M. (1961). The empirical determination of game-theoretical strategies. *Journal of Experimental Psychology*, **6**, 462–468.

Keynes, J. M. (1921). "A Treatise on Probability". Macmillan, London.

Kmita, J. and Nowak, L. (1970). The rationality assumption in human sciences. *Polish Sociological Bulletin*, **21**, no. 1, 43–68.

Knorr, K. and Verba, S. (Eds) (1965). "The International System". Princeton University Press, Princeton.

Khun, H. W. (1962). Game theory and models of negotiation. *Journal of Conflict Resolution*, **6**, no. 1, 1–4.

Khun, T. (1962). "The Structure of Scientific Revolution". Chicago.

Kyburg, H. E. and Smokler, H. E. (Eds) (1964). "Studies in Subjective Probability". John Wiley, New York.

Lieberman, B. (1960). Human behavior in a strictly determined 3 × 3 game. *Behavioral Science*, **4**, 317–322.

Lieberman, B. (1962). Experimental studies of conflict in some two and three person games. *In* "Mathematical Methods in Small Group Processes" (Eds J. H. Criswell, H. Solomon and P. Suppes), pp. 203–220. Stanford University Press, Stanford.

Lorenz, K. (1966). "On Aggression". Bantam Books, New York.

Luce, R. D. (1959). "Individual Choice Behavior". John Wiley, New York.

Luce, R. D. and Raiffa, H. (1958). "Games and Decisions". John Wiley, New York.

Lumsden, M. (1968). Studies in the Psychology of Strategic Thinking. (Mimeograph). Diss., Departments of Psychology and Sociology, University of Bergen.

Lyon, E. S. (1970). Notes on the Explanation of Aggressive Behavior. Unpublished paper, Department of Sociology, University of Lund.

March, J. G. and Simon, H. A. (1963). "Organizations". John Wiley, New York.

Mark, V. H. and Ervin, F. R. (1970). "Violence and the Brain". Harper & Row, New York.

Messick, D. M. (1967). Interdependent decision strategies in zero-sum games: a computer-controlled study. *Behavioral Science*, **12**, no. 1.

Messick, S. and Brayfield, A. (Eds) (1964). "Decision and Choice. Contributions of Sidney Siegel". McGraw-Hill, New York.

Midgaard, K. (1965). "Strategisk tenkning". Norsk utenrikspolitisk institutt, Oslo.

Midgaard, K. (1968). Some comments on the meaning and use of game theory. *Conflict and Cooperation*, **2**, no. 2.

Milnor, J. (1954). Games against nature. *In* "Decision Processes" (Eds R. M. Thrall, C. H. Coombs, and R. L. Davis). John Wiley, New York.

Minas, J. S., Scodel, A., Marlowe, D. and Rawson, H. (1960). Some descriptive aspects of two person non-zero-sum games, part II, *Journal of Conflict Resolution*, **4**, no. 2, 193–97.

Mises, R. von (1957). "Probability, Statistics and Truth". Macmillan, New York.

Morin, R. E. (1960). Strategies in games with saddle points. *Psychological Reports*, **7**, 479–485.

Mosteller, F. and Nogee, P. (1951). An experimental measurement of utility. *Journal of Political Economy*, **59**, 371–404.

Murray, E. J. (1964). "Motivation and Emotion". Prentice-Hall, Englewood Cliffs. (Swedish translation, 1968.)

Neumann, J. von and Morgenstern, O. (1964). "Theory of Games and Economic Behavior". John Wiley, New York.

Nicholson, M. (1970). "Conflict Analysis". The English Universities Press, London.

Ofshe, L. and Ofshe, R. (197). "Utility and Choice in Social Interaction". Prentice-Hall, Englewood Cliffs.

Olweus, D. (1970). "Prediction of Aggression". Skandinaviska testförlaget, Stockholm.

Ploog, D. (1967). Verhaltensforschung und Psychiatrie. *Psychiatrie der Gegenwart*, **1**, 292–443.

Quine, W. V. O. (1953). "From a Logical Point of View". Harvard University Press, Cambridge, Mass.

Raiffa, H. (1953). Arbitration schemes for generalized two-person games. *In* "Contributions to the Theory of Games" (Eds. H. W. Kuhn and A. W. Tucker), vol. II. Princeton University Press, Princeton.

Rapoport, A. (1960). "Fights, Games and Debates". University of Michigan Press, Ann Arbor.

Rapoport, A. (1964). "Strategy and Conscience". Harper, New York.

Rapoport, A. (1966). "Two-person Game Theory. The Essential Ideas". University of Michigan Press, Ann Arbor.

Rapoport, A. and Chammah, A. M. (1965). "Prisoner's Dilemma". University of Michigan Press, Ann Arbor.

Rapoport, A. and Guyer, M. A. (1966). A taxonomy of 2×2 games. *General Systems*, **11**, 203–214.

Richardson, L. F. (1960a). "Statistics of Deadly Quarrels". Boxwood Press, Chicago.

Richardson, L. F. (1960b). "Arms and Insecurity". Boxwood Press, Chicago.

Riker, W. H. (1962). "The Theory of Political Coalitions". Yale University Press, New Haven.

Rutherford, D. E. (1965). "Introduction to Lattice Theory". Oliver & Boyd, London.

Ryle, G. (1960). "The Concept of Mind". Barnes & Noble, New York.

Savage, L. J. (1954). "The Foundations of Statistics". John Wiley, New York.

Schelling, T. (1963). "The Strategy of Conflict". Oxford University Press, London.

Scodel, A., Minas, J. S., Ratoosh, P. and Lipetz, M. (1959). Some descriptive aspects on two-person non-zero-sum games. Part I. *Journal of Conflict Resolution*, **3**, no. 2, 114–19.

Scodel, A. (1962). Induced collaboration in some non-zero-sum games. *Journal of Conflict Resolution*, **6**, no. 4, 335–40.

Scott, J. P. (1962). Hostility and aggression in animals. *In* "Roots of Behavior" (Ed. E. L. Bliss), pp. 167–178. Harper, New York.

Shubik, M. (1963). Some reflections on the design of game theoretic models for the study of negotiation and threats. *Journal of Conflict Resolution*, **7**, no. 1, 1–12.

Shubik, M. (Ed.) (1969). "Game Theory and Related Approaches to Social Behavior". John Wiley, New York.

Shubik, M. (1970). Game theory, behavior and the paradox of the prisoner's dilemma: three solutions. *Journal of Conflict Resolution*, **14**, 2, 181--194.

Siegel, S. (1956). A method for obtaining an ordered metric scale. *Psychometrica*, **21**, 207-16.

Siegel, S. (1964). *See* Messick and Brayfield.

Simon, H. A. (1957). "Models of Man". John Wiley, New York.

Suppes, P. (1961). Philosophical relevance of decision theory. *Journal of Philosophy*, **58**, 605H-613.

Suppes, P. and Atkinson, R. C. (1960). "Markov Learning Models for Multiperson Interactions". Stanford University Press, Stanford.

Swensson, R. G. (1967). Cooperation in the prisoner's dilemma game. I: The effects of a symmetric payoff information and explicit communication. *Behavioral Science*, **12**, no. 4, 314-22.

Thrall, R. M., Coombs, C. H. and Davis, R. L. (Eds) (1954). "Decision Processes". John Wiley, New York.

Verba, S. (1965). Assumptions of rationality and non-rationality in models of the international system. *In* "The International System" (Eds K. Knorr and S. Verba), pp. 93-117. Princeton Universtiy Press, Princeton.

Weber, M. (1966a). "General Economic History". Collier-Macmillan, London.

Weber, M. (1966b). "The Theory of Social and Economic Organization" (Translation of Wirtschaft and Gesellschaft, I). Collier-Macmillan, London.

Wright, G. H. von (1963). "The Logic of Preference". Edinburgh.

Wright, Q. (1942). "A Study of War". Chicago.

9

Ethology and Human Behaviour [1,2]

Mario von Cranach

This chapter is written in the belief that psychology, in seeking to understand man, must take into account the findings of ethology. We can
confidently assume that numerous human behaviour patterns show
similarities with animal behaviour which can be traced back to evolutionary relationships. The scientific problem is that of determining how
these similarities can be established with certainty, of describing how
phylogenetically transmitted behaviour patterns fit into the behavioural
systems of social man and his culture, and of discovering how we can
take account of these factors in shaping our social existence. Psychology
(and the other human sciences) must either tackle these questions independently or take note of how they are dealt with by biologists. The
following discussion will accordingly concentrate rather on the evolutionary origins of human behaviour patterns than on the cognitive value
of analogies and the applicability of ethological concepts in psychology.

[1] Translated from the German by H. B. Nisbet.
[2] We are grateful to the publishers, S. Moos, R. Piper & Co. and Droemer-Knaur, all of
Munich, L. Stocker of Graz, and to the publishers of *The Scientific American* for their kind
permission to reproduce the figures in this chapter.

1   Considerations of principle

Our approach is based upon certain assumptions of a more general nature. Some of these assumptions concern the relatedness of man and animals and have the function of postulates within the argument. The others are reflections on the properties and behaviour of systems.

1.1   ASSUMPTIONS CONCERNING THE RELATEDNESS OF ANIMALS AND MAN

We consider the theory of evolution to be one of the most fully authenticated theories in biology (cf. Heberer, 1967, for points of detail). This theory furnishes our enquiry with the following assumptions:

a. In the course of evolution, genetically stored information, which manifests itself in morphological and behavioural structures, is transmitted with variations from one species to another.

b. Man has emerged from a long series of animal ancestors; these species have disappeared, but a series of species which are also descended from them, and which are consequently related to man, that is, the primates, have survived.

c. Man is the most highly organized mammal; his individual and social behaviour and his social systems are more complex than those of all other mammals.

1.2   ASSUMPTIONS CONCERNING THE PROPERTIES, BEHAVIOUR AND DEVELOPMENT OF SYSTEMS

If we regard living organisms and their societies as systems and individual organs or behaviour patterns as sub-systems, we can apply more general principles to them and thereby attain a clearer understanding of them. In the following paragraphs we shall discuss the structure, function and development of systems on the basis of general system theory. To prevent the argument from becoming too abstract, we shall illustrate it with the following examples, and these will be kept in view, wherever possible, throughout the entire discussion:

1. An example from morphology: the thumb in the structure of the primate hand.

2. The evolution of an artificial organ, the "swallow's nest" in the uniform of a military trumpeter.

3. The evolution of a human behaviour pattern, that of kissing.

This demonstration will concern itself only with limited areas because the development of various sub-systems of human morphology and of human behaviour took place relatively independently, so that separate analyses are required in the case of sub-systems.

1.2.1   *The concept and properties of systems*

The term "system" is used to signify "a complex of elements and their interrelations" (Bertalanffy, 1956), or, in a global sense, "everything that can be regarded as a separate whole" (Toda and Shuford, 1965). The interaction of the elements within a system gives rise to phenomena which cannot be described in terms of the classical sciences but only by means of concepts such as wholeness, organization, directedness, control and regulation. Systems possess an *environment*—that is "the sum total of all objects, changes in whose properties influence the system, and of those objects whose properties are in turn influenced by the behaviour of the system" (Hall and Fagen, 1956)—and also *sub-systems*, which are perceived when the system is sub-divided in accordance with the criterion of specific kinds of object relations. Such distinctions as are among elements (i.e. objects) and relations will depend on the analytical powers of the observer, and the way in which they are divided up into environment, systems, and sub-systems will depend on his point of view and aims.

Open systems, unlike closed systems, stand in reciprocal relationship with their environment. The principle of equifinality, which holds true in the case of closed systems, means that such systems can arrive at the same final state, albeit in different ways and from different initial conditions. Open systems are not subject to the principle of entropy, but exhibit the phenomena of *evolution* and *differentiation*.

1.2.2   *Structure and function*

Systems (and sub-systems) possess structures and functions. The *structure* of a system can be defined as the totality of relations between its sub-systems (Toda and Shuford, 1965), and the same applies to the structure of sub-systems themselves. The structure is thus a map or diagram of relations, and to that extent has a static quality. The concept of *function*, as in everyday parlance, has two uses and can signify:

    a. The action of one unit on another unit, whether the relationship between these units is that of element and system or of system and environment. ("In the case of dynamic systems, particularly cybernetic systems, the function of a system-element consists in the transformation of a specific input into a specific output." Klaus, 1968.)

b. The behaviour of a structured whole. ("The function of a dynamic system is the class of abstraction of the possible behaviour patterns of this system . . ." Klaus, 1968.)

Both concepts of function accordingly denote a dynamic aspect of the system. The two are fundamentally similar, for, in the second case, the concept of "behaviour patterns" in open systems must be taken to include interaction with the environment of the system. The second definition however, is narrower, for it stipulates some kind of behaviour, whereas the first requires no more than existence. In the following remarks, the concept of function will be used in the first sense.

The relationships between structure and function should become clear from our examples shown on p. 374.

The structure and function of any given system are interconnected for they are two aspects of the same thing. But this does not mean that a particular structure must always possess a particular function, or that a particular function can only be fulfilled by a particular structure. On the contrary, the evolution of systems nearly always presents variations in the relationship between structure and function.

1.2.3   *The development of systems*

We speak of a development whenever a new and different kind of system arises out of an earlier one. But this presupposes that structures of the first system are preserved, since it is this which constitutes the difference between a development and an entirely new construction. Linguistic usage, in this case, gives a fair reflection of the distinct processes which occur in both natural and cultural contexts. Natural and cultural development proceeds slowly, as a rule; only a small proportion of those structural characteristics which have hitherto stood the test are threatened, while the overwhelming majority are preserved: *natura non facit saltus*.

Thus we can understand the process of development once we have comprehended the two processes it involves, that is, if we can understand how the old structures in the system are preserved and how the new structures are created. The one is as important as the other.

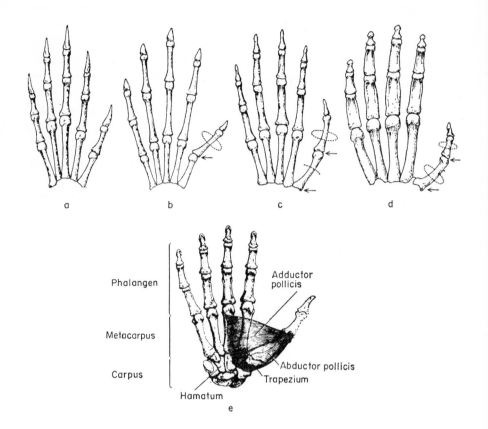

Fig. 1. *The hands of extant primates*. (a) The hand of the tree-shrew (tupaia) already shows the beginnings of that specialization of the thumb which characterizes the primates. (b) In the tarsier (tarsius) the thumb is already separated from the other fingers and can rotate around the joint which it forms with the metacarpus. (c) in the South American capuchin monkey (cebus) the angle between the thumb and the other fingers is wider and the thumb can now move from the base of its metacarpus. (d) In the African gorilla the thumb metacarpus is linked by a joint to the first wrist bone (trapezium), which permits a rotary movement of the thumb metacarpus. (e) The hand of modern man. The development from (a) to (d) has progressed even further. The thumb is very long in relation to the index finger, and set at a wide angle. Powerful muscles move it towards and away from the surface of the hand. Joints between the thumb and metacarpus and between the metacarpus and trapezium enable the thumb to rotate 45 degrees around its longer axis, and thus to act as a counterpart to the other fingers. The broader terminal phalanges make the firm thumb-and-finger grip possible. (From Eibl-Eibesfeldt, 1967, after Napier, 1962.)

A development can be initiated from within the system, as occurs in the course of natural reproduction; in other cases, as with the development of a cultural artefact, it takes place through the action of an external, formative force of the environment. In both cases, the transfer of the old structure to the new system requires a medium which will pass on this structure in the shape of some kind of information. Similarly, the formation of new structural characteristics means that new information must be introduced into the system. To understand the process of development means, therefore, among other things, that one must comprehend the processes whereby old and new information is brought into the system. In biology this is the province of evolutionary theory, which concentrates, however, on the manner in which new information is acquired. The workings of evolution can best be summed up, in universally valid terms, as a combination of three phases: variation, selection and preservation. These phases can also be distinguished in the process of trial-and-error learning (the evolution of a behavioural system—cf. Pringle, 1951, and Ashby, 1952), as well as in socio-cultural evolution (Campbell, 1965). Since the process of selection begins with functions, it should be possible to gain an insight into the basis of the evolution of structures by examining these functions, at the same time bearing in mind the environment with which the system is interacting. This has further implications for the analysis of structures, for since the functions are among the conditions governing the genesis of structures, and since they show the structure in action, they must be included in any analysis of structures: even the structure of a kitchen ladle cannot be properly understood without some knowledge of its function. Conversely, functions are closely associated with structures and cannot be explained without reference to them. Structural analysis and functional analysis are therefore inseparable, which is a truism in biology, anatomy and physiology, and a widely held opinion in linguistics (as applied to syntax and semantics—although function here appears in the guise of "meaning").

1.2.4 *Structural and functional change*

If the link between particular structures and particular functions were a constant one, the study of the evolution of systems would be easier. In reality, the connection between them is in many respects variable. Even an analysis of homogenous systems will usually show a *variability of structures with identical functions.* The information which underlies a given structure will usually tie it down only to a specific range of possible variations, but not to a specific shape. (Thus it is not the morphological characteristic or the innate behaviour pattern but rather their range of variations which is genetically predetermined; not the social behaviour, but its scope, is fixed by rules; not the exact tonal quality of a word, but the relationship of the individual sounds to each other, with a specific tolerance, is subject to the phonetic norm.[1]) A further difficulty is that *different combinations* are frequently possible: for a structure can have several functions and a function can be associated with different structures. But when we examine evolutionary sequences we encounter decisive changes in the shape and combinations of particular structures and functions. Such changes can be described as *structural and functional* transformation; that is, structures can change and disappear, and new functions can arise.

The ideas advanced in this section have long been taken for granted in science, although psychology, for some unknown reason, has largely ignored them. Even Geoffroy St. Hilaire and Georges Cuvier studied the connections between function and structure, and in Goethe's scientific writings, despite his idealistic morphology, we can find numerous quotations which show how familiar he was with the relationships within organized systems. The following passage, which conveys the idea of the hierarchic organization of systems, may serve as an example:

> All living things are not units but pluralities; even when they appear to us as individuals, they nevertheless remain collections of independent living entities. These are ideally and potentially identical, but can manifest themselves in the world of experience either as identical and similar or as different and dissimilar . . . The less perfect a creature is, the more its parts will resemble each other and the whole. The more perfect the creature becomes, the less its parts will resemble each other. In the former instance, the whole is more or less the same as the parts, but in the latter, the whole does not resemble the parts. The more the parts resemble each other, the less their degree of subordination to each other will be. The subordination of parts indicates a more perfect creature.   Goethe, 1817

In this last sentence, we find not only the principle of hierarchic system-organization, but also a criterion for assessing the degree of organic development or differentiation. Let us consider some examples to clarify these various instances:

[1] "That which, on an ideal level, is identical, can appear in the world of experience either as identical or similar, or even as totally different and dissimilar—this is what constitutes the dynamic life of nature." (Goethe, 1817.)

a. *Structural change.* The transformation of forms in Fig. 2 affords examples of structural change. The connections between forms (a), (h) and (i) could not be recognized unless the intermediate forms, and hence the course of the development, were known. The primate hands depicted in Fig. 1 show different stages in the development of the grasping hand (although not in a directly related series). The structure of the kiss in Fig. 3(g), (h) and (i) varies according to the parts of the body in contact (oral kiss, kiss on the cheek, kiss on the hand; but in this case too, the structural characteristic of closed eyes is present). A particularly common form of change is *structural reduction,* which is often accompanied by loss of function. (The human appendix is an example.)

b. *Integration of structures.* The integration of structures into other structures can be seen, for example, in Fig. 2(h) and (i), in which the pattern of the "trumpeter's wings" is transferred to the sleeves. But an extremely common form of integration is that whereby simple and often older structures are assimilated into more complex and often younger structures. This can be seen from the way in which a simple group-consolidating behaviour pattern (cf. Fig. 3(g)) is assimilated into rituals of greeting and departure governed by cultural rules (Fig. 3(h) and (i)).

c. *Functional change.* Examples of this are the repeated changes in function of parts of the sleeve in Fig. 2 from ornament to sign and back again to mere decoration (cf. Koenig, 1969, pp. 63–64; 1970, pp. 69–78), and the well-documented change in function of mouth-to-mouth feeding from group-consolidating kiss to cultural ritual (cf. Wickler, 1969a, pp. 107–108; Eibl-Eibesfeldt, 1970, pp. 150–164). Whether hand-kissing really belongs to the same series of development or not is uncertain.

d. *Loss of function.* The illustrations in this chapter contain no examples of the emergence of new function; the appearance of a new function can often be distinguished from functional change only when a structure has remained functionless over a certain space of time. An example of this is the transformation of the structural characteristic of the divided railway carriage with separate entrances, originally taken over from the mail coach, into a means of social segregation (through the introduction of different classes). (The evolution of the railway carriage, incidentally, affords good examples of the various kinds of structural and functional change described above.)

The fact that functions and structures are subject to change compels us to study their relationships and variations in time, that is, to examine the *history* of the systems in question.

N

2 The transformation of animal behaviour structures into complex human behaviour

2.1 THE PHYLOGENESIS OF BEHAVIOUR PATTERNS AS THE EVOLUTION OF SYSTEMS

Behaviour patterns are systems in the sense defined above. In other words, they possess structures and functions. As we have seen, the evolution of systems depends on the transference of information. In the case of the evolution of human behaviour out of animal behaviour, this can only take place genetically, for transference by tradition (i.e. ritualization and individual learning) is out of the question, and no third possibility exists. Genetic transference has been demonstrated beyond doubt in the case of numerous behaviour patterns (on the relevant

Fig. 2. The development of "swallow's nests." (a) and (b) Young Frenchmen with fur-trimmed jackets whose slit sleeves reveal the sleeves of the under-jacket; (b) shows how it is already possible to reach out through the slit. (c) Burgundian duke. The sleeves of the top jacket are now so long and wide that their function is purely decorative. The arms, therefore, normally protrude from the very long slits. (d) French nobleman. The puffed sleeve-tops of examples (a) to (c) have become shoulder pads. The sleeves themselves are completely open, and hang down only as decorative strips. (e) and (f) Costumes of French commoners with the remnants of the old slit sleeves serving purely as a decoration. In (f) the swallow's nest shape is already clearly recognizable. The plaits could well be the rudiments of the later vertical ornamentation. (g) Trumpeter of a Dutch cavalry detachment of around 1600. Since trumpeters had special importance in battle as signallers they were dressed conspicuously and nearly always rode on white horses. For the same reason, they retained the old costume with the slit sleeves as their insignia. The open sleeves would fly out behind them as they galloped along, thus making the wearer more conspicuous. Hence the name "trumpeter's sleeves". It is now obvious that the sleeve-tops are developing into the later "swallow's nests". The sleeves are also conspicuously decorated by extremely pronounced seams. (h) The coat of a trumpeter of the Bavarian cavalry around 1720, with "trumpeter's wings". These were created by lengthening the remnants of the open sleeves into long bands and transferring them to the back of the coat. Since their colour contrasted with that of the coat itself, they stood out conspicuously as they fluttered behind the rider. (i) The coat of a Prussian drummer of around 1760 with swallow's nests. The fluttering trumpeter's sleeves have disappeared, but their decorations have been transferred to the real sleeves. The military musicians inherited the trumpeter's tradition. (k) Oboeist of the Prussian Fusilier Guards, around 1704. (l) Musician of the German army of the Second World War. The ornament descended from the plaits of the (originally puffed) sleeve-tops has been taken over in its old form. (From Koenig, 1969.)

Fig. 2

Fig. 3

literature, cf. Wickler, 1961, p. 306). In fact, behaviour patterns are often more stable than morphological characteristics (e.g. in Wickler, 1961, Example 1, p. 14, the bristling of hair which is no longer present), and they are adduced for this reason by zoologists as a means of solving systematic problems whenever morphological characteristics do not permit any reliable conclusions to be reached (cf. Wickler, 1961, pp. 348–352).

The evolution of behaviour patterns thus corresponds to that of systems, and what applies to the latter can also be applied to the former, as we have seen in the example of the kiss developing out of mouth-to mouth feeding. The same is true of the development of human behaviour from animal behaviour.

2.2 IMPLICATIONS FOR THE EVOLUTION OF HUMAN BEHAVIOUR PATTERNS

In considering the development of human behaviour from animal behaviour, we can expect, with a high degree of probability, to encounter structural and functional change. Of the various forms which this can take, the commonest instances are discussed below.

The *reduction* of behaviour structures is often accompanied by a reduction of the corresponding morphological structures (cf. in Wickler, 1961, Example 1, p. 14, the bristling of hair which is no longer present, or the baring or closing of teeth in fits of anger to expose the no longer extant canines). But, since these behaviour patterns have often lost their function, they have no great significance (unless they have been ritualized so as to acquire a symbolic function).

Structural integration, on the other hand, which is usual in phylogenetically long-lived human behaviour patterns, is genuinely important. We have already concluded that this is a phenomenon typically associated with the development of complex structures from simple ones. In considering the integration of animal behaviour patterns into human

Fig. 3. The development of kissing. (a) and (b) Mouth-to-mouth feeding and greeting in the chimpanzee. (c) and (d) Mouth-to-mouth feeding: an Uruku Indian woman and a piglet; a Papuan mother and child. (e) An Ituri Indian performs the ritual of distributing pieces of elephant-fat to his fellows from mouth to mouth. (All after Wickler, 1969b.) (f) Mouth-to-mouth feeding. (g) A mother kisses her child. (h) Khrushchev embraces his American host. (All after Eibl-Eibesfeldt, 1970.) (i) How to kiss a lady's hand. From a book of etiquette (Hilgendorff, 1961).

ones, we must therefore bear in mind the difference between man and the other mammals, including even closely related species. In greatly simplified terms, we can define this difference as consisting of three interrelated characteristics: the development of special motor and of special cognitive capacities in the individual, and the tradition of information as a means of creating cultural systems.

Motor and cognitive capacities. These are so often cited as constitutive characteristics of man that little need be said about them here. The most important new acquisitions in the field of motor capacities are the development of the hand and of the organs of speech. The cognitive powers created by the unique development of the human cerebrum make possible, in conjunction with the organs of speech, the development of language and the free use and recollection of symbols and cognitive information; and secondly, in conjunction with the hand, they facilitate the growth of technologies, which allow the species to adapt to the most varied living conditions.

The social tradition and the construction of social and cultural systems. (Most psychologists and scientists pay lip service to these, but many fail to take them into account in their practical activities.) The complicated social behaviour patterns made possible by a viable system of communication, together with the handing down of acquired behaviour patterns, cognitions, and technologies, eventually create durable social systems. These cultures influence the behaviour of individuals even in the smallest details and should be regarded as superordinate systems with their own sets of laws.

What is particularly important for our purposes is that the many innate (i.e. phylogenetically determined) behaviour characteristics are largely integrated into the complex new individual, social and cultural systems. Still recognizable in their detailed characteristics, they have become part of these larger systems and interact with the other elements in them. They have acquired a cognitive character and a cultural significance: in short, something new has emerged.

The example of space-oriented behaviour. The above remarks may be clarified by the following examples of space-oriented behaviour. As a result of their ability to move freely in space, animals at a relatively early stage develop a tendency to concentrate important organs of sensation and activity on a particular side of the body. This side becomes the animal's front, and gains importance as the seat of perception and interaction in social behaviour. Further spatial factors of importance in social behaviour are distance from the partner, and localization within the group and environment: orientation, distance and localization become the fundamental dimensions of social behaviour, and we may therefore conclude that, among social animals, there is no social behaviour without a spatial aspect and no space-oriented behaviour without a social significance. The minimal definition of an animal society requires only that the group should be distributed in space, in deviation from a random model, independently of non-social stimuli (McBride, 1971).

The dimensions of orientation, distance and localization constitute an internally articulated structure whose components interact with one another. Orientation includes such factors as the turning towards or turning away of the body, head and eyes. Distances from objects in various directions to the body add up to form an asymmetrical personal zone, which is larger towards the front than towards the rear; they correspond to the social structure of the group, and complex systems of precedence are evolved. Localization will determine the opportunities available for communication and for satisfying other needs.

All these structures are encountered in human society too. Several books and collections of articles on the significance of human spatial behaviour have appeared in recent years, summarizing the results of numerous empirical studies (cf. Hall, 1959; Sommer, 1969; and Esser, 1971).

The dimensions in question (orientation, distance and localization) are themselves an index of the individual's cognitive and affective attitudes towards his fellows, and of the manner in which a society views itself. But they are closely linked with other communicative behaviour patterns, and have new functions within this context. Thus the direction in which the eyes are turned governs floor apportionment in conversation (Kendon, 1967). Verbal communication can be paralleled by a kind of spatial dance of the participants (Scheflen, 1964; Condon and Ogston, 1966; Birdwhistell, 1968). Spatial metaphors have entered language as a means of characterizing social relationships (for example, "to turn one's back on someone"; "to go along with someone"; "to turn a cold shoulder"; "inclination"; etc.) Explicit and implicit rules for spatial behaviour are a permanent ingredient of cultural norms; spatial constellations symbolize social relationships (for example, judge and accused); and spatial requirements and preferences determine the structure of our material culture. Indeed a separate monograph could well be devoted to man's spatial behaviour.

In short, communication is a time-honoured manifestation of social existence, and human communication is an indivisible compound of ancient elements, some of which have acquired new functions.

Consequences of structural integration. From the fact of structural integration, certain consequences follow both for scientific thinking and for linguistic usage. Man's phylogenetically determined genetic legacy does not constitute a particular *layer* which is built over with "higher" dispositions and abilities. We convey the wrong image and the wrong impression if we speak of a phylogenetically ancient *core*, or an animal *basis* under a human and cultural superstructure. Wherever phylogenetically older behaviour is encountered, it is part of a new unit formed by inter-penetration with behaviour patterns peculiar to man. It is therefore unwise to attempt to treat inherited and culturally acquired behaviour patterns as if they belonged to *different levels of analysis*. They should rather be approached as a holistic system, with due regard for the structural and functional changes which have occurred in the course of history. Just as there is no purely "animal" behaviour in man, neither is there likely to be any purely "human" behaviour; on the contrary, the integration of the two is something new, and it is this which constitutes their truly human quality.

3   Methodological problems

"Natural history is based entirely on comparison" (Goethe, 1795), and everything said in this chapter presupposes that this is in fact the case. But any scientific discussion of the links between human and animal behaviour will involve comparisons of the most varied kinds, and the following distinctions can be made:

a. *In the form of the comparison*, implicit or explicit parallels, and emphasis on similarities or differences.

b. *In the object of comparison*, narrowly circumscribed bodily movements; complex behaviour models; culturally ritualized behaviour patterns and human artefacts; cognitive schemes and social dispositions; societies.

c. *In the manner of explanation*, structural similarities, functional parallels and evolutionary relationships.

Given this variety of possible modes of comparison, let us look at the question of methodology more closely.

3.1 COMPARATIVE METHODS IN BIOLOGY

Comparative methods are of interest here in so far as they can throw light on phylogenetic origins. They have long been used for this purpose in biology.

"Similarity and kinship are not identical concepts in biology" (Remane, 1952.) The "natural system" in biology, founded on similarities in morphological structures, was actually elaborated before the theory of evolution was propounded, and it is possible to translate systematic groups into an evolutionary scheme. Systematics is accordingly one of the bases on which the history of evolutionary descent rests, but the correspondence between the two is imperfect for two reasons: dissimilar structures can have a common ancestry, and similar structures can have a different ancestry. When two distinct species display common characteristics as a result of common descent, we speak of *homology;* *analogy*, on the other hand, denotes a similarity which has come about through the *convergent* development of the characteristics in question.

The central problem in tracing the course of phylogenesis is that of identifying homologies. The criteria employed can only be outlined briefly here, but Remane (1952) and Wickler (1961) can be consulted for further details.

3.1.1 *Homology criteria*

It is usual to look for homologies in the elements of structures and not in the complete structures themselves. Various criteria have been developed for this purpose.

The criterion of situation. This is also a general criterion of similarities between systems as a whole. Elements in two separate systems are identified by their links with other elements (similarity of situation within the structure (cf. Fig. 4, after Wickler, 1961). Since behaviour patterns are

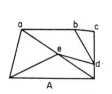 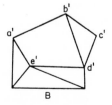

Fig. 4.   a =a', c =c', etc. (structural similarity).

structures in time, the placing of their elements must also be defined in relation to a temporal structure. In the case of behaviour patterns, additional confirmation can be obtained by identifying the organs involved in the temporal structure (Wickler, 1961).

The criterion of position can be applied only if two conditions are met: *the number of components in the two systems must correspond,* otherwise it will not be possible to identify the separate elements accurately, and *the connections between them must be constant in time.* (This latter condition means that the criterion of position cannot be applied to structures whose elements have continually changing connections.)

The criterion of the specific quality of structures. This criterion is fulfilled when the structures share a maximum number of peculiar characteristics (cf. Fig. 5, after Wickler, 1961). It might therefore more aptly be called "the criterion of the specific quality of elements". According to Wickler

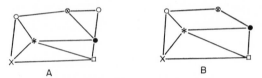

Fig. 5. One corner in B (point o) has dropped out.

(1961), this criterion **is** nearly always applicable. Although it works independently of the number of components involved, it can easily lead to a confusion of homologies and analogies and is never sufficient in itself.

The criterion of relatedness through intermediate forms. This criterion can only be applied in a second operation after the first two criteria have been tried. Two distinct structures can be regarded as homologous if they are linked by sufficient intermediate forms satisfying the above homology criteria. These intermediate forms must be descended from organisms whose overall organization lies between that of the organisms to be compared. It is necessary to ensure that the first and last characteristics in the series represented by the two structures are not simultaneously present in one of the intermediate forms (cf. Fig. 6, after Wickler, 1961).

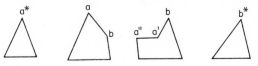

Fig. 6. a* and b* are not homologous (as the intermediate forms indicate).

Along with these main criteria there are other auxiliary ones; for example, simple structures are likely to be homologous if they occur in a large number of closely similar species, or if the species in which they occur exhibit further similarities which are not functionally and ecologically correlated. Remane gives a rule of thumb to the effect that homologies are more likely to be found in complex organisms whose structural similarities extend to the minutest details (Remane, 1952, p. 59).

3.1.2 *Analogy criteria*

Homologies and analogies are mutually exclusive. It is therefore useful to have criteria for identifying analogies too. Unlike homologies, which by definition presuppose a relationship, analogies can have many causes, and it is accordingly more difficult to lay down unambiguous criteria for identifying them. They can only be identified if one has knowledge of functions as well as of structures, for analogy criteria take account of the way of life or *environment* of an *organism*. Structures are most likely to be analogous if they are found in large numbers in species sharing a particular way of life or a particular environment, independently of any relationship (Wickler, 1961). The same will be true if they occur in species with the same environment or way of life, whose relatives in other environments or with a different way of life lack the structures in question. Neither criterion can rule homologies out altogether.

3.1.3 *The comparison of elements as a means of tracing descent*

The homology criteria mentioned above depend upon judgements as to the similarity (or identity) of elements. The criterion of position discovers homologies in elements or component structures within larger structures, which means that components of the separate structures compared must be identified and shown to be the same; the criterion of specific quality compares elements in different structures and looks for similarities between them; and the criterion of relatedness is derived from the two other criteria.

Thus we always compare *elements within a structure;* this can be done by further analysis or by making holistic judgements.

In the former case, we treat the elements themselves as systems; we analyse them into their subordinate elements and then compare these.

If a sufficient number of subordinate elements can be equated, we can treat the elements to which they belong as similar or identical. This procedure can lead to an infinite regress, and must therefore be terminated at some stage by a judgement or supposition.[1]

In the second case, we compare the elements by applying Gestalt-perception (Lorenz, 1959 and 1965) to their visible similarities. The judgement, depending on the skill of the person making it, can be astonishingly accurate, for it takes account of incomparably more (and subtler) characteristics and their relationships than any other methods. Its disadvantage is that it cannot readily be tested. (In everyday existence, we unhesitatingly stake our lives on our perceptions, but as trained psychologists, we refuse to base hypotheses on them.)

We therefore find that comparisons of structures on a given level nearly always include analyses on the next highest level (to take in the environment) and the next lowest level (to take in the elements).

3.2   THE SCOPE OF EXISTING METHODS OF COMPARING HUMAN AND ANIMAL BEHAVIOUR

3.2.1   *The comparison of behaviour patterns*

Only the methods outlined above are available so far for tracing human behaviour back to animal behaviour. They rest on the basic postulate that the information which determines the structures compared was transmitted by genetic means.[2]

If this postulate is granted, human and animal *behaviour patterns* can be treated as homologous (the more detailed our knowledge of them, the better); and knowledge of their origins could lead to new insights, above all in developmental psychology, social psychology (communicative behaviour), and psychopathology. Other possible means of information transference, for example that of cultural traditions, must be systematically ruled out for human behaviour patterns. For this purpose, new

---

[1] This has no real disadvantage, since *all* methods of dealing with elements involve acts of decision; this is the case even in traditional methods of measurement, in so far as the units of measurement are treated as equal. Holistic (or structuralistic) methods are, however, "arbitrary", at least in so far as they define the limits of structures.

[2] If we wished to extend the range of the homology criteria to include systems of all kinds, this postulate would run as follows: "the structures under comparison are determined by the *same* information". Such an assumption would mean that we would have to identify the paths which the information takes.

homology criteria must be developed, and these are indeed implicitly contained in methods of investigation already in use, for example in studies of isolated individuals and societies (Eibl-Eibesfeldt, 1968; in most of the cases discussed, the aim is in fact to discover the genetic basis of human behaviour patterns).

Furthermore, homology criteria should be developed in such a way that they can be applied to structures whose relations are *relations of probability* (probabilistic structures). And finally, as already mentioned, the general principles of structural and functional change in the integration of behaviour patterns into human behaviour should be investigated. (The ethological concept of *ritualization* could be taken as an example.)

3.2.2 THE COMPARISON OF COGNITIVE AND MOTIVATIONAL DISPOSITIONS

The work of human ethologists extends beyond comparisons of behaviour patterns. In the above remarks, behaviour patterns were used as an example to describe the evolution of systems. Such behaviour patterns are manifestations of neurophysiological forms of organization whose actual structures cannot easily be grasped. Thus comparisons of behaviour patterns must act as a substitute, so to speak, for comparisons of their neurophysiological substratum. But there is no reason why the principles of system evolution should be applied exclusively to those neurophysiological structures whose workings activate behaviour which can be perceived by the senses. They ought rather to be applied to all neurophysiological structures, and it can be theoretically justified to look for the phylogenetic origins of cognitive schemes and social (or other) motives. A detailed discussion of these theoretical problems would necessitate an examination of the extensive literature, for which no space is available here. We must confine ourselves to a few remarks on the methodological problems involved.

Cognitive schemes in animals (e.g. innate releasing mechanisms) can only be understood as reactions to particular configurations of stimuli. If we were to apply this model to man in turn (which would be an unjustifiable simplification of psychological problems), we would still have to compare *stimulus configurations as well as reactions* in both animals and man, which would take us far beyond the scope of the comparative methods hitherto discussed.[1] An added difficulty is that innate releasing

---

[1] This is also true of comparisons of elementary acts of perception such as taxis.

mechanisms are modified by experience, even in relatively primitive animals, not to speak of man; the relationship between environmental constellations and actions is overlaid by cultural influences, which are but one of many other complicating factors.

Motivational dispositions cannot be observed, but only inferred from behaviour patterns. Even within a single species, the abstraction of common factors from behaviour patterns is problematic. At least in men, socially important motives may be considered as complicated systems of cognitions, attitudes and beliefs, as well as need-like components. And the further step of applying techniques originally devised for comparing single characteristics to theoretical combinations of whole complexes of characteristics is difficult to justify methodologically.

It would thus appear impossible to identify homologous structures in cognitive schemes and motivational dispositions by existing methods;[1] parallels observed between man and animals in such cases have merely the status of analogies, whose heuristic value must not, however, be underestimated. They are valuable in that every careful operation of analogical reasoning will seek to understand the functions of the structures which are being compared. Besides, ethological models are often of value to the psychologist because they are less distant from physiology.

4   Conclusions

With the aim of understanding the significance of animal behaviour studies for psychology (and other human sciences), we first examined the main features of the evolution of systems. We then considered the methods available for comparing human and animal behaviour. We must now ask finally what implications the whole enquiry has for psychology.

Psychology can either by-pass the findings of ethology, as it has done in the past, or it can try to make use of them. Certain arguments, which we cannot afford to ignore, would advocate the former course. They are as follows:

1. The evaluative argument.
2. The methodological argument.
3. The political argument.

[1] I am nevertheless prepared to accept the assertions of certain ethologists (e.g. K. Lorenz) on the evolutionary history of complex dispositions, because I know from personal experience that these individuals have an *expert vision*.

The *evaluative argument* does not deny in principle that it is possible to gain knowledge of Man from ethology, but maintains, from an onto-logical or pragmatic point of view, that the behaviour patterns so explained are of little value for understanding human behaviour. What is really important are the cognitive acts of the individual, and social and historical factors in society, which should provide the main means of explaining individual human behaviour patterns and social condi-tions. This argument thus makes a more or less *a priori* distinction between what is essential and what is not. But it can be pointed out in reply that, as already stated, animal behaviour patterns are inseparably integrated into human nature, so that a realistic picture of man is impossible without some reference to these inherited characteristics, even if culturally acquired characteristics do predominate.

The *methodological argument* takes the following form. The phylogenetic transmission of behaviour patterns from animals to Man is not sus-ceptible to verification, and cannot therefore be an object of scientific investigation. But this argument is not tenable, because, although tradi-tional methods designed to falsify hypotheses are certainly unsuitable for bringing to light similarities between structures, this should rather encourage us to press on with the development of a general theory of comparison. No science can afford in the long run to let its problems be dictated by its methods. On the contrary, the path we must follow is determined by questions for which we must find appropriate methods of solution. This does not mean, of course, that the mere availability of inadequate comparative methods justifies us in declaring that certain forms are similar without submitting our pronouncements to systematic tests, as has often happened in the past.

Lastly, the *political argument* states that the appeal to biological factors, and in particular to inherited factors, is part of a conservative syndrome, and that any attempts to popularize knowledge relating to the biological determinants of human behaviour will encourage conservative or even "faschistoid" tendencies in society.

It was indeed possible in the past to detect a correlation between politically conservative and faschistoid forms of society on the one hand, and the tendency to give credence to biologistic theories on the other. (We speak of *biologistic* theories, because these were nearly always mis-understood biological theories, as can be shown with the many varieties of social Darwinism.) To this argument it can be replied that the suppression of genuine biological discoveries or the repudiation of knowledge cannot bring any practical or political advantages in the long run. The political role of science has undergone many changes in the past, from that of a pacemaker of social progress to an instrument of government. In our opinion, a biologically based theory of man would help to counteract the exaggerations of the most diverse political doctrines today.

We may therefore conclude that, while they must be taken seriously, these arguments against the biological approach are not tenable. Besides, the consequences of neglecting evolutionary elements in human behaviour are bound to be serious, especially in the field of *theory*. A theory which ignores the biological nature of man must be to a certain (but hitherto indeterminate) extent mistaken. But a mistaken theory will also lead to mistaken *practice*, for mistaken assumptions as regards human nature will encourage mistaken procedures in the care of the sick, in criminology or child education—a false picture of man will lead to a false morality and ethics.

Furthermore, recent advances in biological knowledge of animal behaviour are so spectacular that their extension and application to human behaviour cannot be prevented. This may well become a serious goal for biologists, who would, however, overlook many important features of Man and of human society simply through lack of knowledge. Or it might be carried out in an over-simplified (and hence distorted) form by commercial agencies. The only proper way to incorporate biological knowledge into a scientific view of Man is for biologists and social scientists to collaborate, and this presupposes that the social scientists will learn to understand and evaluate biological data. It might then be possible to describe satisfactorily how old inherited behaviour patterns, human cognitive abilities and culturally transmitted behaviour patterns are blended together to form institutions; for, as we have repeatedly emphasized, it is the combination of these elements which alone constitutes the essential character of man. This path is full of methodological difficulties, and is ambitious and arduous in terms of theory, but no easier way presents itself.

In a situation such as this, we can only console ourselves with the words of Bertolt Brecht: "Practice moves forward one step at a time, but theory must complete the whole march at once."

References

Ashby, W. R. (1952). "Design for a Brain". John Wiley, New York.

Bertalanffy, L. von (1956). General systems theory. *In* "General Systems Yearbook, Vol. I".

Birdwhistell, R. L. (1968). Kinesics. *In* "International Encyclopedia of the Social Sciences". Collier-Macmillan, New York and London.

Campbell, D. T. (1965). Variation and selective retention in socio-cultural evolution. *In* "Social Change in Developing Areas" (Eds H. R. Barringer, G. T. Blanksten and R. W. Mack). Schenkmann, Cambridge, Mass.

Condon, W. S. and Ogston, W. P. (1966). Sound film analysis of normal and pathological behaviour patterns. *Journal of Nervous and Mental Diseases*, **143**, 338–346.

Eibl-Eibesfeldt, I. (1967). "Grundriss der vergleichenden Verhaltensforschung – Ethologie". Piper-Verlag, München.

Eibl-Eibesfeldt, I. (1968). Zur Ethologie des menschlichen Grussverhaltens. *Zeitschrift für Tierpsychologie*, **25**, 727–744.

Eibl-Eibesfeldt, I. (1970). "Liebe Und Hass". Piper-Verlag, München.

Esser, A. (1971). "Environment and Behavior". Plenum Press, New York.

Goethe, J. W. (1817). "Bildung und Umbildung organischer Strukturen". *In* dtv Gesamt-Ausgabe, 13d. 39, 1963. München.

Goethe, J. W. (1820). Erster Entwurf einer allgemeinen Einleitung in die vergleichende Anatomie, ausgehend von der Osteologie. *In* "Goethes Naturwissenschaftliche Schriften" (1920). Insel-Verlag, Leipzig.

Hall, E. T. (1959). "The silent language". Doubleday, Garden City, New York.

Hall, A. D. and Fagen, R. E. (1956). Definition of systems. *In* "General Systems Yearbook, Vol. 1", pp. 18–28.

Heberer, G. (1967). "Die Evolution der Organismen". Fischer-Verlag, Stuttgart.

Hilgendorff, G. von (1961). "Manierlich, Erfolgreich, Beliebt". Stocker-Verlag, Graz.

Kendon, A. (1967). Some functions of gaze direction in social interaction. *Acta psychologica*, **26,** no. 1, 1–47.

Klaus, G. (1968). "Wörterbuch der Kybernetik". Dietz-Verlag, Berlin.

König, O. (1969). Verhaltensforschung und Kultur. *In* "Kreatur Mensch" (Ed. G. Altner). Moos-Verlag, München.

König, O. (1970). "Kultur und Verhaltensforschung." DTV-Verlag, München.

Lorenz, K. (1943). Die angeborenen Formen möglicher Erfahrung. *Zeitschrift für Tierpsychologie*, **5**, 235–409.

Lorenz, K. (1950). "So kam der Mensch auf den Hund". Borotha-Verlag, Wien.

Lorenz, K. (1959). Gestaltwahrnehmung als Quelle wissenschaftlicher Erkenntnis. *Zeitschrift für experimentelleu angewandte Psychologie*, **6**, 118–165.

Lorenz, K. (1963). "Das sogenannte Böse". Borotha-Verlag, Wien.

Lorenz, K. (1965). "Ueber tierisches und menschliches Verhalten", Bd. II. Piper-Verlag, München.

McBride, G. (1971). Theories of animal spacing: the role of flight, fight, and social distance. *In* "Environmental Space and Behavior" (Ed. A. Esser). Plenum Press, New York.

Napier, J. (1962). The evolution of the hand. *Scientific American*, **207**, no. 6, 56–63.

Ploog, D. (1964). Verhaltensforschung und Psychiatrie. *In* "Psychiatrie der Gegenwart". Springer-Verlag, Heidelberg.

Pringle, J. W. S. (1951). On the parallel between learning and evolution. *Behaviour*, **3**, 175–215.

Remane, A. (1952). "Die Grundlagen des natürlichen Systems der vergleichenden Anatomie und der Phylogenetik". Akademische Verlaggesellschaft Geest und Portig, Leipzig.

Scheflen, A. E. (1964). The significance of posture in communication systems. *Psychiatry*, **27**, 316–321.

Sommer, R. (1969). "Personal space". Prentice-Hall, Englewood Cliffs, New York.

Toda, M. and Shuford, E. H. (1964). Logic of systems: introduction to a formal theory of structure. *General Systems Yearbook*, **10**, 3–27.

Wickler, W. (1961). Oekologie und Stammesgeschichte von Verhaltensweisen. *Fortschritte der Zoologie*, **13**, 303–365.

Wickler, W. (1969a). Gruppenbildung bei Mensch und Tier. *In* "Kreatur Mensch" (Ed. G. Altner). Moos-Verlag, München.

Wickler, W. (1969b). "Sind wir Sünder? Naturgesetze der Ehe". Droemer-Verlag, München.

Wickler, W. (1966). Ursprung und biologische Deutung des Genitalpräsentierens männlicher Primaten. *Zeitschrift für Tierpsychologie*, **23**, 422–437.

Wickler, W. (1970). Ursprung und biologische Deutung des Genitalpräsentierens mannlicher Primaten. *In* "Stammesgeschichte und Ritualisierung". Piper-Verlag, München.

10

The Cognitive Structures of the Scientist[1]

Claude Flament

1 Foreword

The scientist cannot remain indifferent to the epistemology of his science. He cannot abandon it to the philosopher who too often confines his interest to scientific publications—a relatively unimportant aspect of scientific activity—while neglecting the day-to-day reality of research work.

The scientist ought, therefore, to contribute to reflection about his discipline. If he has been trained in philosophy—as is still often the case in the behavioural sciences—if need be, he will be able ("one day in the year", advised Descartes) to take a distance from his work and to reflect on its raw materials, the results of his own research. But if he lacks such training, being only a scientist with limited horizons, he may find himself confronted with meta-theoretical problems when difficulties arise in his research, often on the occasion of a painful reverse in his experiments. This has been my fate.

[1] Translated from the French by Alice Stroup and Henri Tajfel.

In the past few years, while I was studying the relationships between cognitive structures and social behaviour and working at the same time on a methodology for opinion polls, it occurred to me that it would be possible to use the same mathematical formalization for the treatment of both sets of problems. It appeared to me that the theoretical conceptions of the issues involved in research were no more than a form— perhaps more elaborate—of the cognitive structures that we were studying, and that, consequently, they were amenable to the same kind of analysis. And thus, leaving aside empirical research for a time, I embarked awkwardly on a problem of meta-theory.

The omens were favourable. If one considers that, notwithstanding differences and shades of terminology (cf. Codol, 1969), the essential problem of psychology (including social psychology) is the problem of cognitive structures and representations, then it follows that the analysis of a scientific theory can be viewed as a special instance of our daily empirical work. If the representation that a subject has of an object is in some way a "naïve theory" (Moscovici, personal communication), then could not scientific theories be considered as more elaborate representations? In that case, the relationship between the scientific observer and the observed subject is merely a slightly peculiar instance of the relationship between two subjects who use cognitive systems that differ a little from one another. And finally, if we push this reasoning *ad infinitum* and use mathematics to help us, we are tackling problems whose solution could guide our work for the remaining 363 days in the year.

2 Formalization of cognitive structures

i. A representation is, at least basically, a system of classificatory features and of relationships among these features; it is frequently convenient to explain these relationships in the form of logical implication (cf., for example, Abelson, 1968). It seems to me that classificatory features do not all simply form definitions in a strict sense: one ought to add to them values, and also behavioural schemes relating to the object of representation. Thus, the description of a set of representations does not appear as a simple dictionary where, for example, "police" would suggest a neutral definition; the representation of the police will require, for some people, elements such as "repressive force", "odious", "those one must oppose", etc.

Such a conception of representations enables one to incorporate into the same cognitive structure concepts and cognitions properly so-called as well as perception of others, attitudes, values, and social norms.

A description of representations which starts from a classificatory principle requires a formalization which uses Boolean algebra.

ii. Boolean algebra $\mathscr{A}$ is distinguished by a set, which we take to be finite, of generating functions $(a_1, a_2 \ldots, a_i, \ldots, a_n)$, and of operations, of which we shall consider three: the "lower" operation, denoted $\wedge$; the "higher" operation, denoted $\vee$; and conjugation, denoted by superscription. With the help of these operations, generators, and some rules of writing, one constructs an infinite class of well-formed formulas; for example: $a = (a_i \wedge a_j) \vee a_k$; $\beta = \bar{a}_i \vee a_j$; etc.

These operations have axiomatic properties which one can indicate by using the isomorphism existing between Boolean operations and set operations (which are well known): the lower operation corresponds to intersection, the higher to union, and conjugation to complementation.

Or again, using the isomorphism between Boolean calculus and the logical calculus of propositions, one will make the following correspond: the lower and AND, the higher and OR, and conjugation and NOT.

With the help of the properties of the operations, one demonstrates that certain different formulas are equivalent; one calls a set of these a *term*. If there are n generators, and $m = 2^n$, our construction gives 2^m terms.

The algebraic interpretation of classes can appear thus: the term a designates the class of objects that have the configuration a of properties. Thus, $(a_i \wedge a_j)$ designates the set of objects having at the same time the property a_i AND the property a_j; $\bar{a}_i$ designates the set of objects *not having* the property a_i; etc.

So constructed, algebra $\mathscr{A}$ is a free algebra: the generators have no relationships among themselves.

iii. A cognitive structure is characterized not only by classificatory features which engender the free algebra $\mathscr{A}$, but also by the relationships among these traits. In order to explain these relationships, let us define "implication" in Boolean algebra: one will say that a implies β, which one will note $(a \rightarrow \beta)$ if and only if $a \wedge \beta = a$ (which amounts to saying that the class a is included in the class β, or that all the objects having property a also have property β).

One sees immediately that if $a \rightarrow \beta$, the class $(a \wedge \beta)$ is necessarily empty, which one notates: $a \wedge \bar{\beta} = \wedge$, $\wedge$ being the Boolean term corresponding to the empty set (θ) in set algebra. Inversely, if $a \wedge \beta = \wedge$, one will put down $a \rightarrow \beta$.

Let us return to our free algebra $\mathscr{A}$; combining in all possible ways the classificatory traits of a cognitive structure, it describes in a sense all the classes that the individual under study can imagine; but in fact many of these classes are not truly conceivable, in the sense that they are obviously empty (for that individual). Thus, if $a_1 =$"to live in the water" and $a_2 =$"mammal", the class $(a_1 \wedge a_2)$ was empty for the zoologists of the past, who thought that the whale was a fish. This can be translated by $(a_2 \rightarrow \bar{a}_1)$: "mammals do not live in the water", or by $(a_1 \rightarrow \bar{a}_2)$: "animals which live in the water are not mammals".

To translate those relationships among generators which are characteristic of the cognitive structure, it is enough then to add to normal Boolean axiomatic the affirmation of the emptiness of a certain number of possible classes in the algebra. It can be demonstrated (cf. Flament, 1965) that the family of empty classes constitutes a very particular sub-set of $\mathscr{A}$, having the properties of what one calls a *Boolean ideal*; $\mathscr{A}$ being a finite algebra, that ideal is entirely characterized by an algebraic term which we shall indicate by $I(\mathscr{A})$.

For the sake of economy, a minimal expression of the term $I(\mathscr{A})$ will be sought, from which it will be possible to extract a *system of implication* characterizing the cognitive structure being studied. The difficult technical problems which this analysis presents are outside the scope of this account (cf. Flament, 1968a, chapter 10).

iv. The determination of a system of (implicational) relationships between classificatory traits (that is to say, of an ideal in Boolean algebra) seems to me to be sufficient for the study of numerous cognitive problems. But one can hope for an instrument of analysis with greater possibilities. This can be done starting with Boolean algebras: (a) leading to an algebra of *quantifiers* ("for all x", "there exists an x") this is accomplished by introducing a new operation into our algebra (cf. Eytan, 1965); (b) leading to a *modal* algebra, permitting notably the expression of the *possible* and the *necessary*—again, it is enough to introduce a new operation (cf. Barbut, 1965); (c) leading to a *deontic* algebra where certain of the generators a are expressed by formulas of the type (xay) where x and y are, for example, individuals, and a an action, so that (xay) then means that "x does the activity a with respect to y" (cf. Anderson, 1962).

These various extensions of our initial algebra enable us to present a fairly exact account of complex cognitive structures and to translate without too much artificiality such opinions as: "If there exists a single upright man in your group, the group ought to be saved".

We shall not examine these possibilities here. What matters is that the results, for which we shall depend on Boolean algebra, can be extended without too much difficulty to more complex algebras than those that have just been considered.

3   Collective representations

i. Concepts of representations and of cognitive structures, such as I have used, seem relatively clear only at the level of an individual A. The concept of *collective representation* needs to be established taking the individual ones as a point of departure.

ii. Let us leave aside the trivial instance where all the individuals of a population would have exactly the same cognitive structure. We will consider a population which is homogeneous in the sense that: all its members use *the same system of generators* $(a_1, \ldots, a_n)$ (and thus the same free algebra $\mathscr{A}$); the ideals $I_1, I_2, \ldots$, of the subjects $S_1, S_2, \ldots$, are *compatible* in a certain way.

Two types of compatibility need to be considered.

1. In studies of semantic structuralization (cf. Miller, 1968), the set of generators is arranged hierarchically (a taxonomic tree); for example, $a_1 =$ "mammal", $a_2 =$ "fish", etc., $a_i =$ "vertebrate", with the inclusion $(a_1 \vee a_2 \vee \ldots) \to a_i$. It can be assumed that all these features are available to all the subjects. But in fact the subjects are not located on the same level of the hierarchy: some will classify as "mammal–fish", without explicitly using the criterion "vertebrate"; others will give a classification which is less refined, using "vertebrate" without distinguishing among the vertebrates. These diverse subjects will have the different ideals $I_1, I_2, \ldots$, in free algebra $\mathscr{A}$ but, given the compatibility of ideals (which is translated by the compatibility of the classifications), the common structure (the taxonomic tree) will be given by the ideal $I = I_1 \wedge I_2 \wedge \ldots$

2. Certain generators translate the subjects' value judgement ("I love", "I want to do", etc.); omitting these for a moment, we can imagine that all the subjects have the same ideal in the algebra $\mathscr{A}_0$ made up of the remaining generators. When the criteria of value are re-introduced one obtains in different ideals $I_1, I_2, \ldots$, the common

structure, individual valuations set apart, which is again defined by the ideal $I = I_1 \wedge I_2 \wedge \ldots$.

For example, in a study on xenophobia, the algebra is constructed from the three following constants (cf. Flament, 1968a, chapter 1):

$a_1 =$ "to accept a foreigner as a companion in leisure";

$a_2 =$ "to accept a foreigner as a neighbour";

$a_3 =$ "to accept a foreigner as a companion at work".

The members of a population of mine-workers consider the following classes not empty: $(a_1 \wedge a_2 \wedge a_3)$, $(\bar{a}_1 \wedge a_2 \wedge a_3)$, $(\bar{a}_1 \wedge \bar{a}_2 \wedge a_3)$, and $(\bar{a}_1 \wedge \bar{a}_2 \wedge \bar{a}_3)$, and also those which result from their combinations by the higher operation. The same workers consider the other classes, such as $(a_1 \wedge \bar{a}_2 \wedge a_3)$ or $(a_1 \wedge a_2 \wedge \bar{a}_3)$, empty. (This corresponds to a Guttman scale which is translated by the scheme of implication $a_1 \rightarrow a_2 \rightarrow a_3$.) This does not mean that each worker accepts *for himself* all the behavioural patterns corresponding to the non-empty classes. A very xenophilic worker will select only the class $(a_1 \wedge a_2 \wedge a_3)$ as a personally acceptable value, while a very xenophobic one will accept for himself only the class $(\bar{a}_1 \vee \bar{a}_2 \wedge \bar{a}_3$.) The same study made on a student population brings out another common structure: $a_1 \rightarrow a_3 \rightarrow a_2$.

To summarize: the workers, like the students, can be more or less xenophobic; but the student population attaches more importance to relationships at work (a_3) than to relationships amongst neighbours (a_2), whereas it is the opposite in our population of mine-workers.

3. If one studies a heterogeneous population, it is sometimes possible to use the concept of *partly common representation*. It can be supposed that the population is divided into homogeneous sub-populations, characterized by the unknown ideals $I_1, I_2, \ldots$; what is directly observed is the ideal $I = I_1 \wedge I_2 \wedge \ldots$. For example, if one combines the worker and student populations previously discussed, one finds an ideal translated by $(a_1 \rightarrow a_2)$ and $(a_1 \rightarrow a_3)$; this is precisely what is common to the two sub-populations. Everyone agrees in giving more importance to relationships of leisure (a_1) than to the other relationships $(a_2$ and $a_3)$. Let us point out that in favourable cases it is possible to break down the observed ideal I into ideals of homogeneous sub-populations. Thus one obtains the algebraic equivalent of Lazarsfeld's analysis of latent structure.

4 Communication

Let us now consider two individuals (or two populations) A and B, making use of classificatory features which are partly or entirely different: the one, $\{a_1, \ldots, a_n\}$, yielding algebra $\mathscr{A}$; the other, $(b_1, \ldots b_m\}$, yielding algebra $\mathscr{B}$. Then the problem of communication—or rather of non-communication—arises; each speaker refers what is being said to his own cognitive system; in fact, words do not have the same meaning for the various speakers (cf. Flament, 1970).

Let us try to define the *algebra of communication*, which we shall call $\mathscr{C}$. In order to do this we take the exact sum of algebras $\mathscr{A}$ and $\mathscr{B}$, that is, we consider the union of the two sets of generators, i.e. $\{a_1, \ldots, a_n, b_1, \ldots, b_m)$; $\mathscr{C}$ is the algebra made up of these $(n+m)$ generators. In $\mathscr{C}$, one finds again all the terms α of $\mathscr{A}$, all the terms β of $\mathscr{B}$, and some terms γ necessarily written with the help of generators a_i of $\mathscr{A}$ and b_j of $\mathscr{B}$. Let there be a term $\gamma = a \wedge \beta$; it denotes the class of objects that are included at the same time in α by the subject A and in β by the subject B. As long as no true communication has been established between A and B, this class γ does not exist for them. It exists only for an observer who has identified the cognitive structures of the two subjects.

It is possible that, while α may not be an empty class for A and β not empty for B, the class $\gamma = a \wedge \beta$ may be empty for both. This may even be necessary for communication to be eventually established: it can happen only if each concept α of A is not diluted through the totality of concepts β of B, and if the objects included in α by A are not divided by B into all the classes β.

It is therefore not enough to identify the ideal $I(\mathscr{C})$ corresponding to empty classes in $\mathscr{C}$; one must also identify the classes γ of $I(\mathscr{C})$ which break down into α not belonging to $I(\mathscr{A})$ and β not belonging to $I(\mathscr{B})$.

Thus we can write $I(\mathscr{C}) = I(\mathscr{A}) \vee I(\mathscr{C}) \vee \Delta$, where Δ corresponds to the empty classes that interest us and which yield relationships between generators of $\mathscr{A}$ and $\mathscr{B}$. Δ *is the dictionary of communication*.

(Let us point out that a minimal expression in Δ is obtained easily when one knows the minimal expressions of the ideals $I(\mathscr{A})$, $I(\mathscr{B})$, and $I(\mathscr{C})$.)

It seems indispensable to establish a typology of possible dictionaries, as a function of the degree and type of the precision of translation. This work remains to be done.

5   Observational techniques

i. Thus we have at our disposal the formal instruments that enable us to analyse cognitive structures and their relationships. But the point of departure for our calculations is not given to us through some miracle; we have no direct access to the properties of the classificatory system characteristic of a subject or to the manner in which he uses it.

Our calculations must start from the standardized results of observations of behaviour, both verbal and non-verbal. Independently of the methods that may be used—such as free interviews, systematic observation, questionnaires or experiments—there are always two phases in the procedure. Their relative importance depends upon the technique that is employed. The first phase is the naïve, almost empathic, stage of research which enables the observer to form some impressions about the subject who is studied. This is the pre-scientific stage of the work; it is followed by a systematization of what is being observed (such as content analysis, the preparation of an observational grid or of a questionnaire, or the planning of an experiment.) The results of this systematization will provide the basis of the genuine scientific analysis.

Our calculations do not deal, however, with the cognitive structure of the subject A but with its translation into the observational system B constructed by the scientist. Because of this, the problem we confront is analogous to that of communication between two subjects A and B; the only difference is that the symmetry between A and B is broken. B is now a reflective system deliberately constructed by the scientist to be as close as possible to A; this has been the aim of the naïve prescientific phase to which reference has been made earlier. But the problem of translation remains; in order to solve it we need to have the "dictionary theory" which still remains to be formulated.

ii. We will now consider some steps we must take to arrive at a theory. The generators $\{b_1, \ldots, b_m\}$ of the system B give a free algebra $\mathscr{B}$. Very often the system itself suggests no more than an empty ideal I $(\mathscr{B})$ (which amounts to the normally empty class notated $\wedge$). This is notably the case in most of the studies using questionnaires. In order to simplify, let us suppose that all the questions are dichotomous; to question j, the positive reply will be b_j, and the negative reply $\bar{b}_j$; in this way algebra $\mathscr{B}$ is defined. In general, the subject who is questioned may reply as he wishes to each question, whatever may be his replies to the other questions. In other words, the subjects may give as non-empty whatever class they please. Then, if the translation between the subject-system $\{a_1, \ldots, a_n\}$ and the questionnaire-system $\{b_1, \ldots, b_m\}$ was perfect, one would have $\mathscr{A} = \mathscr{B}$, and the ideal $I\ (\mathscr{B})$, observed after drawing up the questionnaire, would be a perfect translation of the structure of A, that is $I\ (\mathscr{A}) = I(\mathscr{B})$.

iii. In such a case (frequent but not universal, as we shall see later) we reduce our problem to that of the type of correspondence that may exist between the (unknown) system of a_i and the system of b_j. It seems that an important problem arises from the different degrees of refinement of the relation between the two classificatory systems. And the dissymmetry between A and B becomes essential.

Let us imagine that the classification of B is more subtle than that of A; for example, the questionnaire B uses the concepts $b_1 =$ "anarchist", $b_2 =$ "Trotskyst", $b_3 =$ "Maoist", while the subject A uses only the cruder notion "leftist" ($a_1 =$ "leftist"). The calculation shows that in such a case the ideal $I\ (\mathscr{B})$ resulting from drawing up the questionnaire will bring about the term $(b_1 \vee b_2 \vee b_3 \vee \ldots)$, and never the terms b_1, b_2, b_3, . . ., separately. The observer will thus conclude that b_1, b_2, b_3, . . ., are not elements in the cognitive structure of A, which in fact comprises the element $(b_1 \vee b_2 \vee b_3 \ldots)$ that cannot be dissociated as far as the subject is concerned. The observer will undoubtedly designate this element by the word "leftist"; thus the element a_1 of A, unknown at the beginning, will be correctly identified at the end of the calculations.

Let us now imagine the opposite situation: the classification of A is more subtle than that of B. The questionnaire speaks of "leftist" (b_1), while the subjects distinguish among "anarchist" (a_1), "Trotskyst" (a_2), "Maoist" (a_3) etc. Let us leave aside the problem that the subjects will have in replying to this questionnaire, and the fact that it will elicit no responses at all or random responses, thus depriving the study of all significance. The classification of the subject can be discovered only if there exist in B the terms b_2, b_3, . . ., such that $(b_1 \wedge b_2)$ means "anarchist", $(b_1 \wedge b_3)$, "Trotskyst", etc. The presence in B of the terms b_2, b_3, . . ., will usually be due to chance. Had it been otherwise, that would mean that the observer had at the outset a rather good idea of the classification of the subject, and therefore it would have been more natural to introduce it in B. The result is that the features b_2, b_3, . . ., which distinguish the feature b_1, are not usually very effective differentiators, and that the terms $(b_1 \wedge b_2)$, . . ., are often less stable in the analysis of I $(\mathscr{B})$, and can be interpreted only with difficulty in terms of the cognitive structure of A.

For example, a questionnaire studying the attitude towards de Gaulle makes use of the feature $b_1 =$"to be a trade unionist". In itself, this feature has no connection with the attitude which is examined. Another feature, $b_2 =$"to be in favour of parliamentary government", makes it clear that the term $(b_1 \wedge b_2)$ corresponds to an anti-Gaullist attitude; this suggests that there are several categories of trade unionists, which is hardly startling, but does not permit a clear definition of these categories, especially as the pattern $(b_1 \wedge b_2)$ is not sustained throughout the analysis (Flament, 1968a, chapter 11).

6 The cognitive structure of the researcher

i. The techniques of observation are no more than mediators (rarely neutral) in a communication which constitutes an essential aspect of the scientific activity: the communication between the subject studied and the scientist who studies him. In our perspective, we shall be concerned with the relationship between the cognitive structures of a subject or of subjects and the cognitive structure of the scientist.

The researcher, guided by a scientific theory, selects a technique of observation, observes and interprets. We shall consider the theory as an aspect of the researcher's cognitive structure. It is true that—as distinct from the naïve and spontaneous representations used by the subjects— a scientific theory needs to strive towards rational coherence, to be open to new ideas, submitted to the control of facts, confronted by other theories. Nevertheless, it remains a part of the cognitive structure of the researcher, and it is therefore in close relationship with his attitudes, norms and values (social and philosophical as well as logical) and with his patterns of behaviour (political as well as technical). It is the totality of this structure, and not simply its scientific aspect—which is, at any rate, difficult to isolate—that ought to be taken into account if we wish to understand the manner in which a researcher translates his observations and makes inferences about their underlying nature and origin. ii. My first example is concerned with genuine scientific hypotheses; it also happens to be a concrete example of the relation between theory and observational technique, and it is capable of being easily and fully formalized in our Boolean algebraic language (cf. Flament, 1963, chapter 3, and 1968b).

The theory of the cognitive bias towards structural balance (cf. Zajonc, 1969) describes the representations that the subjects have of groups of individuals who entertain friendly or hostile relations; for example, (x and y are friends) and (y and z are enemies) $\rightarrow$ (x and z are enemies). One can conceive of non-reciprocal feelings: "x likes y, but y does not like x"; the theory rejects this relation as unbalanced and many studies have shown that the subjects exhibit a bias towards reciprocity.

Two kinds of questions can be asked in order to study a problem of structural balance:

1. Are x and y friends or enemies?
2. Does x like y? Does y like x?

For the sake of economy and because of the belief in the existence of bias towards reciprocity, questions of type 1 are generally used. But when new aspects of the problem are studied (such as the relations between friendship structures and hierarchical structures, cf. Flament, 1970b), one cannot be sure that bias towards reciprocity is really active in the subjects' cognitive structures. The use in such cases of questions of type 1 amounts to imposing—with the help of the instrument of observation—the hypothesis of reciprocity on a structure of events which is perhaps very poorly translated in this fashion.

iii. My second example is more general and less easily formalized. It seems to me that at present all behavioural theories are essentially *adaptive* in the quasi-biological sense of the term. This applies to a whole series of scientific concepts: adaptation, equilibration, tension-reduction, balanced structure, cognitive consistency, assimilation, accommodation, etc. To group these concepts in a category of "adaptive theories" suggests a category of "non-adaptive theories"; it then becomes obvious that this remains an empty class in the behavioural sciences.

Let us, however, suppose that a non-adaptive process is at work in the evolution of an individual or a collective cognitive structure. This process would have to be translated into the language of adaptation— the only language which is at present available to us; and thus the process would be broken down into its various aspects, some of which would, for example, imply equilibration and others accommodation. Some phenomena will remain uninterpreted; but this is always the case, and the researcher has available to him concepts such as "random variation". (An entire statistical technology has been worked out for these concepts; but it is theoretically no more neutral than any other scientific technique.) It follows from this that there is practically no chance for a non-adaptive process to be brought to light through research, even if such a process exists and manifests itself in the phenomena which are studied.

But let us imagine that a madman contrives a non-adaptive theory of behaviour that would be acceptable according to the rules of proof which are commonly in use. This would bring into question not only old habits of scientific thinking and a vast amount of studies with conclusions which have been generally accepted, but undoubtedly also an entire conception of man and of social relations together with a whole set of professional, personal and even political practices.

If the adoption of a new theory is likely to entail a vast transformation of our cognitive structures, we must realize that the retention of old theories is due not solely to scientific values; it must also be due to a close interplay with all the other values which happen to be threatened.

7 *Ad infinitum*

I have outlined a formal theory of the relations between the cognitive structures of the researcher and a selected object of study, the cognitive structures of subjects or of populations; in this sense, the argument has been meta-theoretical.

But this line of reasoning immediately suggests that this meta-theory should itself be considered as a cognitive structure of someone like a meta-observer; and we can resume our formalization in order to study the relations between meta-theory and theory to end up with a meta-meta-theory. Once this line of argument is started, there is no reason why it should not be pursued *ad infinitum*.

This is quite obviously mathematical and epistemological fiction since the number of real observers is finite as is the number of theories that each can invent. But this fiction is not entirely devoid of interest when it is considered from at least two points of view. First, it puts us on guard—in a manner which is perhaps provocative—against an opinion which seems rather widespread at present. There is a belief that some kind of absolute truth has been obtained when the extra-scientific values, which make our scientific knowledge relative, have been identified (as Einstein said: "The only absolute is the relative"). It is my view that the identification of these extra-scientific values is itself a labour of cognitive analysis that can in turn be made relative by values which are "extra-meta-theoretical"—and thus we are embarked once again upon our journey towards the infinite.

However, once the problem has been posed within the context of a formalization (the present one, or one which is more complex), it ought to be possible to establish theorems pertaining to this infinite succession of translations. The dictionary theory, of which at present we only possess a few rudiments, ought to enable us to define the deviation between the versions n and $(n+1)$ as a function of the type of relationship between these versions. It would then be useful to know under what conditions the deviation diminishes or increases as a function of n.

In this way, our journey towards the infinite could guide a journey towards knowledge, even if the meaning of "knowledge" had to change a little. At any rate, the meta-theoretical problem would be posed mathematically.

References

Abelson, R. P. (1968). Psychological implication. *In* "Theories of Cognitive Consistency: A Source Book". (Eds R. P. Abelson *et al.*) pp. 112–140. Rand McNally, Chicago.

Anderson, A. R. (1962). Logic, norms and roles. *In* "Mathematical Methods in Small Group Processes" (Eds J. H. Criswell, H. Solomon and P. Suppes), pp. 11–22. Stanford University Press, Stanford.

Barbut, M. (1965). Topologie générale et algèbre de Kuratovski. *Mathématique et Sciences Humaines*, **12**, 11–27.

Codol, J.-P. (1969). Note terminologique sur l'emploi de quelques expressions concernant les activités et processus cognitifs en psychologie sociale. *Bulletin de Psychologie*, **23**, 63–71.

Eytan, M. (1965). Qu'est-ce qu'un quantificateur? Le point de vue de l'Algébriste. *Mathématique et Sciences Humaines*, **10**, 47–65.

Flament, C. (1963). "Applications of Graph Theory to Group Structure". Prentice Hall, New York.

Flament, C. (1965). L'analyse booléenne de questionnaire. *Mathematique et Sciences Humaines*, **12**, 3–10.

Flament, C. (1968a). "L'analyse algébrique de questionnaire" (mimeograph). Laboratoire de Psychologie Sociale, Aix-en-Provence.

Flament, C. (1968b). Structural balance theories. *In* "Algebraic Models in Psychology" (mimeographed), chap. 6. University of Leiden.

Flament, C. (1970). Structures cognitives et communication. *In* "Colloque de Psycho-linguistique". Alger.

Flament, C. (1971). Image des relations amicales dans des groupes hiérarchisés. *Année Psychologique*, **71,** 117–125.

Miller, G.-A. (1968). Algebraic models in psycholinguistics. *In* "Algebraic Models in Psychology" (mimeographed), chap. 5. University of Leiden.

Zajonc, R. B. (1969). Cognitive theories in social psychology. *In* "The Handbook of Social Psychology" (Eds G. Lindzey and E. Aronson), chap. 5. Addison-Wesley, Reading, Mass.

11

The Analysis of Episodes[1]

Rom Harré

1 Introduction

Social psychology will begin to be truly a science only when it ceases to be concerned almost exclusively with the identification of patterns of overt behaviour, and the conditions under which they occur. The established sciences are distinguished by the fact that they always seek to answer the question as to *why* the observed patterns among phenomena prevail. And they always proceed to answer that question by discovering, or imagining, the causal mechanisms which produce the phenomena. Social psychology has yet to reach this stage; that is, it has yet to pass from critical natural history to science. In this chapter we shall outline the method by which this transition can be achieved. The study of the causal mechanisms of social interaction will be called ethogeny.

The mechanisms responsible for the observed patterns of social interaction are the interrelations of meanings as perceived by the interactors. The way people respond is determined by the way in which they have understood the meaning of the situations in which they find themselves, and by the rules and conventions they accept with respect to those meanings.

[1] For further developments of the material in this chapter, see R. Harré and P. F. Secord (1972). "The Explanation of Social Behaviour". Blackwell, Oxford.

The structure of the meaning relations can be discovered by studying accounts that people give from their own special point of view, of social interactions in which they have taken part. It follows that, in order to discover the nature of these meaning relations, accounts must be collected and analysed. Philosophical psychology has shown that a great many episodes in human life are best understood as the performance of certain acts. There are conventions or even explicit rules, which determine which series of actions are required for the performance of any particular act. These may be the formal rules of a ceremony; for instance, they may determine which actions have to be performed in order that the ceremony (or act) of marriage may be carried out. They may also be the informal conventions which determine the words, the tone, and the gestures, with which an insult is delivered. The interaction which prescribes the actions performed and the acts thereby achieved will be defined here as the Aa-structure of the episode. The ethogeny of a formal episode like a marriage ceremony is easily uncovered because the people involved need refer only to the explicit rules in giving an account of what they each did. Here we will attempt to develop a methodology for the discovery of the ethogeny of less formal social interactions.

First an endeavour will be made to devise a system of concepts for understanding social interactions, and to check this system against reality. Possibly after generations of human ethogenists have studied the real lives of men, women and children, it may become apparent that certain very subtle patterns of interaction have the force of causal laws. Although our methodology cannot assume this, it must be designed so that it may ultimately lead to a knowledge of these laws. However, the analysis of episodes should not be undertaken in the hope of discovering laws of nature, but of identifying patterns in human life against which and with the help of which the adequacy of a conceptual system can be checked.

Looked at in more detail, "checking-out" can be seen to involve two stages. The first stage is exemplified by the structure of a quarrel-pattern. Since it must first be established that the episode is one in which what happens is mediated by the perception of meanings, only the broadest categories are involved, and these are implied by questions such as: "Did he do it?" "Did he mean it?"

A movement, such as a hand coming into contact with a face, is fitted into a quarrel-pattern if the striker can be said to have meant it to hurt, and the sufferer to have understood it as being meant to hurt, and so on. At this stage we are concerned with identifying a pattern of actions, i.e. movements for which an account can be given. At stage two of the checking-out process, the *Aa*-structure begins to be made explicit, that is the actions are seen to hang together as parts of an effort to achieve something, i.e. the acts mentioned in the accounts of stage one come under scrutiny. By introducing explanatory metaphors, for instance, by treating the interactors as performing a ritual and so introducing the liturgical model, *intelligibility* and *coherence* are imported into the pattern of actions via the scrutiny of the acts. This kind of explanation, checked out by whether it makes the actions of the interactors intelligible and coherent, is quite similar to the role of theories in such sciences as chemistry. In chemistry empirical patterns have the force of laws, and the theory is a sketch of the causal mechanisms which produce the patterns of phenomena described in the laws. In real life, where the people are behaving ritualistically, for example, the application of the liturgical model identifies the mechanism of interaction exactly as the molecular theory does in the physical sciences. Of course, meanings and rules come to form a coherent "mechanism" in a quite different way from the *mechanical* mechanism of molecules.

2   Possible conceptual systems of role and rule

The use of liturgical and game models for understanding accounts of episodes involves the deployment of the concepts of role and rule. For the moment we shall assume an intuitive understanding of these notions, and of their obvious conceptual connection. We will now develop, *a priori*, an account of all possible conceptual systems based upon role and rule, that is an account of all possible models for the understanding of formal episodes of the liturgical and game type.

The episodes of human life can be distinguished by whether they have an outcome, or whether they do not. A football match is an episode with an outcome. It is so designed that it leads to a result. All episodes of this kind, whether structured by formal rules or not, can be identified by the fact that some of the actions performed in the course of the episode admit of the question: What are you doing that for? Proper answers in terms of the accepted outcome may be: "to score a goal", "to pass sentence", "to confer a degree", and so on. To all such episodes we can, *a fortiori*, apply the concepts of plan and intention, that is, we can ask for and expect to receive accounts from the actors.

o

Outcome is not to be confused with a simple temporal end or simple effect. The episode of listening to a concert has an end, and may lead to a pleasant euphoria, but in the sense I am defining here it does not have an outcome, that is to say, there is no conventional act which it achieves. Driving around the countryside with no particular destination in mind, and solely for entertainment is not an episode with an outcome. The former may be defined as consummatory episodes and the latter as non-consummatory.

Consider those rules which "guide" the actions of the people involved. They may be so specific as to lay down in advance the particular action to be performed. It may be required that the censer be swung 30 degrees to left and right by someone facing in a East-West direction. No detail is too small to be of social importance. There was a bitter war in Russia over whether three or two fingers should be raised in blessing. It may even be *required* that actions be done in a certain style, for instance reverently rather than flippantly. Restrictions upon the style of a performance are more often made explicitly in the stage directions of a drama than in the order of service, but implicit principles of style may be made explicit by a priest when these are violated by the altar boys. Rules of these varying degrees of specificity contrast with those which specify only the kind of actions that are to be performed. For instance, the rules of Association Football specify only the kinds of ball handling that are permitted. For many purposes this distinction runs parallel with that between those rules which prescribe actions and those which permit them. Injunctions tend to be specific and permissions to be general; but this may not necessarily be the case. For instance, in order to score a leg bye in cricket, one must make some shot at the ball, but no particular shot is specified. The permission to take British currency abroad was once specifically limited to £15. This preliminary classification of rules is broadly three-dimensional: (i) the actions which come under the rule may be specified, in some degree of detail, or only their general kind delineated; (ii) whatever the degree of specificity of the actions the rules may be injunctions or permissions; (iii) there is also the distinction between explicit rules and tacit conventions, but this distinction will not loom large in the present context. In terms of Shwayder's (1965, pp. 263–274) well-known classification of rules, my distinction between the specific and the general is similar to the distinction he makes between the *constitutive* and *non-constitutive*, while all the rules with which these models are concerned are included in his *enabling* rules. Our distinction between rules used to account for the actions of people involved in consummatory episodes and those adopted to account for actions in non-consummatory episodes closely parallels Shwayder's differentiation between enabling rules which constitute rules for succeeding and those which do not.

For example, elaborate rules may govern the way patball is played, but because a game of patball is not a consummatory episode, they cannot be said to include "rules for succeeding".

These distinctions permit the following possibilities:

1. The rules are *specific* as to the actions required and the end-state is *determined*; thus (a) the episode is consummatory and defines a *ritual*, or (b) the episode is non-consummatory and defines a *routine*.

2. The rules are *general* as to the actions required and the end-state is *undetermined*; thus (a) the episode is consummatory and defines a *game*, or (b) the episode is non-consummatory and defines an *entertainment*.

A marriage ceremony is a ritual since the specific actions required of the participants are determined: when they are performed the bride and groom are married, and their coming to be married consists in the performing of the actions. A performance of a play is a routine because the specific actions required of the participants are laid down in advance, the script acting like a rule; but no act is really performed in the course of carrying out the actions. Footballers follow certain general rules in the course of the episode in which they take part, but the winners are not determined beforehand; if they are it is no longer considered to be a game. This last point is illustrated, for instance, by the ambivalent status of professional wrestling.

All of these are formal episodes in which there is clearly no difficulty about the identification of role and rule. From these considerations we are able to deduce that the four main kinds of formal episodes are restricted to those described above. It follows, *a priori*, that the principal types of derivative models for informal and enigmatic episodes are the liturgical model, the routine and the game model; the concept of entertainment is included to take up the analytical slack. We are not concerned with the classical philosophical problems of rules, that is with the questions of how we know whether a rule is being followed, and how we can tell which rule is being followed, problems discussed extensively by Wittgenstein (1959). Rules make their appearance in ethogeny in the giving of accounts. They are not inductive generalizations of behaviour; they are the principles used by the participants and the observers of an episode to account for, explain, justify, or excuse, their conduct. When we watch a church service from the nave we do not attempt to derive a meaning from the ritual being followed; but after the priest has performed some action we ask him, or someone else involved, to explain its meaning. The explanation we receive will have reference to an instruction in the liturgy. Were ethogeny still intent on the induction of laws of nature, the notion of rule would be of no advantage, since the classical problems of rules are no different from the classical problems of induction. But if rules are what the players and other participants refer to in the course of accounting for their actions, we are free of the tiresome shackles of traditional inductive scepticism.

This principle means, in effect, that liturgical and game concepts form the basis of explanations people give of their *own* activities. Also, role–rule concepts are fundamental to the accounts which people (including social psychologists) give of the activities of *others*.

The most explicit discussion of the role–rule conceptual system, and of the liturgical and game group of models, hereafter called the *R-r* model group, since the widespread use of these notions from the sixteenth to eighteenth centuries, is in the work of Goffman (1959) to which we shall refer in demonstrating how the *R-r* model group can be used in ethogeny. The appropriateness of the use of these models is explained by Goffman, not just as an analytical tool, but as a reflection of a feature of real life. The models have a double role in that they are both explanatory of and constitutive of real episodes. They are both applied to and derived from the observation of actual episodes. This can be expressed in two principles.

1. *The Constitutive Principle.* For definite purposes, either consciously or unconsciously, people adopt *R-r* roles and rules which they then superimpose upon other activities. For instance, work may be carried out in a manner which is in accordance with certain conventions in order that an inspector or manager should gain a certain impression of the workers.

2. *The Explanatory Principle.* In order to interpret the details of what people are doing, it is necessary to explain their activities in terms of one or more of the *R-r* set of models; for instance, eating cannot adequately be described as *just* eating, nor working as *just* working.

The necessity for the adoption of (2) follows from the generality of the application of (1). Even in those cases where we can hardly claim that the participants are even tacitly imposing an *R-r* structure of role and rule upon their actions, it may be illuminating to use concepts in explaining their actions, those concepts which would be employed if (2) had been adopted on the basis of the assumption of an explicit application of (1).

How do we know what is going on in the episodes of everyday life? Most of these episodes are neither causal, like the course of a disease, nor formal, like the course of a trial; they are *enigmatic*. The *dramaturgical model* provides the methodological breakthrough. The development of the dramaturgical standpoint is the main burden of Goffman's "The Presentation of Self", and it is for this reason that Goffman has been called the Copernicus of the human sciences. To adopt the dramaturgical standpoint is to take a generalized form of "role-distance" from an episode, and to ask how we would perceive the episode were we taking part in it while deliberately following explicit rules. In this way it becomes possible for us to give a monitoring commentary; that is if we are able to see which of the R-r models is appropriate for the episode. In short, the dramaturgical standpoint is created simply by taking role-distance from whatever one is doing. The dramaturgical standpoint is thus logically connected with the possibility of taking role-distance. Since philosophers, for instance Hampshire, connect being an agent with the power to give a monitoring commentary on one's actions, and those who advocate participant observation as a method in social psychology must do the same, the dramaturgical standpoint is connected both with agency and with the philosophers' methodology. For the social scientist acting as an observer, the adoption of the dramaturgical standpoint enables him to think of the participants *as if* they were actors and to imagine the script they might follow.

Thus adopting the dramaturgical model (or better, standpoint) is a way of attaining the general standpoint from which it becomes possible to discover the ethogeny of an episode, the rules and meaning which explain what is done and what is said. But in "Where The Action Is" (Goffman, 1969), particularly in the first and last chapters, explicit liturgical and game models come to the fore. The bulk of the essay, "On Face Work", is the exploitation of the liturgical model, under which the various means by which "face" is maintained and saved are treated as rituals. The general structure of "face" rituals is expressed in the sequence, "challenge, offering, acceptance and thanks" (Goffman, 1969, pp. 14–15, 17). In this sequence of acts we have an *Aa*-structure in terms of which all "face" episodes can be analysed and understood, i.e. have meaning as actions. A great many sequences of the actions of rituals, that is rites, will be found to express this structure. Although, unlike real rituals, the initiation of a specific rite will not necessarily be followed by the proper, subsequent steps. Goffman observed (op. cit., p. 18) that the emotional flux may interpenetrate the Aa-structure in that, at certain points in a rite, it may be proper to express a particular emotion. This expression may be realistic or it may be merely conventional, or any degree between. This is the E-structure, the real emotional flux in an episode; it is not necessarily related to those expressions of emotion which appear as part of the Aa-structure, in speech acts, gestures, facial expressions, etc. That someone properly says "I'm sorry" certainly does not necessarily mean that he feels any degree of sorrow. We generally *express* grief when we are *supposed* to express it, that is, when it is proper, and not when we actually feel it. Indeed, among Anglo-Americans it may be improper to express grief when it is felt, and proper to express it when it is not. There is a complex Anglo-American style of behaviour at funerals, in which the overt expression of grief is a means of concealing whatever real grief is felt, and must be seen to be so.

Goffman's use of the full spectrum of R-r models can be seen in his development of a game model for understanding certain episodes that involve face-work. He observes that sometimes the conditions that are necessary for the fruitful application of a game model are satisfied. He states: "Every face-saving practice which is allowed to neutralize a particular threat opens up the possibility that the threat will be wilfully introduced for what can be gained by it." (Loc. cit., p. 18). The awareness of this step as a ploy by the putative victim initiates the "game" sequence, so that an episode whose Aa-structure is at the beginning ritualistic, or liturgical, can be transformed so that the latter parts of its Aa-structure must be seen in the light of a game model. Explicitly introducing the game-model concepts Goffman writes: "The purpose of the game is to preserve everyone's line from an inexcusable contradiction, while scoring as many points as possible against one's adversaries and making as many gains as possible for oneself." (Op. cit., p. 19.) Finally, he offers, as the deepest and subtlest level of analysis of the Aa-structure of "face" episodes, an explicitly *joint* liturgical and game model. This combination is perfectly feasible. In the past there were semi-formal episodes which were literally *sacred games*, having both a liturgical and a sporting element. The actions performed were the means by which certain acts were carried out, but the *Aa*-structure did not determine the outcome for any particular individual, although, of course, it fully determined the nature of the outcome. Thus, what was for the individual a game, albeit a deadly one, became from the point of view of the judges, spectators and others involved, a rite, since there was a victory, and a victor, and through that victory, by whosoever's hand, the act was achieved. The ball courts of Yucatan, and the *stadia* of Greece were equally the scenes of episodes whose *Aa*-structure can only be understood by the application of a joint liturgical and game model. This combination is possible only if the actions are so arranged that it is possible to distinguish the fact that there will be an outcome from the fact that a particular person is the actor in that outcome. In the sacred games, as in the everyday saving of face, the ritual is employed competitively by the individuals involved; but whoever the victor may be, because his victory has been achieved within the rite his face has assuredly been saved. This is beautifully described by Goffman (op. cit., p. 25).

Finally, in the eponymous essay of "Where The Action Is." Goffman makes explicit use of a specific game model, by employing concepts appropriate to episodes which are games of chance in the analysis of episodes which, at first sight, do not appear to be games at all. For instance, mental health is what is hazarded by those who take psychedelic drugs in the bravado spirit of gambling, and so on. In his "Presentation of Self" he employs the constitutive principle[1] to show that people construe certain episodes as having the *Aa*-structure of a game of chance. He writes: "Given the practical necessity of following a course of action whose success is problematic and passively awaiting the outcome thereof, one can discover an alternative, howsoever costly, and then define oneself as having freely chosen between this undesirable certainty and uncertainty at hand." (Op. cit., p. 125.) Thus, someone represents himself to himself, and perhaps to others, as a "gamblin' man."

In short, Goffman's method is the explicit and subtle exploitation of the dramaturgical standpoint as a basic methodology, and of the *R-r* group of models as the basis of a conceptual system for making an analysis of the *Aa*-structure of episodes. He justifies this method both by showing the force of the analyses, and by demonstrating that some

[1] Another interesting use of an explicit game model is in Scott and Lyman's (1968) analysis of the state of mind of those stigmatized people who seem paranoid.

episodes are structured as they are because the people involved bend the course of events so as to present the episode as a drama, a ritual, a game or some blend of all three. Finally, it should be added that there are those for whom only the fourth in our group of models can provide a life structuring, namely those for whom every episode is but an entertainment. For instance, Wilfred Sheed (1967) gives an account of the former life style of the English upper middle-class in which effort, feeling, commitment and the like were hidden under a measure of effortless superiority.

3   The epistemology of the *R-r* group of models

How do we know when it is appropriate to apply one of these models to an episode, or whether to use a conceptual system in the description of an *Aa*-structure that may be some suitable combination of concepts derived from the group as a whole? Do we know whether we have analysed the situation well or badly, correctly or incorrectly? Can we discover what roles are being filled in the course of an episode, and what the litany, script or rule book is? Do we know if there is a litany, a script or a rule book? Of course, for formal episodes which are literally rites, performances or matches there is no problem: the roles and rules are quite explicit and known to many.

In the application of the *R-r* group of models to informal episodes it should now be clear that the actions and movements carried out are secondary to what is believed to be their object: the true significance lies in what acts are performed. Thus we must gain some insight into the attitude of those involved. This can best be achieved through a anticipatory, retrospective or contemporary monitoring commentary made possible by taking the dramaturgical standpoint. The problem for the social psychologist is when to apply the models to cases where the actual commentary does not report an *Aa*-structure of this kind, or to cases where there is no commentary at all. The *R-r* group of models equip the social psychologist with a conceptual system for superimposing a dramaturgical monitoring commentary when no commentary is provided by the actors. These models also enable him to gain a deeper insight into the situation than the usual commentary allows by making it possible for him to take the dramaturgical standpoint vicariously for the actors and to see the episode simultaneously from the point of view of author, producer and director.

But how can we judge the validity of our insight? How can we evaluate vicarious commentaries?

Before attempting to answer these questions we must realize that the R-r group of models and the dramaturgical standpoint not only enable the actions of the performers to be construed within an Aa-structure but also involve the idea of spectators, congregations, audiences, that is people before whom a *performance* takes place, and in many cases for whose benefit it is given. A social psychologist, by adopting the dramaturgical standpoint automatically creates an audience and thereby automatically achieves role-distance from the episode; he makes the episode objective for the participants. It is very important to understand that one or more of the players may also have the role of members of the audience. A play-reading in a private house, where everyone present reads a part, is *not* a performance without an audience for players and audience are the same people. The most profound discoveries of social psychology will be made by those who, while playing a part, filling a role and so on, can be their own audience. In the study of informal episodes the whole array of R-r models may need to be deployed complementarily. For instance, there may not merely be a simple transformation from priest to competitor; an individual may shift his role from member of congregation to spectator to audience. In the succession of models there is not only an alternation between the actors and the other people participating; there is also a differentiation between the categories of those who look on and those who perform because the relation between the spectators of a game and the players is not the same as that between the congregation and the priest, nor are either identical with the relation between the audience and the actors in a play. Indeed, this last relation is itself a complex of various different possible relations from participation to alienation. As Eric Bentley put it: "The mirror on the wall is only one, the mirrors in the mind are many." (Bentley 1965, p. 150.)

In formal episodes will be found a clue for the verification of our assumptions. When an episode is in reality a rite, a drama or a match the account given by the participants is definitive, since they are carrying out precisely the actions laid down in the liturgy, script or rule book for the achievement of a specific act. In formal episodes the commentary given by the audience, congregation or spectators must coincide with that given by the actors since their view about what acts are being performed must coincide exactly with the views of the actors, otherwise they cannot assume the role of audience, spectators or congregation.

There are two ways of checking an account of a non-formal episode given from the dramaturgical standpoint in terms of one or more elements of the R-r group of models. When the social scientist is himself an actor, a player or acolyte, or could be considered to be such in accordance with the model, then his account as a member of the audience must coincide with his perception of his own role and the rule-convention which defines it. But a difficulty may be encountered in that the disparity between the account he gives and his perception of the situation as an actor may be eliminated by his realization that the performance is itself not what it seems. An admirable fictional account of this resolution of such an ambiguity is given by John Fowles (1966) when he describes the gradual discovery by the hero that what he takes to be play-acting is actually (or is better perceived as) a rite. In the course of the book there are also brief shifts into both game and entertainment perspectives. The very same actions can be used for the performances of different acts, and therefore the same episode can be seen as possessing different Aa-structures. All this allows for negotiation between actor and audience as to what the Aa-structure is. The most that we can make of the question "What is the *real* Aa-structure?" is what description of the Aa-structure is most frequently negotiated between audience and actors for a given episode. When the social scientist stands apart from the episode, verification will be reduced to a negotiation between himself and the participants concerning the Aa-structure; in some instances this may involve the question of whether or not there is an Aa-structure at all. The only possible sense that can be given to the concept of "the rightness of an account by an ethogenist" is that his account should be the most stable element in a negotiation of accounts when discrepancies exist. The flux of powers and liabilities and of emotions are not like this, since they have physiological connections of various modes and degrees, so that with respect to these models they contain a non-negotiable component.

4   Theories as to the origins of *Aa*-structures

The attempt by some social psychologists, in particular by Biddle and Thomas (1966) to unify this kind of social psychology on the basis of a single concept of "role" is a serious error. There is no single concept that can survive extraction from the *R-r* group of models and examination from the dramaturgical standpoint which can be applied broadly to formal and informal episodes alike. In their definition of "role" as "the generic idea of the particular behaviour of persons" they have weakened the concept so drastically as to make it useless, since it would appear that this peculiar definitional phrase means no more than "what people do" which is not a concept with which any significant distinctions can be made. If this is what "role" in "role theory" means then "role theory" is just another name for a broadly conceived psychology. This attempt to understand their definition is based upon my construal of their phrase "emitting behaviour" to mean "doing something". The roles people play or adopt must be a more specific notion than merely the general style of their behaviour. One might be tempted, from the argument so far presented in this chapter, to identify the roles people play with styles of life that are maintained by explicit or implicit rules (conventions). But the notion of role is narrower. For instance, the use of language is capable of specification by rules, although the origin of regularities in language use are in fact more often by paradigm imitation than by adherence to rule. But there is no role of language-user. This is because the mere use of language does not, of itself, constitute a formal episode, although it plays a very significant part in most of human life, not least its formal episodes. The burden of the argument so far suggests that only for formal episodes and for non-formal episodes that resemble formal episodes in having an *Aa*-structure do we have a use for the concept of role. There is a confusion in role theory as interpreted by Biddle and Thomas between similarly patterned actions in general and what one might call rule or paradigm determined styles of acting; also the latter category is insufficiently distinguished into those styles which are intelligible as features of an episode with an *Aa*-structure (as for instance the role of the priest in a marriage ceremony is filled by someone who, in doing certain things in a certain sequence, brings off the act of marriage), and the acting out of a role where the actions performed are not done so as to give the episode a particular *Aa*-structure. It is only in this latter sense that there is a female role, although it may be necessary for the Morris Radiators Spring Queen to be female, and presumably accustomed to the female role. The *R-r* group of models when applied to informal episodes isolate roles only in the former sense. Even when this point has been dimly perceived most role theorists (for instance, Merton, 1957) have failed to perceive the enormous differences between the roles typified by priests, those typified by actors and those typified by players. In failing to make this distinction they have failed to distinguish between those *Aa*-structures which are consummatory and those which are not: that failure is vitiating. Role theory, one might say, was a crude and undifferentiated ethogeny. We can do better. The role-theorists' notion of "position" catches something of this sense, but not all positions endow their occupants with powers to perform acts, though very many do. Goffman himself strengthens a rather weak general notion of role by qualifying it as "the typical response of individuals in a particular position" (Goffman, 1969, p. 47). Observe that by this definition there could be the role of Spring Queen, but not the "female role". There just might be the role of mother, since motherhood, being a relative concept, would be construed as a position, and women might show a recognizable style of behaviour that could be identified as typical of the position.

Role is surely a normative concept. We are not just interested in what people typically do as priests, centre-halves or women, but rather what it is proper for them to do. Typical ways of behaving are only indicative of the proper ways of behaving if in their accounts of their actions priests, centre-halves, and women cite the rules, conventions and paradigms in giving their reasons for doing these things, or for having acquired the habit. An important methodological innovation, which is implicit in the work of Goffman and explicit in ethogeny, is that the identification of the structure of an episode cannot be achieved by identifying in it common elements with other episodes. It can only be properly analysed by reference to the monitoring commentaries of the participants, or of the engaged audience, i.e. from the dramaturgical standpoint. The distinction between two different notions of role by which, for instance, the priestly role can be distinguished from the female role had better be marked by a definite terminological distinction. Unfortunately this distinction has not been maintained unwaveringly by psychologists or sociologists, so there is no term in common use in the human sciences. "Style of life" catches most of the nuances of the sense of role in which there is a female role. There are very important overlaps between these two concepts, in that as a matter of empirical fact every genuine role has one or more associated styles

[1] As played, for instance, by "Agnes" (cf. Garfinkel, 1967). Note Garfinkel's careful restriction of the degree to which Agnes' playing the female role can be understood with a game-model.

of life, failure to conform to which may lead to loss of plausibility of the incumbent in the role. Celibacy, for instance, amongst Roman Catholic clergy is part of the priestly style, but not part of the priestly role. The distinction is most easily preserved in just those cases like the priesthood where the role is defined by reference to the carrying out of the actions by which certain acts are performed in formal episodes. In occupations that are more commonly taken to be jobs, the two interpenetrate, and are not easy to disentangle. In the life of a manager in a business, role and style are closely interwoven. Nevertheless they can always be disentangled in analysis by reference to the actions necessary to the performance of the acts with respect to which the role exists, e.g. the legal and institutional demands upon a manager. It may be the case that these are more easily or more effectively carried out if the manager adopts a certain style, say that of effortless superiority. But we know that the effectiveness of a style is in part a function of the historical setting, and we know that there is no necessary connection between the adoption of a certain style and the power to perform certain acts, which is the essence of role.

Failure to keep this distinction unwaveringly is partly due to the fact that the acquisition of *both* role and style, that is the learning of what is proper behaviour, occurs in two wholly distinct ways. They are both acquired by a combination of imitation of paradigms, and positive and negative injunctions.[1] The passage from this thought to the empirical investigation of the means by which roles are learned and styles acquired must be mediated by a careful conceptual investigation amongst the various concepts of imitation. Piaget (1951) discusses varieties of imitation. Some conceptual guidelines can be found in Austin (1961, pp. 201–219.)

The mode of analysis of episodes which reveals their Aa-structure through taking the dramaturgical standpoint and the application of the R-r group of models is not without implications as to the nature of those individuals whose interactions are episodes. The inability of the mechanical model of man to cope with the essential features of people such as their linguistic powers, which endow them with the capacity for commenting upon their actions and so making episodes with Aa-structures possible, with all that this implies, should be clear. In applying the R-r group of models for the analysis of episode the

[1] The broad distinction between learning by imitation and learning by injunction is well established in empirical studies (cf. Hartley, 1964; Strauss, 1959).

ethogenist may, on occasion, have to consider people as priests, actors, or players. There are important respects in which neither actors, priests nor players are like the kind of entities which fit the mechanical model. The notion that the attributes of entities can be treated as parameters implies that some attributes can be maintained constant while one chosen to be the independent variable is deliberately varied. This is an essential feature of this model. At the heart of it is the idea of logically independent properties, which co-vary. From this derives the idea of experimental design in which there are dependent and independent variables. As has often been pointed out, the attempt to treat social phenomena as the interaction of entities which are essentially fitted to the parametric model has been characteristic of the mistaken attempt to model psychology on physics, (cf. Louch, 1966, chapters 1 and 2). It stands in great contrast to the R-r group of models. If these are adopted an ethogenist looks for the equivalent of scripts, liturgies, books of rules, and not for correlations, statistics and significance measures. He proceeds in a wholly different way: he looks for the relations of meanings. The advantages of the ethogenic approach can be summed up in the advantages of the R-r group of models.

Since there are episodes in human life which really are the performance of plays, the carrying out of ceremonies and the playing of games, the R-r group of concepts does have *literal* employment in some episodes. This important point has been overlooked in naïve role theory (cf. Biddle and Thomas, 1966, pp. 41–44.) The analogies that justify the metaphorical employment of the conceptual system are based upon likenesses and differences between entities of the same kind, namely episodes in human life, and between people acting and "acting". The mechanical parametric model has *no* literal employment in human life, not even, it seems, in medicine (Laing, 1969.) The analogies that would justify its employment would have to be made between highly incomparable entities, that is between language-using, act-performing organisms, and such entities as fit the parametric model, such as confined samples of gas, or short lengths of electrical conductor.

The parametric model is strongly deterministic: it depends upon a strict application of the principle that a particular change in a parameter *always* leads to an identical consequential change in another parameter. In this context "always" means that should there be a change in a parameter not followed by the expected change in some other parameter, then a third parameter has broken loose, as it were, and is varying. The R-r system is not deterministic in this way. It allows for the introduction of some very important backstop concepts, such as decisions and wants. We may choose to act out this or that episode in a dramatic way, or we may not. Of course these choices are subject to the giving of accounts, but this itself must terminate, and the final step in a sequence of reasons may be the final backstop of the bloody-minded, that of "I just don't want to". In the R-r group of models similarities in people's behaviour do not originate in similarities in external manipulation or change of a parameter, or from internal modifications of physiology, but from shared conventions, rules and paradigms. Rules of behaviour do not have the status of laws of nature since they can be ignored, defied or changed, as Goffman (1969) has emphasized, and because adherence to them is not a reflection of the presence of identical or very similar causal mechanisms in the entities involved. A hydrogen atom always emits light of just such and such wavelengths because it has precisely such and such a structure, and that structure is the causal mechanism responsible for that behaviour. Similar behaviour has *no* necessary implications of similarity of reasons for that behaviour (cf. Goffman op. cit., p. 9.)

References

Austin, J. L. (1961). Pretending. *In* "Philosophical Papers". Clarendon Press, Oxford.

Bentley, E. (1965). "The Life of the Drama". Methuen, London.

Biddle, B. J. and Thomas, E. J. (Eds) (1966). "Role Theory: Concepts and Research". John Wiley, New York.

Fowles, J. (1966). "The Magus". Jonathan Cape, London.

Garfinkel, H. (1967). "Studies in Ethnomethodology". Prentice-Hall, Englewood Cliffs, N.J.

Goffman, E. (1959). "The Presentation of Self in Everyday Life". Anchor Books, New York.

Goffman, E. (1969). "Where the Action is: Three Essays". Allen Lane, London.

Hartley, R. E. (1964). *Merrill-Palmer Quarterly*, **10**, 3–16.

Laing, R. D. (1969). "Self and Others". Tavistock, London.

Louch, A. R. (1966). "Explanation and Human Action". Blackwell, Oxford.

Merton, R. K. (1957). "Social Theory and Social Structure" (Revised edition). Free Press, Glencoe, Illinois.

Piaget, J. (1951). "Play, Dreams and Imitation in Childhood" (translated by C. Gattegro and F. M. Hodgson). Heinemann, London.

Scott, M. B. and Lyman, S. M. (1968). Paranoia, homosexuality and game theory. *Journal of Health and Social Behavior*, **9**, 179–187.

Sheed, W. (1967). "A Middle Class Education". Sphere Books, London.

Shwayder, D. S. (1965). "The Stratification of Behaviour". Routledge & Kegan Paul, London.

Strauss, A. (1959). "Mirrors and Masks". Free Press, New York.

Wittgenstein, L. (1959). "Philosophical Investigations". Blackwell, Oxford.

Author Index

Numbers in italics refer to pages where references are listed at the ends of chapters

Subject Index

A

Act of speech, 219, 231, 233, 236, 239

Adaptive processes, 403–404

Advertising, 273–274

Aggression, 8, 72–73, 87, 265, 349, 351–359, 362
  inhibition of, 355–356, 358, 360–361
  instrumental, 356–357

Analogy models in social sciences, mechanistic, 144–147, 174, 202–203, 421–423
  organic, 147–149, 150–151, 267
  process, 149–150, 151, 168–169

Arms races, 359, 363

B

Behaviour,
  conscious, 347
  definitions, 343–345
  innate, 345–346, 353–356, 361
  social, 35–36, 49–50

Behaviourism, 20, 125, 131–133, 224, 225, 231, 238

"Biologistic" theories, 10, 389–390

Bodily engagement (*Leibengagement*), 215, 219, 220, 221, 222, 223, 231, 236

Boolean algebra, 10, 395–397, 402

C

Change,
  action, 204–205
  definition of, 172, 205
  diachronic analysis and, 172–173
  open systems in, 178

Cognitive bias theory, 403

Cognitive consistency, 116–117

Cognitive decentration, 108, 220–221, 223

Cognitive determination of emotion, 76, 107

Cognitive dissonance theory, 31, 44–45, 90, 91, 102, 104–105, 109–110

Common-sense assumptions, 18–19, 37–38, 123–124, 340–341

Communication,
  community of interpretation in, 221, 224, 226, 228, 234, 249, 250
  decoding in, 234
  encoding in, 234
  formal representation of, 399
  grammar of, 240–254
  in conflict, 339
  in production, 282
  intention in, 220, 224, 230, 232–234, 236, 246
  nesting of message elements, 248, 250–251
  non-verbal, 79, 246
  paralinguistic, 236
  persuasive, 50, 51, 53